P9-AQN-505

Introduction to Psychotherapy
4th edition

This fourth edition of *Introduction to Psychotherapy* builds on the success of the previous three editions and remains an essential purchase for trainee psychotherapists, psychiatrists and other professionals. It has been revised and extended to capture some of the current themes, controversies and issues relevant to psychotherapy as it is practised today.

Bateman has added new chapters on attachment theory and personality disorder and has developed further the research sections on selection and outcome. His new chapter on further therapies covers a variety of therapeutic movements and establishes links between these and classical psychoanalytical therapies.

Introduction to Psychotherapy is a classic text that has been successfully updated to provide a relevant and essential introduction for anyone interested in psychotherapy.

Anthony Bateman is a Consultant Psychotherapist at St Ann's Hospital, London. **Dennis Brown** worked at the Group Analytic Practice in London and at the Institute of Group Analysis in London. **Jonathan Pedder** was Consultant Psychotherapist at the Maudsley Hospital in London.

Introduction to Psychotherapy
4th edition

An outline of psychodynamic
principles and practice

Anthony Bateman, Dennis Brown,
and Jonathan Pedder

Routledge
Taylor & Francis Group
LONDON AND NEW YORK

RC
480
.B3178
2010
Science
Library

First published 1979 by Tavistock Publications

Second edition published in 1991 by Routledge

Third edition published 2000 by Routledge

Fourth edition published 2010
by Routledge
27 Church Road, Hove, East Sussex BN3 2FA

Simultaneously published in the USA and Canada
by Routledge
270 Madison Avenue, New York, NY 10016

Routledge is an imprint of the Taylor & Francis Group, an Informa business

© 1979, 1991, 2000, 2010 Anthony Bateman, Dennis Brown and
Jonathan Pedder

Typeset in Times by Garfield Morgan, Swansea, West Glamorgan
Printed and bound in Great Britain by TJ International Ltd, Padstow,
Cornwall
Cover design by Sandra Heath

All rights reserved. No part of this book may be reprinted or reproduced
or utilized in any form or by any electronic, mechanical, or other means,
now known or hereafter invented, including photocopying and recording,
or in any information storage or retrieval system, without permission in
writing from the publishers.

This publication has been produced with paper manufactured to strict
environmental standards and with pulp derived from sustainable forests.

British Library Cataloguing in Publication Data
A catalogue record for this book is available from the British Library

Library of Congress Cataloging-in-Publication Data
Bateman, Anthony.
   Introduction to psychotherapy : an outline of psychodynamic principles
and practice / Anthony Bateman, Dennis Brown and Jonathan Pedder. –
4th ed.
      p. cm.
   ISBN: 978-0-415-47611-9 (hardback) – ISBN: 978-0-415-47612-6 (pbk.)
1. Psychotherapy. I. Brown, Dennis. II. Pedder, Jonathan. III. Title.
   RC480.B3178 2010
   616.89'14–dc22

                                                        2010004610

ISBN: 978-0-415-47611-9 (hbk)
ISBN: 978-0-415-47612-6 (pbk)

4360030487

Contents

Foreword to the first edition

We have often been asked to recommend some introductory text in psychotherapy, and felt at a loss. Freud's papers on technique (1912a, 1913a) or Bion's (1961) *Experiences in Groups* make fascinating if not essential reading for those embarking as therapists on formal individual or group psychotherapy. Yet we were not aware of any one book – certainly none written by psychotherapists in this country – which answered basic questions such as 'what is psychotherapy about?'. This book was born out of our attempts to answer that question and to convey something about dynamic psychotherapy to medical students and newcomers to psychiatry from various disciplines. We have been unashamedly simple in trying to delineate basic psychodynamic principles in Part I. We have described something of the range of methods based on these principles in Part II. We do not say very much about the practice of psychotherapy – that is 'how to do it' – for we believe that this can only really be learnt by embarking on the journey of exploration, either as patient or as therapist under regular supervision.

We are both psychoanalysts working part-time as consultant psychotherapists in a teaching hospital psychiatric unit where all current opinions and treatments in psychiatry are represented. In our view Freud's work and psychoanalysis have provided the spring which has nourished all later forms of dynamic psychotherapy, be they individual or group psychotherapy, marital or family therapy. With the proliferation of new forms of psychotherapy, both within and beyond the fringe of psychiatry, we felt some simple statement of basic aims and principles would help to orientate ourselves and, we hope, others.

The psychoanalytic view is, among other things, essentially a developmental one. It sees man against the evolutionary background of his long pre-human and especially more recent primate past; it sees man in his historical and social setting; and lastly, it sees each individual in his own unique cultural and developmental context, which is our particular concern in psychotherapy. The present can only be understood in terms of the past. The past is ever-present.

Dennis Brown
Jonathan Pedder
St Mary's Hospital, London
1979

Foreword to the second edition

The Foreword to the original edition began by explaining that there was a gap in the literature. Before 1979 there were no simple, comprehensive, introductory texts to which we could direct new-comers to psychotherapy. Clearly others were thinking along similar lines. In the same year Bloch (1979) edited a multi-author book describing a range of psychotherapies, and Malan (1979) produced *Individual Psychotherapy and the Science of Psychodynamics* which sums up in vivid everyday language years of working in this field at the Tavistock Clinic. In 1979 Whiteley and Gordon (1979) published a comprehensive survey of group methods in psychiatry, and Storr (1979) an account of his own approach to individual psychotherapy. Six years later came Casement's (1985) lively description of the interactional process in psychoanalytic work. This was followed by Symington's (1986) Tavistock Clinic lectures on key contributors to modern psychoanalysis, and Frosh's (1987) exposition of different developments within the psycho-analytic tradition, and their implications for culture. All of these we would recommend to students of psychotherapy at different points in their professional development. Two other books have appeared which are of particular use to lay-people and potential patients: Knight's *Talking to a Stranger* (1986) and *Families and How to Survive Them* by Skynner and Cleese (1983).

Nevertheless, the steady interest in our book leads us to believe that it is of continuing value. It is regularly included in the reading lists for trainee psychotherapists, psychiatrists, and other profes-sionals, and it is often recommended to interested lay-people and prospective patients.

It was meant as a brief and simple introductory overview to the many forms of dynamic psychotherapy and their origins in and links with psychoanalysis. It traces the similarities and differences between individual, group, family, and social therapy and some of the 'newer' therapies. In updating we have continued the original aim, taking into account developments since 1979, including valuable new additions to the literature for those who want to read further, with an expansion of the sections on selection and research. We have touched on shifts in the social climate and impending changes in the organization of psychotherapy practice and training in the United Kingdom.

We wish to thank Dr Robin Skynner and Dr Don Montgomery for their comments on family therapy and gender assignment respectively; and Mrs June Ansell for her ready and efficient help with the manuscript.

Dennis Brown
Institute of Group Analysis, London
Jonathan Pedder
Maudsley Hospital, London
1991

Foreword to the third edition

Our first edition appeared in 1979, the second in 1991. The book has maintained its place on reading lists for trainee psychiatrists, psychotherapists, and counsellors. Interested general readers and potential clients have found it a useful overview of the increasing range of psychotherapies available today. So far it has been translated into nine languages. Yet psychotherapy itself is developing, and we want this to be reflected in a third edition for the new millennium. The original authors (DB and JP) therefore invited AB to join them in rewriting the book. He is already an established teacher and writer, as well as an experienced clinician within the NHS from which both DB and JP have now retired.

The passage of time has not lessened our belief that psychoanalysis provides the basis of all dynamic psychotherapies (individual, group, family and couple, and social) and that many of the 'newer' therapies owe their basic ideas to some aspect of psychoanalytic theory and practice. Since the first two editions, some such therapies have declined and others have become more prominent. Behaviour therapy, essentially non-analytic, has largely given way to cognitive-behavioural therapy (CBT), now a major part of the psychotherapeutic armamentarium, especially within psychiatry. Having earlier differentiated itself from psychoanalytic therapy, in its more recent development CBT has become closer in its methods to the psychodynamic, analytically based therapies. There has been further development in other therapies such as interpersonal psychotherapy, cognitive analytic therapy, and conversational therapy. These have developed out of the search for brief forms of therapy, considered in more detail in this edition. One effect of the rise of CBT and other therapies has been to stimulate more outcome research in all therapies including psychodynamic therapy.

This is in line with a more serious questioning of the cost-effectiveness of different therapies, especially the longer-term therapies which are often needed for radical change and sustained personal growth. We welcome such questioning and have extended our section on selection and outcome. Changes in emphasis in modern understanding of therapeutic relationships are reflected, along with recognition of changes in society and the patterns of the individual's relationships with others. Consideration is given to current issues such as the proliferation of counselling, the recovered memory controversy, and the increasing influence of attachment theory in therapy and research.

We wish to thank Dr Harold Behr and Dr Stuart Whiteley for their comments and suggestions regarding the sections on family therapy and social therapy respectively; and Mrs June Ansell for continuing practical help with the manuscript.

AB, DB, JP

Foreword to the fourth edition

Dennis Brown and Jonathan Pedder asked me to join them when they were preparing the third edition of this book. *Introduction to Psychotherapy* was already an established text popular with trainee psychiatrists, psychologists, medical students, counsellors, and others because of its broad and inclusive approach to psychotherapy. One of my explicit roles was to maintain the tradition of developing the book in accordance with changes in psychotherapy, mental health services, and training requirements. The fourth edition is the result of my endeavours.

It is a decade since the publication of the third edition. Both Dennis Brown and Jonathan Pedder have sadly died, entrusting the text, as we left it in the third edition, to me. This has turned out to be more of a problem than I had initially appreciated. The practice of psychoanalytic psychotherapy, the organization of psychotherapy services, and the requirements of psychotherapy training have all changed over the past decade. Yet the basic concepts underpinning practice have stood the test of time and to a large extent the test of empiricism. Dennis Brown and Jonathan Pedder had already artfully and comprehensively summarized the tortuous edifice of psychoanalytic theory in previous editions and between us we had tried to establish links between the practice of some of the 'newer', yet now well-established, therapies and the 'older' psychodynamic therapies in the third edition. So what was to be done for a fourth edition?

Looking back at previous editions it seemed to me that each edition captured a particular moment in the history of psychological therapies. So I have tried to capture some of the current themes, controversies, and issues relevant to psychoanalytic psychotherapy as it is practised today. Now is a time of flux, crossover, recombination of ideas, and challenge. For some, biological understanding continues to trump psychological understanding, genes are more powerful determinants of character and mental function than environment, and yet for others biology and environment are no longer in competition but mutually interactive. This is reflected in the extensive research on attachment and child development, much of which has confirmed earlier psychoanalytic theory. I have therefore extended the discussion on attachment and its importance in understanding mental development. In doing so I have introduced the concept of mentalizing and more detail about attachment theory and its use in psychotherapeutic treatment, and highlighted some aspects of neurobiology relevant to psychotherapy.

Cross-fertilization of theories of mental function and crossover of practice of therapies have become increasingly apparent. This is a double-edged sword. Psychoanalytic theory and practice is in danger of becoming appropriated by other therapies. Ideas and techniques once thought of as specific to dynamic therapy, for example an emphasis on emotions and an understanding of how the past influences the present, have all become part of other therapies, often with little reference to their origins. So I have tried to emphasize the core of psychoanalytic therapy whilst adding sections which are relevant to wider developments in theory and practice. Psychoanalytic psychotherapy as a treatment has always tried to offer a pathway for permanent psychological change to give individuals the best chance of negotiating the considerable stresses and strains of everyday life. As a result it has been adapted for the treatment of personality disorder, which by definition is a problem in relationships and social function, the very targets of psychoanalytic therapy. Many psychoanalytic psychotherapy services and practitioners have embraced this new interest in personality disorder. So I discuss treatment of personality disorder in detail.

The contemporary research paradigm of 'evidence-based medicine' and 'empirically supported treatment' remains a challenge to psychoanalytic psychotherapy. In the current climate the apparent lack of evidence of effectiveness remains one of the greatest challenges to its acceptance as a treatment within the National Health Service and other mental health services. It remains my view that whilst there is merit in the arguments against the sole use of empirical methods in the study of psychoanalysis and psychoanalytic psychotherapy we are best served by developing and adapting them in a meaningful way. We cannot simply avoid empirical research. Indeed when we embrace the gold standard of randomized controlled trials they seem to show us in a favourable light. I have therefore developed further the sections on selection and outcome and added a brief summary of relevant research at the end of each section on the main forms of psychotherapy. In keeping with the continued research interest in the therapeutic alliance I have placed greater emphasis on this aspect of therapy in both parts of the book.

Finally the lasting success of *Introduction to Psychotherapy* is, I believe, due to the remarkable ability of Dennis Brown and Jonathan Pedder to convey the essence of the theory and practice of psychoanalytic psychotherapy without losing its depth and sophistication. I hope this new edition does justice to their legacy.

Anthony Bateman
Barnet, Enfield and Haringey Mental Health NHS Trust, London
2009

Prologue

What is psychotherapy? It is essentially a conversation which involves listening to and talking with those in trouble with the aim of helping them understand and resolve their predicament. Psychotherapeutic conversation can only take place successfully in the context of a trusting relationship. Only then can the process of personal revelation, exploration, understanding, and resolution of problems flourish. An experience of being understood generates an experience of security, which in turn facilitates mental exploration, the primary focus of all psychotherapy.

> *Mrs A. went to her family doctor complaining of bouts of tearfulness and acute attacks of panic and anxiety. She considered herself to be happily married and could not account for her symptoms. Her doctor regarded them as the manifestations of a depressive illness, that is to say of some physical disease process of presumed, but as yet undiscovered, biochemical origin. He prescribed various antidepressants in turn, but these had little effect; rather Mrs A. began to feel that something dreadful was happening to her which nobody understood and that perhaps she was even going mad.*

Are there other ways of trying to understand such problems?

When an alternative point of view of her predicament was sought, the following aspects of her life and its history emerged. Her symptoms had begun when her only child (a daughter) was 6 years old. At that time Mr and Mrs A. had been discussing the possible need for their daughter to go away to a boarding school because of their remote situation in the country. It seemed likely that Mrs A. was far more depressed over this projected separation than she herself had acknowledged. Moreover when Mrs A. herself had been 6, her parents had separated and she was sent to live with an aunt, so that the possibility of separation from her daughter in the present had re-awakened the heartache of her own separation from her parents at the same age long ago. When Mrs A. reviewed her recent experiences in relation to the past within this suggested framework, her tearfulness and anxiety began to make sense to her and to resolve. She no longer felt prey to some mysterious and frightening disease process beyond her control, but began to recognize herself as a diseased person, discomforted by a situation that only too painfully reminded her of the past. As she explored her past in relation to her current feelings, what had been an overwhelming emotion without any representation in her mind became a more complex representational experience, giving her a personal narrative of her symptoms and allowing her to represent what had been implicit information in her mind of which she was unaware as explicit knowledge to her mind.

Symptoms that patients bring to doctors may often be the expression of unacknowledged feelings in the present, which remain hidden because of painful associations with the past. One of the central aims of this book will be to try to provide a framework within which to understand such problems and begin to approach them psychotherapeutically.

Part I

Psychodynamic principles

INTRODUCTION TO PSYCHODYNAMIC PRINCIPLES

It is widely agreed that about a third of all patients who go to their family doctor have primarily emotional problems. About half of these will have a recognizable psychiatric condition, with two-thirds of them having unmet needs. But only one in twenty is referred to a psychiatrist (Boardman, Henshaw, & Willmott, 2004). A still smaller proportion will be referred on for formal psychotherapy in the National Health Service (NHS). However, psychotherapy at varying levels will be appropriate for some patients at each of these stages. We will discuss these different levels and types of psychotherapy in further detail in Part II. The term 'psychotherapy' is used in both general and special ways; it includes forms of treatment for emotional and psychiatric disorders that rely on talking and the relationship with the therapist, by contrast to physical methods of treatment (such as drugs and electroconvulsive treatment).

Most psychotherapy in the general sense is carried out informally in 'heart-to-heart' conversations with friends and confidants. 'Everyone who tries to encourage a despondent friend or to reassure a panicky child practices psychotherapy' (Alexander, 1957, p. 148). Well-worn sayings such as 'a trouble shared is a trouble halved' make sense to everyone. Such help is more likely to be sought in the first instance from the most readily available help-giver, such as a friend, family doctor, priest, or social worker, rather than from a psychiatrist or psychotherapist. In the medical field, the art of sympathetic listening has always been the basis of good doctoring. There has been a risk that this might be overshadowed by the enormous advances in the physical sciences and their application to medicine, which have resulted in an increasing attention to diseased organs, to the relative neglect of the whole diseased person. In the last generation, interest has shifted back again to the individual as the focus of stress in the family and community, and psychodynamic principles have helped to illuminate this interest. While it is correct that many acute and major forms of psychiatric disturbance are best treated by physical methods, the addition of psychotherapeutic treatments may enhance outcomes both quantitatively and qualitatively. But the reverse is also true. Many less acute forms of neurotic and interpersonal problem are better helped by psychotherapeutic methods and in some disorders pharmacotherapy is relegated to a secondary level of intervention. For example, borderline personality disorder, a disorder characterized by marked interpersonal problems, can only be successfully treated using psychological treatment (Oldham, Phillips, Gabbard, *et al.*, 2001; NICE, 2009). We shall take up this issue further in Part II, particularly in discussing levels of psychotherapy (p. 109) and selection (p. 238).

Historically there have been two major approaches to psychotherapy in the special sense, competing with varying mixtures of rivalry and cooperation. These are psychodynamic psychotherapy, which has its historical origins in Freud's work and psychoanalysis, and behavioural psychotherapy, which involves an application of learning theory and stems from the work of Pavlov on conditioning principles. Here we are principally concerned with psychodynamic rather than with behavioural psychotherapy (though see p. 111 and p. 228). Basically the approach of the behaviourist was that of a physiologist or psychologist studying the patient from the *outside*. He* was interested in externally observable, and preferably scientifically measurable, behaviour and in manipulating (by suitable rewards and punishments) deviant or maladaptive behaviour towards some agreed goal or norm. Behaviour therapy has now been modified and developed and joined with cognitive science to form cognitive-behavioural psychotherapy. Over the past decade, despite the hybrid name, this approach has become less behavioural

---

* Where the sex of the therapist or patient is not defined by the particular circumstance described, he or she is referred to, for convenience, in the masculine gender throughout this book; such references should be taken to imply male or female.

and more cognitive, focused on inner states of mind and how cognitive processes influence behaviour. We discuss this on page 229. The dynamic psychotherapist is more concerned with approaching the patient empathetically from the *inside* in order to help him to identify and understand what is happening in his inner world, in relation to his background, upbringing, and development: in other words, to fulfil the ancient Delphic injunction 'Know Thyself'. Dynamic psychotherapy has been the major influence in the field of mental health, and has appealed more to doctors, social workers, and those psychologists immersed in the complexities of relationships with patients or clients, and to patients wishing to understand themselves and their problems rather than to seek symptomatic relief alone. Sutherland (1968, p. 509) wrote:

> By psychotherapy I refer to a personal relationship with a professional person in which those in distress can share and explore the underlying nature of their troubles, and possibly change some of the determinants of these through experiencing unrecognized forces in themselves.

(Those unclear about the respective training and role of psychiatrists, psychologists, psychoanalysts, and psychotherapists will find them briefly described in the Appendix).

Perhaps what is more surprising is that dynamic therapy and cognitive-behavioural therapy share aspects of theory and practice themselves and overlap with other therapies. So before we move on it is worth commenting on the increasing integration of psychotherapy that has taken place over the past few years. Despite the tensions between schools of therapy, integration has taken place within theory and everyday clinical practice. Theory has become increasingly intertwined, with concepts being borrowed or even appropriated from one therapy to another; different therapies are often organizationally integrated, for example offering family therapy with cognitive therapy for a patient with schizophrenia, and practitioners are integrating techniques into their own amalgam to tailor the approach to the patient.

The phenomenal growth of psychotherapies is largely a manifestation of these integrative tendencies at their most promiscuous. In the 1960s there were about 60 different forms of psychotherapy, by 1975 there were over 125, by 1980 there were 200, and by the mid-1980s there were over 400 variants (Bergin & Garfield,

1994). Few, if any, of these new psychotherapies have received the systematic appraisal that is required in the present climate of evidence-based practice. Many use techniques from more than one theoretical orientation and are commonly described as 'eclectic' rather than integrative.

Theoretical integration has been formalized into hybrid therapies such as cognitive analytic therapy (CAT, see p. 230) or interpersonal psychotherapy (IPT, see p. 222), which explicitly bring together elements from other known therapies into new free-standing types of psychological treatments with their own methods and evolving traditions. CAT, which was originally devised as a brief therapy suitable for NHS practice and accessible for inexperienced therapists, explicitly combines cognitive elements such as diary-keeping and self-rating scales with an analytic attention to transference and countertransference. IPT was devised as a brief, manualized, and therefore researchable therapy for depression.

A further facet of integration in psychotherapy – which might be referred to as 'integration in practice' – refers to the flexibility which is to be found in the practice of mature clinicians, whatever their basic training, in which they will often consciously or unconsciously bring in elements of technique or theory borrowed from other disciplines. Thus psychodynamic therapists present cognitive challenges to their patients, or make behavioural suggestions, while therapists with a cognitive-behavioural background, as their therapies extend in time, may well work with transferential aspects of their patients' behaviour such as non-compliance with homework tasks or persistent lateness.

Despite this increasing unification of psychotherapies it will be our contention first that all forms of dynamic psychotherapy stem from the work of Freud and psychoanalysis, which has produced many offshoots, and second that there are aspects to psychodynamic therapy that are specific, singular, and unique. Jung and Adler broke away before the First World War to found, respectively, their own schools of analytical psychology and individual psychology. Between the wars Melanie Klein and Anna Freud, applying analytic ideas to the treatment of disturbed children, developed child analysis. During the Second World War, Foulkes and others explored the use of analytic ideas in groups and developed group psychotherapy. Since the last war further developments have included family, couple, and social therapy. Rogers in the Encounter Movement, developments such as bioenergetics, and other forms of humanistic and integrative therapy have been seeking new ways of encouraging direct interpersonal contact to help free people from a sense of isolation and alienation from themselves and others. (Some of the links between these developments are traced in the 'family tree' of Figure 10 on p. 223.)

However, despite their apparent diversity and different theoretical formulations within dynamic therapies themselves, we believe that all schools of dynamic psychotherapy hold in common certain key concepts. These basic concepts are briefly introduced now and each is expanded in later sections of Part I.

Basic concepts

People become troubled and may seek help with symptoms or problems when they are in *conflict* over unacceptable aspects of themselves or their relationships. This is contrasted with the traditional medical model where symptoms are viewed solely as an expression of disordered anatomy and physiology.

Aspects of ourselves which so disturb us that they give rise to *anxiety* or *psychic pain* may be consciously rejected, and become more or less *unconscious*. We all employ a number of *defence mechanisms* to help us deny, suppress, or disown what is unacceptable to consciousness; these may be helpful or harmful.

Unacceptable wishes, feelings, or memories may arise in connection with basic *motivational drives*. The different psychodynamic schools may disagree over how to categorize human drives or as to which are the more important and troublesome: for example, those associated with eating, attachment, or sexual or aggressive behaviour. The central importance of conflict over drives and their derivatives remains.

Again, although *phases of development* have been conceptualized in a number of different ways, it is widely agreed that how we handle our basic drives begins to be determined in infancy by the response of others to our basic needs, our urges, and our states of mind. This is commonly at first mother, but subsequently others of emotional significance (father, siblings, teachers, etc.) have increasing influence, although how we respond to these people may be partly determined by the earlier pattern of interaction between mother and child. The developmental understanding of the interaction between mother and child has flourished as *attachment theory*, which now forms an increasingly important aspect of psychodynamic theory and practice.

It is in *models of the mind*, or theorizing about the structure of the psyche, that greatest disagreement has arisen. Freud revised his theories several times. At first he saw the psyche simply in terms of conscious and unconscious levels; later he introduced the concepts of super-ego, ego, and id. In more anthropomorphic terms Berne (1961) has written of the parent, adult, and child parts of each one of us. Yet running throughout is the idea of different psychic levels, with the potentiality of conflict between them.

Inevitably models of the mind have become mixed, although authors continue to emphasize particular elements of a model, with some concentrating on ego function and others emphasizing unconscious process. These differences are not necessarily oppositional. No single theory adequately explains all aspects of human function. One model that has had considerable influence both within and without psychodynamic therapy is *object relations*. Despite the harshness of the term, objects are essentially mental representations of current and past relationships and the emotions associated with them. But percolating the model yet again is the idea of conflict within or between representational 'objects'.

Aspects of the *therapeutic relationship* will be the last of the theoretical principles dealt with, and it naturally leads us on to the area of practice. We will distinguish between the therapeutic or working alliance, transference, and countertransference.

HISTORICAL BACKGROUND TO DYNAMIC PSYCHOTHERAPY

Before developing each of these concepts further, let us take a brief look at the historical background, where we are much indebted to Whyte (1962) and Ellenberger (1970). Although it might be broadly true to say that all modern forms of dynamic psychotherapy – whether psychoanalysis, individual or group psychotherapy, or family or marital therapy – stem from the work of Freud and others at the turn of the century, it would not be true to say that Freud 'invented' psychotherapy.

The idea of a talking cure through catharsis of feelings is at least as old as the Catholic confessional, and current idioms such as 'getting it off your chest' testify to the widespread belief in its value. A work on Aristotle's concept of catharsis was being much talked of in Vienna in the 1880s and may have influenced Breuer and Freud.

Nor is there anything revolutionary in the idea that we are often in conflict with our feelings, wishes, and memories. In 1872, a year before Freud entered university, Samuel Butler (1872, p. 30) wrote:

> There are few of us who are not protected from the keenest pain by our inability to see what it is that we have done, what we are suffering, and what we truly are. Let us be grateful to the mirror for revealing to us our appearance only.

Writers down the ages, who have attempted to penetrate the complexities of human motivation, have known this intuitively. Shakespeare, for example, recognized unconscious conflicting wishes in *King Henry IV Part II*:

PRINCE: I never thought to hear you speak again.
KING: Thy wish was father, Harry, to that thought.

Pascal (1623–1662) in his *Pensées* knew that 'The heart has its reasons, which reason knows not.' Rousseau (1712–1778) wrote: 'There is no automatic movement of ours of which we cannot find the cause in our hearts, if we know well how to look for it there.' Writing in the 1880s Nietzsche anticipated Freud: '"I did that" says my memory. "I could not have done that" says my pride, and remains inexorable. Eventually the memory yields' (Whyte, 1962).

Freud's achievement, combining the gifts of a great writer and scientist, was to address these ideas to a medical context, in such a way that they have since been given continuing and increasing, if at times faltering, attention. Yet as we have said, Freud did not invent psychotherapy any more than Darwin invented evolution. Darwin too had his forerunners; yet it was the added impetus of the evidence he collected for his new causal explanations of natural selection that gave a fresh weight to already current ideas on evolution.

Ellenberger (1970) has traced the ancestry of dynamic psychiatry from its origins in exorcism, and its evolution through magnetism and hypnotism. In primitive times, disease, both psychic and somatic, was commonly thought to be due to possession by evil spirits. Healing was expected to follow exorcism and such treatment was naturally in the hands of religious leaders or traditional healers, such as shaman, witchdoctor, or priest.

Alternatively, it was thought that disease might arise from infringement of taboos. Then again cure was expected to follow confession and expiation. Healing by exorcism and confession have both played a part in the Christian tradition. However, with the rise of Protestantism, the Catholic monopoly on confession weakened. There was an increased interest among lay-people and some doctors in the idea of the 'pathogenic secret' formerly disclosed only to priests at confession. Thus, by around 1775, the time of the last executions for witchcraft in Europe, exorcism as practised by priests such as Gassner (1727–1779) gave way to new techniques (which we would now call hypnotism) stemming from the work of the physician Mesmer (1734–1815). We might now find Mesmer and his disciples fanciful in their theories about magnetic fluid as an explanation for what they called magnetic sleep, but increasing attention was being paid to such phenomena. The similarity between magnetic sleep and natural somnambulism (or sleep-walking) led to its being first re-named artificial somnambulism, and later hypnotism.

Towards the end of the nineteenth century there was further acceleration of interest in all sorts of psychic phenomena (which we would now see as different examples of dissociation within the psyche) such as hypnotism, spiritism, mediumistic trances, automatic writing, and states of multiple personality, all of which suggested split-off unconscious psychic processes. Phenomena that were formerly thought to be caused by possession and therefore to be cast out by exorcism were now attributed to unconscious agencies to be reached and revealed by hypnosis. Accounts of possession were replaced by clinical accounts of multiple personality. In 1882 the Society for Psychical Research was founded in London to examine such phenomena. In the same year Charcot gave an important lecture to the Academy of Sciences in Paris, which brought a fresh respectability to hypnosis in medical circles, and helped to dispel some of the scepticism psychiatrists had felt towards it.

Throughout the century there was an increasing interest among writers in such phenomena, particularly that of dual or multiple personality, a well-known example being Stevenson's *The Strange Case of Dr Jekyll and Mr Hyde*, published in 1886. By the 1880s there was also considerable interest in the importance of repression of emotional and instinctual life in determining human conduct. For example, Schopenhauer (1788–1860) had already anticipated psychoanalysis; in Freud's own words, 'not only did he assert the dominance of the emotions and the supreme importance of sexuality but he was even aware of the mechanism of repression' (Freud 1925a: p. 59). Benedikt (1835–1920), a Viennese physician known to Freud and Breuer, was among the first medical men to suggest that the origin of neuroses, and especially hysteria, often lay in a painful pathogenic secret involving sexual life. Nietzsche (1844–1900) emphasized the importance of instincts and their sublimation, of self-deception, and of guilt feelings arising from the turning inwards of impulses which could not be discharged outwardly. In literature and drama, Dostoevsky and Ibsen were exploring the theme of passions that lurk below the surface and dictate the actions of men who may deceive themselves that they are rational beings. Ellenberger (1970) refers to this as the 'unmasking trend' that was prevalent in the 1880s. Ibsen's father had been a miner and his tomb bears a miner's hammer put there by his son to emphasize how he had continued the mining tradition of digging away at what lies below the surface – similar to the archaeological metaphor that Freud was fond of using.

Sigmund Freud (1856–1939) was born at Freiberg in Moravia (now part of Slovakia and named Pribor); when he was a child of 4, his family moved to Vienna. At school Freud had some leanings towards the law, but as he wrote in his autobiography, 'the theories of Darwin, which were then of topical interest, strongly attracted me, for they held out hopes of an extraordinary advance in our understanding of the world' (Freud, 1925a, p. 8). He was later to consider that, following Copernicus and Darwin, he had himself delivered the next major blow to man's self-esteem and view of his central position in the universe. It was on hearing Goethe's essay on nature read aloud just before he left school that he decided to become a medical student.

He entered medical school in Vienna in 1873 but did not qualify until 1881 because he spent some time working in Brucke's physiology laboratory while considering an academic career. This was a time when the rational hope was high that the ills of mankind would yield to discoveries in the basic physical sciences. Brucke had pledged, 'No other forces than the common physical and chemical ones are active within the organism' (Jones, 1957a, p. 45). Freud shared that hope early on and to some extent never quite abandoned it since he later predicted the more recent vogue for drug treatments in psychiatry.

The name of Freud is so closely identified with psychoanalysis that it is often not appreciated that he had an established reputation in several other fields before he ever came to his psychoanalytic discoveries in his forties. As a medical student he had already done original work in neurohistology; as a neurologist he had made important contributions and written on aphasia and on cerebral palsies in children; and he had been associated with the introduction of cocaine, as a local anaesthetic, into ophthalmology.

Freud felt that he encountered some anti-semitic prejudice in his ambition to achieve a university post. He had been engaged for some time and, impatient to get married, determined to set up in private practice in Vienna as a neurologist. Before doing so he obtained a grant to visit Charcot in Paris in 1885.

Charcot at that time was giving grand theatrical demonstrations of neurological cases, amongst which there were hysterical patients with paralysis, anaesthesia, or bizarre gait. Freud noted that Charcot could create by hypnosis conditions identical to those arising spontaneously in hysterical patients, and that furthermore the pattern of the disorder followed the idea in the patient's mind rather than any anatomical pathway (as seen in true neurological lesions). He therefore concluded that if hysterical disorders could be created by hypnosis, perhaps they arose spontaneously by autosuggestion – in response to an idea in the patient's mind of which he was *unconscious*.

Freud returned to Vienna and married in 1886. In his private neurological practice he found the usual proportion of hysterical cases. At first he used hypnosis as a treatment in an attempt to dispel the symptoms by suggestion. Through his association with Breuer, with whom he wrote the *Studies on Hysteria* (Breuer & Freud, 1895), he found that by putting patients into a light hypnotic trance and encouraging them to talk freely, memories or ideas might be revived that had become repressed and unconscious because they were unacceptable to conscious ideals. Hence the 'talking cure', as one of Breuer's patients called it, was born. Freud soon abandoned hypnosis as a direct method of intervention and not long after gave up using it even as a lubricant to talking, relying entirely on free association (p. 145). The couch remained in psychoanalysis because of its original use by Freud the neurologist, and its convenience to Freud the hypnotist. He himself slowly withdrew from the position of active examining doctor beside the patient, to that of accompanying ally on a voyage of self-examination sitting behind him. He thereby rescued the neurotic patient from the public theatre of Charcot's demonstrations, where only external appearances counted, and created the private space of the analytic consulting room where hitherto unmentionable and unacknowledged aspects of man's inner world could be faced. Symptoms that had been taken for meaningless by-products of as-yet-undiscovered somatic processes could be viewed afresh as meaningful communications about inner states of conflict.

THE CONCEPT OF CONFLICT

The idea of conflict over unacceptable aspects of the self is central to the psychodynamic point of view. Indeed, the very expression 'dynamic' itself was borrowed by Freud from nineteenth-century physics to convey the idea of two conflicting forces producing a resultant third force acting in another direction.

In the classical psychodynamic model the mind is seen as a battlefield with opposing forces vying for supremacy; the child is continually challenged by internal dissonance and opposing demands of internal wishes and external requirement. Whilst this sounds at best uncomfortable, it is seen as constructively developmental and impels compromise between differing internal desires and between internal and external demands allowing adaptation. Much of the conflict is transitory. But some may be inherently insoluble and create inner tension, for example conflicts that push the child or adult towards courses of action which are equally desirable but incompatible – wishes of dependence and independence, masculine and feminine identifications. As we will discuss (see p. 28), conflict is managed through the use of *defence mechanisms* which when used excessively or inappropriately may result in bodily symptoms, implying that conflict itself can lead to the experience of physical illness.

So long as medical students were only taught anatomy and physiology (or their subdivisions, such as histology and bio-chemistry) it was natural that doctors should try to understand their patients' complaints as symptoms of disordered anatomy and physiology and, therefore, treat them physically. But there is

widespread agreement that about one-third of all patients presenting to doctors have primarily emotional problems which cannot be
understood in this way, with much resulting frustration to both
patient and doctor. It is a romantic view to think that this is some
new phenomenon due to the pressures of modern life; Cheyne, a
London physician writing in 1723, estimated that one-third of his
patients had no organic disease.

If we bear in mind (as in the case of Mrs A., p. xvii) that
patients' complaints may not be symptoms of a discrete disease
caused by an external agency alien to the person, but indicative of
a conflict in someone who is diseased or alienated from a part of
himself, we may be better equipped to understand the puzzling
complaints of some people in distress. The discovery of micro-
organisms in the last century was a vast advance in the
understanding of disease, but also satisfied man's need to blame
forces *outside* himself (an updating of devil theories of disease)
rather than accept responsibility *within* himself.

The importance of conflict in human distress is not only relevant
to psychiatry, but to the whole field of medicine. If a child
complains of abdominal pain, this might well be symptomatic of a
physical disorder such as appendicitis; or alternatively it might be
the child's way of saying that he does not want to go to school for
some reason that he cannot acknowledge or admit for fear of adult
reactions.

This idea of conflict is not just a fanciful one dreamt up by man
to understand himself. Ethologists now well recognize its importance in understanding animal behaviour. A bird exhibiting territorial behaviour may approach another aggressively at the edge of
its territory, then become afraid, retreat, and go on to repeat the
pattern of approach-avoidance conflict several times; or it may turn
aside and begin pecking at the ground as an indirect outlet for the
aggression. This behaviour, which ethnologists term re-direction, is
what psychoanalysts call displacement (p. 36).

Which aspects of the self give rise to such conflict? We shall
discuss this at greater length in the section on motivation, but a
common misrepresentation of Freud is to assume that he attributed
all problems to sex and thereby to dismiss psychoanalysis as
culture-bound to bourgeois Vienna of the 1880s, and not of general
relevance. Indeed Freud found that many of his female hysterical
patients were suffering from sexual conflicts, but it is instructive to
quote his actual words about this (Freud, 1894, p. 52):

In all the cases I have analysed it was the subject's sexual life that had given rise to a distressing affect . . . Theoretically, it is not impossible that this affect should sometimes arise in other fields; I can only report that so far I have not come across any other origin.

Since then we have indeed come to recognize the immense importance of conflict 'in other fields', for example, aggressive feelings, which may be turned against the self (in depression and suicidal attempts) or converted into psychosomatic symptoms. What is significant is not only the centrality of conflict as a mental process but also the manner in which the mind of the individual manages the conflict. Physical and psychological symptoms arise when mental processes cannot resolve anxiety. When this happens there is an intensification of emotions leading to the formation of symptoms. Depression itself, or the grief that follows bereavement or some other loss vital to self-esteem, may feel overwhelming to an individual and not be consciously acknowledged; attempts to resolve the intensity of the feelings of loss (mental symptoms) may find outlet in physical symptoms. This commonly occurs when a patient presents symptoms at the anniversary (possibly unacknowledged) of a bereavement.

It is in conditions such as borderline psychoses and profound character disorders and personality disorders that Anna Freud (Freud, 1976) suggested we are dealing with early harm inflicted on the ego by endowment, environment, and vagaries of internal maturation, that is, by influences beyond its control which impair the ego's strength and therefore its capacity to contain and manage primitive anxieties and impulses. Many forms of trauma, including early separation and loss (Bowlby, 1969, 1973, 1980) and the many forms of child abuse, are increasingly recognized today as important for healthy psychological development (Lyons-Ruth, Dutra, Schuder, et al., 2006; Bureau, Easterbrooks, & Lyons-Ruth, 2009). Early traumas have been shown to influence development, and the effects of later trauma, for example in studies of survivors of the Holocaust and other disasters (Kestenberg, 1982; Pines, 1986; Menzies Lyth, 1989; Garland, 1998), are of considerable significance.

It should not be thought that all forms of psychiatric disturbance can be explained as the result of conflict. There is considerable genetic predisposition to functional psychoses such as schizophrenia and manic depression. But placing too much explanatory value on these important developments can lose sight of the person himself who may continue to experience considerable conflict in relation to himself and his loss of function. Indeed some patients may be more vulnerable to conflict and its effects as a result of their mental illness. There are also some rare forms of organic psychosis caused by physical cerebral dysfunction, such as by brain tumour or vitamin deficiency. The concept of conflict is of more especial importance in understanding neurotic disorders, where we are dealing with the internal damage which the ego in the later course of development has inflicted on itself by repression and other defences. Neurotic conflicts ultimately originate in personal relationships during a person's formative years, which become internalized and determine the sort of relationships formed with others thereafter, although the outcome may depend on what is happening in current close relationships, as will be discussed especially in considering family and couple therapy (p. 176).

UNCONSCIOUS PROCESSES

The concept of the unconscious forms a cornerstone of psycho-dynamic theory and practice. Freud was the first to explore sys-tematically the role of the unconscious in normal and abnormal mental functioning. Some philosophers have objected to Freud's ideas about the unconscious on the grounds that only conscious phenomena should be considered as mental events. Yet the idea of the unconscious had been increasingly discussed throughout the nineteenth century. Psychologists such as Herbart (1776–1841) emphasized the conflict between conscious and unconscious ideas; and the philosopher Schopenhauer (1788–1860), anticipating Freud, wrote: 'The Will's opposition to let what is repellent to it come to the knowledge of the intellect is the spot through which insanity can break through into the spirit' (Ellenberger, 1970, p. 209).

As the authority invested in man's idea of God declined in Europe from the Middle Ages onwards, there was a corresponding increase in human self-awareness which reached a particular intensity around 1600. The word 'conscious' first appeared in European languages in the seventeenth century. The dualism of Descartes (1596–1650), separating mind from body and thought from feeling, marked the high tide of this movement with its assertion that mental processes are limited to conscious awareness. This emphasis on rational thinking was one of the forces that led to the Enlightenment of the eighteenth century and many positive achievements in the spread of education and political freedom; but it devalued imaginative and emotional life so that a natural reaction was the Romantic movement of the early nineteenth century typified by poets such as Wordsworth, Keats, and Shelley. The idea of unconscious mental processes was 'conceivable around 1700, topical around 1800, and became effective around 1900' (Whyte, 1962, p. 63). By 1870 'Europe was ready to discard the Cartesian view of mind as awareness' (White, 1962, p. 165). If anything, Freud made the idea of the unconscious temporarily less popular by his early emphasis on its sexuality.

There are four basic ways in which the term is used. First, it is used to imply that there is a mysterious realm of mental function, often called *the system unconscious*, which is quite separate from the rest of the functioning of the mind. Unconscious becomes a 'thing in itself', a noun – *the* unconscious – rather than an adjective, and is used to describe a component of the mental apparatus which Freud originally hoped would be shown to have a neuro-biological basis. The therapist becomes akin to the anatomist trying to dissect a component of the mental structure. Second, unconscious is considered descriptively, an adjective – unconscious process, unconscious affect – rather than a noun, a reservoir of latent meaning about which the individual is unaware, yet which has a profound influence on his understanding self and others. This is *the dynamic unconscious*. The therapist becomes an explorer of multiple meanings which are found in all narratives. Third, the unconscious has been used to describe a quasi-mystical aspect of human experience not so much related to the individual but more a part of all human kind. Jung described a collective unconscious which he considered to be innate and generalized, finding evidence in beliefs, symbols, and mythology found to be common in widely differing cultures. Finally, the unconscious has been linked to the past and present. Sandler and Sandler (1984) considered the unconscious process to have two primary elements: the past unconscious which related to those aspects on unconscious process that continued from childhood in an unmodified form to have an influential role in determining the adult's responses; and the present unconscious which modifies the past unconscious through the use of defence mechanisms, allowing childhood wishes some expression, albeit in an attenuated form.

Current usage tends to emphasize unconscious mental processes and it is preferable to think in terms of *different levels* of consciousness and use the word unconscious as an adjective rather than a noun. Aspects of ourselves which conflict with consciously held ideals may be denied, suppressed, or disowned and become more or less unconscious. Something may be unconscious merely because we are not aware of it at a particular time, for example, the colour of our front door at the moment of reading these lines; or because we find it easier to function by suppressing disagreeable feelings or painful memories, though we might easily be reminded of them. These levels Freud called *preconscious*. Alternatively an idea may be unconscious because it is actively repressed owing to its unthinkable nature – a memory, fantasy, thought, or feeling which conflicts with our view of ourselves and of what is acceptable, and which would cause too much anxiety, guilt, or psychic pain if it were acknowledged. Freud suggested it was this process that led to the formation of the dynamic unconscious. Repression may weaken at times so that previously unconscious mental contents become manifest, usually modified by defensive elements, for example, during sleep in the form of dreams, at times of stress in the form of symptoms, or in the emergence of apparently alien impulses under the influence of drugs or alcohol.

The idea of different psychic levels parallels that of different neurological levels, with higher centres controlling and inhibiting more primitive ones which, in turn, might find expression if higher controls were relaxed. Freud, with his own neurological background, had always been impressed by the saying of the neurologist Hughlings Jackson (1835–1911): 'Find out all about dreams and you will have found out all about insanity.' In dreams and insanity we get the most direct insight into deeper levels of the psyche. Our idiom 'I wouldn't dream of it' seems to imply the idea of several levels: there are things we would dream of but not do; then, more deeply, things we would not even let ourselves dream of.

Perhaps the idea of the unconscious is now so much a part of our thinking that no further argument is needed, but evidence in support of the notion of unconscious psychic activity comes from the following sources, one of which is dreams.

Dreams

Freud always regarded dreams as 'the royal road to the uncon-scious' and *The Interpretation of Dreams* (1900) as his greatest work, of which he wrote: 'Insight such as this falls to one's lot but once in a lifetime' (Freud, 1900, p. xxxii). He drew a distinction between the often apparently absurd manifest content of a dream and the *latent content* hidden behind it by a censorship which could be by-passed by free association. Dreams were the 'disguised fulfilment of a repressed wish'. This wish-fulfilling function of dreams is a commonplace. Children dream of feasts or treats, adults of forbidden pleasures or of lost persons or places they long to see again. Dreams may also be attempts to master unpleasant experiences or to solve problems. Rycroft (1979) emphasizes the creative and imaginative aspects of dreaming, rather than just the conflictual and neurotic, and regards dreaming as the non-discursive mode of communication of the non-dominant cerebral hemisphere. This suggestion of a link between dreams and brain functions has become of increasing interest to dynamic therapists and neurobiologists. Emphasizing brain function rather than meaning, neurobiologists have investigated the formation of dreams and initially findings appeared to contradict Freud's theories. In 1977 Hobson and McCarley, citing animal data, put forward an 'activation–synthesis' hypothesis of dreams suggesting that rapid eye movement (REM) sleep is associated with dreams. This brain activation is instigated by chemical changes in the pons, which they asserted refutes Freud's theory that the dreams are disguised wish fulfilments which would require the activation to arise at a higher level of brain function. In REM sleep ascending excitatory waves – the activation component – stimulate higher midbrain and forebrain cortical centres, producing rapid eye movements and randomly activating parts of the association cortex in which memory traces are stored. Since the images and memories are random they suggested that they do not in themselves convey any meaning. On waking the dreamer pieces together aspects of the dream – the synthesis component – to integrate it into his life and to make sense of it. Emotions in the dream were considered as a response to the content but this was later modified as it became clear that emotion itself could actually shape the content of the dream (Hobson, 1999). But there are a number of problems with this approach, which neither confirms nor refutes Freud's theory.

First, to some extent there is a philosophical problem in confusing the study of matter and material things with mental and immaterial things. Second, other work by Mark Solms has suggested that REM sleep and the experience of dreaming are not necessarily associated with each other and that dreams can be initiated from areas of the brain closely related to motivational systems, suggesting that Freud's theory may have some neurobiological as well as psychological credence (Solms, 2000; Kaplan-Solms & Solms, 2007). The use of dreams in general psychiatry has been usefully reviewed by Mitchison (1999) and Reiser (2001).

Artistic and scientific creativity

Many writers, artists, and composers, in describing their own creative processes, have told of how they feel taken over by some inner force not entirely within their conscious control. Often the creative process actually takes place during sleep or dreaming. Kekulé, wrestling with the problem of the structure of benzene, dreamt of a snake eating its tail and then immediately saw that the benzene molecule must have a ring structure (Findlay, 1948). Coleridge is said to have conceived his poem 'Kubla Khan' while dozing under the influence of opium (Koestler, 1964). The playwright Eugene O'Neill claimed to have dreamt several complete scenes and even two entire plays; he urged himself as he fell asleep by saying, 'Little subconscious mind, bring home the bacon' (Hamilton, 1976). Mozart described in a letter the vivid experience of his own creative genius when his ideas seemed to flow into him at a rush:

> Whence and how they come, I know not – nor can I force them
> . . . Nor do I hear in my imagination the parts successively, but I
> hear them, as it were, all at once . . . All this inventing, this
> producing, takes place in a pleasing lively dream.
>
> (Vernon, 1970, p. 55)

By contrast to the flash of inspiration experienced by Mozart, Bertrand Russell writes of a slower process of 'subconscious incubation' preceding the final sense of revelation:

> It appeared that after first contemplating a book on some
> subject, and after giving serious preliminary attention to it, I

needed a period of subconscious incubation which could not
be hurried and was if anything impeded by deliberate thinking.
. . . Having, by a time of very intense concentration, planted
the problem in my subconsciousness, it would germinate
underground until, suddenly, the solution emerged with blind-
ing clarity, so that it only remained to write down what had
appeared as if in a revelation.

(Storr, 1976, p. 65)

Apart from the creative activity actually occurring in dreams,
dramatists and writers have described how in a waking life too
their characters emerge from within them with a life of their own.
Pirandello, whose play *Six Characters in Search of an Author*
illustrates this process, wrote in his journal: 'There is someone who
is living my life. And I know nothing about him' (see foreword in
Pirandello, 1954).

Hysterical symptoms

We have already seen how, on his visit to Paris, Freud developed
the idea that hysterical conditions – paralysis, anaesthesia, ataxia –
could be caused by an idea of which the patient was not conscious.
This could arise from the suggestion of an outsider (by hypnosis)
or from inside (by autosuggestion). Such hysterical symptoms,
Freud proposed, are constructed like dreams as 'compromises
between the demands of a repressed impulse and the resistance of a
censoring force in the Ego' (Freud, 1925a, p. 45):

*A young woman walked into the casualty department of a
hospital complaining of weakness of her left arm. It transpired
that she had just come from a psychotherapy group at the same
hospital, where she had felt extremely angry with the male
therapist sitting on her immediate left, but too frightened to say
so. The weakness of the arm was a compromise between her wish
to hit him and her fear of doing so, though she was then able to
complain about him indirectly to the casualty doctor. It was
necessary to know her story to explain this fully. She was angry
with the therapist because he had just announced he was leaving
the group. She had been abandoned as an infant and adopted
from an orphanage by an elderly couple. They could not tolerate*

any 'bad behaviour', and if she were 'naughty' would threaten to send her back there.

This explanatory account of an unexplained phenomenon implicating the unconscious process has its origins in attempts to understand paralyses seen in casualties from the Franco–Prussian war which seemed to relate to traumatic experiences at the battlefront. Abreaction or talking about the experience, during which the sufferer was able to remember the events he had gone through, relieved the symptoms. Freud suggested that it was not only current trauma that could lead to hysterical symptoms but also childhood trauma, and he speculated that this was because the emotions associated with early trauma could not be processed by an immature mind. The idea that emotional states were frozen in time and 'dammed up' and could threaten the equilibrium of mental function became known as the *affect-trauma model* of the mind. It remains an implicit model of change, albeit with only limited evidence, for therapists who encourage emotional catharsis in therapy.

Post-hypnotic phenomena

A subject may be hypnotized and given the suggestion that when he awakens he will forget consciously what the hypnotist has said, but that after an interval, when the hypnotist snaps his fingers, the subject will cross over to the window and open it. The subject awakes and, on being given the signal, opens the window. When asked why he did so, he looks briefly confused and then says that it was too warm in the room. This illustrates how a complicated sequence of behaviour (opening the window) can be under the control of an idea (implanted by the hypnotist) of which the subject is not conscious and furthermore that when a conscious explanation is demanded, a rationalization follows (that it was too warm).

Parapraxes

When we make a slip of the tongue or forget something, it could be due to a simple mistake in the machine of the brain, but often, on further examination, as first suggested by Freud in the *Psychopathology of Everyday Life* (1901), it turns out to be emotionally motivated. For example, we may forget an appointment or the name of somebody we are annoyed with and wish to forget, but all this happens outside consciousness.

> *A young woman had not been able to come to a meeting. Later she met the chairman and apologized, saying that, 'Dr X raped . . . I mean roped . . . me into doing something else'.*

Was this a simple mistake, or the expression of a fear, or most probably the expression of a resentful feeling of having been coerced into doing something against her will? Beyond the 'psychopathology of everyday life' many everyday phenomena indicate the co-existence of different levels of consciousness. Drivers often find they are 'miles away' in their thoughts, especially on motorways, and 'come back' to find they have been negotiating traffic without conscious awareness. People commonly find themselves singing a popular song for no apparent reason, until they discern an associated link triggered by a preceding mood, impulse, word, or preconscious perception.

Subliminal perception, selective attention, and perceptual defence

Below a certain threshold, light or sound stimuli can lead to psychophysiological responses without consciously being noticed. Thirty years ago there was a furore in the USA about the use of subliminal advertising; messages like 'Eat Popcorn' were flashed onto cinema screens for a fraction of a second, an exposure too short for recognition by the public but long enough for sales of popcorn to be dramatically increased. There is a great deal of experimental evidence (Dixon & Henley, 1991) that the threshold of perception is influenced by motivation; below a certain level of stimulation we can see what we want to see, but be blind to what we do not want to see (e.g. words giving rise to fear or embarrassment flashed momentarily onto a screen). It would seem that there is a selective and discriminating filter mechanism at work, which operates below the level of awareness in much the same way as Freud suggested that the censor operates in dreams.

Sometimes those fresh to the psychodynamic way of thinking question how remote events remain unconscious and dormant for years before causing any effects for good or ill, in the way that streams flow underground before suddenly breaking to the surface. This idea of dammed-up feeling causing trouble, the affect-trauma model mentioned earlier, seems less of a mystery to writers such as Thomas Hardy, who wrote 'I have a faculty for burying an emotion in my heart and brain for 40 years, and exhuming it at the end of that time as fresh as when interred' (Gittings, 1975, p. 5).

The social unconscious

In recent years the *social unconscious* has been recognized (Hopper & Weyman, 1975; Dalal, 1998) as influencing both individual and group life through deeply embedded cultural and historical assumptions, attitudes, values, traumas, ideologies, and myths. Through them, identity and self-esteem, both individual and collective, are supported or undermined. Defences against the recognition of current social conflicts and trauma can prevent their recognition and resolution, as in dealing with issues of ethnic discrimination or other destructive stereotyping (Brown, 1998a; Volkan, 1998). African Americans reliably report whether they experience someone as racially prejudiced against blacks or not. When individuals whose self-report is genuinely non-prejudicial are tested, those who are experienced as prejudiced by an African American process negative information associated with a black face faster and more accurately, suggesting that even if a person is unaware of it the presence of mental processes consistent with a prejudicial attitude is reliably sensed and responded to by an observer (Fazio, Jackson, Dunton, *et al.*, 1995). For a further discussion of 'automatic' attitudes, see Gawronski (2007).

The biological unconscious

It was as long ago as the 1950s (Scoville & Milner, 1957) when it was discovered from careful clinical observation of an amnesic patient that specific areas of the brain, the hippocampus and the medial temporal lobe, mediated explicit (now known as declarative) memory, a conscious memory for people, objects, and places. It then transpired that even though the same patient had no conscious recall of new memories of people, he could continue to learn new perceptual and motor skills. These memories are completely unconscious and are evident in action rather than via conscious recall and are now known as procedural or implicit memory. Individuals use the two systems together and repetition can transform declarative memory into procedural memory (e.g. driving a car). Procedural memory is now known to be a collection of integrated processes involving different brain systems, suggesting that we now have a biological example of one element of unconscious life. As we discussed earlier, Freud used the term unconscious in a number of different ways and he was clear that aspects of functioning of the ego are unconscious even though it is not repressed. These components of the mind are concerned with habits and perceptual and motor skills, thereby mapping onto procedural memory systems – a sort of procedural unconscious.

This correspondence between psychodynamic principles and neurobiological understanding has been developed further to enhance understanding of the effects of emotion on memory and how emotional states during psychotherapy may bring about change. Stern (1998) and others (Sander, 1998) have provided evidence suggesting that change during therapy is not related to conscious insight but more to expansion of unconscious procedural, non-verbal, knowledge and behaviour. They propose the idea of moments of meaning in which instances in the interaction between patient and therapist represent achievement of new implicit memories enabling change in behaviours that allow an increase in procedural strategies in ever-widening contexts.

ANXIETY AND PSYCHIC PAIN

Aspects of ourselves and our experience sometimes cannot be readily assimilated into our conscious view of ourselves and our world, because of the anxiety or psychic pain they arouse. The notion of psychic pain may at first seem strange to those used to thinking of any pain as physical. They may believe that pain is either real (physical) or imagined (psychological). However, any experience of pain is ultimately a psychic experience, whether the origin of the pain is somatic or psychological. Furthermore the experience of pain of physical origin depends on our mood and attention at the time; in the heat of battle severe wounds may pass unnoticed; and psychological treatment for chronic pain relies on distraction and management of mood. The older English expression 'sore' unites the two realms of psyche and soma, since we talk of 'feeling sore' in both areas. We also speak of being injured in both body and feelings; and our idioms describing a problem as a 'headache' or a person as 'a pain in the neck' acknowledge that seemingly physical pain may reflect a relationship between psychic and somatic pain.

For brief periods we may be able to tolerate considerable anxiety (e.g. coping with an emergency) or to bear considerable psychic pain and depression (e.g. following bereavement). Alternatively we may try to ward off such emotional discomfort by employing a number of defence mechanisms. Yet again, the stress may prove too great and defences fail; a state of decompensation follows and we may fall ill either psychically or somatically.

The experiencing of anxiety is not of course necessarily abnormal. Anxiety accompanies autonomic arousal, which is the normal response of an individual to threatening situations and prepares him for fight or flight. This has obvious original evolutionary survival value in the wild and we all still experience anxiety in competitive situations such as athletic competition, examinations, or interviews. This helps key up the individual for optimal performance; only if the anxiety is excessive or out of proportion is it maladaptive and abnormal. The anxiety aroused in a situation such as public speaking may be disturbing for the very reason that there is no motor outlet for its discharge.

The problem of anxiety and how we deal with it in ourselves is seen as central in most formulations of the origin of neurosis. Freud offered different formulations of the origin of anxiety in the early and later phases of his career. At first he thought defence caused anxiety, and later that defence was provoked by anxiety.

His earlier model (Freud, 1894) was a more physiological/ hydraulic one; he suggested that anxiety was the expression of undischarged sexual energy or libido. His classic example would be an individual practising coitus interruptus (withdrawal during intercourse to avoid conception), whose undischarged sexual tensions were then thought to be expressed in the form of anxiety symptoms. He referred to the resulting conditions as the *actual neuroses*. Although the model has now generally been discarded, there are still situations in which it has application. For example in a situation of danger, where autonomic arousal is appropriate and has obvious survival value, we may be unaware of anxiety as long as we are occupied in taking avoiding action. When action is blocked or ended we may become more aware of anxiety. In addition, considering anxiety as the result of undischarged aggressive drives is still useful in relation to psychosomatic disorders (Schoenberg, 2007).

However, Freud (1926b) later revised this view of anxiety (as undischarged libido) and came to see anxiety as the response of the ego to the threat of internal sexual or aggressive drives. Anxiety was a signal alerting the individual to the presence of danger in the unconscious, for example, that an inhibited wish was becoming increasingly powerful. If the ego could not prevent or defend against unacceptable thoughts, ideas, or wishes entering consciousness then persistent anxiety or neurotic symptoms would result.

Freud also developed a useful hierarchical taxonomy of anxiety, ranging from primitive to mature, based on how the mind of the child could manage anxiety at different stages of development. The baby has fewer mental resources to cope with fear than a 2-year-old, the 4-year-old has different resources than the 2-year-old, and so on. The psychological level at which an individual manages anxiety will determine the severity of the psychological illness. We can all use primitive mechanisms to cope with problems when we feel we are under dire threat. The earliest anxieties are paranoid or persecutory, intermediate anxieties relate to separation, and higher level anxieties include anxieties related to self-esteem and super-ego anxiety, commonly related to guilt. Clinically, what is important is to consider the level of conflict evidenced by the patient, as this will inform treatment and how the therapist talks therapeutically to the individual.

The individual with persecutory anxiety will at best be oversensitive to slights from others but at worse become paranoid and dangerous as he tries to manage the anxiety. At times this may result in fragmentation and disintegration of psychological function and the patient collapses into a psychotic state of mind. The patient with separation anxiety shows a fundamental conflict between the need for a person and fear of losing him, which can lead to overdependency, agoraphobic and avoidant symptoms, or conversely excessive detachment. The use of the concept of castration anxiety has understandably had a bad press and the term has been discarded. The original formulation of castration anxiety was in terms of the Oedipal fear of the little boy that his punishment for loving his mother and challenging his father would be castration and humiliation to what Freud erroneously presumed was the position of the woman. But it is important not to throw the baby out with the bathwater and the concept has been developed in relation to the themes of powerlessness within a phallocentric society, fears of success, and anxieties about assertion (Benjamin, 1990).

Super-ego anxiety is related to conflict between different components of the mind, particularly between the guardian of our conscience and our conscious desires. People with excessively high standards worry constantly about their inability to meet their own requirements and may become tormented to the extent that they have an obsessive-compulsive disorder. Others may become depressed with a constant feeling of failure.

Bowlby has offered some very interesting comments on the connection between anxiety, mourning, and defence. His influential work is considered in more detail on p. 55. A young child who has developed an attachment to a mother-figure shows distress, when separated from her, in three recognizable phases of *protest*, *despair*, and *detachment*. Bowlby (1973, p. 27) writes: 'the phase of protest is found to raise the problem of separation anxiety; despair that of grief and mourning; detachment that of defence'. The thesis that was then advanced (Bowlby, 1960) was that the three types of response – separation anxiety, grief and mourning, and defence – are phases of a single process and that only when they are treated as such is their true significance grasped. Yet these three processes of separation anxiety, mourning, and defence were encountered in the reverse order by Freud. He first became aware of the significance of defence (Freud, 1894); later of mourning (Freud, 1917b); and lastly came to the revised view of the significance of anxiety (Freud, 1926a).

Initially Freud was preoccupied with the problem of anxiety and the defences used against it as he observed them in the neurotic conditions he saw, such as hysterical, obsessional, and phobic states. Only later did he turn his attention to depression, which is a much larger clinical problem; in psychiatric practice about half of all patients seen are depressed. A simple way of stating the relationship between anxiety and depression is to say that whereas anxiety is the reaction to the threat of loss, depression is a consequence of actual loss.

It was not until 1917 in *Mourning and Melancholia* that Freud (1917b, pp. 243, 251) drew attention to the similarities between bereavement and depression, such as sadness, despair, loss of interest in the outside world, and inhibition of activity. Whereas:

mourning is regularly the reaction to the loss of a loved person, or to the loss of some abstraction which has taken the place of one, such as one's country, liberty, an ideal and so on . . . in melancholia, the occasions which give rise to the illness extend for the most part beyond the clear case of a loss by death, and include all those situations of being slighted, neglected or disappointed, which can import opposed feelings of love and hate into the relationship or reinforce an already existing ambivalence.

In other words, in melancholia or depression the loss may not be an obvious external one, but more of an internal one involving a loss of self-esteem. Depression, for example, may follow failure to achieve some longed for ambition or position vital to self-esteem (Pedder, 1982).

Another way of expressing this is to say that a painful discrepancy has arisen between the subject's ideal self or ego-ideal (myself as I would like to be) and his actual self (myself as I am). This discrepancy gives rise to a state of psychic pain (Joffe & Sandler, 1965), to which there may be one of several responses. A normal response might be to protest – 'fight' rather than 'flight' – to direct aggression against the source of pain. The subject may attempt to master the pain in an adaptive way, or in the case of a mature, robust individual may be able to bear the pain and work through the ensuing disappointment and loss of self-esteem. Alternatively there may be one of several less healthy responses to this central state of unbearable psychic pain. If the wished-for state cannot be restored there may ensue a state of helplessness which Joffe and Sandler suggest (1965, p. 395) may:

represent a fundamental psychobiological response which could be conceived of as being as basic as anxiety. It has its roots in a primary psychophysiological state which is an ultimate reaction to the experiencing of helplessness in the face of physical or psychological pain in one form or another.

One response to this state of helplessness might be to give up and relapse into physical illness, described by Engel (1967) as the 'giving-up, given-up complex' which often precedes somatic disease. Another would be for the psychic pain to become converted into psychogenic bodily pain (Merskey & Spear, 1967). A third is to relapse into depression itself.

Alternatively, defence mechanisms, such as denial of a loss, may prove sufficient to cope with the pain – at any rate for a while.

> *A middle-aged woman presented with depression. She knew that her father had died when she was 10; she thought she believed what she had been told as a child that he had been reported missing, presumed dead, on active service during the war. This allowed her to go on hoping that perhaps after all he was not dead and might one day turn up, so that for 30 years she had hoped every knock on the door might be her father. During psychotherapy she one day recalled with horror a memory of her brother coming into the kitchen when she was 10 and saying, 'There's a man in the garage with blood all over him.' At that moment she realized that her father had killed himself but simultaneously denied the knowledge; the memory remained, though buried, for years. Only by painfully accepting the fact of his death and its horrifying circumstances could she begin to work through the process of mourning and to move forward again.*

In the following section we consider further mechanisms of defence commonly used to manage anxiety

DEFENCE MECHANISMS

One way of dealing with aspects of the self that, if consciously experienced, might give rise to unbearable anxiety or psychic pain is by using a variety of defence mechanisms.

Everyone needs and uses defences at some time – the question is, 'to what extent and when?'. Sometimes, overenthusiastic workers in psychiatry or its fringes appear to feel that no one should have any defences, regarding them as a modern form of sin; but an uninvited attack on someone's defences is as unjustified as any other form of assault. Defences are normal psychological mechanisms and help to maintain an individual's mental stability. To attack them insensitively is likely to be harmful.

Defences are often categorized according to developmental stages – immature/early/primitive, neurotic, and mature (see Table 1). This is not to say that someone who uses immature mechanisms is an

Table 1 Mechanisims of defence

Primitive/immature	Neurotic	Mature
Idealization	Denial	Humour
Projective identification	Depersonalization	Sublimation
Splitting	Displacement	
Projection	Intellectualization	
	Rationalization	
	Reaction formation	
	Regression	
	Repression	
	Phobic avoidance	

immature person, more that we default to increasingly immature mechanisims as our anxiety increases and as we become more psychologically desperate and terrified about our mental survival. Maturity includes a capacity to acknowledge and tolerate problematic feelings and thoughts within ourselves without acting on them, except when appropriate. We gradually develop a separation between thinking and doing and no longer need to use early mechanisms of defence excessively as we develop more mature defence styles. Use of a more mature mix of defences is associated with better general adjustment (Erickson, Feldman, & Steiner, 1996) whilst recurrent use of more immature styles leads to psychiatric disturbance (Vaillant, 1992). Regression increases the risk of suicide and violence, displacement differentiates violent from non-violent patients, projection and denial turn aggression outward, and repression has been linked to inwardly directed aggression (Apter, Plutchik, Sevy, *et al.*, 1989). This supports the idea that some defences are more primitive than others, representing earlier developmental psychological processes which were appropriate at a specific stage of development. But when they are used inappropriately or excessively at a later stage of development this suggests underlying psychological disturbance. The more primitive mechanisms are considered to be splitting, projection, projective identification, omnipotence, and devaluation. In short, the sort of person who sees things in black and white and fails to take into account the views or experiences of others.

Freud (1894) first introduced the term 'defence' to describe the specific defence mechanism operating in the cases of hysteria he was then studying; he later termed this particular defence 'repression' and went on to describe others. Repression has been suggested to be the primary mechanism of defence and that other defences are only called into operation when it fails and unaccept-able impulses or wishes become more conscious – the return of the repressed. By 1936 Anna Freud (1936), his daughter, was able to list nine mechanisms of defence (regression, repression, reaction-formation, isolation, undoing, projection, introjection, turning against the self, and reversal). She added a tenth normal mech-anism (sublimation) and one or two more (such as idealization and identification with the aggressor). Melanie Klein emphasized the defences of splitting and projective identification (Segal, 1964) occurring in both normal and abnormal development.

Further development of the concept of defences has taken place over the years. In contrast to this classical picture, relational models see defence mechanisms as a protective shield within which the authentic self is held: Defences form part of the attempt to facilitate the development of a 'true' (Winnicott, 1965) or 'nuclear' (Kohut, 1971) self in the face of a defective relational environment. In keeping with Freud, clinicians consider some uses of defence as developmentally necessary. The boasting of the little boy becomes a powerful force in overcoming inferiority and attaining manhood; omnipotent and paranoid defences, rather than avoiding inherent destructiveness or innate division and conflict, are desperate attempts to overcome and recover from states of terror and despair resulting from environmental failure.

Bowlby reframed defences in interpersonal terms, basing his view on attachment theory (Holmes, 1993). Secure attachment provides a positive primary defence whilst secondary or pathological defences retain closeness to rejecting or unreliable attachment figures. In 'avoidant attachment' both neediness and aggression are split off and the individual has no conscious knowledge of the need to be near the attachment figure, appearing aloof and distant; whilst in 'ambivalent attachment', omnipotence and denial of autonomy lead to clinging and uncontrolled demands. For clarity we follow a more classical exposition in discussing the specific defences often referred to in the literature. Our list of defences that follows is not exhaustive but made up of those we find ourselves thinking of most commonly in everyday clinical work.

Repression

As described at the beginning of the previous section, we all at different times *suppress* inconvenient or disagreeable inner feelings, or totally *repress* what is unacceptable to consciousness. Commonly suppression is considered to be mostly a conscious act whilst repression takes place outside awareness. There is nothing abnormal or pathological about either of these processes, unless carried to extremes. Before the days of anaesthetics, a sensitive surgeon had consciously to ignore and then suppress feelings about the screams of patients in order to be effective. In extreme cases though, people who declare they have never felt angry or sexually aroused may be severely repressed.

The concept of repression has been brought back into focus more recently with the controversy surrounding recovered memories of abuse. The issue has been polarized by labelling the memories as true or false, recovered, or discovered. False or pseudo-memory implies that all of these memories are untrue and based on fantasy or wish fulfilment. Recovered memories imply that the memories are accurate and have been 'stored' in the unconscious only to be uncovered by therapy. Others have labelled the memories as discovered memories to attempt to neutralize the controversy.

As our knowledge about memory has become more extensive, so also has the complexity of the debate. Selective forgetting is a well-known phenomenon of the memory system, retrieval of memory can occur for the first time long after the event, anxiety and trauma interfere with the storage of memories, and the motivated distortion of recall has become a central component of cognitive theories and behavioural accounts of psychopathology. Of course, as in any debate, there is also evidence that memories can be remembered clearly but be proven false. One well-known personal pseudo-memory was described by Piaget, the well-known Swiss developmental and cognitive psychologist. For many years Piaget described a clear visual memory of someone trying to kidnap him from his pram when he was 2 years old and of his nanny chasing away the kidnapper. Years later, when Piaget was 15, the nanny returned to the Piaget family and confessed that the incident had never occurred. Her motive in reporting the event had been to enhance her position in the household, but she subsequently suffered guilt about the fabrication and about the watch she had received as a reward (Piaget, 1962). So the question is not so much related to whether or not repression exists but more about what its role is as a hypothetical psychological process in psychological disturbance and the functioning of memory.

Denial

We may deny or forget unpleasant external events: for example, an unhappy affair or an examination failure. It has been reported that, following bereavement, up to 40 per cent of widowed people experience the illusion of the presence of their lost spouse and 14 per cent actually imagine they have heard or seen the lost partner (Parkes, 1972). This could be seen as a form of denial of a painful loss which is fairly normal, that is, common in exceptional circumstances. The experience of a phantom limb following amputation (sensations suggesting the limb is still there) may have neurological origins, but may also be understood in the same way as a denial of the loss. This view is supported by reports that phantom limb is experienced more commonly after sudden and unexpected amputation (e.g. following a road accident) than when there has been time to prepare for it psychologically. Both these examples illustrate the difference between repression and denial. In contrast to repression, which aims to remove an aspect of internal reality from consciousness, denial or disavowal (Freud, 1940) deals with external reality and enables an individual to repudiate or to control affectively his response to a specific aspect of the outside world. Denial involves splitting of the mind in which there is cognitive acceptance of a painful event while the associated painful emotions are repudiated. The protective aspect of denial is illustrated by Greer, Morris, and Pettingale's (1979) finding that women with breast cancer who showed denial (or defiance) when told the diagnosis, following mastectomy, had a significantly higher survival rate than women who reacted with hopelessness or depression.

Projection

We commonly externalize unacceptable feelings and then attribute them to others: 'The pot calling the kettle black.' Christ knew this well: 'Why beholdest thou the mote that is in thy brother's eye, but considerest not the beam that is in thine own eye?' It must be as old as time to blame our neighbours, or neighbouring village, tribe, country, etc., for our own shortcomings. This is a normal though tragic and dangerous human trait. In extreme forms it amounts to paranoia, for example, when individuals disavow their own hostile or sexual feelings but declare that others have hostile or sexual designs upon them. This is manifest in the extreme in paranoid psychoses, delusional disorders, and erotomania, for example.

Sometimes people behave as though not only feelings but important aspects of their own selves are contained in others; for example, the mother who unconsciously deals with the deprived-child part of herself in caring for her baby may spoil it and prevent it growing towards greater independence. This helps mother to cope with the pain of her own frustrated longing for closeness and dependence, but the baby's developing needs may be thwarted by mother seeing in the child an aspect of herself and provoking the child to enact it. In the technical language of Kleinian psychoanalysis this is an example of projective identification (Sandler, 1987).

Closely associated is the phenomenon of splitting, which involves the complete separation of good and bad aspects of the self and others, as illustrated by the perennial interest of children in heroes and monsters, good fairies and witches (Bettelheim, 1975). Clinically we see it in splitting between good and bad feelings, between idealization and contempt of self and others.

Splitting and projection are considered to be behind many of the symptoms which are characteristic of borderline personality disorder and other severe personality disorders (Kernberg, 1984). Dynamic therapy has been modified for these conditions (see p. 235) according to this understanding and focuses on the consequences of excessive use of splitting and projection (Kernberg, Clarkin, & Yeomans, 2002).

Reaction formation

Reaction formations go to the opposite extreme to obscure unacceptable feelings. They may be highly specific, for example showing excessive deference to someone whom one hates or caring excessively for others when one wishes to be cared for oneself, or more generalized, in which case they form part of a character trait. Conscientiousness may be an example of this when associated with obsessional personality; excessive precision and tidiness may hide a temptation to lose control and to be messy. Extreme cleanliness may have its usefulness, for example, 'scrubbing up' in an operating theatre. Out of context it can be crippling, for example in obsessional neurosis where many hours a day may be spent in washing rituals. The psychodynamic view of such obsessional states is that hostile feelings are usually being concealed.

Reaction formation is related to identification with the aggressor which Freud (1920) had alluded to when describing the behaviour of a child towards an adult in which there was a total submission to the adult's aggression and a resulting internalization of profound feelings of guilt related to the inwardly directed aggression. But it was Anna Freud (1936) who described the mechanism in detail. Since then it has often been known as the Stockholm syndrome after the siege in Stockholm in which bank robbers held bank employees hostage for 6 days in 1973. In this case, the victims became emotionally attached to their victimizers, and even defended their captors after they were freed from their 6-day ordeal.

Rationalization

An example of this has already been given in discussing post-hypnotic phenomena (p. 20) when the subject justifies an unconscious impulse and is unaware of its source. Our idiom 'sour grapes' is a further example deriving from Aesop's fable of the fox who could not reach the grapes and consoled himself with the rationalization that they were sour anyway. In other words an individual gives himself a logical and plausible explanation for what is happening or for irrational behaviours that have been prompted by unconscious wishes. Not surprisingly this mechanism is common in politics, business, and medicine when things go wrong. Sometimes this is differentiated from intellectualization in which emotional anxiety is managed by cognitive appraisal. For example a young person anxious about sexual performance might discuss the morality of pre-marital sex with a friend rather than mention his underlying anxieties.

Conversion and psychosomatic reactions

Unacceptable feelings or affects may be converted into physical symptoms as in hysterical conversion or psychosomatic disorders. We have already given a classical example of hysterical conversion above (p. 19). Such hysterical disorders are becoming increasingly uncommon in developed societies, almost as if people now know that the deeper meaning would be rumbled. On the other hand, psychosomatic disorders have gained increasing attention in recent years. Bottling up of rage may, for example, contribute to an attack of migraine.

A conscientious but inhibited nursing sister could never express her exasperation with her junior nurses whenever they made a silly mistake, for fear she would be too destructive. On such an occasion she would bottle up her rage and typically have an attack of migraine later that evening. During the course of psychotherapy she became more in touch with her anger and more able to express it. One day she reported that she had been able to tell off a nurse at fault and was surprised but delighted to find that no migraine had then followed.

In hysterical conditions there may be a symbolic element to the symptoms, which hints at an underlying fantasy, as in the example of the girl whose paralysed arm represented a defence against her wish to hit her therapist (p. 19). Psychosomatic disorders are now less often thought to have this symbolic significance, but to occur in those restricted in their fantasy life, whose emotions are expressed physically and whose thinking tends to be concrete and conversation circumstantial. The word 'alexithymic' has been introduced to describe such people who have no words for their feelings (Nemiah, 1978). These qualities are now recognized as occurring in post-traumatic states and in some people with addictive problems and sexual problems, as well as those prone to psychosomatic disorders and reactions (Taylor, 1987).

Uncertainty remains about the underlying psychological processes involved in hysterical conditions and psychosomatic disorders. The descriptive term somatization disorder is now often used and is part of the official classification system for the *Diagnostic and Statistical Manual for Mental Disorders* (American Psychiatric Association, 1994). Patients have a history of many physical complaints, including symptoms of pain, gastrointestinal complaints, sexual symptoms, and pseudo-neurological complaints, all with no clear medical explanation. The overlap with hysteria and character problems is well described and the presence of histrionic personality traits, conversion and dissociative symptoms, sexual and menstrual problems, and social and interpersonal impairment (Cloninger, 1994) suggests that unconscious determinants are important, especially as the affected individuals are genuinely distressed and experience terrible psychological anguish.

Displacement

When we are too afraid to express our feelings or affects directly to the person who provoked them, we may deflect them elsewhere. A cartoon example is the office hierarchy: the boss is angry with his next-in-command, who in turn takes it out on the one beneath him, and so on till the office boy is left kicking the office cat. The phenomenon of displacement is widespread in other animals and known to ethologists as re-direction. A common type of displacement is the 'turning on the self' of affects such as anger, as seen in self-destructive behaviour and masochism; it is particularly prominent in depressive conditions and suicide attempts.

Regression

It is perfectly normal and indeed desirable on holiday to abandon our more usual adult responsibilities and go back (regress) to the less mature joys of childhood, such as swimming, games, etc. In the face of disasters with which we feel unable to cope – such as severe illness or accidents – we may also regress to more child-like and dependent ways of behaving. Then we look for adults or leaders in whom we can repose our trust (see Transference, p. 70), although this may also leave us vulnerable to domination by demagogues.

Sleep might be seen as a normal daily form of regression from the challenges and responsibilities of waking life. A child who has achieved bladder control may, following the birth of a younger sibling, regress to bed-wetting again. The condition of anorexia nervosa (severe weight loss and amenorrhoea in teenage girls caused by dieting) can be partially understood as a retreat from the difficulties of coping with adolescent sexuality (Crisp, 1967).

Depersonalization, confusion, and dissociation

These are terms with a well-recognized meaning in general psychiatric phenomenology. Depersonalization is the name given to a state in which someone feels to be outside himself, as if separated from his feelings and from others by a glass screen, like an outside observer of his own mental processes or body; this may occur in any psychiatric state but is a special feature not surprisingly of anxiety disorders and depersonalization disorder and other dissociative disorders. Confusion, in contrast, is the term given to a state of disorientation in time and place, in which the subject may not know the date or where he is; this is the hallmark of an organic psychiatric state due to underlying somatic cerebral dysfunction.

However, although these are both well-accepted terms in general psychiatry, which we do not wish to challenge, patients much more often complain of feeling confused when they have no such organic state. They are usually in intense conflict between opposing feelings, say of love and hate, and confusion has descended like a sort of defensive fog to deal with the unbearable conflict. This mechanism operates in many cases of depersonalization. Like confusion (in our sense), depersonalization occurs during intense emotional arousal and the subject may notice quite a sudden moment of 'switching off' of feelings within himself and a withdrawal from the outside world. This is also known as pretend mode functioning (see p. 84). There is evidence from psychophysiological studies in line with this; measures of arousal suggest abnormalities of stress-response systems, which may themselves be a cause of some of the symptoms but equally might be the result of the dissociative processes (Giesbrecht, Smeets, & Merckelbach, 2007; Simeon, Knutelska, & Yehuda, 2007). Dissociation is a hypothetical mental process, like repression, that disrupts connections between a person's thoughts, memories, feelings, actions, or sense of identity. It is a normal response to trauma, and allows the mind to distance itself from experiences that are too much for it to process at that time. Dissociation is still encountered in clinical practice, occurring in cases of hysterical fugue or amnesia. In war-time, a soldier might come wandering back from the front line in a fugue state having had to obliterate the intolerable memory of seeing all his comrades killed by a shell. In peace-time, a person may appear in a casualty department declaring that he does not know his name, address, or anything about his past life. This may have followed some imbroglio or misdemeanour, such as hitting his wife in a row or being discovered committing a fraud, the emotional consequences of which cannot be faced because of the shame and blow to self-esteem involved.

Sublimation

This was defined by Anna Freud (1936, p. 56) as, 'the displacement of the instinctual aim in conformity with higher social values'. It is the most advanced and mature defence mechanism, allowing partial expression of unconscious drives in a modified, socially acceptable, and even desirable way; for example, murderousness may be given a partial outlet in work in abattoirs or in field sports. The suggestion often made by older people that restless or aggressive young men should be made to join the army for a time suggests that sublimation as an idea has cultural acceptance. The drives (p. 39) are diverted from their original primitive and obviously aggressive and sexual aims, and are channelled into a 'higher order' of manifestation.

An intellectual young man of 18, brought up in an emotionally confusing family, was outwardly very inhibited and unassertive. His pleasure in self-display, competition, and sexual curiosity were so stunted by conflicts that he avoided girls and was shocked to read a biological account of reproduction at 16. However, from an early age he had built up a remarkable collection of tin soldiers, and was fascinated by the flamboyant costumes of historic times. They seemed to give expression to the otherwise repressed but healthy parts of himself. Until he worked through his neurotic inhibitions, his curiosity and his exhibitionistic and competitive impulses were dealt with as though intolerable except in this indirect and sublimated form.

Beyond neurosis, sublimations enrich both individuals and society. Freud saw culture as a sublimation of our deepest and darkest urges as well as an embodiment of our highest aspirations, as in sport or drama. The writer Kafka (1920) said something similar in an aphorism: 'All virtues are individual, all vices social; the things that pass for social virtues, such as love, disinterestedness, justice, self-sacrifice, are only "astonishingly" enfeebled social vices.'

Vital parts of an individual may only be expressed in dreams or pastimes. Through cultural activities we can participate indirectly and vicariously in propensities otherwise unexpressed; carnival is a time-honoured example. A society's culture is the outcome of its life at all levels, from instinctual roots to highest ethical ideals; unconscious drives press for expression. Social defences develop to channel this expression and reduce associated conflict and anxiety.

MOTIVATIONAL DRIVES

Any attempt to understand the springs of human behaviour in all
its complexities in both health and disease must, sooner or later,
confront the problem of human motivation. Dramatists, novelists,
and poets were exploring the fields of human love and hate,
heroism and destructiveness, long before scientists began to turn
their attention to such concerns. Clearly there are many types of
innate behaviour, from simple in-built reflexes to complicated
patterns which depend more on learning, such as maternal caring
behaviour. There are also basic physiological needs for air, food,
and water, which, if not satisfied, lead to powerfully motivated
behaviour. But ordinarily, in contemporary Western society, we are
not deprived of such needs and they do not give rise to conflict. We
are concerned more with those areas of motivation where conflict
does arise.

In talking about motivational drives we come immediately to
a central problem for the language of psychotherapy (Pedder,
1989b), which is the same whenever we try to grapple with the
mysterious relationship between psyche and soma (or mind and
body). From the side of the psyche we can use the language
of human experience and speak of urges or wishes; from the side of
the soma we can talk like biologists or scientists about instincts or
drives. Sandler and Joffe (1969) distinguished between the experiential and non-experiential realms. In the experiential realm lie all
our sensations, wishes, and memories: all that we 'know' through
subjective experience, whether conscious or unconscious, at any
given moment. By contrast, the non-experiential realm of instinct
and drive remains intrinsically 'unknowable'.

Instinct has been defined as 'an innate biologically determined
drive to action' (Rycroft, 1972). The term has been in use since the
sixteenth century and derives from the Latin for impulse (*Shorter
Oxford English Dictionary*). In the nineteenth century the notion of
an instinct or drive was coloured by the language of the physical
sciences and seemed to convey the oversimplified idea of hydraulic
pistons pushing an animal forward. Nowadays biologists prefer to
speak of innate patterns of potential behaviour, acknowledging
their greater complexity. Such patterns, or 'motivational systems'
(Rosenblatt & Thickstun, 1977), require particular external triggers
or releasers for their activation. Yet at times we do still subjectively
experience our drives or impulses as welling up from inside us,

perhaps against our will. We have chosen to use the expression 'motivational drives' to try to convey elements of both the psychic experiential side and the somatic biological side.

We have already said in the Introduction that different psycho-dynamic schools may disagree over how to categorize motivational drives and which are the more important or troublesome, but all agree about the central importance of conflict over drives and most give prominence to sexual and aggressive drives. Other drives considered important are those associated with eating, attachment, parental, and social behaviour. A brief historical sketch seems the best way of reviewing the problem.

As we have seen (p. 12), Freud was at first impressed by the frequency of conflict over sexual feelings, particularly in his female hysterical patients. Jung (1875–1961) reacted against what he considered to be Freud's excessive emphasis on sexuality, and thought more in terms of some general life force or libido (p. 129). Adler (1870–1937) gave more importance to aggressive strivings and the drive to power (p. 131). Initially Freud believed the stories his patients told him of sexual seduction by adults in infancy and felt that it was the repression of such traumatic memories that gave rise to neurotic conflict. Before long, however, prompted by his self-analysis (from 1897) and thinking that child seduction could not be as common as his theory required, he felt he must be mistaken. He believed that what he was hearing from his patients, if not true historical accounts, was the expression of childhood fantasies of wished-for occurrences. Now he thought that *psychic reality* was often far more important than actual historical reality. However, more recently the pendulum has swung back with the increasing recognition of the reality of child sexual abuse. Freud has been criticized for revising his views and been accused of withholding evidence supporting the reality of childhood seduction to bolster his theory about the pathogenic influence of fantasy (Masson, 1985).

The ensuing discovery of the importance of infantile sexuality led to the publication of *Three Essays on the Theory of Sexuality* (Freud, 1905). Up until this time the accepted view of the develop-ment of normal heterosexuality was that it arose de novo at puberty (the myth illustrated by Botticelli's painting of the birth of Venus arising from the waves as a fully formed woman). Freud saw that this account took no notice of the phenomena of homo-sexuality and bisexuality nor of infantile masturbation and sexual curiosity. He came to see the sexual drive as present from birth and developing through a number of different stages (oral, anal, phallic, etc.), pleasure being derived from different erotogenic zones at different stages (p. 46). The best known of all these must be the Oedipal phase (around 3–5) named after the myth of Oedipus who unknowingly killed his father, married his mother, and then blinded (symbolically castrated) himself on discovering his crime.

In his later years, perhaps following the influence of Adler and the destructiveness of the First World War, Freud paid more attention to man's aggressiveness. The debate continues as to whether aggression is innate in man (primary aggression) or a response to frustration and deprivation (secondary aggression). Both views are valid: on the one hand there is a healthy assertiveness that man needs for survival and competition (e.g. in work or sport); on the other hand there is a more pathological destructiveness (e.g. football hooliganism) born of frustration.

The theme of aggression between members of the same species has been taken up and explored by ethologists (e.g. Lorenz, 1966). One example of such aggression is territorial behaviour. In circumstances where food supplies are not abundant, individuals or separate groups need to be spread out widely to ensure their food supply. Intra-specific aggression may have developed to achieve this. The bright colours of some coral fish or the song of birds has evolved, Lorenz suggests, as a warning signal to others of the same species to 'get off my patch' as it were. These assertive signals serve to delineate the territory of an individual; only if a rival does not heed them does fighting arise and the owner of the territory react aggressively to drive the intruder away. Another function of intra-specific aggression, especially between males, is to ensure the sexual selection of the best and strongest animals for reproduction. This is more common in animals living in nomadic herds (antelope, bison, etc.) where there is less need for territorial jealousy, as food supplies are abundant, but selective pressure operates to produce strong males to ensure the defence of the herd against predators. In social animals, particularly the higher primates and man, another important function of aggression is in status-seeking and the maintenance of dominance hierarchies; it contributes to the social stability of a group if everyone 'knows their place' and is afraid of their superior. While this is valuable in facing and meeting acute dangers, as in the discipline of the military hierarchy in war-time, or the operating theatre team in surgery, at other times hierarchical behaviour can be stultifying to individual growth and initiative.

The early psychoanalytic view of sexuality as a pleasure-seeking drive present from birth has had considerable explanatory value. However, to some it appeared to be too much centred on the individual and his gratifications. 'Object relations' theorists (Fairbairn, 1952; Guntrip, 1961; Winnicott, 1965; Balint, 1968; Greenberg & Mitchell, 1983a) have suggested that the primary motivational drive in man is to seek relationship with others. Rather than the individual finding satisfaction through different means at different stages (beginning with the oral stage), the individual seeks relationship with the other (at first, mother) through different means at different stages. This search would necessarily be carried out through the means appropriate to the stage of development (at first via the feeding relationship). Rather than an infant seeking gratification of an oral impulse, we have a couple finding satisfaction through a feeding relationship.

Harlow's (1958) well-known work on infant chimpanzees dramatically illustrates this drive for attachment to objects. When taken away from their mothers and provided with 'surrogates' composed of metal frames representing heads and bodies, either covered with simulated fur or incorporating milk-filled bottles and teats, the infants clung to the soft furry ones or returned to them when startled; they only turned to those with bottles when hungry. In other words, holding had primacy over feeding. It was the tactile substitute 'mothering experiences' that were crucial in providing a sense of security. It formed a base from which to develop relatively normally, although without the company of other young chimpanzees normal sexual and social behaviour did not develop in later life.

Bowlby (1969), following his work on maternal deprivation (1952) and the effects of separation of mother and infant, came to view attachment as an important primary drive in higher primates, including man, and considered that attachment behaviour should be conceived as a class of behaviour that is distinct from feeding behaviour and sexual behaviour and of at least equal significance in human life. Attachment behaviour reaches a peak between 9 months and 3 years, and probably evolved in 'man's environment of evolutionary adaptedness' (for example, the savannah plains in Africa) to ensure the protection of the helpless infant from predators. The work of Bowlby, who trained as a psychoanalyst, has

stimulated major developments in our understanding of infant–
mother interaction and has become one of the more productive
areas of psychodynamically based research. We discuss this in
more detail on p. 55.

Exploratory and attachment behaviour have a reciprocal
relationship. An infant or growing child, for example a toddler
playing on the beach, will explore further and further away from
mother (or home base) until he becomes anxious about separation
from her. He then returns to base for security and reassurance,
to recharge his batteries, as it were, before setting off to explore
once more.

We need a base throughout life; man is a social animal. Of
another, the honey bee, Maeterlinck (1901, p. 31) romantically
wrote:

> Isolate her, and however abundant the food or favourable the
> temperature, she will expire in a few days not of hunger or cold
> but of loneliness. From the crowd, from the city, she derives an
> invisible aliment that is as necessary to her as honey.

There seems little doubt that man has a natural tendency to seek
out others, and that in so doing he finds and fulfils himself. How
much this can be called a primary social instinct, in the sense of a
biologically determined drive to action, is debatable, although
modern evolutionary studies, both biological and neurological,
indicate that our social nature is built into our genes and our
central nervous system (Edelman, 1989; Ridley, 1996). In more
developed societies social behaviour transcends biological necessity; it is more of a psychological necessity. Social networks provide
the setting in which individuals struggle to find significance for
themselves through relating with others. At first the network is the
mother–child attachment, then the family, and then developing
networks of school, work, sexual relationships, the new family, and
the wider community. Man's sense of self and of his own value
depends on the presence of others and his interaction with them
throughout life.

In the last few decades, so-called self-psychology has emphasized
our need for others, not only to gratify our instinctual demands.
Other people are needed to affirm our sense of self by appropriate
mirroring, allowing stage-appropriate infantile grandiosity to compensate for our helplessness and powerlessness. Later we need

models with whom to identify, to promote our sense of agency. Kohut (1971, 1977) saw others fulfilling the role of *self-objects*. The self-object is one's subjective sense of a sustaining intimate relationship with another whose security and interest maintains the self, that is, fused aspects of the self which allow the development of *healthy* as opposed to *pathological* narcissism (Kohut & Wolf, 1978). Self-object needs were initially described in the treatment of narcissistic patients, but are now considered to be ubiquitous and enduring and a requirement of the normal psychological functioning of the self.

Yet still this list of biological drives or relationship-seeking behaviours does not exhaust the range of human activity. There is the curiosity and exploratory drive of the human infant which Piaget (1953) has emphasized. In psychoanalysis Klein (1928) had already discerned what she called an 'epistemophilic instinct', later to be developed by Bion (1962) in his concept of K (knowledge) as a primary personal function alongside Love and Hate. Whatever its status, should this be seen merely as a derivative of sexual curiosity, later to be 'sublimated' in scientific and artistic exploration; or is it a drive in its own right which leads to some of our more unique human creative achievements? Storr (1976) argues that the retention of the capacity for childhood playfulness into adult life is one of the mainsprings of creative activity.

The psychoanalyst George Klein (1976) wrote of the ego requiring a complementary concept, the 'we-ego'; and the sociologist Norbert Elias (1991) wrote of the changing 'we–I balance' in sociocultural history. Even today we see great variations in this balance between different cultures. For example, studies comparing personality in the USA, India, and Japan have distinguished between co-existing individualized, familial, and spiritual selves, each an organizer of motivational drives and influenced in different cultures by varying 'ego ideals and superegos' (Roland, 1988) (see sections in Models of the Mind).

The group known as Neo-Freudians that arose in the USA in the 1930s (Fromm, Horney, Sullivan, and Erikson) particularly emphasized this interpersonal dimension in contrast to the intrapsychic dimension stressed earlier by Freud (Holland, 1977). This has been continued by psychoanalysts and others who have pioneered developments in group, family, social, and interpersonal therapies (see appropriate sections in Part II). Those interested in some of the recent academic thinking which applies psychoanalytic ideas to a wider social context are referred to Burkitt (1991), Frosh (1987), Parker (1997), and Rustin (1991).

Conflict and breakdown in these supportive and self-defining relationships cause distress and even illness. We are now increasingly aware of the need to combat isolation and to find substitutes for disintegrated family and social groupings: in other words, to promote and channel a drive towards cooperation and cohesion in both individuals and societies (Kraemer & Roberts, 1996; Mulgan, 1997).

Whatever formulation of motivation is preferred, the central dynamic concept of conflict over primitive impulses remains. Freud himself revised his own theories of instinct several times, although throughout his work the idea of an opposing duality persisted. At first he saw the struggle to be between self-preservative and reproductive instincts, later between self-love (narcissism) and love of others, and finally he spoke more poetically of a clash between life and death instincts. His first formulation is not unlike that of the poet Schiller, who said that till the influence of the spirit governed the world, it was held together by 'hunger and love'.

Science and literature will continue their attempts to fathom the complexities of human motivation. Perhaps it is premature at this stage in our knowledge, and unnecessary for the purpose of this book, to be more precise in classifying motivational drives. Psychotherapy is more concerned with the impulses, urges, and fantasies which cause people distress and conflict. The force behind them comes from deep within us, with a driving quality which justifies the term 'unconscious peremptory urge', coined by Sandler (1974). Failure to come to terms with these vital parts of our nature can be the basis of overt mental illness or personality disorder, or lesser degrees of neurotic suffering and inhibition.

DEVELOPMENTAL PHASES

> So was it when my life began;
> So is it now I am a man;
> So be it when I shall grow old,
> Or let me die!
> The Child is father of the Man;
>   (Wordsworth, from *My Heart Leaps Up*, 1802)

The way in which we handle our basic drives begins to be determined in infancy by the response of mother, or mother substitutes, and subsequently by significant others (father, siblings, teachers, etc.). In the last two decades important observational studies have been conducted on infant development which emphasize the importance of mutual attunement and reciprocity between mother and infant (Stern, 1985; Emde, 1988; Gergely & Watson, 1996).

Stages in development extend through and beyond infancy, and have been conceptualized in many different ways. But the concept of successive phases, each needing to be negotiated at the appropriate and critical time to allow satisfactory progression to later phases, is widely held. Shakespeare wrote of the seven ages of man long before anyone in a more scientific field of psychology attempted their own classifications. The very existence within psychiatry of different areas of specialization dealing with childhood, adolescence, adulthood, and old age testifies to the existence of different problems at different ages. The idea of different phases proceeding from simple to more complex as maturation and learning progress is somewhat analogous to the idea of different neurological levels building up from simple to complex. As earlier stages or levels are negotiated they may be left behind or incorporated into later patterns, but there remains the potentiality of reversal or regression to more primitive levels in psychology, as in neurology, especially when difficulties of an earlier phase were not fully resolved.

Freud's (1905) classical psychoanalytic theory of libidinal or psychosexual development is one such theory of phases. He viewed adult sexuality as the outcome of a libidinal drive present from birth and developing through a number of pre-genital phases, pleasure being derived from different erotogenic zones at each stage. First, he proposed an oral phase (>1 year) where satisfaction is derived by the infant via the mouth from sucking, for example, nipple or thumb, which appears to be independent of, and to go beyond, nutritional needs; second, an anal stage (1–3 years), where gratification is derived from gaining control over withholding or eliminating faeces; third, a phallic-Oedipal phase (3–5 years) when the child begins to be more aware of his or her own genitalia, with consequent curiosity and anxiety about sexual differences. He or she may develop a passionate attachment to the parent of the opposite sex, with rivalrous and hostile feelings to those who stand in the way. This is followed by latency, a period of relative quiescence of sexual interest, perhaps even prudishness, while interests are turned more to the outside world and to intellectual development at school. Latency ends with puberty, when hormonal changes re-fire the sexual drive and the genital phase begins.

Nowadays, we would add that although an individual may be physically capable of reproduction from puberty, a further period of adolescence follows before a person's final sexual identity is established and sexual adulthood reached at around 20–21 years (Laufer, 1975). Erikson has referred to the 'psychosocial moratorium' of adolescence, following the 'psychosexual moratorium' of latency, before more adult responsibilities are expected. Another important theory of stages in development is that of the psychologist Piaget (1953), who focused more on cognitive and intellectual (rather than emotional) development. He has described intellectual development as proceeding from an early sensorimotor stage (0–2 years) before the development of language, through the stage of pre-operational thought (2–7 years) to concrete thinking (7–11 years), and not arriving at a capacity for formal abstract thinking till around 11 years or so. Piaget's ideas have particularly influenced educationalists, who now recognize that a child's readiness to learn depends upon the stage of development he has reached. A child can only be taught what he is ready for; the effect of any experience depends upon the individual's developmental phase.

Erikson's (1965) eight stages of psychosocial development are somewhat reminiscent of Shakespeare's seven ages of man. They are summarized alongside other phase theories in Table 2. It will be seen that each stage may be resolved for good or for ill: for example, in the first stage towards the establishment of trust or of mistrust. It may be noted that the first five of Erikson's stages correspond roughly to the stages of Freud's classical theory of libidinal development. The last three of Erikson's stages correspond more to those of Jung (p. 129), who was particularly interested in man's later development and his individuation as maturity and old age approach, with all the problems of success and achievement or disappointment and resignation.

Can we find common ground between these developmental theories – the classical Freudian theory with its possible over-emphasis on the individual and his gratifications, Erikson's more socially orientated viewpoint, and others, such as object relations theory (p. 61)? Let us consider the newborn infant and his developing relationships through the early years of childhood. Broadly speaking, three stages can be delineated: (1) a phase of

Table 2 Developmental phases

Ages	Shakespeare's seven ages of man	Freud's classical libido theory	Erikson's eight stages of psychosocial development	This book
0–1	At first the infant mewling and puking in the nurse's arms	Oral	Trust vs mistrust	Dependent (two-person)
1–3		Anal	Autonomy vs shame and doubt	Separation– individuation
3–5		Phallic- Oedipal	Initiative vs guilt	Rivalry (Oedipal three-person)
6 to puberty	The whining schoolboy unwillingly to school	Latency	Industry vs inferiority	Psychosexual moratorium
Adolescence	The lover sighing like a furnace	Puberty	Identity vs identity diffusion	Psychosocial moratorium
Early adulthood	A soldier full of strange oaths	Genitality and later stages of individuation emphasized by Jung	Intimacy vs isolation	Marriage
Middle adulthood	The justice full of wise saws		Generativity vs self- absorption	Parenthood
Later adulthood	Lean and slipper'd pantaloon		Integrity vs despair	Involution
	Sans everything			

more or less total dependence on mother at 0–1 years; (2) a phase of growing separateness and individuation at 1–3 years; (3) a phase of increasing differentiation and rivalry from 3–5 years.

Phase 1 In the first year of life the infant gains a growing awareness of the outside world and of self as distinct from others, within the context of a feeding and nursing relationship. At first he has only to cry when hungry, cold, wet, or uncomfortable and, provided 'good-enough mothering' (Winnicott, 1965, p. 145) is available, his wishes will appear to be satisfied magically; the infant may even be encouraged to believe in the omnipotence of his wishes. With the beginnings of awareness that mother's breast, smile, comforting arms, smell, and warmth are not his own but belong to another, the infant begins to be anxious that she might go away, especially if he feels he has been too greedy or demanding and, as teeth develop, that he may have bitten and hurt mother and caused her withdrawal. How mother responds to the infant's basic needs is bound to affect how he feels thereafter about them.

This first phase has been called the oral phase in classical psychoanalysis. Certainly the infant begins to explore the world by putting things into his mouth, but to subscribe all that happens under the label 'oral' is too narrow. This is the stage when (as Erikson has indicated) basic trust in other people is established, trust that others will continue to provide support and comfort. Gross failures (by the environment) at this early stage can lead to the most severe forms of psychiatric disturbance later (Lyons-Ruth, Dutra, Schuder, *et al.*, 2006).

Phase 2 Towards the end of the first year, the infant begins to be more aware of himself as separate from mother and those who supply his needs; Margaret Mahler has called this the separation–individuation phase (Mahler, Pine, & Bergman, 1975). Developmentally a 'switch' occurs, moving the infant from being primarily self-directed to being other-interested. This change is biologically driven and when it does not occur, for example in autism, the effect on social development is severe. Stern (1985) argues that this process of differentiation even begins soon after birth. The sense of self is developing; ego boundaries are being established between self and others, between 'me' and 'not-me'. Classical psychoanalysis called this the anal phase, but it is too restricting to focus solely on the pleasure derived from withholding or releasing faeces. Certainly, as this is a phase of establishing independence from mother, there may be battles over toilet training, but so there are over eating, dressing, or other activities as the child begins to exert his own will, often to the point of considerable negativism or contrariness. The story of banishment from the Garden of Eden might be seen as the story of loss of a state of bliss (mother's breast) when man first learnt to say no to God (the father) and discovered sexuality. However, to reduce all these strivings to the concept of anality seems too narrow. Indeed, an excessive preoccupation with elimination or soiling in the child is more likely to be the consequence of deprivation in other areas. Moreover, in normal development there are other important things happening. There is the development of speech and cognitive functions, exploration and locomotor development, and increasing mastery of the environment.

This is Erikson's second stage, when autonomy is established. The infant begins to separate from mother but is still largely dependent on her, not only for food and locomotion but primarily for protection from danger. The period from 9 months to 3 years is the time of maximal attachment behaviour (Bowlby, 1969). It is Bowlby's contention that this type of behaviour evolved largely to furnish protection from predators (p. 56). Any premature or imposed disruption of attachment at this stage, such as might be caused by prolonged separation or hospitalization of mother or infant, may lead to later anxieties about the reliability of attachment figures, such as difficulty in trusting people in relationships both personal and professional.

Phase 3 By the age of about 3, the infant is well aware of himself as a separate person, of his parents as separate and different people, and of his siblings (if any) as rivals in his environment. The role of sibling relationships in development and pathology continues to receive renewed interest within psychoanalysis (Volkan & Ast, 1997). The child of 3 is aware of sexual differences in a broad sense and more specifically is becoming curious about actual genital differences within the family and outside. We now know about the distorting effect on development of sexual seduction and abuse. A vast amount has been written about the development of psychosexual identity and gender role, as distinct from genetic sex, and the extent to which this is determined by inbuilt genetic or hormonal differences in contrast to postnatal social and cultural factors. In brief, as we ascend the animal kingdom, biological factors such as hormones have less influence, and psychological and environmental factors have a much greater one. The work of Harlow and Harlow (1962), for example, has shown that monkeys separated from their parents at birth and reared in isolation, so that they have no opportunity to learn by observing sexual behaviour in adults, may later be sexually incompetent themselves as adults.

Money, Hampson, and Hampson (1957) and Hampson and Hampson (1961) studied the effects of re-assigning the sex of a human child when it has been wrongly assigned at birth in intermediate sex types. Normally, humans have either male (XY) or female (XX) sex chromosomes and corresponding external genitalia to match. In some intermediate types there may be male genetic constitution with apparent female external genitalia, or vice versa. At birth, sex is always assigned on the basis of external genitalia, although in these hermaphrodite and pseudo-hermaphrodite cases the apparent genitalia may be incongruent with the chromosomal sex and the gonadal sex. Money and the Hampsons demonstrated that it is comparatively easy to re-assign the sex correctly before 1 year, but almost impossible after about 5. They suggested that somewhere between 1 and 5 years a gender role is established by cultural expectation whatever the actual genetic sex, and that this process can be likened to a permanent 'imprinting'. However, although all researchers in this field acknowledge the importance of sex of assignment in determining gender identity, a number of writers have produced evidence that in some cases genetic and hormonal factors can overcome the sex of rearing long after the age of 5 (Hoenig, 1985). This gender interchangeability is in accord with Plato's and Freud's view of man's inherent bisexuality or Jung's view that the opposite is concealed by appearances, the anima by the animus (or vice versa). The complexity of gender identity development has been extensively studied over the last decade (Chodorow, 1994; Di Ceglie, 1998).

The strength of sex drive may be determined by both biological and psychological factors, and indeed to some extent follows androgen levels in both male and female. However, gender role, like gender identity and sexual object choice, is determined by a combination of psychological and cultural factors acting on a biological substrate.

This phase (3–5 years) of increasing sexual differentiation, as we have already said, was called the Oedipal phase by Freud after the myth of Oedipus, who unknowingly killed his father and married his mother. The 'Oedipal complex' has, unfortunately, tended to become one of those frozen cliches of psychoanalysis which can easily be ridiculed if taken too literally and concretely to mean that every child wishes to murder the same sexed parent and have intercourse with the opposite sexed parent. Children do not have exactly an adult's concept of either death or intercourse, but certainly they may wish their rivals (parent or siblings) out of the way so as to enjoy greater intimacy with mother or father. This period of childhood is undoubtedly a time of passionate love and hate, rivalry and jealousy, the outcome of which can have a decisive effect on later character formation. It would be a Utopian dream to imagine children could be protected from conflicts at this (or earlier) stage. If all goes well, conflicts may be weathered; but if a rival parent or sibling, whose presence is resented at that time, becomes ill, dies, or is absent through hospitalization, divorce, or war, the child may fear that hostile wishes have magically come true and grow up fearful of the intensity of his jealousy. The neurotic, like the child, fails to distinguish between fantasy and reality, between thought and deed, between the wish and its realization. This phase corresponds to Erikson's third stage, when the crucial issue is whether initiative prevails over guilt.

An advantage of thinking in terms of these three broad stages of childhood development (although of course each merges into the other) is that they can be roughly related to different kinds of clinical problem. Neurotic disorders, such as hysterical and phobic states, are classically thought to derive from problems at the Oedipal phase of development (3–5 years). Some severe psychiatric disorders, such as borderline psychoses and gross character disorders, are thought to result from disturbances in the earliest phase (0–1 years) of the mother–child relationship. Disturbances in the intermediate phase (1–3 years) may later contribute to problems of self-determination (e.g. resentful compliance) or problems over separation and loss (e.g. anxiety and depression). In general terms the earlier the stage in development at which the problem arose, the more difficult it will be to treat psychotherapeutically before verbalization is possible.

By the time of entering middle childhood the child has come to adopt his own ways of integrating internal and external pressures and the conflicts they engender. He has begun to deploy a characteristic range of coping strategies and defences, as described in a previous section. How he does this will be dependent on how the earlier stages have been negotiated, and that negotiation itself is dependent on the quality of the mother–infant interaction. Recognition of the importance of the mother–child interaction and its influence on psychological development transcends the stages of development and reconciles many of the different developmental perspectives. We discuss this in the next section on attachment theory.

Development does not stop with middle childhood, but whether early crises have been resolved for good or for ill, towards or away from the establishment of sufficient trust, autonomy, and initiative, will determine an individual's attitude and response to subsequent challenges. One of the first of these is starting school, when separation from mother, new disciplines, and exposure to rivalry with peers test earlier solutions. In adolescence, pressure comes from the internal upsurge in strength and sexuality, fired by hormonal changes which give new impetus to primitive drives. At the same time, the young person is having to face detaching himself from the family, both for social reasons and because sexuality in the family runs counter to the universal taboo on incest. The adolescent has to work out a new psychosocial identity for himself; the task of separating from the family and establishing his own individual identity repeats the task of separating from mother in the earlier separation–individuation phase. Earlier problems of dependency, autonomy, rivalry, and sexual differentiation are reactivated in a way that accentuates the crisis, and may lead to disturbances of feeling or of behaviour such as delinquency, promiscuity, or experimentation with drugs. However, adolescence provides a second chance for the solution of these problems, as Anna Freud (1958) has pointed out.

The middle childhood years and adolescence are times of identity development, as well as changes in motivational drives, anxieties, and defences. Engagement with peers in social groups at school and in so-called youth culture provides opportunities to identify with people and ideals outside the family. In terms of self-psychology, or self-object theory, new self-objects – mirroring, idealizing, and twinning 'alter egos' – help the developing self to re-fashion itself as a young adult. Problems on the way may lead to 'identity diffusion', which accounts for some of the vulnerability of adolescence (see Table 2) and helps explain the instability that can lead to serious breakdown. But adolescents can also rapidly recover, particularly if earlier phases were mastered positively, with short-term psychotherapeutic intervention.

The table of developmental phases (Table 2) shows what everyone learns from experience: that each phase of life involves fresh opportunities and challenges. Marriage and parenthood will appear desirable and possible, and be achieved more or less easily, according to our resolution of earlier crises. Attitudes to them will be influenced by our experience of our own parents in these roles. Success at a later stage can help to correct earlier imbalances. For example, attainment of a successful marriage, through learning to trust oneself and the other in an intimate relationship, can modify the effect of mistrust learned in the earliest dependent stage. In other words, the past shapes the present, but the present can also re-shape the influence of the past. This is the basis of development and change in life and in psychotherapy.

Many people experience more or less of a 'mid-life crisis' (Jaques, 1965) when the fires of enthusiasm and optimism begin to abate and when the discrepancies between aims and achievements dawn on them. Some change their career, or their sexual partner, in an attempt to regain their sense of youth and purpose, sometimes successfully, at least for a time. Contacting the yet unexpressed aspects of themselves, or going back to those parts they have lost touch with because of the demands of career and parenthood, can lead to enrichment and completion, as Jung (1933) has emphasized.

Eventually, however, everyone has to face the death of their parents, the involution or running down of physical and mental powers, the relinquishing of children, the loss of career at retirement, and the death of friends and eventually of themselves. At this final stage the balance is between despair and a sense of completion or fitting into a scheme in which death and birth are part of the same cycle of renewal. How the scale tips depends not only on our current circumstances, but on the individual's attitudes, which represent the summation of solutions to every earlier crisis, and on social attitudes.

Since the first edition of this book in 1979, society and social attitudes have been changing fast. They influence all Erickson's stages of development described above. For example:

• A trustful mother–infant bond can be threatened by immaturity and lack of support, with rising teenage pregnancies and poor child-minding facilities.

- A childhood sense of autonomy, initiative, and industry need fostering by still inadequate and unequal educational facilities, and encouragement by parents not too indifferent or over-pressurizing.
- Adolescent identity formation can be distorted by parental divorce, and by commercial and peer pressures in regard to early sex, drugs, etc.
- Job insecurity and unemployment, along with such factors already mentioned, can delay the establishment of intimate partnerships and thus the ability to plan for children in a secure setting.
- In later years, redundancy, unemployability, an unplanned retirement, as well as broken marriages and the scattering of families by increased social mobility add to the difficulty of facing the later years with integrity rather than despair.

But as Erickson notes, each stage is a crisis to be met, as a challenge. Many older people now find a new lease of life through creative, planned retirement. They, like many younger people, are finding less formal arrangements than marriage, and introduction agencies and advertising columns are used nowadays without shame. Sexual plurality, the depathologizing of homosexuality, and the acceptance of multi-culturalism and feminism are all part of moves towards a freer, more tolerant society which creates gains as well as strains.

ATTACHMENT THEORY

Bowlby's ideas were probably stimulated by his work as a young man in a home for maladjusted boys. He was profoundly affected by his clinical work with boys whose relationships with their mothers had been disrupted and he later went on to study 44 juvenile thieves. He found that one factor that distinguished the thieves from other children was evidence of their prolonged separation from their parents and that this was particularly striking amongst those whom he termed affectionless. This led to his suggestion that disruption of the early mother–child relationship was a forerunner of later mental disturbance. Whilst this seems to be commonsense nowadays, it was far from the case then. Development was seen, as we have already discussed, as an almost intrinsic process of internal psychological struggle and biological drives, only marginally influenced by the mother and environment. Now a new emphasis propelling development was being suggested in which the mother influenced the infant and the infant stimulated responses from the carers.

Further study over a number of years, which included the documentation on film of the impact on 18–48-month-olds of separation from their parents during admission to hospital or residential nursery by colleagues (Robertson, 1952), led to Bowlby's view that the infant is born with a predisposition to engage in social interaction and that the crucial aspect to developing this ability is an unbroken (secure) attachment to the mother. Bowlby thought that the child who does not experience this was likely to show signs either of partial deprivation, such as an excessive need for love, or of complete deprivation indicated by listlessness, unresponsiveness, and retarded development. He later considered these reactions in terms of separation, as we have already mentioned – protest, despair, and detachment.

Bowlby initially gave a biological focus to attachment, emphasizing the survival value of the attachment process by ensuring proximity with a protector. But later he focused on intrinsic behavioural aspects and the role of the attachment process in regulating the infant's internal states. So attachment was even possible to abusive caretakers because the goal of attachment is to regulate an internal state stimulated by fear. Proximity-seeking takes place as soon as a child is fearful; when the closeness is achieved, the fear is assuaged and supplanted by a psychological goal of feeling close to someone. Thus the response of the caregiver is crucial. Fundamentally the attachment system is organized around reciprocity – a behaviour in the child stimulates a response in the mother, and vice versa. *Care-seeking* behaviours are met by *care-giving* behaviours. The child cries and reaches out for the mother and the mother reaches out in response to pick up the child. In doing so she soothes the child's fear. In this way a secure base develops from which further exploration can take place. The exploration will come to an abrupt halt at the point at which the child becomes fearful, and so the presence or absence of the attachment figure has a profound influence on how much exploration takes place. Separation therefore has two stressful features: the child experiences the fear of exposure and does not have access to the source of protection. Bowlby reserved the term anxiety for the experience of the child when the fear system is aroused during exposure in the absence of mother.

The three behavioural systems of attachment, exploration, and fear create the context in which development takes place and are now known to have a profound effect on the cognitive, affective, and social development of the child. Bowlby suggested that the appropriate availability of the mother led to the development of *internal working models*, which are in effect mental representations and expectations related to oneself and others. Over time it has become apparent that children and mothers show different patterns of attachment. Mary Ainsworth, a developmental psychologist at one time working at the Tavistock Clinic in London, developed a test known as the Strange Situation, based on the separation of the infant from the mother (Ainsworth & Wittig, 1969). Infants are briefly separated from their mother in a situation unfamiliar to them. Initially the infant is allowed to explore with his mother in the room. A stranger enters the room, usually a nice research assistant, who converses with the parent and then approaches infant. At this point the parent leaves the room inconspicuously. The stranger's behaviour is then responsive to that of the infant. Shortly after, the mother re-enters the room and greets and comforts the infant. This pattern is repeated again but with the stranger entering after the child has been alone for a short time. When the parent re-enters she picks up the infant after greeting him and the stranger leaves the room inconspicuously. Two aspects of the child's behaviour are observed: the amount of exploration (e.g. playing with new toys) the child engages in throughout the experiment; and the child's reactions to the departure and return of his mother. Four patterns of behaviour are apparent:

1 *Secure* infants explore readily when they are with their mother but are anxious in the presence of the stranger and avoid her; they are distressed by their mother's brief absence and rapidly seek contact with their mother afterwards and are reassured by this contact, returning to their exploration.

2 *Anxious/avoidant* infants appear to be made less anxious by separation, may not seek proximity with their mother after separation, and may not appear to prefer her over the stranger.

3 *Anxious/resistant* infants show restricted play, tend to be highly distressed by the separation, and do not settle afterwards, showing stiffness, tearfulness, and fussing in a passive way.

The mother's presence does not reassure them and the infant's anxiety and apparent anger interfere with his capacity to derive comfort from the proximity.

4   *Disorganized/disorientated* infants show freezing, head banging, and a desperate wish to escape from the situation even in the presence of the mother. They may even attack the stranger and are not comforted by the return of the mother.

It is generally thought that in these cases the mother serves both as a source of comfort and fear. As a result, anxiety stimulated by the Strange Situation produces confusing states of mind.

The stability of attachment patterns of childhood has been demonstrated by following children assessed using the Strange Situation into adolescence and young adulthood and re-assessing their attachment using the Adult Attachment Interview (AAI) developed by Main and Goldwyn (1991). The AAI is a structured clinical interview which elicits a narrative history of childhood attachment relationships from the person by asking about early relationships, separations, loss, punishment, and episodes of mal-treatment. Again, a number of different categories become appar-ent. *Autonomous/secure* individuals value attachment relationships and coherently integrate memories into a meaningful story and regard them as formative. *Insecure/dismissing* people tend to deny memories and idealize or denigrate those that they talk about, whilst *insecure/preoccupied* individuals tend to be confused or angry or somewhat bewildered about their memories of attachment figures. A final group of *unresolved* individuals display significant disorganization, showing semantic or syntactic confusions in their narratives: for example, at one point saying that their mother betrayed them and they have never forgiven her; and yet, when describing a further memory, saying that their mother was their best friend.

It is those infants with disorganized attachment and adults with significant disorganization who are receiving the most attention. Attachment research has become increasingly concerned with child maltreatment and neglect. The disorganized attachment was linked to maltreatment of the child and unresolved trauma histories of the parent. The traumatized mother becomes both the signal of safety and the source of anxiety or danger which undermines the whole of the attachment behavioural system. Longitudinal investigations have linked infant disorganization to later dissociative states and to adult mental health problems and personality disorder. But the link between childhood experience, the attachment process, and adulthood is complicated. Studies of low-risk groups have failed to identify any simple relationship between insecure attachment, for example, and behavioural problems in middle childhood. By contrast, studies of high-risk groups have been more successful in finding a relationship between insecure attachment and externalizing problems (e.g. aggression, poor peer relations) in the school years and between ambivalent attachment and anxiety disorder in adolescence (Raikes & Thompson, 2006). The effects of attachment trauma may be mediated through failures in the development of mentalizing, which is discussed on p. 82.

Finally, the question for clinicians is how attachment theory and research contribute to the practice of psychotherapy itself. Psychotherapy is, at its base, an attachment relationship. We will discuss this in the final section on the therapeutic alliance (see p. 68) but first we consider models of the mind. How the mind functions is highly dependent on the attachment relationship and the context in which the developing infant and child finds himself.

MODELS OF THE MIND

We need some sort of working model of the mind as a framework within which to organize our experience, much as we need a map when embarking on a journey in unfamiliar territory. It is probably in this area of the theories of psychic structure, or metapsychology, that most disagreement has arisen among the different psychodynamic schools. It must be remembered that these are theories or models of how the mind works; we should expect constant revision of such theories in the light of advances in our understanding of man, comparable to the revisions in other scientific fields such as in the theories of the structure of matter or of the nature of gravitation.

Freud revised his own theories several times, although fundamental to his thinking and that of other psychodynamic schools is the idea of different psychic levels. Here there is more than a hint of Freud's neurological background and the influence upon him of the neurologist Hughlings Jackson. At first (in the 1890s) he described the psychic apparatus simply in terms of *conscious* and *unconscious* levels. Next (in *The Interpretation of*

Dreams, 1900) came his topographical theory with the idea of conscious, preconscious, and unconscious realms. Consciousness would correspond to what we are immediately aware of at any given moment. The preconscious would include all those memories or sense impressions, of which we are not immediately aware, but which can fairly easily be brought to full consciousness. The unconscious would include repressed memories and sensations, which are not so readily available, as well as more primitive impulses and fantasies (p. 14).

In 1923 (in *The Ego and the Id*) Freud introduced his structural theory with the now familiar concepts of *super-ego*, *ego*, and *id* (ego and id corresponding roughly to conscious and unconscious respectively, and super-ego approximating to conscience). This is a much more complex theory than the previous one. The conscious, preconscious, and unconscious labels of the topographical theory describe different levels or areas of experience. The structural theory is a hybrid that attempts to combine biological, experiential, and interpersonal dimensions. For example, by id is meant the basic biological aspect of the psyche, the inherited instinctual and constitutional aspects which we share to a large extent with other higher primates. It recalls Darwin's closing words in *The Descent of Man* (1871): 'Man with all his noble qualities . . . still bears in his bodily frame the indelible stamp of his lowly origin.'

The ego (corresponding roughly to consciousness) is concerned with rational thinking, external perception, and voluntary movement. It may be noted that there is some correspondence between such ego functions and cortical activity (in neurophysiological terms). The former are mostly waking functions, concerned with external reality, and are largely suspended in sleep. Other functions such as defence mechanisms (p. 28) operate at a more unconscious level, but are also relaxed during sleep and fatigue or under the influence of drugs and alcohol. The ego is at the centre of object relations, both as they are represented in our inner world and met in the outer world. The ego is the mediator between the needs and demands of the inside world and the realities and opportunities of the outside world. In performing this refereeing task it has to heed the super-ego, which is roughly equivalent to conscience, both in its conscious and unconscious aspects.

The super-ego is built up from the internalized representations and standards of parental figures from infancy onwards, with contributions from later relationships with teachers and other admired or feared figures. We can distinguish further between the more primitive and punitive aspects of the super-ego ('Thou shalt not . . .') and the more positive ego-ideal or those precepts we may try to follow. The primitive super-ego and the ego-ideal are somewhat like the Gods of the Old and New Testaments, respectively. It must be remembered that not all the operations of the super-ego are conscious. We may think out for ourselves, as adults, our attitudes to major issues of the day, such as abortion, euthanasia, etc., but more frequently in many (often trivial) ways, such as queuing in shops, we operate according to the less conscious dictates of conscience. Indeed, society could hardly survive without them. Difficulty arises when the unconscious super-ego (unnecessarily) represses feelings and impulses which may then give rise to symptoms, as in the case of the paralysed left arm of the young woman who wanted to hit her therapist (p. 19).

We have already said that the structural theory is a hybrid. The id is more of a biological concept that refers to the instinctual processes within a single person. The super-ego is an entirely different sort of concept, which moves away from one-person psychology towards family and social psychology. It is a concept which implies an interpersonal dimension including others in the external world who become internalized and set up as internal representations or images. These internal images people our dreams, but may be externalized and experienced in our ready response to myths, fairy stories, and drama. Such images are not exact representations of real past external figures, but, coloured by our feelings towards them, may become exaggeratedly good or bad objects. This process has been particularly emphasized by the followers of Melanie Klein (Segal, 1964). These idealized and denigrated figures become the heroes and demons of our dreams and mythology.

From the 1920s onwards there was a movement in theory-building away from models involving physical notions of psychic energy, towards more interpersonal models involving relationships between people. The object-relations theorists (Fairbairn, 1952; Guntrip, 1961; Winnicott, 1965; Balint, 1968; Greenberg & Mitchell, 1983a) whom we have already mentioned (p. 42) were an example of this movement.

The term *object-relations* theory is ill-defined despite its significant influence in psychotherapy. Greenberg and Mitchell (1983b) undertook a definitive assessment of the concept and suggested it was a theory concerned with the relationship between real, external people and the traces they leave in the mind of the other in terms of internal images, relationships, representations, and emotions. During childhood we build up images of our relationships with our parents, family, friends, and important caregivers. These develop in complexity over time. We internalize a representation of the relationship we have with them, that is, we lay down a memory of the interactions and the emotions associated with them. These representations gradually become mentally active internal working models which guide us in future relationships because we can use them to predict interactions with others. When people vary from our internal expectations based on previous experience, we become more alert and wary because the interaction does not map easily onto an internal representation. We look for reciprocity between external and internal and avoid jarring clashes which create anxiety.

From an object-relations perspective there is neither a need to consider the balance of the ego, super-ego, and id nor a requirement to consider basic motivational drives. Nevertheless practitioners have tended to combine models with the result that, over time, mixed models of the mind have become predominant. For example it is accepted, as we have suggested, that patterns of objects relations are shaped by the early interactions with the caregivers, that they become increasingly complex through the stages of development, and that they may be distorted by aggressive drives as well as external experience.

With the development of object-relations theory, psychoanalysis has moved increasingly towards an experiential perspective in terms of understanding the interaction between the patient and therapist as a representation of their internal object relations. In other words, what happens between the patient and therapist is a residue of the patient's relational past, an enactment of his internal object-relational states, and indicative of how he forms his current relationships. The focus of therapy has therefore become the relationship rather than an understanding of the interaction between forces. In the next section we consider this in more detail in relation to the transference (see p. 70).

Self-psychology, or self-object theory (p. 138), is a further development of object-relations theory and conceives of the self as over-and-above ('super-ordinate') the tripartite division of ego, super-ego, and id. In developing a strong and resilient self, we need others not only as sources of gratification and as objects to rely on and internalize, but also as self-object mirrors of ourself. The self is envisaged as having two poles, leading from modified grandiosity to realizable goals. An adequate self thus feels good about itself, and when disappointed and 'narcissistically wounded' does not fragment and resort to 'narcissistic rage' or denial and self-destructive behaviour. Attempts have been made to integrate self-psychology with object-relations theory (Kernberg, 1975; Bacal & Newman, 1990).

By placing *relationship* at the centre of human experience, self-psychology has more in common with object-relations theorists such as Fairbairn and Guntrip than with classical Freud and Klein. However, as Bacal and Newman have pointed out, Freud foresaw the central role of an object-relations perspective, perhaps even the self-object function of others and, even further, possibly attachment theory itself. In a footnote in *Three Essays on the Theory of Sexuality* (Freud, 1905, p. 224) he tells a story:

> I once heard a three-year-old boy calling out of a dark room: 'Auntie, speak to me! I'm frightened because it's so dark.' His aunt answered him: 'What good would that do? You can't see me.' 'That doesn't matter', replied the child, 'if anyone speaks it gets light'. Thus what he was afraid of was not the dark, but the absence of someone he loved; and he could feel sure of being soothed as soon as he had evidence of that person's presence.

Eric Berne, in *Games People Play* (1966), has given a popular account of a serious psychodynamic school in the USA known as transactional analysis (see p. 221). His use of the concept of 'ego states' representing the adult, parent, and child parts in each one of us is a particularly graphic way of expressing psychic structure in terms which will also be helpful when considering the phenomenon of transference in the next section. If we consider the different levels of the psyche (Figure 1) as described by psychoanalytic and transactional analytic theory we can discern: a rough correspondence between the primitive child part of us and the id; a closer correspondence between the ego and the adult, rational, reality-orientated part of us; and the closest correspondence of all between the super-ego and the parent within ourselves. Among the advantages of using these terms is that they have immediate meaning to

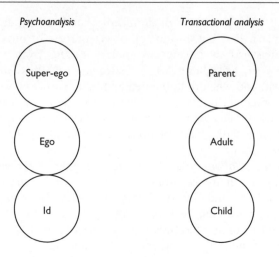

Figure 1

most people. To speak of conflicts between super-ego and id may be thought to give a scientific ring to discussions amongst professionals but would make little sense to most patients; to talk of conflicts between the parent and child parts within us makes sense to most people.

We have emphasized repeatedly the notion of different psychic levels and, in particular, the frequent dualities which ran throughout Freud's thinking and appear also in other psychodynamic formulations (Table 3). For example, Freud contrasted conscious and unconscious; ego and id; secondary process thinking (rational and logical) as characteristic of consciousness and primary process thinking (illogical and irrational) as characteristic of the unconscious; the reality principle, which dictates the workings of the ego, and the pleasure principle dictating the id. There may be conflict between the present and the past and between culture and instinct. There is a conflict between the outer world or external reality and our inner world or psychic reality. Jung wrote of the contrast between the persona or mask which we present to the world and the shadow or darker side of our nature which we wish to hide. Winnicott (1960) and Laing (1960) have written similarly of the false self which hides the inner true self. In Berne's terms the adult obscures the child.

Table 3 Dual levels of psychic structure

Conscious	Unconscious
Ego	Id
Secondary process thinking	Impulse
Reality principle	Primary process thinking
Outer world	Pleasure principle
External reality	Inner world
Present	Psychic reality
Culture	Past
False self	Instinct
Persona	True self
Adult	Shadow
	Child

Table 4 Dual levels of awareness between self and others

	Known to self	Unknown to self
Known to others	A Public self	B Blind self
Unknown to others	C Secret self	D Unconscious self

We have specially emphasized how this way of thinking in terms of different psychic layers or levels is common to all psychodynamic schools. Sometimes there are things we admit to ourselves but hide from others; sometimes we also hide things from ourselves. This is common human experience which any theory of the psyche has to meet. Table 4 (modified from Luft, 1966) illustrates how such dual levels of awareness within the individual relate to similar dualities between people in everyday life.

As will be discussed in Part II, psychotherapy involves information being communicated from C to A (self-disclosure), from B to A (contributions from others), and from D to A (in more intensive treatments).

So far we have tended to speak of personality dynamics as self-contained, the ego working to integrate the diverse pressures from id, super-ego, and external reality as perceived by the sensory apparatus of the individual. This model portrays the individual as essentially isolated, with the external world represented by images and memories based upon interpretations of his experiences. Although this model is extremely useful in explaining *intrapsychic* phenomena, it has limitations when we come to more complex *interpersonal* phenomena. This is not surprising; scientists have long been discovering that events cannot be fully understood without taking into account the environment or setting in which they occur. Just as the malfunctioning of an organ may be part of the distress of the whole person, so a malfunctioning individual may be part of a whole family in trouble, or a family disturbance may be part of a social malaise. A disturbance may permeate all three levels: for example, a child may develop abdominal cramp which keeps him off school so that he can remain reassuringly close to mother, who is depressed and talking of suicide because of her husband's inability to get employment.

The model of the individual mind can be seen as a system inside a wider system, that of the family, inside another, that of society. These systems are not enclosed in watertight boundaries; they inevitably influence each other. In talking of one person and his impulses, the concept of psychic 'energy' may be useful. When considering the effect of early relationships on the interaction between two individuals, object-relations theory (p. 42) may be more helpful, with its emphasis on the role of internal images or representations of people in the outer world. In discussing more complex interpersonal and social phenomena, notions of communication and information (Watzlawick, Beavin, & Jackson, 1968) are more relevant. The contrasts between these three levels of interaction are more spurious than real. People function on all three levels at once; the isolated individual is an abstraction.

General systems theory (Bertalanffy, 1968) has been developed over the last few decades to study and explain interactions in a wide range of fields from cybernetics to sociology, and more recently psychiatry. A system is a set of interacting elements within a hypothetical boundary which makes it more or less open to mutual influence with the environment; in sociology and psychology this influence is largely effected by informational communication. Systems theory allows us to think more clearly about the well-known fact that a setting determines what happens inside that setting, and that parts cannot be understood without considering the whole, as expressed in John Donne's view that 'No man is an *island*, intire of itself – every man is a peece of the *Continent*, a part of the *maine*'. It helps us to understand self-regulating processes, which depend on control and feedback, and the interaction of cause and effect.

Traditionally, in the physical sciences, and therefore in medical thinking derived from them, effect was always thought to follow cause and it was considered illegitimate to suggest that the effect might be the cause. The cause of a symptom had to be sought in the physical lesion which resulted in the symptom: for example, abdominal pain caused by appendicitis. However, where there is no physical lesion the effect of the symptom may itself be the cause. This way of thinking – to consider the effect of the symptom in seeking its cause – has often been dismissed as shoddy teleological reasoning. However, as Bowlby (1969) has shown, it is now perfectly legitimate in many complex scientific spheres to think in this way. The trajectory of an old-fashioned cannon ball or bullet will be described by its velocity aim, and so on, when fired. The end is determined by the start. This is the 'billiard ball' universe of Newtonian mechanics. However, in more complex systems, such as a guided missile, the trajectory will be constantly adjusted according to whether or not the desired end point is being achieved. Similarly, in living organisms, complex behaviour is often 'goal-corrected'; abdominal pain, the effect of which is to miss school, may be caused by unwillingness to go to school.

Human beings exist in a series of systems. From the start they are part of a system (the mother–child pair) which is part of a larger one (the family) which in turn is part of further overlapping and concentric systems (the extended family, school, the neighbourhood, the wider community, etc.). These are termed 'open systems', in that their boundaries are permeable to influences from the smaller sub-systems they comprise and the larger supra-system of which they are a part. We can discern hierarchies of systems in which smaller ones are subject to the rules and expectations of large ones: for example, the individual to the rules of the family, the family to those of society. Furthermore, each system contains a 'decider sub-system' with functions of communication, control, and coordination, such as the central nervous system or ego in the individual, the parents in the family, or government in society. In trying to understand phenomena at any level, we have to decide where to focus attention. Can we understand someone's headache or high blood pressure in terms of an isolated physical system, or do we have to include the whole person (body plus mind)? Can we adequately explain an underlying anxiety or rage without taking into account the family network or relationships at work? Finally, can we explain a person's condition fully without taking social

phenomena into account, for example, whether his social conditions, such as poor housing or unemployment, are contributing to
the poor family relationships and thus to his emotional disturbance?

> Observe how system into system runs,
> What other planets circle other suns.
>   (Alexander Pope, *An Essay on Man*, 1733)

A systems theory approach allows us to conceptualize the organization of such interacting levels and to clarify where we can
usefully concentrate therapeutic intervention. For example, we
might not accept a family's view as to who the sick person is. A
child brought with bed-wetting or school-refusal may be best
helped by looking at the whole family; the arrival of a new baby,
mother's depression, or parental discord may need to be considered
in order to help the child. Until we look at the wider system we
cannot see the meanings and messages, overt and covert, which the
patient is conveying or to which he is responding. Unless we look
at the whole family, we might be unable to explain why, following
treatment, beneficial change in one member leads to a detrimental
change in another – for example the husband of an agoraphobic
housebound wife becoming depressed when she gives up her
helpless role.

Similarly, we may not understand what is happening between the
patient and doctor until we recognize that the patient is treating the
doctor as though he were somebody from the past, from the earlier
family system, as will be discussed in the following section in
considering transference.

THERAPEUTIC RELATIONSHIPS

In considering the total doctor–patient or therapist–client relationship, we feel it is helpful to distinguish four elements. These
are the *therapeutic or working alliance, transference, countertransference*, and *mentalization*.

Therapeutic alliance (see Table 5)

The therapeutic or working alliance refers to the ordinarily good
relationship that any two people need to have in cooperating over

Table 5 Elements of the therapeutic alliance

Patient
    Affective interaction with the therapist
    Perception that therapist interventions are relevant and helpful
    Recognition of significance of goals of therapy
    Personal bond with the therapist
Therapist
    Ability to be responsive, sympathetic, and helpful
    Sensitive and appropriate intervention
    Respectful of patient
    Affective interaction with patient
Patient and therapist
    Collaborate on aims of therapy
    Congruence between expectations
    Development of shared understanding

---

some joint task. In medicine it has often been known as establishing a good rapport with a patient. It is an everyday affair, fostered by friendliness, courtesy, respect, and reliability, as any good tradesman or professional person unselfconsciously demonstrates. In therapy it is defined as 'the relatively non-neurotic, rational relationship between the patient and the analyst which makes it possible for the patient to work purposefully in the analytic situation' (Greenson, 1967, p. 46).

The importance of the therapeutic alliance in psychotherapy has been repeatedly demonstrated in research literature. In an important conceptual article, Gaston (1990) suggested that both therapist and patient bring elements to the alliance and described four components: the patient's affective relationship with the therapist, the patient's capacity to work purposefully in therapy, the therapist's empathic understanding and involvement, and the patient–therapist agreement on the goals and tasks of therapy. One way to identify the importance of these factors in therapy is to look at all the studies that measure the therapeutic alliance and combine the data to make a larger sample size on which to perform a statistical analysis. This is known as a meta-analysis and was developed in psychotherapy research because samples from individual studies tended to be small. Martin, Garske, and Davis (2000) did this and found that the therapeutic alliance was consistently related to outcomes, suggesting that the alliance not only reflects positive change but may also produce it. The importance of the alliance is not restricted to psychotherapy and may improve outcomes in other treatments. In the NIMH Depression

Study (see p. 264) the relationship between the alliance and outcome was equal across pharmacological and psychotherapeutic treatments, accounting for nearly a quarter of the variance in combined self-report and expert-related outcomes. The same is likely to be true even for surgical procedures. So, the take-home message for doctors is that focusing on the relationship with the patient is an essential part of good treatment.

Whilst the positive aspects of the therapeutic alliance are important for the effective implementation of therapy, it has become apparent that negotiating a breakdown in the alliance is also of importance (Safran & Muran, 2000). No therapy goes smoothly. Sometimes the therapist will slip up and at other times the patient will feel demoralized. How the patient and therapist manage these situations in which the collaboration is lost is of considerable importance. They are known as ruptures in the alliance. Therapists need to acknowledge their own contribution to any breakdown in the quality of the relationship and to explore what has happened. Done sensitively, the rupture can become a significant learning point for both patient and therapist rather than an overwhelming negative experience leading to ending therapy. Hence difficulties in therapy become an opportunity to enhance understanding of the interpersonal process. This is not dissimilar to how we manage our closer relationships in life – when we encounter difficulties, we try to sort them out rather than running away from them.

Transference

The concept of transference, like psychotherapy itself, has both general and special meanings, though some would use the term only in the restricted sense to refer to a special phenomenon which arises in psychotherapy. In a general sense we respond to every new relationship according to patterns from the past. We transfer feelings and attitudes developed in earlier similar experiences, especially where there are no particular clues available as to how we should react; this is what psychologists call 'set'. For example, in a new job, we may find ourselves reacting inexplicably strongly to a male or female supervisor, until it becomes apparent that the supervisor reminds us of, and re-awakens feelings about, an authoritarian father or domineering mother.

This phenomenon is intensified when we are anxious due to illness or disaster. All mothers know that a child, when ill or frightened, reverts to behaviour characteristic of an earlier age and needs more cuddling and attention. As adults, too, when severely ill we tend to regress emotionally to earlier, more child-like, levels of functioning and react to doctors or nurses as if they were parents or figures from the past. This usually causes few problems in medicine, because it is reversible as the acute phase of illness passes. After all, in traditional medicine much of nursing is a mothering function – feeding, dressing, washing, comforting – and much of doctoring, from a patient's emotional viewpoint, is more of a paternal function – visiting the ward to see how nurse/mother is coping. This holds true psychologically whether the nurse or doctor is actually male or female.

More particularly, in any developing psychotherapeutic relationship, patients may begin to experience feelings towards the therapist as if he were a significant figure from the past. Transference then becomes a tool for investigating the forgotten and repressed past or as something that helps to understand how the patient has become sensitized by earlier relationships. Greenson (1967, p. 155) has defined transference as:

> the experiencing of feelings, drives, attitudes, fantasies and defences toward a person in the present, which do not befit that person but are a repetition of reactions originating in regard to significant persons of early childhood, unconsciously displaced onto figures in the present. The two outstanding characteristics of a transference reaction are: it is a repetition and it is inappropriate.

Let us go back to using the terms of Berne and transactional analysis (p. 63) and consider various situations where any person seeking help (Figure 2, left) may consult any help-giver (Figure 2, right). Parent, adult, and child parts of each are represented by P, A, and C. If, for example, we take our car to the garage for a service, this should remain an emotionally neutral and therefore purely adult–adult transaction or working alliance (see Figure 3).

However if, for example, we go to our bank manager to ask permission for an overdraft, we might think we have perfectly good grounds and that this will be a purely adult–adult transaction (A↔A) and then be taken aback to find the bank manager behaving like a heavy-handed and lecturing parent, as if we were a demanding child (C←P, Figure 4a). On the other hand, we might go along feeling like a guilty child asking for more pocket money

Help-seeker   Help-giver

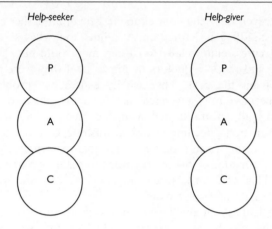

Figure 2

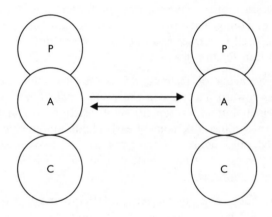

Figure 3

and expecting a stern parental refusal (C→P); we may then be pleasantly surprised to find that the manager treats us straight-forwardly as another adult (A←A) (Figure 4b).

If we consult a doctor about a fairly trivial and emotionally neutral problem (e.g. an ingrowing toenail) this should remain a straightforward adult–adult transaction (Figure 5a). But when we are more anxious about ourselves, or when acutely ill, we tend to regress to more child-like levels of functioning and invest doctors or nurses with whatever good or ill we may have felt towards parental figures in the past (Figure 5b). As we have already said,

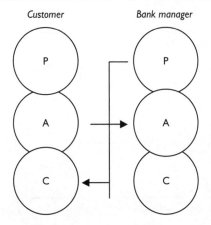

Figure 4a

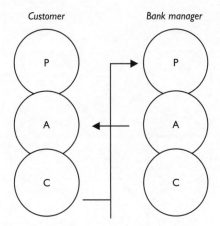

Figure 4b

this matters little in acute illness as it is readily reversible. How, indeed, could a patient requiring emergency surgery permit a stranger to cut into his flesh unless the child part of him were capable of considerable basic trust and of investing the surgeon with goodwill as a benevolent parent figure?

However, the same regressive phenomena may cause problems in less acute medicine and not be so easily reversible. For example, in the past the admission of patients to remote mental hospitals for long periods robbed them of their adult responsibilities for feeding,

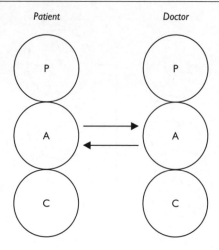

Figure 5a

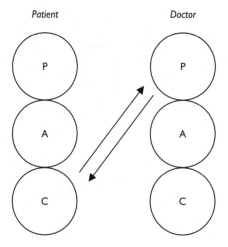

Figure 5b

clothing, and supporting themselves. Treating them as children, and thereby infantilizing them, exposed patients to the risks of institutionalization and added to whatever underlying disease process there may have been.

We now move on to the occurrence of transference in the special field of psychotherapy. One of Breuer's famous cases, described in the *Studies on Hysteria* (Breuer & Freud, 1895), was that of Anna

O, who had numerous hysterical symptoms, including paralyses and disturbances of vision and speech. Breuer found that these could be relieved by putting her into a light hypnotic trance and inviting her to express in words the repressed feelings and unacceptable thoughts that she had experienced at the time of nursing her sick and dying father. Anna herself called this her 'talking cure' or 'chimney-sweeping'. Towards the end of treatment, erotic feelings emerged towards Breuer, which alarmed him as he took it for an adult–adult (or frankly adulterous) reaction. He is said to have taken his wife for a second honeymoon to reassure them both; and thereafter he withdrew from further explorations in this field (Jones, 1953, ch. 11).

Freud, on the other hand, puzzled over this reaction, particularly when a patient flung her arms round his neck (Jones, 1953). When other patients began to express towards him feelings of either affection or hostility that he felt he had done nothing to provoke on the adult–adult level, it occurred to him that perhaps it was the child part of the patient re-experiencing him as some parent figure from the past. At first he thought such feelings were an obstacle to the treatment and to the smooth flow of free associations. Soon he realized that this was an invaluable new tool for investigating the forgotten and repressed past. As inner representations of figures from the past become superimposed onto the image of the therapist, feelings are expressed towards him that belong to the past. The consciously forgotten past becomes re-enacted in the present of the transference. This re-enactment has been called the 'private theatre' of transference (Pontalis, 1974).

In analytic psychotherapy (Figure 6) the therapist first sets up a therapeutic or working alliance between the adult part of the patient and the adult part of himself (A↔A) in order to investigate the way this relationship is distorted by the child part of the patient, which colours his feelings towards the therapist with residues of feelings about important people from the past (C→P or the transference). Sometimes the working alliance itself has been called the positive transference, but this is confusing and it is useful to distinguish between the working alliance and positive and negative aspects of the transference (Sandler, Dare, & Holder, 1973).

It follows that analytic psychotherapy can only really work satisfactorily in an unmodified form when the patient has sufficient adult capacity or 'ego strength' to recognize, tolerate, and sustain the paradox that, although he may have intense feelings towards the

Patient   Therapist

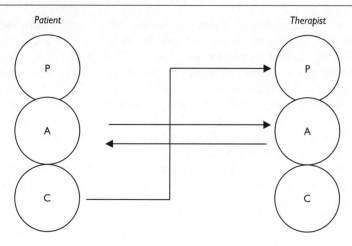

Figure 6

therapist 'as if' the latter were a parent, in reality this is not the case. This capacity to appreciate the paradox is similar to that needed by the audience in the theatre (Pedder, 1977) or to the 'conscious acceptance of the as-ifness' (Milner, 1971) needed to enjoy any form of art. There may be insufficient ego strength for this in the immature or in those of markedly low intelligence; and in the psychotic the 'as if' quality may be lost, and the transference become psychotic, so that the therapist really is confused with the parent (p. 241). This does not mean that analytic therapy is unhelpful in these cases but that the therapist may need to adapt the standard technique.

In individual psychotherapy or analysis, the most likely manifestation of transference will be when the patient begins to experience the therapist as if he were an aspect of mother or father, even regardless of the sex of the therapist. However, feelings about other family members from the past may also be transferred into the present, as for example when a patient begins to experience the therapist's other patients as siblings to whom he may feel intensely rivalrous. The re-enactment of forgotten feelings about siblings may become even more obvious in a psychotherapy group (Brown, 1998a).

A young adult woman started in a group because she was chronically depressed. She was the elder of two children brought

up in an old-fashioned family who (it was presumed) had longed
for a son as the first-born child. The second child, born three
years after her, was a boy and his arrival probably much feted, so
that she may well have felt intensely jealous or even frankly
murderous towards him. Perhaps to a certain extent she over-
came these feelings and as they grew up came to appreciate him
as a companion. But when she was about 20 he was killed in a
road accident and it was then that she became chronically
depressed. A psychodynamic formulation would be that her
brother's actual death in the recent past had awakened guilt
about her childhood feelings of hostility in the remoter past, as if
her earlier murderous feelings had somehow come magically true,
leaving her feeling weighed down by guilt and thus depressed.
However, when at first any suggestion was made to her along
these lines in the group, she dismissed it contemptuously. Then
after a few months a new male patient, slightly younger than
herself, joined the group. She attacked and criticized him merci-
lessly in a way which, to everyone else in the group, was evidently
out of proportion to any real characteristics the unfortunate
newcomer may have had. Then she began to see that she was
reacting to this new arrival in the family of the group with all the
repressed and forgotten hostility she had felt towards the arrival
of her brother in her original family. But it was only re-
experiencing these buried feelings in the transference here and
now that enabled her to get in touch with them.

Transference phenomena are directed towards the therapist and
towards others in the therapeutic situation – for example, fellow
group members as in the example just cited, where the transference
was to the group as family and to a new group member as an
unwelcome newborn brother. The setting – the couch, the consulting room, the continuity of sessions, the group as a whole, the
therapeutic community, the hospital – can become charged with
powerful feelings and fantasies that we need to consider if otherwise incomprehensible actions are to be understood. For many
patients the hospital or other institution is experienced as an
extension of the therapist (Main, 1989, ch. 3), so feelings and
actions directed towards one or the other are similar. In contrast,
they may be very different, as when disturbed, often 'borderline'
patients split staff into good and bad aspects of themselves and the
staff represent their own 'internal objects'. This causes rifts and

disagreements in the staff that need to be recognized if they are to be healed.

The development of positive transference to an institution and its staff can make it difficult for patients to leave, but for chronically dependent and damaged patients it can ensure that they are sufficiently sustained. The diffusion and generalization of transference enables them to feel secure in the availability of help if they should need it, despite the inevitable change of staff over the years; the six-monthly rotation of junior psychiatrists can otherwise be devastatingly disruptive to the chronically disturbed patients who are left to their care.

So far we have talked about transference as an 'as if' phenomenon in which patients experience someone in the present 'as if' they are someone from their past. This is the most basic definition of transference and critics have suggested that understanding transference in this way leads to the danger of undermining a patient's current feeling and experience by implying that it is not relevant to the current context and is primarily a distortion of the present by the past. There is merit in this and it is often better for psychotherapists to consider transference not so much as the inexorable manifestation of unconscious mental forces from the past, but rather as the emergence of latent meanings, organized around and evoked by the intensity of the therapy relationship. This involves examining how the details of present-day wishes, character formations, and personal expectations are influenced by the past – how the individual is sensitized in his current life by his past; it does not accept the idea of infantile neurosis as the only explanation for adult pathology, nor does it see transference neurosis as a simple pathway to cure – hence it de-emphasizes reconstruction as a therapy technique. Transference has thus become a much wider concept involving the interplay between the patient and the therapist, representing the conflicts of the mind and reflecting the interactions of the internal object representations; it is a medium through which the individual's internal drama is 'played out' with the therapist; it is a new experience influenced by the past, rather than a repetition of an earlier one.

To summarize, there are a number of ways in which transference is considered: as a distortion of reality or as a valid representation of a present unconscious situation coloured by experiences from the past; as a general or specific therapy phenomenon; and as the whole or only part of the therapeutic situation. We discuss these aspects of transference further in the later section in psychoanalytic psychotherapy.

Countertransference

In discussing the general aspects of transference, we have largely been considering the patient's feelings and attitudes towards the therapist. What about the latter's feelings towards the patient, which in the field of psychotherapy are generally referred to as *countertransference*? Sometimes doctors and nurses seem to feel guilty that they have any feelings towards patients or that they have failed to rise above them. Yet if young people were not moved by the sufferings and plight of others, the helping professions would be seriously denuded. Certainly there are times, such as when attending bad accidents or acute emergencies, when professional people need the help of their training in disciplining themselves to face the situation without fainting or running away. Yet we need not be ashamed of our feelings and in less acute situations can learn a lot from them.

For example, a medical student who had been interviewing a very withdrawn schizoid patient said, 'I'm very sorry but I could get nothing out of the patient.' Now this might have been a reflection on the student's poor interviewing technique, as he feared, or it could have been the response any human being would have experienced with this particular uncommunicative patient. Provided we can be sure that we are in a reasonably good humour, not too distracted by our own problems, or too pressurized by badly organized workload, then our feelings about a patient can be most instructive. Clearly such a concept can easily be abused since people react differently, and if the doctor got out of bed on the wrong side, all patients that day might be dismissed as hysterics. But by acknowledging such feelings in ourselves and reflecting on them – rather than by immediately acting on them and showing the patient the door – we can begin to wonder what it is in the patient that is making us feel this way.

Within the special field of psychotherapy, the concept of countertransference, like transference, has had various meanings; we find it helpful broadly to distinguish two uses. As in the development of the concept of transference, countertransference was at first thought of as an obstacle. Any strong feelings the therapist might have had about the patient were thought to represent his own unresolved conflicts and problems, from his own past or present life, transferred onto the patient. For this reason, among others, it is desirable for anyone specializing in any form of psychotherapy to first undergo a personal psychotherapeutic experience himself. This then is one meaning of countertransference, when the therapist contaminates the field with his own problems from elsewhere.

However, assuming that the therapist comes to the patient not unduly ruffled by his own problems and is able to maintain an attitude of 'free-floating attention' or 'listening with the third ear' in order to hear the message behind the patient's surface communication, then the therapist's own spontaneous feelings and emotions, as his unconscious 'tunes in' to that of the patient, may provide the key to understanding what is at first incomprehensible. Heimann (1950) was among the first to begin turning attention to this second aspect of countertransference, which, far from being an obstacle, becomes an important tool in psychotherapy. She assumed that the analyst's unconscious understands that of the patient, and that rapport at this deep level stirs feelings which it is the analyst's task to sustain and use as a source of insight into the patient's conflicts and defences.

About the same time Little (1951) was developing similar ideas in her work with severely disturbed patients, whom she recognized were often as exquisitely sensitive to the analyst's unconscious countertransference as to his intentional communications. Such patients test out the analyst's capacity to sustain the consequent tensions (Little, 1957). Winnicott (1947) described patients' capacity to evoke feelings of hatred in their helpers which are in some measure 'appropriate'. He usefully distinguished between such 'objective' countertransference, and 'subjective' aspects which stem more from situational or unresolved personal issues in the therapist. Since those early papers much has been written about the usefulness of analysing our countertransference reactions to patients (e.g. Racker, 1968; Sandler, 1976; Brown, 1977; Epstein & Feiner, 1979; Searles, 1979; Casement, 1985; Giovacchini, 1989; Baranger, 1993; Jacobs, 1999).

As Michael and Enid Balint (1961) put it, what the doctor feels may help him to understand his patient's illness. In other words, what the therapist feels may be part of the patient's communication, conscious or unconscious. The patient may feel more threatened, and therefore cut off from his feelings, than the therapist, whose capacity to tolerate conflict and anxiety should be less restricted. By putting himself empathically in the other's shoes, the therapist allows himself to feel what the patient has been unable to acknowledge in himself, such as anxiety or grief; or the therapist may experience feelings appropriate to the person the patient is treating him as in the transference (e.g. a protective or rejecting parent). In short, the therapist's countertransference feelings may be a reflection of what the patient feels about, or is doing to, the therapist, consciously or unconsciously.

In the treatment of a young woman struggling to free herself from a destructively critical and possessive elderly mother, the therapist found herself being drawn into feeling critical and controlling towards the patient. Recognition of this by the therapist in supervision enabled her to comment upon it and led to the patient herself recognizing how she repeatedly drew women into relationships of this sort.

This is an example of what Racker (1968) calls '*complementary* countertransference'; the therapist reacted in the way the patient expected her to behave, as a critical mother, drawn into it by the patient's unconscious provocation. The latter doubtless felt the aggrieved and hurt child. Indeed it was the therapist's ability to detach herself from the complementary countertransference sufficiently not to act on it, but instead to reflect about it, and her capacity to tune in empathically to how the hurt child felt – which Racker calls '*concordant* counter-transference' – that got them both beyond re-enacting the pathogenic early relationship.

In discussing transference we have tried to relate the phenomenon to other areas of experience in order to emphasize that this was not just something peculiar to psychoanalysis and psychotherapy. Can we do the same for countertransference? At times it may seem to imply something rather mysterious to suggest that the therapist is able to pick up feelings of which the patient is unaware, or disowns. But as Darwin (1872) argued in *The Expression of the Emotions in Man and Animals*, this is a basic mammalian capacity to pick up non-verbal cues about the emotional state of fellow beings so as to be able to know whether they are friend or foe. And the everyday prototype of what the analyst does in sensing the patient's feelings is surely what the mother does for her infant, who is literally 'in-fans' or without speech and cannot yet put feelings into words.

At first the infant is entirely dependent on mother for identifying states of distress and doing something about them, without words being exchanged. A little later mother begins to name the baby's feelings for him so that he can begin to think about them for himself. All infants must pre-verbally pass through a developmental phase of alexithymia, or having no words for feelings, which we see perpetuated so strikingly in psychosomatic patients. Just as mother helps her baby become acquainted with his feelings and eventually able to symbolize and talk about them, so does the analyst/therapist help his patient achieve the same via the use of the countertransference.

In recent decades we have deepened our understanding of therapeutic relationships as *mutually involving* – far from the notion of therapist as a blank screen, although we still have to be able to step back and reflect on our own as well as our patients' experience. A significant but still to some extent controversial trend in psychoanalysis has been the focus on the *mutually created* 'intersubjective relational matrix' (Atwood & Stolorow, 1984; Ogden, 1994; Dunn, 1995; Jones, 1997; Kennedy, 1998). This could be seen as resembling the joint exploration of the *multi-person matrix* created in the therapeutic setting in analytically orientated group and family therapy, and to some extent in social therapy (see relevant sections in Part II). In addition, the focus on intersubjective interactional process has been linked with attachment research in the development of the concept of mentalization.

Mentalization

Jerome Frank (1961, p. 232) wrote decades ago in his classic book, *Persuasion and Healing*, that:

> much, if not all, of the effectiveness of different forms of psychotherapy may be due to those features that all have in common rather than to those that distinguish them from each other.

It has been proposed that mentalizing – attending to mental states in oneself and others – is *the most fundamental common factor* among psychotherapeutic treatments and may account for the fact that different psychotherapeutic treatments may be equally effective for the same condition. So what exactly is mentalizing? We are mentalizing when we are aware of mental states in ourselves or others – when we are thinking about feelings, for example. The core of mentalizing is *holding mind in mind*. We give a mental quality to people in everyday life, for example interpreting a puzzled face as perhaps indicating we are not explaining things well; in psychotherapy we cultivate an awareness of self and other in terms of mental states, for example asking a patient what he makes of what we have said. But 'mental states' is a rather vague term and covers a large domain, including needs, desires, feelings, emotions, thoughts, beliefs, imaginings, dreams, hallucinations, delusions, and such like. To fully understand someone's mental state we have to understand many of these aspects of their inner experience, which is extremely difficult, if not impossible, and so we often use our imagination about how they feel and why they feel as they do. Mentalizing is restrained imagination in that sense – we obtain evidence and extend it using our imagination to further our understanding. We do not 'guess' with our imagination but place their mind in ours to see if we can place ourselves in their shoes. Mentalizing in this way entails interpreting behaviour as *based on* mental states, or involves inferring the mental states that lie *behind* overt behaviour as if 'behaviour' and 'mental states' are always separable. So when we are talking to someone and tears start to stream down his face, we ask him what is making him cry and gradually build up a mental framework around our observation. In doing so we also scrutinize how his behaviour and emotional expression affect us. Piecing it all together we gain a better understanding of someone and their motivations. Often, however, mental states and behaviour are inseparably *conjoined*, that is, so thoroughly intertwined that one cannot be disentangled from the other – as in a cry of pain or in leaning forward when paying keen attention and engaging in rapid-fire conversation.

This brief discussion of mentalization illustrates a number of important features of the process. First, there is an interactional component in which appraisal of both the other person's mental state and one's own is required. There is a reciprocity with the expectation that learning about someone's mind will change one's own mind and that this will be reciprocated. Second, there is a controlled and explicit element – we ask questions, we suggest people explain to us how they feel, we watch their movements carefully – and yet there is an automatic aspect. We do not consciously spend our time fathoming everyone's mental states or, for that matter, our own, just as we do not spend our time concentrating on how we walk. We 'just' walk. In the same way we 'just' mentalize. It is below the level of consciousness most of the time. Third, there are cognitive and affective components: cognitive in the sense that we ask specific questions about what someone is thinking; affective in the sense that we subjectively feel our and others' emotional states – we are moved by someone's expression of love and happiness for example. Fourth, we can focus our mentalizing on external features (e.g. facial expression) or on internal experience (e.g. asking someone to explain exactly what is going on in their mind whilst remembering that mental states are in fact opaque and can never really be known by someone else). We can lie, for example, about what we think, although of course someone might suspect we are telling a lie if other information, particularly subjective sensitivity, does not match. A person might say they feel fine and yet external observation suggests they are miserable – they look down, their voice is low and toneless, and they make us feel sad. So mentalizing as a process is more complex than a number of other ideas in psychology and psychotherapy that are used to describe mental processes within or between individuals – empathy (see p. 92), psychological mindedness (see p. 247), and mindfulness (see p. 206), for example.

It is inevitable that any individual will be better at some aspects of mentalizing than others because of their developmental experiences, and that problems with mentalizing are likely to be a handicap particularly to everyday human interaction. We will misinterpret people if we misunderstand their motives, become distrusting if we assume that people are malevolent, and be unable to love and feel love if we cannot find ourselves in someone else's mind. But everyday events also affect our capacity to mentalize – fatigue, feelings, drugs, alcohol – and we have all experienced a sense that we are not in our right minds when we become very upset. Emotional states rapidly overwhelm our abilities to remain rational and sensible, affecting our decisions and our social and professional responses. So it is inevitable that psychiatric illnesses, particularly those that are characterized by disturbance in emotions (e.g. depression and anxiety), are also characterized by problems in mentalizing. Conversely, those with mentalizing difficulties are more likely to find it difficult to manage their emotions and to engage constructively in social interaction. People with personality disorder are an example. Personality disorder is primarily a disorder of social relationships, which become disordered because of persistent failures of mentalizing in the affected individual. We will discuss this in a later section of the book (see p. 235).

The seeds of later problems with mentalizing can be traced back to childhood and the attachment relationship (see p. 55) with the mother. In the second half of the first year of life, albeit long before they conceive of mind as such, infants take a critical step towards mentalizing in perceiving action as being goal directed. At this point, infants develop a sense of self and others using a naive, albeit developmentally appropriate, theory of rational action. It is evident in the infant expecting a person's actions to achieve goals efficiently within the constraints of physical reality. For example, at 9 months, infants take it as a matter of course that one computer-animated agent takes a straight path to make contact with another, or the agent jumps over an obstacle if need be; surprise is expressed if the agent deviates from the constraints placed on him by physical reality. The infant is not informed by mental reality, and understanding of the actions of the other is based solely on physical reality, that is, whether there is an obstacle or not. Gradually this changes and by the age of 2 years infants interpret others' actions as stemming from desires, wants, and intentions; they have an implicit understanding of true and false beliefs (Onishi & Baillargeon, 2005); they point to objects while engaging an adult's attention and, at 18 months, visually check to ensure that they have the adult's attention before pointing – what Franco (2005) termed 'the seed of mentalizing' (p. 142); they engage in shared imaginative play that facilitates cooperative skills (Brown, Donelan-McCall, & Dunn, 1996); and they begin acquiring a language to represent internal states (Repacholi & Gopnik, 1997). Nonetheless, at this early stage, infants are unable fully to separate mental states from external reality; the distinction between internal and external remains blurred.

It is between 3 and 4 years of age when children develop a fully-fledged explicit understanding of representational mental states, as exemplified by their passing false-belief tasks that require linguistic articulation (i.e. anticipating that a child will look for something on the basis of where he wrongly *believes* it is located rather than on where it is *actually* located). The most common example of these tasks is the Sally–Anne task. Children are told or shown a story involving two characters. For example, the child is shown two dolls, Sally and Anne, who have a basket and a box, respectively. Sally also has a chocolate, which she places in her basket, and then leaves to take a walk. While she is out of the room, Anne takes the chocolate from the basket and, rather than eating it, puts it in the box. Sally returns, and the child is then asked where Sally will look for the chocolate. The child passes the task if she answers that Sally will look in the basket, where she originally put it; the child fails the task if she answers that Sally will look in the box, where the child knows the chocolate is hidden, even though Sally cannot know, since she did not see Anne hide it there. In order to pass the task, the child must be able to understand that another's mental representation of the situation is different from their own, and the child must be able to predict behaviour based on that understanding. The results of research using false-belief tasks have been fairly consistent and most normally-developing children are unable to pass the tasks until around age 4. People with developmental disorders may have more or less ability to complete the task successfully. Individuals with Down syndrome develop a mentalizing capacity but over 80 per cent of children with autism are unable to complete the task.

The crucible for the emotional and cognitive development of mentalizing is the attachment relationship. Secure attachment is conducive to mentalizing for a number of reasons. First, challenges, conflicts, and fears in the mother–child relationship will prompt mentalizing, and the emotional containment the relationship provides will modulate the emotional arousal, which will allow further mentalizing. Excessive emotion undermines our mental capacities and so if the child is fearful he will panic rather than reflect. If the mother understands the fears of the child then the child will be able to understand his own fears. Second, a secure attachment relationship promotes positive emotional experience, which induces a sense of importance about trying to understand experience. Third, and most crucially, in a secure attachment relationship the attachment figure is frequently mentalizing the child, and mentalizing is conducive to further mentalizing. In effect, the secure attachment relationship is the ideal practice ground for mentalizing. Without this stable crucible for development, we now know that development can become diverted along a less favourable path: maltreated children are less inclined to engage in symbolic play, suggesting that they cannot understand this more complex level of representation; they are less likely to respond empathically to other children's distress; they show more emotionally dysregulated behaviour; they talk about internal and emotional states less often; and they have difficulty understanding emotional expressions.

Finally, we now discuss a number of reasons why we consider mentalizing to be a central clinical component of psychotherapy. First, since the work of John Bowlby it has generally been agreed that psychotherapy invariably activates the attachment system and, when well applied, generates a secure base experience. In our view this is important because the attachment context of psychotherapy is essential to establishing a virtuous cycle of synergy between the recovery of mentalization and secure base experience. Second, the experience of being understood generates an experience of security, which in turn facilitates 'mental exploration' – exploration of the mind of the other to find oneself represented. Third, therapists continually construct and reconstruct in their own mind an image of the patient's mind. They label feelings, they explain cognitions, and they spell out implicit beliefs. Importantly they engage in this mirroring process, highlighting that what they are expressing is their understanding of the mind of the patient. Fourth, mentalizing in psychotherapy is prototypically a process of shared, joint attention – it is the mental state of the patient where the interests of patient and therapist intersect. The shared attentional processes undertaken in psychotherapy in our view serve to strengthen the patient's mental stability. It is not simply what is focused on that we consider therapeutic from this point of view, but the fact that patient and therapist can jointly focus on a shared content of subjectivity. Fifth, the explicit content of the therapist's intervention will be mentalistic as he is principally concerned with increasing understanding of the patient's mind, whether this be through understanding transference reactions in psychoanalytical therapy or identifying automatic negative thoughts in cognitive therapy (see p. 228), or explicating reciprocal roles in CAT (see p. 230). All these techniques entail explicit mentalization so that they succeed in enhancing coherent representations of desires and beliefs in the patient. That this is the case is supported by the common experience that such efforts at explicit mentalization will not be successful unless the therapist succeeds in drawing the patient in as an active collaborator in any explication. Implicit and explicit mentalization are brought together in an act of 'representational redescription', the term Annette Karmiloff-Smith (1992) used to refer to the process by which 'implicit information in the mind subsequently becomes explicit knowledge to the mind' (p. 18). Sixth, the dyadic nature of therapy inherently fosters the patient's capacity to generate multiple perspectives. For example, the interpretation of the transference may be seen as presenting an alternative perspective on the patient's subjective experience. We view this as optimally freeing the patient from being restricted to the reality of 'one view'. Gradually the patient becomes less certain and, in being so, is less restricted and more creative.

Generating different perspectives can be powerfully promoted through engagement in group psychotherapy in which group members hold multiple perspectives between them, all of which require consideration. In either the individual or group setting, mental states are by necessity represented at the secondary level and are therefore more likely to be recognized as such, as mental representations. It should be remembered that this will only be helpful if implicit and explicit mentalization have not been dissociated and feelings are genuinely felt rather than just talked about.

In sum, it is our belief that the relatively safe (secure base) attachment relationship with the therapist provides a relational context in which it is safe to explore the mind of the other in order to find one's own mind within it. It is quite likely that this is an adaptation of a mechanism provided to us, probably by evolution, to 'recalibrate' our experience of our own subjectivity through social interaction. The engagement in a psychotherapeutic context, either individually or in groups, thus does far more than provide nurturance, warmth, or acceptance. The therapist, in holding on to their view of the patient and overcoming the patient's need to externalize and distort the therapist's subjectivity, simultaneously fosters mentalizing and secure attachment experience. Feeling recognized creates a secure base feeling that in turn promotes the patient's freedom to explore herself or himself in the mind of the therapist. Increased sense of security in the attachment relationship with the therapist, as well as other attachment relationships possibly fostered by the therapeutic process, reinforce a secure internal working model and, through this, as Bowlby pointed out, a coherent sense of the self. Simultaneously the patient is increasingly able to allocate mental space to the process of scrutinizing the feelings and thoughts of others, perhaps bringing about improvements in fundamental competence of the patient's mind-interpreting functions, which in turn may generate a far more benign interpersonal environment.

These are lofty claims and it is to the question of how to achieve them in therapy that we now turn.

Part II

Psychodynamic practice

INTRODUCTION TO PSYCHODYNAMIC PRACTICE

In Part I we argued that people may become ill and present problems to a potential helper, such as a doctor, when in unbearable conflict with unacceptable and often unconscious aspects of themselves and their relationships or struggling with the effects of harmful early experiences. The basis of dynamic psychotherapy is the provision of a setting in which a person may begin to be reconciled with these disowned aspects of himself and his experience. Essentially, the setting for this process is the relationship with the therapist; without it, psychotherapy cannot begin.

From the time of Hippocrates it has been recognized that the doctor–patient relationship must involve trust and confidentiality if the physician is to be permitted to examine a patient and do what is needed to heal effectively. In this century and the last, following Freud, psychoanalysts and other psychotherapists have developed the potential of trust and confidentiality in the consulting room, which has become their theatre of operations – not an operating theatre where an active doctor works on an inert patient, but a shared space in which patient and therapist engage together in exploring and resolving pathogenic conflicts and mitigating the effects of early failure and trauma.

Although this special kind of relationship has been formalized in psychoanalysis and psychotherapy, in part through the therapeutic alliance we have just discussed, the role of attentive listener has always been played by the good doctor. In 1850 the American novelist Nathaniel Hawthorne described it vividly in *The Scarlet Letter*:

If the latter (the doctor) possess native sagacity, and a name-less something more, – let us call it intuition; if he show no intrusive egotism, nor disagreeably prominent characteristics of his own; if he have the power, which must be born with him, to bring his mind into such affinity with his patient's, that this last shall unawares have spoken what he imagines himself only to have thought; if such revelations be received without tumult, and acknowledged not so often by an uttered sympathy, as by silence, an inarticulate breath, and here and there a word, to indicate that all is understood; if, to these qualifications of a confidant be joined the advantages afforded by his recognized character as a physician; then, at some inevitable moment, will the soul of the sufferer be dissolved, and flow forth in a dark, but transparent stream, bringing all its mysteries into the daylight.

The capacity for empathy, or putting oneself intuitively in another's shoes and identifying emotionally with him in his predicament, is clearly not restricted to psychotherapists, doctors, or other pro-fessionals. It is doubtful that this capacity is wholly inborn, as Hawthorne suggests, rather than learnt from early experiences of parents and others and from its later encouragement in professional training. Moreover it is essential that the capacity to relate intu-itively is balanced by the ability to view both the sufferer and our response to him objectively. With these qualifications, the passage from Hawthorne describes well the *facilitating* role of the therapist. The experience of someone trying to understand, rather than judge or control, provides the sense of safety and space in which to begin to be oneself. Then the person in distress can feel secure enough to share his problems and to explore what he dared not think or speak of before; in effect, a therapeutic alliance has developed which acts as foundation for continuing therapy.

Therapeutic listening is not passive, 'but involves alert and sympathetic participation in what troubles the patient' (Bruch, 1974). It is in this sense that psychotherapy is a conversation; it is not a superficial chat and does not seek quick, temporary relief by reassurance and suggestion. It involves talking honestly and with increasing familiarity and intimacy, between people who are equally committed to understanding the sufferer and his problems, with the aim of bringing about change. It requires tactful challenge and confrontation, and is never straightforward.

Both therapist and patient will, at times, have to struggle to maintain the therapeutic alliance and to cope with resistance to understanding and change. Cooperation requires trust and a sense of 'being on the same wavelength'. Going too fast can provoke resistance in the patient – a phenomenon described by Malan's law that a 'good' session is followed by an increase in resistance (Malan, 1979, p. 104). Crises of confidence will occur at times, but usually with lessening frequency, intensity, and duration.

Patients with disturbed personalities will make greater demands on the therapist's resources. The latter may have to cope with attacks on the therapeutic process and even his ability to think. This is true whatever the level of modality or therapy, making an understanding of the principles of psychodynamics and of therapeutic relationships relevant to them all.

In Part II we will deal in turn with the main therapeutic *elements of psychotherapy*, the different *levels of psychotherapy*, and then the different types of dynamic psychotherapy practised at present. Several distinctive forms of treatment have emerged during this century and the last. We have traced their evolution in the 'family tree' in Figure 10 (p. 223). *Psychoanalysis* developed in the private consulting rooms of a few pioneers early in the century, but continues to be the major form of intensive treatment and study, though for a relatively small number of patients and trainees. In the 1920s and 1930s, child analysis developed in child guidance clinics, using play material to engage the child's imagination and promote communication. Following the social upheavals of World War I, briefer face-to-face methods of *analytic psychotherapy* emerged in general hospital out-patient departments and clinics, to help the mass of non-psychotic patients who could no longer be ignored. These clinics were named Departments of Psychological Medicine so that patients could avoid the stigma of madness. With more liberal legislation, psychiatry was moving out of the mental hospital. One no longer had to be labelled insane to get help with psychological problems. In the 1940s and 1950s, partly under the impact of World War II, psychoanalytic principles were applied in the development *of group psychotherapy* for the treatment of neurotic and personality problems, so releasing new therapeutic potential, and making help available to more people. More recently, as the interaction between people in groups (such as families and institutions) was seen to cause as well as to reflect individual disturbance, group psychotherapy was joined by *family and couple therapy* and by *social therapy*.

Since the first edition newer developments, to some extent spawned by dynamic psychotherapy, have had a marked influence on mainstream psychotherapeutic practice; these include *interpersonal psychotherapy*, *cognitive-behavioural therapy*, *cognitive-analytic therapy*, and the *conversational model*. In addition there have been a number of changes to the generic model of dynamic psychotherapy we describe in this book as practitioners treat a wider group of patients, in particular people with personality disorder; transference-focused psychotherapy and mentalization-based psychotherapy for borderline personality disorder are two examples and we discuss all these later (see pp. 236–237).

Outside the mainstream, for some 40 years methods such as *Encounter* have claimed to free 'normal' people from social alienation, and forms of counselling (p. 118) and self-help (p. 110) are developing for many sorts of human problem and predicament. One no longer has to be labelled a psychiatric patient in order to be helped. Finally, we shall finish this outline of the practice of psychotherapy by firstly considering some of the issues of suiting the therapy to the patient in discussing *selection*, and then by considering the data about process and outcome of therapies in a section on *outcome and research*.

Historians could get some idea of the time sequence in which the main types of analytic psychotherapy emerged in the UK from the dates when the principal journals dealing with them were founded. The *International Journal of Psycho-Analysis* was founded by Ernest Jones at the same time as the British PsychoAnalytical Society in 1919. The *British Journal of Medical Psychology*, now *Psychology and Psychotherapy: Theory, Research, and Practice*, the journal of the Medical Section of the British Psychological Society, which was a meeting place for psychotherapists between the two world wars, was founded in 1920. *Human Relations*, the journal of the Tavistock Institute of Human Relations, was founded in 1947; the *Journal of Child Psychotherapy* was first published by the Association of Child Psychotherapists in 1963; *Group Analysis*, the journal of the Group Analytic Society (London) which set up the Institute of Group Analysis, appeared in 1969; the *Journal of Family Therapy*, journal of the Association of Family Therapists, started in 1979; and the *International Journal of Therapeutic Communities* started in 1980. In the mid-1980s, three journals in our field appeared at roughly the same time in 1984–1985: *Psychoanalytic Psychotherapy*, journal of the Association for Psychoanalytic Psychotherapy in the NHS; the *British Journal of Psychotherapy*; and *Free Associations*. The journal of the Society for Psychotherapy Research, *Psychotherapy Research*, was first published in 1991.

ELEMENTS OF PSYCHOTHERAPY

The personality, like the body, has a natural tendency towards healing and growth; the fundamental task of psychotherapy, like that of medicine and surgery, is to create conditions which facilitate these processes. It is because they are threatening or painful that aspects of the self and relationships are treated as unacceptable and therefore disowned, whether by individuals or groups such as families; for example, an individual may repress unwanted feelings, or a family may project them into the 'black sheep' of the family or into the 'big bad world outside'. The process of psychotherapy involves discovering the unreality of the fears of calamity if they are allowed into awareness, expressed, and owned. It also involves finding new ways of integrating such feelings in order to function and develop more freely and effectively.

Figure 7 illustrates the way in which conditions provided by the treatment setting initiate and interact with dynamic processes in the patient. A *relationship of trust*, allowing *communication in words*, promotes the *understanding and integration* of previously unacknowledged aspects of self and relationships.

Relationship of trust

Seeking help from a stranger is bound to arouse anxieties and provoke conflicts additional to any already underlying a patient's symptoms. What is this person like? Will he understand? Will he be able to help? Will he want to help me? Will he think I'm wasting his time? Will he judge me harshly as too bad or too mad to be helped? The patient's wish to protect himself from the dangers implicit in questions such as these can conflict with his intention to be honest. Reticence and mistrust at interview exist over and above unconscious defence mechanisms (p. 28). How the therapist meets the

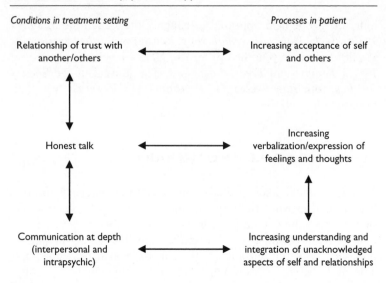

Figure 7

patient and responds to his tentative approaches helps to determine whether the patient feels the necessary initial trust.

To foster such a relationship and the therapeutic alliance the doctor/therapist needs to be respectful and non-judgemental. By conveying his recognition of a patient's anxieties, particularly those stirred up by the consultation, the therapist can help the patient to relax and speak more openly. Aware that the patient may be communicating *indirectly* about his real concerns, the doctor/ therapist is ready to broaden the inquiry with a few questions such as 'how are things at home?' or 'are you worrying about anything else?'. If and when the patient finds that the doctor can be trusted with his confidences, and is on his side, further foundation is laid for a *working or therapeutic alliance* (p. 68). This does not always come easily. For a while a patient might feel it safer to remain detached from the problems presented, for example joining in a collusive assumption that they are physical rather than human problems of living with himself and others. Sometimes it is only after such a contact has been established and tested that the boundaries of trust can be extended, and then only if the doctor seems ready to allow it. Sometimes it takes months or years for people to learn sufficient trust to take the opportunity to unburden themselves of their real problem.

A woman in her thirties, living with a man by whom she had two children, and now again pregnant, had attended her GP for two years with recurrent headaches for which no organic cause could be found. She was finally able to confide that the man beat her and virtually made her a prisoner in the house. Airing the problem and releasing her suppressed rage brought her some relief, and opened up the possibility that something could be done for the disturbed family.

It so happened that this family was from a minority ethnic group. We cannot be sure whether this affected the delay in getting at the psychological truth behind the patient's physical symptom, but there is increasing recognition that anxiety and mistrust are widespread between clients and professionals on different sides of a gender or ethnic divide, as well as one based on social class. So deep are these attitudes, often justified by ignorance or at least unconscious prejudices embedded in our society (Ashurst & Hall, 1989; Littlewood & Lipsedge, 1989), that they have led to some radical innovations in the provision of psychotherapy for women and for minority ethnic groups (Ernst & Maguire, 1987; Acharya, Moorhouse, Kareem, *et al.*, 1989). There is something natural about seeking out people similar to ourselves on the basis that they are more likely to have experienced comparable difficulties. But this does not mean that if patients and therapists share common values, have similar attitudes, and are of the same gender, sexual orientation, or ethnicity that outcomes of treatment for particular problems will be better. In fact the evidence is against such a simple idea. For example, studies looking at such variables as ethnic match between patient and therapist rarely found any differences in outcomes between matched and unmatched clients (see Zane, Nagayama Hall, Sue, *et al.*, 2004, for review). What is probably more important is mutual respect.

For the doctor/therapist, meeting a stranger who seeks help can also create anxiety, more so perhaps in the novice wanting to prove his efficacy to himself and the patient. It is important for the therapist to recognize this in order to understand the patient's communications and his own responses to them (see Counter-transference, p. 79). Beyond this, however, the development of therapeutic ease and skill involves the ability to trust one's own responses and intuitions; and it is because most of us grow up with some blind-spots, distortions, or inhibitions that supervision and a personal therapeutic experience are so valuable a part of training in psychotherapy, and mandatory in further specialist training in dynamic psychotherapy.

If the initial barriers to trust are overcome, then therapy can begin. It will be recalled that in individual development as viewed by Erikson (p. 49) basic trust should be attained in the first phase of the mother–child relationship. Of course many were not so fortunate in their earliest experiences, so distrust may infiltrate any relationship with a potential helper; rejecting help may be an ultimate defence against a world seen as treacherous. But the discovery that the doctor/therapist does not fail him can be an important corrective experience for a patient. Bowlby (1977) has spoken of this as the provision of a *secure base* (a temporary attachment figure) from which the patient can explore himself and his relationships.

It is noteworthy that the earliest, seventeenth century, meaning of the word conscious was *knowing together with another (Shorter Oxford English Dictionary)*. Discoveries about oneself are difficult to establish unless they are shared with another person. Freud's self-analysis was a heroic enterprise since he ventured alone into the dark, with no one present to accompany him and affirm his often disturbing discoveries. Nevertheless it is questionable whether he could have managed without the sounding board of his friendship and correspondence with Fliess (Jones, 1952, ch. 13). The difficult task of accepting and coming to terms with previously unacknowledged aspects of the self is eased by the experience that they are being accepted and understood by another person. The therapeutic relationship provides the safe space in which confidence can be tested and confidences entrusted. What has been private or unknowable becomes known together with another. It can be explored and evaluated within the counterpoint of subjective and objective experiences; the therapist provides, as it were, a mirror through which the patient is enabled to see himself and the way he sees others. The experience of mutual reflection within the therapeutic relationship reinforces the patient's own capacities for reflective thinking.

Communications in words

Putting things into words makes them explicit. It involves a commitment to communication, which a patient may be reluctant to make until he has found out more about the doctor's response to his problems, especially those he feels bad about. The doctor/ therapist tries to 'read between the lines', and to judge whether or when to indicate that he realizes there is more to talk about. A tactful question may then open up a difficult topic by providing the right words.

However, the initial communications between patient and doctor, which are crucial in determining whether a relationship of trust develops, may very well be non-verbal, conveyed by manner, facial expression, gesture, or posture (Argyle, 1972; Fraser, 1976) in the same way that infant and mother communicate and establish a relationship before attaining a common verbal language. Interest, respect, and reliability are not conveyed by words alone. Yet the attainment of a common language in therapy can initiate changes comparable to those brought about by the development of language in the child. Speech makes communication immeasurably richer, subtler, and more accurate. Words develop as symbols representing such things as ideas, shades of feeling, and moral attitudes. The fact that words can also be used to conceal the truth is a sign of their power, which is why we use the more primitive and sometimes more truthful non-verbal signs to check on the validity of communications. The lack of marked discrepancy between what is said and how it is said is a sign of genuineness looked for by both parties in the developing patient–therapist relationship. The presence of discrepancies alerts us to things not yet spoken of, or being avoided, perhaps unconsciously.

Psychotherapy is a voyage of discovery. The patient tries to put his findings into words and communicate them to his travelling companion, the therapist. One patient referred to her therapist as her Sancho Panza; she could not have embarked on the frightening inner journey without his comforting companionship. The patient's perceptions and misperceptions of the therapist's attitudes and feelings, based on transference, are powerful aids in exploring aspects of the past which distort current relationships. When spoken of by the patient and 'received without tumult' by the therapist, as Hawthorne put it, isolating experiences and fears can be stripped of their power. The Grimm brothers' story of Rumpelstiltskin illustrates the relief that can be gained by naming a threat (Rowley, 1951).

The move from unconscious, primitive, and often bodily experiences – based on primary process thinking, and located in the id

(p. 60) – to ideas about the self and relationships expressible in words – based on secondary process thinking located in the ego – is often a rocky path and awareness is not achieved with ease. The nature of an unspeakable conflict takes a long time to work out and resolve. The move from allusion and metaphor to usable and clear verbal communication may be slow.

> *A young woman had developed such a fear of her own developing independence and sexuality that she had starved herself for several years. Even when the clinical condition of anorexia nervosa had receded, she continued to purge herself daily with huge quantities of laxative. It was only when she had been in a psychotherapy group for over a year, gradually overcoming her distrust and her conviction that the therapist did not like her, that she was able to link her purging with her guilt feelings. These were about her adolescent use of sexuality to find a sense of being wanted and to take revenge on her mother. She had experienced mother as critical and rejecting, particularly after the birth of a brother whom she could not bear to see mother breast-feed; yet she still wanted her approval and love. As the patient's self-esteem grew through greater acceptance, under-standing, and assertion of herself, she was finally ready to use the group's interpretation of the link between guilt and purging. She was able to forgive herself and renounce her childhood tie to her mother. Then she discovered to her own surprise that she no longer needed to purge herself, literally and metaphorically. Her conflicts had become the stuff of conversation.*

Talking is not an end in itself; if it becomes so then it is being used as a defence against real communication and change, like the parliamentary filibuster (Langs, 1979a). Used creatively, talking is the channel through which the patient's discoveries can be expressed and examined with the therapist and any other com-panions in the therapeutic enterprise, such as fellow members of a group or family.

This emphasis on talking by the patient stems from psycho-analysis, with its accent on finding meaning where there had been ignorance and confusion. Freud discovered that deep fears moti-vate the avoidance of disowned experiences and wishes, and that these have to be gradually faced and worked through. However, in recent years some schools of psychotherapy, notably Encounter,

Psychodrama, Gestalt, Bioenergetics, and Primal Therapy (pp. 209–218), have attempted to avoid the defensive use of rational talking by inducing direct confrontation between people and by encouraging the physical expression of feelings and relationships. Their methods, which involve active techniques of catharsis, re-enacting, touching, and bodily expression, often promote very intense experiences and require a more obviously active and directive role of the therapist. They can sometimes reach people for whom talk is not an easy medium or who use it predominantly defensively. Such methods emphasize doing rather than thinking, in order to avoid the danger of defensive talk and rationality, but run the converse risk of defensive doing and feeling. Both feeling and talking are ultimately necessary for full expression; Shake-speare's Malcolm urges Macduff, who had been told of the slaughter of his wife and children, to 'Give sorrow words; the grief that does not speak/Whispers the o'er-fraught heart and bids it break' (*Macbeth*, Act IV, Scene III).

A young woman of 30 was extremely inhibited in a psycho-therapy group, and characteristically became silent instead of expressing anger. This could be understood in terms of her parents' inability to understand or tolerate her rage at the arrival of a baby sister when she was 18 months old; they had responded by taking her to see a child psychiatrist with whom she would not share even the few words she had at that time. She had stopped trying to talk in the family for a long while. One day in the group, members noticed she was withdrawing again and tried to help her to express her anger. She was so tongue-tied that the therapist handed her a cushion which, against intense internal resistance, she was eventually able to pummel. Only when she experienced the relief of giving vent to her feelings, within a supportive environment, was she able to put words to her destructive fantasies and to her fear of the group's shock and abandonment, as though the group were her early family. Then she could begin to understand her fears and to integrate her anger in a modified form.

Understanding and integration

Understanding a problem is usually the first step in its solution. However, the true nature of a problem may be deliberately hidden by a patient, because of fear or feelings of shame or guilt, or it may be outside his conscious awareness. Sometimes a person wants to be *passively* 'understood' by someone else without wishing to understand himself; then, the 'understanding' expected of the doctor is likely to be a misnomer for benevolent sympathy. The dynamic forms of therapy seek to engage the patient in *actively* understanding himself and his problems. They involve exploration of the origin and meaning of his symptoms and the human problems they reflect. It has been suggested (Home, 1966; Rycroft, 1966) that this properly implies a hermeneutic rather than a mechanistic view of behaviour, that is, one concerned with discovering meaning in phenomena rather than with the deterministic cause and effect linkages characteristic of the physical sciences. As he explores disowned aspects of himself and his relationships, the patient gains new clues for the deeper understanding of his problems. If authentic, this understanding is reinforced by the way it links and makes sense of many experiences or leads to fresh discoveries. But what is to be done with this self-knowledge? To be therapeutic, discovery and understanding have to be paralleled by a process of integration and change.

For example, the young woman who purged herself (p. 100) needed to see the meaning of her symptoms as an expression of conflict in her relationship with her family, and *re-experience* it in the transference with the therapist and 'sibling rivals' in the group, before she could understand it emotionally and at depth, that is, with *emotional as well as intellectual insight*. Then, by reassessing her problems and the possibilities of change, she was able to forgive herself and free herself from the hostile dependent tie to her mother, and begin to use her self-assertive impulses in a more outgoing way. She was now more fully aware of what had previously been unconscious.

As in artistic and scientific creativity (p. 18), understanding is arrived at in psychotherapy in all sorts of ways – sometimes in a seemingly spontaneous flash of realization, but often in slow stages and with a good deal of struggle against resistance. It is promoted by interaction with the therapist or others in the enterprise, and is mediated by both non-verbal and verbal communication. Three specific types of verbal communication contributing to therapeutic understanding have been delineated: confrontation, clarification, and interpretation (Greenson, 1967). *Confrontation* – a misnomer because the aim is not to argue with the patient but more to *challenge* his assumptions about himself and others – draws the patient's attention to what he appears to be doing, often repeatedly and seemingly unaware: for example, coming late to sessions, showing hostility to a certain sort of person, or engaging in self-punishing behaviour. *Clarification* helps to sort out what is happening, by questioning or rephrasing. *Interpretation* offers new formulations of unconscious meaning and motivation.

Interpretation links the conscious and unconscious determinants of an experience, act, or symptom and thus extends the patient's understanding of himself and his relationships, including those in the therapeutic setting. Interpretations play an important part in psychoanalysis and the forms of dynamic psychotherapy deriving from it, which are sometimes called *interpretative* or *insight-orientated* psychotherapy. As Rycroft (1966, p. 18) puts it, the analyst is someone

> who knows something of the way in which repudiated wishes, thoughts, feelings and memories can translate themselves into symptoms, gestures and dreams, and who knows, as it were, the grammar and syntax of such translations and is therefore in a position to interpret them back again into the communal language of consciousness.

An interpretation is not a dogmatic assertion delivered *de haut en bas*, but rather a suggestion or tentative hypothesis offered in the spirit 'could it be that . . .?' or 'I get the feeling that . . .' This has been called 'framing speculations as an invitation to a mutual exploration' (Meares & Hobson, 1977). Increasingly, as treatment progresses, patients become able to understand and interpret their own experience and behaviour.

The dynamic concept of insight supposes an awareness of the interaction between external and internal reality, that is, between objective and subjective experience. Health involves awareness of both. The balance between the two can be disturbed either way: extreme withdrawal, introversion, or even psychosis cuts a person off from external reality; and excessively extraverted or constricted personalities may be cut off from subjective feelings or inner reality. The correction of such imbalances plays an important part in the analytic psychology of Jung (1946). All psychodynamic schools of thought agree that partial failures of insight result from the operation of defences: for example, denial of an external fact such as a painful bereavement, or the projection of an unwanted internal impulse.

Just as understanding between people can lead to reconciliation, so self-understanding and insight can lead to reconciliation with disowned aspects of oneself. In other words, understanding has an integrating function. Freud's (1933) dictum 'where id was, there ego shall be' implies the integration of external and internal realities. Less mature defences may be given up or superseded by sublimation. Repressed and split-off parts can be restored to the self in the new climate of experimentation and growth if the therapeutic relationship provides the necessary security and flexibility. The person is enabled to discover the extent of his internal world, perhaps even to discover for the first time that he has one. We know from studies of sleep that those who do not remember their dreams, or even claim never to have dreamt, spend a fifth or more of their sleep in dream activity; if woken during periods of rapid eye movement (REM) sleep they are usually able to describe dreams (Berger, 1969). Those who do not may show characteristics of alexithymia (Kalucy, Brown, Hartman, *et al.*, 1976). It is striking how often people in therapy start remembering dreams for the first time.

It is arguable how necessary insight is for therapeutic change to take place, at least for limited change. Patients may recover and be none the wiser, knowing only that they were helped by medication or the psychiatrist. Even so, factors such as suggestion and satisfaction of the need to be helped by a reliable parent-figure are likely to be operating. These are part of the non-specific placebo effect of much medicine, including psychiatry and psychotherapy. Perhaps a significant aspect of therapy is engaging in a process of personal discovery with someone that one trusts. When looking below the surface or becoming more deeply involved with the therapist is too threatening, some patients in psychotherapy get better quickly as a defensive 'flight into health'; such an improvement may be short-lived, unless circumstances and important relationships change the whole balance of the individual's adjustment.

Many patients prefer to see their emotional disturbances as 'illnesses', unconnected with themselves or their relationships; they are only too glad to receive physical treatment with drugs or electroconvulsive therapy (ECT), and to get relief as rapidly as possible. This is understandable and appropriate for many people, particularly in severe crisis or psychosis. It is probably also right for others with less acute and severe disturbances whose wish or capacity for introspection and verbalization is limited, although techniques such as psychodrama and art and music therapy may enable some people to enter gradually into the sphere of 'insight therapy'; so also may massage, yoga, and other forms of body work (p. 216). However, such methods can be used non-analytically and may be useful when deep exploration is best avoided, for example in those too threatened by the intimacy of a therapeutic relationship or the fear of opening a Pandora's Box inside themselves. The assessment of these criteria of motivation and 'ego strength' will be considered in discussing Selection (p. 238).

Given the wish to explore and the capacity to bear what is discovered, understanding and integration still have to be achieved and maintained in the face of resistances. These can be very powerful, since they involve defences against anxiety and psychic pain. This is why by-passing resistances, by exploring people's problems under hypnosis or drugs, is so often of little use, because their need for defences has not been removed; they are not ready to use what has been discovered.

Psychotherapy is much more than doing clever detective work, fishing around in the unconscious, and making shocking revelations. It must involve the establishment of a working alliance in which trust, talk, and understanding help a person to accept the hitherto unacceptable. The patient needs a fully conscious and cooperative ego, not one lulled off its guard by drugs or hypnosis. For much the same reason the beneficial effects of some of the more active techniques such as Encounter (p. 209), which stimulate the experience and discharge of very intense feelings, may be no more than transient because they are not integrated and followed through. The patient's need for symptoms and defences has to be explored, understood, and *worked through* – repeatedly experienced and resolved – before he can give up what has been called the *primary gain*, that is, the advantage in terms of immediate freedom from emotional discomfort.

If they are prolonged, as with any disability, the sufferer may learn to make the best of his neurotic symptoms and defences. They come to have a social function, maintaining certain roles and relationships which might bring advantages: for example, sympathetic consideration may be gained, along with covert revenge for its having been previously withheld. In some families it is difficult to gain attention, and illness may be the only means of being noticed as a person with special needs. Once gained, the advantages of receiving sympathetic consideration may need to be maintained by the same methods. A gross example of such 'secondary gain' is the so-called compensation neurosis following an industrial injury, when a pension may depend on the perpetuation of a lifetime of suffering. The secondary as well as primary gain might have to be understood and relinquished before therapeutic change can take place. Finally, change in one person may depend on change in others in his family network, who may resist if they need the patient to be 'ill' in order to maintain their own adjustment. To allow the patient to change, other members of the family may need to be involved in family or marital therapy, or individual or group treatment in their own right.

A joint consultation with husband and wife showed that a recurrently depressed woman was subtly undermined by her husband, who seemed to need her to remain the weak incompetent one. This ensured him the role of strong trouble-free protector, without which he was thrown back on his own self-doubts and depression, related to the early loss of his mother. He needed to let his wife become more assertive and less dependent upon him, by facing his own problems in individual therapy.

In therapy, the relationship of trust and the realization that one can talk about what seemed to be unspeakable, and think about the unthinkable, act as powerful antidotes to such resistances. Nevertheless understanding often has to be struggled for by both patient and therapist. The therapist needs to be able to tolerate uncertainty and ambiguity, sometimes for long periods of time, without jumping to premature conclusions. Of course there are human situations, such as surgical emergencies, which demand quick decisions and actions and when it is right to say, 'don't just stand there, do something'; but in psychotherapy we need more often to remember the opposite, 'don't do something, just be there' or 'don't just say something, just sit there'. In other words we require what Keats (1817) called 'Negative Capability', 'that is, when a man is capable of being in uncertainties, mysteries, doubts, without any irritable reaching after fact and reason'. Even surgeons, when withholding an operation, sometimes speak of 'masterly inactivity'. In psychotherapy too there are times when the most that the therapist can do is just be there, tolerating anxiety and uncertainty, surviving as a reliable concerned person (perhaps also surviving the patient's hostility and demands for immediate action and gratification) until such time as things become clearer and understanding is finally reached. Sometimes the therapist's survival is the crucial corrective experience for the patient as the parents' is for an adolescent; 'the best they can do is to *survive*, to survive intact, and without changing colour, without relinquishment of any important principle' (Winnicott, 1971, p. 145).

Although many people do not want to know the truth about themselves, because they fear what they avoid, quite a few patients referred for psychiatric treatment feel an urge to understand what has happened to them. A survey by Michaels and Sevitt (1978) revealed that almost one in three of a series of patients referred to a psychiatrist clearly hoped to gain insight into their problems, expressing this in such statements as, 'I want the psychiatrist to help me to see things I couldn't see myself', and, 'I want to understand why I feel this way so that I can do something about it'. Because dynamic psychotherapy seeks to understand a person in a developmental way – integrating what they were with what they are and what they are becoming – the insight gained fosters a sense of continuity of identity. It allows the work of psychotherapy to be continued and extended beyond the termination of therapy sessions; the patient learns his own way of understanding and working at problems.

Integration implies wholeness. A person becomes *at one* as he brings together and consolidates his previously divided parts, in keeping with the origin of the word *atonement*: at one in harmony (*Shorter Oxford English Dictionary*). Integration of previously unknown aspects of the self and relationships demands adjustment, as with any discovery, be it the earth's roundness or atomic power. Patients need to harness previously unexpressed impulses into their functioning. New facts and feelings have to be incorporated into a person's view of himself in relation to others, such as finding that enemies and parents are human, and can be at least partially forgiven, like himself. However modest, these changes amount to a reorganization of personality.

A married woman had for 10 years been crippled by a fear of thunderstorms. She lived in dread that every weather forecast or rumbling lorry heralded a storm. When first seen, she described how, the eldest of a large family, she had married early to escape from being a skivvy to a strict and domineering mother. In childhood, despite her frustration and rage, she had been unable to stand up for herself. The phobia started soon after marriage, when unplanned pregnancy threatened an end to her briefly enjoyed freedom. She was able to admit that she had felt some dismay and resentment, but had had to disown any murderous feelings towards the baby inside her.

It could be postulated that this child, and the others who followed, provoked the patient's fury at being restricted and cheated, which revived her childhood conflicts, when the arrival of successive siblings evoked feelings which could not be expressed for fear of retaliation by mother; feelings and retaliation were therefore now symbolically externalized in the form of the phobia. The intensity of the patient's anxiety and her resistance to insight were contra-indications to dynamic psychotherapy at that time. Instead she was treated by a behavioural technique of reciprocal inhibition (exposing her to imagined thunderstorms while deeply relaxed). After some 35 sessions she was free of the phobia, and had come to trust the therapist towards whom she had developed a positive affectionate transference. A few months later, when preparing a birthday party for her eldest child, she had a panic attack, with none of the previous precipitants (such as a thunderstorm, weather forecast, or the sound of a lorry). The patient was dismayed when she arrived for a follow-up appointment a few days later, but was now able to trust herself enough in the therapeutic relationship to question her previous understanding of the phobia as a habit related to the occurrence of thunderstorms during her pregnancy with this child. The acceptance of intense disappointment and resentment towards the therapist, for whom she also felt warm affection, enabled her to admit to ambivalence too in her relationship with her child and the rest of her family, both past and present.

The truth, as it were, was out; but she was now able to think of owning her destructive feelings, and in five further sessions of more dynamic psychotherapy, one with the whole family, this mother made rapid changes in her view of herself and her relationships. She now understood herself and what had gone wrong over the last 10 years much more fully. Instead of splitting off an important aspect of herself, she was able to integrate it and make changes in attitude which freed herself and her family from her

role as resentful martyr, locked in a prison of dutiful devotion.
She was able to demand more time for herself and her interests,
and to expect more help from her family in carrying out domestic
chores. Thus she was able to re-establish her relationships on a
more honest and secure basis, which at follow-up 15 years later
had withstood the test of time.

This case illustrates three things. First, before the patient could
change herself and her adjustment enough to outgrow her symptoms, she needed in her current life situation to integrate feelings
previously disavowed because of neurotic conflicts based in early
relationships.

Second, the case demonstrates that psychotherapy requires an
optimum level of anxiety and tension, like many other sorts of
learning. This is reminiscent of the Yerkes–Dodson law of experimental psychology (Yerkes & Dodson, 1908). Moderate levels of
anxiety facilitate learning, as everyone knows who has studied for
examinations; too much and performance falls off; too little and
nothing gets started. The same is true in psychotherapy. Insufficient anxiety can reduce motivation for serious work; too much can
prevent it, as in the early stages of this patient's therapy.

Finally, the case shows how the level of therapy is determined by
the depth and extent of self-knowledge which the patient seeks and
the therapist fosters, and by the amount of simultaneous internal
and external change sought in reaching a new adjustment. This
question of the level of therapy will be pursued in the next section.

LEVELS OF PSYCHOTHERAPY

Broadly, psychotherapy is the use of personal relationships to help
people in trouble. This can occur in many different contexts and at
variable levels of skill. A lot of informal psychotherapy takes place
between friends and confidants. Such relationships have neither the
advantages nor disadvantages of the formality and relative distance
of a professional relationship.

The value of airing problems, expressing feelings, and of
receiving support, encouragement, and advice is common knowledge, as witnessed by colloquial expressions such as 'getting it off
your chest'. The friends who are sought out by distressed individuals are those who know intuitively the value of the principles

described in the last section: they are trustworthy, willing to listen, and they try to understand.

Informal groups, also, are widely recognized as having a pro-phylactic or therapeutic effect based on mutual encouragement and the provision of a sense of identity. The sharing of common interests or problems unites people: for example, in work or sport, in religious or political groups, and in self-help groups such as Alcoholics Anonymous.

The *relief* and *support* offered by such informal relationships, with individuals or groups, are of great value in themselves, and are more acceptable to many who would be reluctant to seek professional help, even if it were available. While sympathetic support can be very helpful, a person can often be helped further if, at the same time, he is also offered some plain speaking. This may confront him with his own contribution to the creation and main-tenance of his difficulties, and encourage him to take action to resolve them. Advice is often of less value than helping people to make up their own minds and be responsible for their own decisions. Principles such as these are known intuitively by many people, but it often requires the relative detachment and socially sanctioned authority of a professional relationship to make them acceptable to those seeking help. A fellow traveller on the train may be entrusted with someone's life story and problems precisely because of the relative distance and anonymity provided by the lack of further personal contact.

At more formal levels of psychotherapy, many types of professional helper may nowadays be involved, although the personality, attitudes, and basic orientation of the therapist are as important as his particular professional allegiance. A number of defining frameworks exist to classify different formal psychothera-pies but none are entirely satisfactory. The simplest method is to group psychotherapies according to their theoretical base and their type of clinical intervention – psychoanalytic psychotherapy, inter-personal therapy, cognitive-analytic therapy, cognitive therapy, cognitive-behavioural therapy, behaviour therapy, systemic ther-apy, and so on. This leads to the erroneous belief that differently named therapies are clearly distinct or that the same named ther-apies are uniform. In fact there is a good deal of overlap between them, and similarly named therapies can be delivered in many different ways given that they are partially dependent on the per-sonality of the therapist. Some argue that therapies are best classified as either cognitive-behavioural or relational. The former would include cognitive, behavioural, cognitive-behavioural, dialectical behaviour, and psychoeducational; the latter would include psychodynamic, psychodynamic-interpersonal, interpersonal, and Rogerian. However, such a broad classification may blur some of the differences between the therapies within the same grouping and also lead to a problem of where to place the integrative therapies, such as cognitive-analytic therapy.

Cawley (1977) provided a helpful classification in delineating four types of psychotherapy. Originally the classification focused primarily on psychodynamic therapy, although behavioural therapy was classified as type 4. But cognitive-behavioural therapy and other therapies may be classified within the same system since types 1–3 are not based on theory but upon the professional background and training of practitioners, the limitations imposed by their specialization, and the intensity of application of therapy. Types 1–3 involve increasing depth of exploration.

Psychotherapy 1 is what any good doctor (or other professional) does and is synonymous with the art of medicine. It involves an awareness of the person as well as the problem he presents, and requires an ability to communicate and empathize with people from different backgrounds. The doctor who decides to refer a patient to a psychiatrist or psychotherapist recognizes the anxieties this may arouse, and helps the patient with them by explaining and dispelling unreasonable apprehensions. So this level of psychotherapy requires good communication skills and a natural interest in others and their predicaments.

Psychotherapy 2 is what a good psychiatrist, social worker, psychologist, or other mental health professional does. It encompasses Psychotherapy 1, but requires ability to understand and to communicate with patients suffering from all types and degrees of psychological disturbance. It involves recognition that an individual's present state and attitude are influenced both by previous experiences and by his ways of thinking about the world and himself, often in ways which are outside his awareness and control. To this extent it incorporates some of the psychodynamic and cognitive principles which underlie Psychotherapy 3. However, while the phenomena of transference or the identification of cognitive assumptions and distortions, for example, may be recognized in Psychotherapy 2, and used to understand patients' behaviour and attitudes, they tend not to be commented on. They are usually used only in the sense of allowing or encouraging a mildly positive transference – seeing the psychiatrist as a good and reliable parent – to reinforce the therapeutic alliance, or to facilitate understanding of underlying cognitive distortions. At this level the practitioner is better able than non-specialists to form a therapeutic alliance with patients with psychiatric illness or with those whose mental processes are distorted.

Psychotherapy 3 would be what many people mean by psychotherapy, especially in its formal or specialized sense. Dynamic psychotherapy is discussed here in more detail but cognitive and other 'brand named' therapies may be included at this level. Nowadays there is increased recognition of the importance of the relationship between therapist and patient to the success of all therapies, including behavioural therapy, thereby potentially dispensing with Psychotherapy 4 altogether in this classification. Psychotherapy 3 includes those characteristics of Psychotherapies 1 and 2 which relate to the therapist's attitude to the patient – respect, understanding, and acceptance – but it puts greater emphasis on helping patients with particular techniques to understand the predisposing, precipitating, and perpetuating factors of their problems and to take responsibility for themselves and their relationships. Dynamic psychotherapy makes the doctor–patient relationship its focus, and uses the psychodynamic principles described in Part I to explore and understand patients' problems. Transference phenomena are encouraged and worked with in Psychotherapy 3, since they throw light on the continuing influence of past relationships, from which the patient can begin to free himself as he comes to recognize them. It is Psychotherapy 3 in its various forms that will concern us mostly in the rest of this book.

Figure 8 (on p. 113) illustrates how Cawley's Psychotherapies 1, 2, and 3 can be seen as changing levels of any psychotherapy, *irrespective of the context* in which they are delivered, and how elements of both dynamic and cognitive-behavioural psychotherapy meet in the fields of family, couple (see p. 176), and some types of group therapy (see p. 153). These schematic links are elaborated further in considering the range of psychotherapeutic methods in Figure 11 (p. 255). There, the existence of newer intermediate forms of therapy, such as cognitive-analytic therapy (CAT) and interpersonal therapy (IPT), complicates the simple picture represented here.

A more recent attempt to classify the psychotherapies is found in the *NHS Psychotherapy Services in England: Review of Strategic*

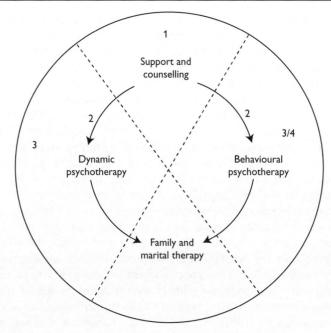

Figure 8

Policy (NHS Executive, 1996). Three types of psychotherapy are identified – *types A, B, and C.* This classification defines psychotherapies both according to the context in which they are delivered and their theoretical base. Each different type may be performed more or less skilfully and at any level of service from primary to tertiary care. It cannot be assumed that specialist expertise in one type of therapy delivery will generalize to another. For example psychotherapy in primary care is in itself a highly skilled activity, but a therapist proficient in giving treatment in that setting may not be able to provide the same expert service in secondary care.

Type A psychotherapy is any *psychological treatment given as an integral component of mental health care.* It is part of a care programme offered by a team or service and is not offered separately. For example a psychiatrist may offer a family intervention in schizophrenia to complement pharmacological treatment, psychodynamic therapy in anorexia nervosa, and a programme targeting weight gain and establishment of a normal eating pattern. Type A psychotherapy may include specialist psychotherapy (type C) but more often is equivalent to Cawley's type 1 and 2 psychotherapy.

Type B is *eclectic psychological therapy and counselling*. A great deal of counselling is eclectic psychological therapy and it is not easy to distinguish between the two, particularly as both interventions require skilled practitioners for effective intervention. The characteristic of type B therapy is that it is informed by more than one theoretical framework and is a complete treatment intervention in its own right. In general, counselling tends to be skills based, used to treat the less severely ill, for example people with adjustment problems, and tends to be delivered within primary care. In contrast, eclectic psychotherapy is used for complex psychiatric problems, formulates problems from basic principles of human development and psychopathology, and takes a problem-focused, multi-model approach to intervention.

Type C includes *formal psychotherapies that are practised within particular models*, with well-developed bodies of theory and protocols for practice: for example *psychoanalytic, cognitive-behavioural, systemic*. They are equivalent to Cawley's type 3 and 4. Practitioners are specialists with further training in one or more of the therapies, usually recognized by the British Confederation of Psychotherapists (BPC) or the United Kingdom Council for Psychotherapy (UKCP) (see p. 276).

It is type C psychodynamic therapy with which this book is primarily concerned although, as mentioned earlier, psychodynamic therapy may also be a type A therapy if delivered by a specialist in the context of an overall treatment plan, illustrating some of the inadequacy of the classification! This classification has now been further developed, linking levels of pathology with organization of services which, to some extent, links with Cawley's proposals made so long ago. In the UK the NHS has begun implementing a plan of Improving Access to Psychological Therapies (IAPT) (CSIP, 2007) in which delivery of psychotherapy takes into account the different needs and requirements of those with mental ill-health using a stepped care approach. The idea is to match type of treatment with frequency of intervention and context of service and training of practitioner to give the best chance of a favourable outcome for the patient. The idea is simple. It is to provide patients with the most cost-effective and appropriate treatment, in the least invasive manner, as close to home as possible. The result of this initiative has been to talk about psychotherapies according to this *stepped care* model. *Step 1* is the recognition of the problem, mostly done in general practitioner (GP) surgeries, social service offices, and so on;

Table 6 Levels of psychotherapy

Cawley's levels		Levels of communication	
1 {	Outer (support and counselling)	1	Unburdening of problems to sympathetic listener
		2	Ventilation of feelings within supportive relationship
2 {	Intermediate	3	Discussion of current problems with non-judgemental helper
		4	Clarification of problems, their nature and origins, within deepening relationship
		5	Confrontation of defences
3 {	Deeper	6	Interpretation of unconscious motives and transference phenomena
		7	Repetition, remembering, and reconstruction of past
		8	Regression to less adult and less rational functioning
		9	Resolution of conflicts by re-experiencing and working them through within therapeutic relationship

step 2 provides brief treatment for mild disorders such as anxiety and depression without complicating features, and so requires practitioners to have only moderate levels of training; *step 3* is for patients with moderate levels of disorder, for example more severe depression and anxiety but still without complications, and so needs more treatment sessions and is provided by practitioners with more experience; finally, *step 4* is for patients with complex disorders who require longer treatments given at a high level of skill. Therapists treating patients at this level are at the level of Cawley's psychotherapy 3.

Whichever classification is used it is clear that psychotherapy can be aimed at any of the different levels of communication which may develop when patient and therapist meet, as depicted in Table 6. The outer levels may indeed be adequate for many patients but the skill of specialist psychotherapy is to move appropriately between the levels depending on the need of the patient.

Outer levels – relief, support, and counselling

Unburdening of problems, ventilation of feelings, and discussion of current problems with a sympathetic and objective helper can enter into all levels of psychotherapy. They are the basis of formal psychotherapy (especially in the early stages), of supportive psychotherapy, and of counselling. The psychotherapeutic aim can very properly be limited, at this outer level, to the relief of airing problems and coming to see them in clearer perspective. It should be emphasized that this support is not synonymous with supportive psychotherapy, which is now considered a specific mode of treatment (Holmes, 1995).

Supportive psychotherapy is a term given to the commonest form of psychotherapy in medical and general psychiatric practice. Its main aim (Van Marle & Holmes, 2002) is to restore or maintain the status quo in two groups of patients. The first group contains those reacting to a crisis such as bereavement, divorce, loss of a job, or academic difficulties, when distress and tension impair their usual ways of coping. In the course of a few weeks of weekly or twice-weekly sessions, the therapist provides support while encouraging the patient in restoring his coping capacities. Here there is an overlap with Rogerian counselling (see p. 119).

The second group contains those severely handicapped, emotionally and interpersonally, by chronic schizophrenia, manic-depressive illness, or extreme personality disorder. While the therapist may see no prospect of fundamental improvement, he responds to the patient's need for continuing help to maintain the best possible adaptation. The therapist provides regular contact at, say, monthly or three-monthly intervals, if necessary over years, and plays a fairly active and directive role in encouraging the patient to capitalize on his strengths, while avoiding pushing him too much. Bloch (2006) rightly points out the danger of inducing dependence in long-term supportive therapy. This can produce difficulties for patients and for therapists when they become burdened by the dependence and try to withdraw from it, or when they leave for another job. In psychiatric units it may be junior doctors who see most of the long-term patients, and their training posts are of limited duration, hence the importance of team-work in supportive therapy so that patients can look to a helping network – for example, the whole psychiatric unit or social services department – rather than to an individual.

Supportive psychotherapy is also characterized by the techniques used. Holmes (1995) identifies holding and containment, an active 'real' therapist, positive reinforcement, working positively with defences, helping with coping, reframing problems, and judicious use of transference and countertransference as important techniques. Holding and containing involves a capacity to do nothing, 'to be with' (Wolff, 1971) the patient, or, during crises, to speak on the phone and to offer emergency appointments when appropriate. An active therapist is more willing to reveal himself, to answer and to ask questions, to direct a session, and to give positive reinforcement with encouraging remarks. A disturbed patient may be helped to modulate affects such as anxiety and depression through relaxation and recognition that they have an illness – an example of working positively with the defence. This increases coping capacities.

Positive reframing of a problem and judicious use of transference and countertransference are advanced skills of supportive psychotherapy. A depressed patient may be helped to realize that her depression is in fact a relationship or interpersonal problem; a borderline patient may be helped to understand that self-mutilation is preferable to death and that she is doing the best she can. Monitoring of countertransference is as important as in formal psychotherapy. The therapist needs to decide when to offer another appointment, when to accept phone calls, when to prescribe, and when to be active or inactive. Recognition of countertransference is essential when making these decisions.

Thus supportive psychotherapy is appropriate for relatively healthy people in a crisis, and for those whose defences are precarious or have broken down. To oversimplify, supportive psychotherapy is for patients at both extremes – the worried well and the severely mentally ill. In both groups, exploration at depth is usually neither necessary nor desirable. In the first group it can usually be avoided, but in the second group it should be avoided. Acutely psychotic patients are already overwhelmed by primitive feelings and unconscious fantasies and their need is to strengthen their defences, not to explore them (p. 241). This level of psychotherapy can be used very effectively by general psychiatrists.

A young man from abroad, bitterly disappointed at failing to gain promotion in his country's Air Force, had to undergo an emergency operation. Post-operatively he complained of chest pain, and the doctor looking after him, thinking the patient would not understand, joked to a colleague that he must have had a heart attack. On hearing this, the patient became acutely anxious and hypochrondriacal. He remained in this condition, despite examination and reassurance by several eminent physicians and surgeons, who, however, never spoke to him more than cursorily.

Eventually he was seen by a psychiatrist who recognized his depression. He supported him in regular sessions, and encouraged him to start going out more. He allowed the patient to talk to him about his feelings and the predicament of his life situation, so enabling him to translate symptoms into problems. The psychiatrist prescribed antidepressant medication and, perhaps more importantly, saved his face by giving him medical grounds for leaving the Air Force, which he had wanted to do in order to make a new life for himself.

The psychiatrist provided him with a supportive relationship on the model of a good father with time to be interested, not aloof and disdainful as the patient imagined his own father would be. What the patient needed to get well was not just reassurance that there was nothing physically wrong with him; he had had a lot of that, to no avail. He needed someone to recognize and help him with the feelings and conflicts provoked by his life situation. On this occasion there was no need to explore whether the patient's problems were more deep-seated, for example, whether they may have been perpetuated by unresolved Oedipal conflicts.

Counselling is another name for a form of psychotherapy at this outer level, which has rapidly developed as a method of help for specific groups of people: for example, Marriage Guidance Counsellors are consulted by those with marital problems; Student Counsellors at universities, colleges, and schools see students with emotional and academic problems; Samaritans are contacted by people in states of suicidal despair. Counselling services have grown up for those with sexual problems, HIV infection, or, in association with abortion services, for women with unwanted pregnancies. Recruitment, training, techniques, and standards of counsellors are inevitably varied, but are coordinated by the British Association for Counselling established in 1976. It is also fair to say that many counsellors are now trained to move between levels of psychotherapy and so are offering treatments for people with more severe difficulties.

It is easier to define what counsellors do than to give a precise definition of what it is; counselling techniques vary from providing information (e.g. about available sources of help in the community) to helping the client understand his attitudes and feelings. There is a balance between non-directive and directive intervention. Rowland (1993) has defined it as 'an ethical task in which the counsellor forms a therapeutic alliance with the client and uses a range of skills to facilitate the client's resolution of his or her problems'. This early definition identifies the problem: counselling is not well defined and incorporates a range of techniques rather than relying on specific techniques which might make it easier to define. Of the psychotherapies it is not alone in this. Only recently have efforts been made to define exactly what psychotherapists do in differently named treatments (Skills for Health, 2009). The British Association for Counselling and Psychotherapy (BACP) defines counselling as 'a systematic process which gives individuals an opportunity to explore, discover and clarify ways of living more resourcefully, with a greater sense of well-being'. Thus, counselling may be concerned with addressing and resolving specific problems, making decisions, coping with crises, working through conflict, or improving relationships with others. The main psychotherapeutic component is usually at the outer level, where ventilation of feelings and discussion of current problems enable a client to make and carry out valid and appropriate decisions. Counsellors recognize that when clients are treated as responsible people, and helped to find their own solutions, opportunities for learning and growth are increased. The counsellor's non-directive role – leaving decisions to the client and withholding direct advice or interpretations – discourages dependency and so tends to ease termination (Mearnes & Thorne, 2007).

A major influence in non-directive counselling techniques has been the client-centred psychotherapy of Carl Rogers (1961), later a pioneer of the Encounter movement (p. 205). Having come to psychology from a theological background, he took a basically optimistic view of the individual's capacity for growth and self-realization when provided with an enabling relationship. He and his colleagues have demonstrated that effective therapists are those with three characteristics: *accurate empathy* (which they can communicate to the client), *non-possessive warmth* (which accepts whatever the client brings of himself), and *genuineness* (self-awareness and ability to be truly themselves in the relationship). The therapeutic process envisaged by Rogers is essentially an increasing frankness and extension of self-awareness within the therapeutic relationship. The counsellor's activity is mainly reflecting what the client says, and paraphrasing his words. Rogers and Dymond (1954) have shown that these methods can lead to greater self-acceptance, expressed as a reduction of the discrepancy between the client's perceptions of himself as he is and how he would like to be. This is not surprising, as the therapist concentrates on accepting and affirming the client's awareness of himself as it unfolds; and he always helps the client to see himself in a favourable light. For example, a therapist might help a client plagued with guilt feelings to convert these into a sense of righteous bitterness at having been wronged, that is, to see badness outside rather than within himself.

Recently there has been an expansion of counselling services in primary care (Tylee, 1997), although the effectiveness of such services remains unclear. Friedli *et al.* (1997) compared Rogerian counselling with routine care from the GP in patients suffering from emotional disorder, and found that all patients improved over time to a similar degree. Satisfaction was greater in those patients who received counselling. A number of other studies have favoured counselling over other interventions for depression and shown that offering it in the context of primary care is effective for patients with mild depression, anxiety, and mixed emotional disorders (Ward, King, & Lloyd, 2000). Overall there is evidence for the efficacy of counselling for depression in primary care for patients with mild to moderate depression of recent onset when it is compared with antidepressants, GP care, and other psychological interventions. There is no evidence of its effectiveness for chronic depression. Interestingly the studies which looked at acceptability to clients of medication and psychotherapy found little preferential difference between them.

Rogerian counselling is certainly psychotherapeutic in that it is based on a relationship of trust, verbal communication, and increase of understanding. However, in general, Rogerian therapists do not confront defences or interpret unconscious processes such as transference phenomena. In other words, they do not explore at such depths, as do more analytic therapists.

Before moving on to consider the deeper levels, it should be emphasized that support is a vital part of therapy at all levels, at least as much at the deeper levels as at the outer. It might therefore be more appropriate to talk not of *supportive* psychotherapy, but *non-exploratory* therapy. Often this would be more a non-exploratory *phase* of therapy, since later, when acute disturbance has passed, the time may be ripe for judicious exploration.

Intermediate levels

Many social workers, psychiatrists, and general practitioners work at this level, clarifying problems within a deepening relationship, and confronting defences and interpreting less conscious motives when appropriate. In deeper levels of therapy, transference and other unconscious processes become the main focus of analytic exploration; they may be manifest even in a first interview and in the outer levels of more purely supportive therapy and counselling. At intermediate levels they are used to assist the psychodynamic understanding of the patient and the way he relates to the therapist. Even when the therapist encourages mildly positive feelings towards himself as a good reliable parent, and avoids the emergence of more intense positive or negative transference feelings, awareness of defence mechanisms and the complexities of transference and countertransference may enable him to engage with the patient more deeply and effectively. An example from Gill (1973, p. 35) illustrates three successive levels of interview with one patient in general practice:

A middle-aged single woman had come to her doctor complaining of feeling tired and cold. He took a full history, examined her and had tests carried out to exclude physical causes such as anaemia ('traditional medical interview'). She still felt ill, so he asked her back for a longer interview, and inquired about her life and circumstances, discovering that she had been dominated by her mother and that her symptoms dated from a recent change in the office where she worked ('detective type of personal interview'); she agreed that this was relevant, thanked the doctor for his interest, but resisted further inquiry. He therefore prescribed anti-depressants and asked her to return in two weeks. When she did so she was even more depressed. The doctor apologetically said, 'Oh dear, we must try again', at which she burst into tears. He was shocked at his own reaction of thinking how ridiculous she looked crying while wearing such a formidable hat, but immediately realised that she might make other people unsympathetic to her in a similar way. This initiated what came to be called a 'flash type of interview' at depth, in which they both shared a new understanding of the way she longed for personal warmth, but hid it and kept people at bay with her stern manner. Before this could happen they both lowered the barriers, the doctor admitting his failure, and the patient letting herself cry. The interview was much warmer than the earlier ones and established a new relationship between doctor and patient, which should be useful in itself but also in helping her to react differently with other people.

A leading part in the promotion of psychotherapy at these levels was played by the seminars for general practitioners started by Michael and Enid Balint at the Tavistock Clinic in London (Balint, 1957; Balint, Ornstein, & Balint, 1972; E. Balint, Courtenay, Elder, et al., 1993; Hopkins, 1972; Sanders, 1986). These seminars continued as 'Balint Groups' for general practitioners. Gradually the views they propounded have been incorporated into training for GPs and so the groups are no longer so common. However, case discussion groups in which patients' problems are formulated using the perspective and emotional experience of the doctor are essential elements of psychiatrists' training programmes (Das, Egleston, El-Sayeh, et al., 2003). The Balints made clear how the doctor's attitude and response to patients, and his explicit and implicit expectations of them, shape what they bring to him. Patients learn the doctor's language. Balint (1957) called this the 'apostolic function' of the doctor, through which he develops in his practice a particular culture of complaining, diagnosis, and treatment. The complaints the patient offers, most often physical, can be accepted at face value or seen as overlying a more personal problem. Some doctors will accept the presenting complaint without question; others give the patient an opportunity to talk about any wider problems to gather the context of the problem and to see if there are any precipating or moderating factors. This is what Balint called 'patient-centred medicine', in contrast and in addition to 'disease-centred medicine'.

The experienced doctor is aware that some patients need to go on indefinitely expressing their need for support, symbolized by visits for repeat prescriptions, and that he himself, or rather the doctor–patient relationship, is a powerful medicine, with its most active agent being the feeling of having a 'good reliable parent'. Social workers have parallel experiences. Whatever their professional background, mental health professionals and others appreciate the opportunities offered by the special nature of the setting in which they work and its influence on their relationship with patients. The general practitioner, for example, has opportunities to understand patients in the context of their families and to learn their various characteristic ways of reacting to difficulties. He can ask about other family members, visit them, or ask them to come and see him. Because he is generally accessible he may choose to provide support over long periods of time. He may also propose deeper exploration of a problem if and when the patient is ready for it. He can offer longer interviews at the end of a 'surgery', a special appointment with himself, or sometimes an appointment with a visiting psychiatrist or psychotherapist. He may refer the patient to a psychiatric clinic, although some family doctors develop skill in working at depth in the five to ten minutes available in the average NHS surgery, as in the example above. Over recent years an increasing number of general practices have incorporated counsellors and psychotherapists into their teams and the IAPT programme (see p. 114) takes place in the community and sometimes in general practice surgeries.

The therapist working at these intermediate levels has learnt to evaluate his countertransference (p. 79), and discriminate between his personal feelings and those evoked in him by the patient. This understanding can assist his treatment of a patient and extend the help he may give. Furthermore, trial interpretation of transference phenomena and cautious confrontation of defences can be used to assess a patient's suitability and readiness for deeper analytic work, should referral be considered for more specialized psychotherapy (p. 125).

Deeper levels – exploration and change

At all levels of therapy, the therapeutic relationship is the context within which therapy takes place, but, at the deeper more dynamic levels, it is also the main focus of therapeutic work. At this level a more specific therapeutic alliance is formed, transference and countertransference phenomena are explored, and unconscious motives, anxieties, and defences are identified, especially as they emerge in the 'here and now'. Many of the processes at this level have been described more fully in the section on Understanding and Integration (p. 101). Briefly, as traced in Table 6, dynamic psychotherapy allows and encourages the re-experiencing, in the transference, of disturbing experiences that can be traced from childhood through to adulthood; such repetition fosters understanding of

Table 7 Similarities and differences between supportive and
          exploratory psychotherapy

Similarities	Unburdening of problems	
	Ventilation of feelings	
	Discussion of problems	
	Support within 'working alliance'	
	Reliability of time and place	

Differences	Supportive (level 1)	Exploratory (level 3)
Defences	Supported and reinforced	Confronted and modified
Anxiety	Kept to minimum	Optimal level sought
Transference	Minimized and accepted	Fostered, revealed, and analysed
Regression	Discouraged	Allowed within sessions
Reporting of dreams	Not encouraged	Welcomed
Advice	Offered as necessary	Withheld
Medication	Offered as necessary	Offered if necessary

their origins but more importantly allows the patient to develop a
coherent narrative of how they have become like they are, which
they can use to understand themselves better (Freud, 1912). The
narrative and understanding is then used to explore at greater depth
the traumas and conflicts linked to present symptoms, aided by
conditions which permit psychological regression to the child inside
the adult: *reculer pour mieux sauter*. When understood, defences,
which are no longer necessary, may be discarded or modified, so
enabling the individual to function more flexibly.

The understanding sought is more emotional than intellectual:
insight has to be an emotional experience to affect deeply a
person's view of himself. Moreover, repetition or working through
is required for a patient to resolve conflicts and establish a new way
of experiencing himself and his relationships in the face of resistance from persistent anxieties and defences. The aim of treatment
at this deeper level is therefore more than symptomatic relief: it is
reintegration and change in personality functioning, both intrapsychic and interpersonal, towards greater wholeness, maturity,
and fulfilment.

Table 7 outlines the similarities and chief differences between
psychotherapy at the outer and deeper levels, that is, between
so-called supportive psychotherapy and exploratory or analytic
psychotherapy. It should be remembered that while support is an
essential and fundamental part of all psychotherapy, exploration at
depth is not; one can have support without exploration, but not
exploration without support. Otherwise it may seem paradoxical

that psychoanalysis, the form of psychotherapy which explores most intensively, provides the immense support of daily sessions. It is often desirable to plan supportive and exploratory phases in treatment: for example, support and management may be emphasized while acute emotional disturbance is contained and reduced, to be followed by exploration of underlying problems. It is important that the level is chosen and timed appropriately for each patient.

In the following sections which describe the distinguishing features of each of the main forms of dynamic psychotherapy, after a brief historical introduction we will consider in turn the therapeutic setting, the role of the patient, the role of the therapist, and the therapeutic processes most characteristic of that form of therapy. These divisions, made for the purpose of exposition, are somewhat artificial and should not be taken too literally; the crux of the therapeutic process is the interaction between patient and therapist in the chosen setting.

PSYCHOANALYSIS AND ANALYTIC PSYCHOTHERAPY

Modern dynamic psychotherapy can be said to have begun with Freud and psychoanalysis, the early development of which has already been briefly outlined (p. 9). To avoid confusion, it may be helpful to distinguish at this point between at least three different meanings and uses of the word *psychoanalysis* (Main, 1968). First, it is a technique for investigating unconscious psychic life, by inviting a patient, lying on a couch, to say whatever comes to mind. Second, it refers to a theoretical body of knowledge built up on the basis of such observations. Third, the term is used to describe an intensive method of psychotherapeutic treatment. Although we prefer to see these three (the technique, the theory, and their application) as intimately connected, logically one does not entail the other. The theory might have explanatory value but the treatment based on it could be ineffective; or the treatment may be effective but for reasons quite other than the theory supposes. It might avoid confusion if the term psychoanalysis were reserved for the theory of psychoanalytic psychology from which various methods of psychoanalytic psychotherapy derive. In the area of treatment we might then talk of intensive analytic psychotherapy rather than psychoanalysis.

Next we come to the much-debated issue of similarities and differences between psychoanalysis (analytic psychotherapy three to five times a week) and the less-frequent psychotherapy. There is a considerable literature on this topic (Rangell, 1954; Wallerstein, 1969, 1989, 1999). We share the view of these authors and others that the differences are blurred and there is a continuous spectrum between the most intensive analytic psychotherapy (or psychoanalysis) through intermediate ranges of exploratory psychotherapy to the less intensive and more supportive psychotherapies. The ends of the spectrum may look sharply different. Analysts who only see patients five times a week will naturally consider what they do to be very different from what other psychotherapists do: for example being 'purer' than psychoanalytic psychotherapy, which may be seen as more eclectic in its approach. There may even be a sense that psychoanalysis is 'better' than psychotherapy, but this is not necessarily the case. Some patients do well with one session a week and may have done worse with more frequent meetings. So it is important for therapists to find the right level and intensity for each individual patient to work at, rather than adjusting the patient to the method: for example, starting one to three times a week, before deciding with the patient what his further needs are.

Full psychoanalysis (or five-times-a-week analytic psychotherapy) is appropriate and feasible as a treatment for only a minority of patients, although an intensive analytic experience remains the core of training for future psychoanalysts and specialist dynamic psychotherapists. In this section, psychoanalysis will be considered together with analytic psychotherapy of less frequency and intensity, since in our view their similarities outweigh their differences. But first let us take a further brief look at some of the developments and influences in psychoanalytic theory beyond the elementary principles set out in Part I.

The evolution of psychoanalytic theory is an immense subject. Many authors have reviewed its first half-century (Jones, 1953, 1955, 1957; Guntrip, 1961; Ellenberger, 1970; Sandler, Dare, Holder, et al., 1997; Bateman & Holmes, 1995). In its earliest phase, psychoanalysis was based on a cathartic model. Most of Freud's early cases were young women thought to have hysterical disorders (now, many would be considered to have borderline personality disorder), whose symptoms were traced to dammed up feelings associated with sexuality. Therapy, at first under hypnosis, aimed to uncover repressed memories and release the feelings held back because they were unacceptable to the patient's conscious view of herself. Freud wrote of 'releasing strangulated affects' and 'of making the unconscious conscious'. As his translator, James Strachey, wrote in the introduction to *Studies on Hysteria* (Breuer & Freud, 1895, p. xviii):

> . . . Freud abandoned more and more of the machinery of deliberate suggestion and came to rely more and more on the patient's flow of 'free associations'. The way was opened up to the analysis of dreams. Dream-analysis enabled him, in the first place, to obtain an insight into the workings of the 'primary process' in the mind and the ways in which it influenced the products of our more accessible thoughts, and he was thus put in possession of a new technical device – that of 'interpretation'. But dream-analysis made possible, in the second place, his own self-analysis, and his consequent discoveries of infantile sexuality and the Oedipus complex.

Freud developed his traumatic theory of the neuroses because, when under hypnosis and later via free association (see p. 145), his patients told him about sexual experiences in early childhood. Believing their stories, he came to the view that early sexual experiences could not be processed psychologically by the individual and so were actively removed from consciousness or repressed, giving rise to neurotic symptoms later. During the 'talking cure' some memories seemed to return, 'the return of the repressed', leading to symptomatic improvement. Later Freud came to the view that these experiences may have been imagined rather than actually experienced and, although Freud has been criticized for changing his mind (Masson, 1985), his recognition of the difficulty of distinquishing between reality and fantasy was a forerunner of a debate that has now reached epidemic proportions and is often referred to as the *recovered memory controversy*.

Recovered memories

It is now believed that child sexual abuse is commoner than originally thought and yet the true incidence remains unknown. Child agencies, judicial process, and epidemiological surveys have suggested that 6–62% of the population have experienced sexual abuse at some point during childhood. Overall, studies suggest that around 15% of the general population and 30% of psychiatric patients have experienced sexual abuse (Palmer, Coleman, Chaloner, *et al.*, 1993). The experience increases the incidence of levels of depression, eating disorders, and self-harm. Many patients attribute loss of trust in relationships, poor self-esteem, sexual dysfunction, and increased hostility to childhood abuse.

There is uncertainty about whether abuse and other traumatic events can be forgotten completely and later return to consciousness. If so, what is the veracity of such memories? If they are untrue then we are faced with the possibility that fantasy itself is a powerful instigator of symptoms since many patients with recollection of trauma and abuse suffer serious mental symptoms. Over the years many clinicians have reported that patients recover memories during clinical sessions. Those working with survivors of traumatic experiences have also noted the existence of psychogenic amnesia, suggesting that loss of memory for traumatic incidents may occur. There is no doubt that people forget things, and no one questions the validity of fugue states in which an individual loses personal memory but subsequently recalls his autobiography accurately.

Most people now accept that traumatic events can be forgotten and then remembered (Fonagy, 1999), although the argument continues. For example, the report of the Working Party on Reported Recovered Memories of Child Sexual Abuse of the Royal College of Psychiatrists (Royal College of Psychiatrists, 1997) was more equivocal. It suggested that there was little evidence for such a view, implying that complete loss of memory of traumatic sexual abuse was unlikely and that there was little evidence for repression.

This raises another question because the controversy is not just about whether memories can be lost and later return but whether they are actively inhibited, keeping them out of consciousness as Freud originally suggested. Some have argued that the mechanism involved is ordinary forgetting and that there is no need to posit a special mechanism such as repression. This seems unlikely since recovered memories and traumatic memories have characteristics which are not the same as those things that we passively forget and later remember. They are often accompanied by extreme emotions, by a reluctance to discuss them, and by deliberate attempts to forget them to avoid painful associations. Further, recent data from neurocognitive science have suggested that there are inhibitory processes in both attention and memory and that these may be especially marked in certain individuals. Abuse itself may interfere with the accurate laying down of memory. Research in hypnosis has shown that people can temporarily block access to certain memories and that unconscious memory can influence present experience and thoughts. Thus whilst more work is needed there is some evidence for the clinical hypothesis of repression and of its importance in psychological function.

It has been suggested that memories recovered in therapy may be the product of inappropriate suggestion. Even if this were the case it does not account for those memories that are retrieved at other times. Surveys of practitioners suggest that memories are often recovered before rather than during therapy and are the stimulus to seek therapy. This alone implies that the hypothesized implantation of memories by misguided practitioners can only account for a small subset of recovered memories, if any at all. Nevertheless the guidelines produced by the Royal College of Psychiatrists warn against the use of certain techniques in therapy, such as literal dream interpretation, body memories, and memory recovery techniques. None form part of mainstream psychoanalytic psychotherapy. Indeed the representation of psychoanalytic therapy as an archaeological dig searching for early memories is related more to Hollywood than to actual practice.

Freud and his followers

Returning now to the history of psychoanalysis and psychoanalytic psychotherapy, Freud's discovery of the importance of Oedipal conflicts may have emerged from his own family situation (Pedder, 1987). He was the favoured eldest of eight children of his father's second wife, whom he also had to share with two half-brothers old enough to be his father. Many ill-informed critics of Freud think mistakenly that he stopped at the point where he emphasized sexuality, which led, by 1913, to his parting from both Jung and Adler.

Carl Gustav Jung (1875–1961) developed his own school of analytic psychology, which moved away from man's biological roots to a study of the manifestation of his psychological nature in myths, dreams, and culture – in part products of the *collective unconscious* and its *archetypes*. These are prototypes of figures to be found in many widely different cultures (Jung, 1964). They include the Animus and the Anima (male and female elements found in members of the opposite gender), the Shadow (unacknowledged aspects of the Self), and the Great Mother, the Wise Old Man, and the Hero. He saw treatment as a process of *individuation*, the unifying of an individual through discovering the hidden or undeveloped aspects of his personality. Born in Switzerland, the son of a country pastor, Jung was an isolated child; his older brother died before he was born and his sister was nine years younger. He became very introverted, and for a time experienced fainting fits which kept him from school. Whereas Freud developed psychoanalysis from a background and private practice in neurology which brought him patients with hysterical *neuroses*, Jung started his psychiatric career working with *psychotic* patients in hospital. He was struck by the universal symbols (or archetypes) in their delusions and hallucinations. After his rupture with Freud, overtly because of disagreement about the importance of sexuality, but perhaps also over father–son rivalries, Jung again withdrew into what Ellenberger (1970) calls a 'creative illness' during which he too conducted a self-analysis. But instead of using free association, as Freud had done, Jung provoked upsurges of unconscious imagery by writing down and drawing his dreams and telling himself stories which he forced himself to prolong. He subsequently became actively involved with others in developing *analytic psychology*, but he had to withdraw periodically to his lakeside retreat for long periods of replenishment, as though alternating between the outer and inner worlds. Jung's concepts of extraversion and introversion have become part of everyday language. His ideas of finding a fuller balance in the personality between its different trends (male and female, thinking and feeling, sensation and intuition), and his emphasis on creativity and imaginativeness, are of value in all psychotherapy. Fordham (1978) and Samuels (1985) provide useful introductions to Jung's ideas. Compared with some psychoanalysts, analytic psychologists tend to view the therapeutic relationship more as a direct encounter between two individuals. They often sit facing their patients and work less with transference, though in Britain, Jungian and Freudian analysts have much in common.

Alfred Adler (1870–1930), in contrast to Jung, moved away from preoccupation with intrapsychic life, particularly at deeper, unconscious levels, towards a more social view of man. Born in Vienna, the middle of three sons, he was acutely aware of sibling rivalry; as with Freud and Jung, his family experiences contributed to his particular insights (Pedder, 1987). In his view, neurosis originated in attempts to deal with feelings of inferiority, some-times based on relative physical handicaps ('organ inferiority'), which gave rise to a compensatory drive to power. Similarly, he saw 'masculine protest' in women as a reaction to their inferior position in society. Adler rejected Freud's earlier view that sexual drive (libido) was primary, and that aggression was merely a response to frustration. He postulated an aggressive drive before Freud did. Although he formed his own school of *individual psychology*, several of his ideas have become incorporated into the practice of many psychotherapists. These include the 'inferiority complex' and the recognition that 'striving for power' may reveal itself by its apparent opposite, that is, its retreat into manipulative weakness. His interest in the interaction of the individual with society, and between individuals in small groups, is taken up again in the section on group psychotherapy. Adler also influenced the development of the 'neo-Freudian' cultural school (Sullivan, Horney, Fromm, etc.) (see Figure 10, p. 223) and of transactional analysis (Berne, 1961). Ansbacher and Ansbacher (1957) have edited a useful anthology of Adler's writings.

Yet at the same time as Jung and Adler were leaving the psychoanalytic movement, Freud's ideas were also changing and developing. Contrary to the view of some of his contemporary critics he had become more convinced of the pathogenic signi-ficance of actual seduction (Freud, 1917a) and by the time he wrote *Mourning and Melancholia* (Freud, 1917b) he was concerned less with instinctual drives as such, and more with internalized rela-tionships with the people towards whom affectionate and hostile feelings are directed. He had recognized, for example, that depres-sion could result from the loss, by death or otherwise, of a valued person or ideal (p. 26). Hostile feelings provoked by the pain of loss may then be turned on to the self through the internalized image of the lost person, with whom the sufferer identifies. Clinically this is seen when a bereaved person, perhaps at an anni-versary, develops the symptoms suffered by the deceased. These ideas led to Freud's (1923) final formulation of the personality structure into ego, super-ego, and id (p. 60).

Post-Freudian developments

Since then, two important developments in psychoanalysis could be said to have emphasized, respectively, the ego and the id. *Ego psychology* has concentrated on studying the ways in which the ego organizes itself, adapts to both external and internal reality, and deploys instinctual drives (Hartmann, 1939). Anna Freud (1936) delineated many of the mechanisms by which the ego defends itself from anxiety and psychic pain (p. 28). However, even in severe neurosis, many ego functions may be conflict-free: for example, someone may be functioning perfectly well at work, though handicapped in his personal life. The early development of ego functions (p. 48), as the infant becomes more aware of his boundaries and of the difference between me and not-me, has been studied by direct infant observation, notably by Mahler *et al.* (1975) and Stern (1985). In recent years ego psychology has tended to move away from abstract disputation about types of psychic energy, to interest in the development of internal representations of the self in relation to others (Kernberg, 1975). This development has brought ego psychology closer to object-relations theory (p. 61).

Melanie Klein (1882–1960) may be said to have furthered 'id psychology'. Born in Vienna, she came to Britain from Berlin in 1926 at the invitation of Ernest Jones, who had founded the British Psychoanalytical Society in 1919 (Grosskurth, 1985). Like Anna Freud, she was a pioneer of child analysis and its use of play as a means of communicating with the child's fantasies and conflicts. In this way she analysed children as young as 2 years of age (Klein, 1932). She became aware of their powerful, unconscious fantasy life, which she viewed as springing directly from instinctual drives. She thought that children have innate knowledge of sexuality and are innately aggressive, so developing Freud's controversial idea of a 'death instinct'. Through her work with young children, Melanie Klein came to realize the early importance of the mother, so complementing Freud's greater emphasis on the role of father; it is perhaps no coincidence that Freud was a man and Klein a woman. In her view, Oedipal conflicts, or their precursors, begin much earlier than in the classical view of the Oedipus complex (p. 51).

Klein especially emphasized primitive mental mechanisms such as introjection, projection, and splitting. In the earliest months, before the infant has clearly recognized the difference between fantasy and reality, between what is inside and outside itself, the death instinct, according to Klein, leads to feelings of destructive rage even without experiences of frustration, and images of a bad mother are split off and projected outside. The good feelings and images are introjected and kept inside, but threatened by the return of the projected 'persecutory' mother – the so-called *paranoid-schizoid position*. As the child learns that it is the same mother who both gratifies and frustrates, it has to cope with ambivalence, that is, loving and hating the same person. This more mature *depressive position* allows for the co-existence of love and hate, and thus promotes concern for the other and a wish to make amends and repair any damage the child imagines it has caused. Inadequately worked through, the depressive position can lead to unreasonable fears in later life that any hatred will damage or destroy a loved person. This is a way of viewing the clinical experience that death of a parent or sibling in childhood can result in the harbouring of deep feelings of guilt in later life (Pedder, 1982). Kleinian analysts, in concentrating on primitive mental functions and fantasies, pay less attention to the real experiences of the developing child than do other psychoanalysts, and consider that an experience of bad mothering can be attributed to projected images of a bad mother created by the child (Segal, 1964).

There has been a continuing to and fro debate within psycho-analytic circles as to whether externally imposed or internally imagined experiences are more important in development. Sigmund Freud had at first thought that the prime causes of neurosis were trauma and seduction, but when he realized that these may have been imagined he considered inner psychic reality to be the more important. Recent awareness of the extent of child abuse (see p. 127) has led to a revision of this view; we consider internal and external realities as of equal importance, and as interacting. Later on, in his structural theory, Freud (1923) re-emphasized the part played by external figures as they became internalized in the super-ego. 'The super-ego enshrines the fact of personal object relations' (Guntrip, 1971, p. 28). The Kleinians have given overriding importance to the role of internal fantasy, to the relative neglect of external reality. It was partly as a reaction to this that Bowlby (1952, 1969, 1973, 1980) set out to investigate the effects of one very obvious trauma, that of maternal separation (p. 55), and Winnicott (1965) began to explore the importance of maternal provision and the 'facilitating environment'.

Object-relations theory views the development of personality as inextricably linked with the internalized early relationships and the feelings associated with them, both good and bad. This schism between internal and external influences on development has polarized psychodynamic practitioners, but there is increasing recognition that it is the interaction of the two that is important and one does not have primacy over the other. It is through the work of Bowlby on attachment and Winnicott on the psychological interplay between mother and baby that this balance has come about.

Bowlby was careful to distinguish between scientific and theoretical aspects of psychoanalysis (Holmes, 1993). As we have already discussed (see p. 55), his main concern was to place object-relations theory on a scientific footing through ethology – the scientific study of animal behaviour. To do so he became more concerned with the effect of the external object on the individual than with the influence of the individual on the object. Rather than considering how a child's inner world shapes his internal perception of the object and thereby governs his responses and experiences, Bowlby considered how the individual's personality was moulded by the inadequacies, absences, and losses of important caregivers. To re-iterate (see p. 56), he formulated a theory of development based on attachment. In essence, attachment theory is a theory of proximity and separation: when I am close to my protector or loved one I feel safe; when I am away from home I may feel sad, anxious, and lonely. It is both a theory of behaviour and of feeling. To feel close is to feel attached, but to be close is not necessarily to be securely attached. Attachment may be secure and insecure. *Secure attachment* allows an individual to miss someone and to be sure of her return. *Insecure attachment* leads to anxiety, to fear of rejection, and to vigilance. Such feeling may lead to proximity-seeking behaviour suggestive of a simultaneous wish to be close and a desire to punish the attachment figure, who is experienced as failing an internal need. This is known as *ambivalent insecurity*. The profound effect that this work has had on the practice of psychotherapy is worth a brief detour. Attachment theory is not the basis of a new therapy but more a 'meta-model' of diverse therapies. Through the lens of attachment, features of psychotherapy can be defined which are relevant to therapy generally, whether it be individual, group, or family interventions.

Attachment and the practice of psychoanalytic therapy

Attachment theory proposes that certain key elements are shared by all therapies. These include the *relationship*, which Bowlby conceived of as a secure base from which to explore, an explanation of difficulties through a *shared narrative*, and an organized method for overcoming the problems. When a patient starts to form a relationship with his therapist it will quickly become apparent that he is bringing to therapy all the uncertainties, suspicions, and upsets that he has experienced in his life and that his attachment patterns will be brought into play in the therapeutic encounter, so it is helpful for the therapist to delineate the predominant attachment pattern of the patient. An insecure pattern will be represented by avoidance, ambivalence, and disorganization, which will mean the therapist has to employ all his skills if a secure base is to be formed from which to explore problems. The patient may attend sporadically, remain uncertain about the value of therapy, and be unable to decide to stay or to leave. If both patient and therapist manage the struggle by continually repairing therapeutic ruptures (see p. 70) and the therapist is attuned to the patient's uncertainties, a more secure base will develop and gradually the patient will build up an internal secure base in himself from which to approach the external world, and in doing so will feel more secure in himself.

The focus on attunement in contemporary psychotherapy stems from the work of Bowlby. It is attunement between mother and baby and, by analogy, between patient and therapist that gives rise to secure attachment and the development of a secure base. Children of parents who are responsive to the child's needs and understand their child's mental states – mentalizing (see p. 82) their child – are likely to be better adjusted socially and interpersonally and more able to reflect on their experiences and integrate them into a coherent whole. Holmes (1992) suggests that three components of psychotherapy make up a secure base phenomenon – attunement, the fostering of autobiographical competence, and affective processing – and that all are required for treatment to be effective. So what is attunement?

Attunement

Stern (1985) sees attunement as the rock on which the infant builds a sense of self. The parent tracks the infant's emotional states in minute detail and in doing so permits a sense of sharing likely inner experience. Through reciprocal interaction, appropriate care-giving behaviours, emotional responsiveness, and emotional expression, the infant gradually develops a sense of himself. This process gives a feeling of connectedness – as Stern says, attunement seeks out the activation contour that is momentarily going on in any and every behaviour and uses that contour to keep the thread of communication unbroken. Brazelton and Cramer (1991) describe the synchrony, symmetry, and contingency from which mutual play and infant autonomy begin to emerge. The translation of these ideas to therapy has led to a focus on patient–therapist interaction. Good therapists mirror their patients, automatically matching their patients' speech patterns and reciprocally changing postures. This has led to questions about the classical technique of a patient lying on a couch with the analyst sitting behind, but even then there is a reciprocity in relation to voice modulation for example.

Bowlby was concerned about separation and initially thought that the best way to prevent problems was to avoid its occurrence early in life, but later he was to realize that the way in which separation was processed was also important. Evidence suggests that if a loss is denied it leads to a dismissive pattern of attachment and, if it cannot be transcended, a preoccupied pattern. Processing is done through the parent–child interaction and how the parent handles the child's response is the key factor – accepting the hurt, anger, and sadness about the separation and allowing its expression, ignoring it, or dismissing it as 'silly' or childish. The lesson for therapy is that the therapist has to encourage appropriate and manageable emotional responses to separations and loss and to past trauma. Being alert to the ways in which patients react to their stories of trauma is as important as listening to the story itself. Some patients will dismiss the importance of current and past events – it is only too common that people who try to kill themselves deny the importance of the event shortly after. Bowlby's answer to this is for the therapist to sensitively counteract the automatic belief, traditionally held as part of the essence of being English, that a stiff upper lip is necessary for survival. Readers interested in Bowlby's understanding of affective processing in relation to early trauma are recommended to read his account of Darwin (Bowlby, 1990), whose mother died when he was 8 years old. Dumped on his older sisters by a busy and grumpy father he was never allowed to mention the death of his mother. As an adult he was plagued with psychosomatic symptoms and even wrote a letter of condolence to a friend sympathizing about the death of his young wife, saying 'I truly sympathise with you though never in my life having lost one near relation, I daresay I cannot imagine how severe grief such as yours must be'. It seems that the emotions and memories associated with her death were not only repressed but also defensively denied.

From Bowlby to Winnicott

Donald Winnicott (1896–1971), who came 'through paediatrics to psychoanalysis', as the title of his collected papers reminds us (Winnicott, 1975), was working at the same time as Bowlby. His focus was especially on the early mother–infant relationship. He developed his concept of the 'good enough mother' (Winnicott, 1965) and the necessity for a degree of 'maternal preoccupation' for an infant to thrive. As Winnicott (1975, p. 99) has said: 'There is no such thing as a baby', always 'a nursing couple'. Without mothering, a child perishes. Mother is needed not only to satisfy and look after his physical needs, but also to sense his emotional needs, to share his feelings with him, and to modify them through her greater awareness of reality. She can feel anxious without feeling overwhelmed and helpless. Ideally, mother will at first encourage her infant's illusions of omnipotence, but later provide for 'gradual disillusionment'. Later in development, mother's presence is still needed to provide a sense of safety and space in which the child can play and be creatively himself, a role paralleled by that of the analyst in psychotherapy. Winnicott recognized that both fact and fantasy influence our development. It is the interplay between external and internal reality which psychoanalysis and its derivatives are uniquely able to investigate.

Winnicott was especially interested in the interplay between mother and infant in the first years of life. He introduced the terms *transitional objects* and *transitional phenomena* for designation of the intermediate area of experience, 'between the thumb and the teddy bear, between the oral eroticism and the true object-relationship' (Winnicott, 1971, p. 2), between dependence and separation. Transitional phenomena ease separation anxiety by representing both the self and the mother. Through the use of transitional phenomena, greater exploration from an attachment figure becomes possible. Winnicott repeatedly asks for the paradox of the transitional object to be respected. We must never ask, 'did you conceive of this or was it presented to you from without?'

(ibid, p. 12). The transitional object is a joint creation of infant and mother; successful therapy is a joint creation of patient and therapist. 'Psychotherapy takes place in the overlap of two areas of playing, that of the patient and that of the therapist' (ibid, p. 38). Together they create a space and a shared language in which the patient comes to understand himself anew, much as an infant first discovers the world and learns to speak through mother. 'We experience life in the area of transitional phenomena, in the exciting interweave of subjectivity and objective observation, and in an area that is intermediate between the inner reality of the individual and the shared reality of the world that is external to individuals' (ibid, p. 64).

In America, self-psychology or self-object theory has in the last 20 years emphasized the role for the developing self of mirroring and idealizing others. These function as 'self-objects' – fused aspects of the self – which provide a sufficient sense of 'infantile grandiosity' and the power to pursue ambitions and aspirations. They are needed to withstand the inevitable blows to the infant's narcissitic vulnerability, which, when severe, can lead to narcissistic rage and loss of cohesion. Optimal disappointments, however, give rise to 'transmuting internalizations' and thus an adequately resilient self-esteem, reflecting Winnicott's view of mother's role in allowing gradual disillusionment of infantile omnipotence.

Although these ideas initiated by the Chicago psychoanalyst Heinz Kohut have been developed within a psychoanalytic context, particularly in North America (Kohut, 1971; Wolf, 1994), not all psychoanalysts accept their technical prioritizing of empathy and their side-stepping or transcending of classical drive and conflict theory (Kohut, 1979). The role of self-objects extends beyond infancy, to peer relationships and group life. They can be used to understand the self-transforming effect of short-term treatments and the therapeutic effect of a single consultation, or so-called transference cures.

All these divergent developments have led to an 'elasticity' (Sandler, 1983) of psychoanalytic concepts and a suggestion that there is not just one psychoanalysis and psychoanalytic psychotherapy but many. However, a number of contemporary themes can be discerned. There has been a greater appreciation of the uniqueness of each patient–therapist relationship and of how analysis takes place in a 'bi-personal field' to which both sides of the partnership contribute (Little, 1951; Langs, 1979b; Klauber,

1981). Therapists are not dummy targets for patients' preformed transference reactions; their emotional and intellectual responsiveness to their patients' needs must vary and their own personalities inevitably obtrude, for good or ill. The increasing recognition of the importance of countertransference as a therapeutic tool (see p. 79) is part of this trend. Deepening appreciation of what the psychoanalyst himself provides parallels understanding of maternal provision in the very earliest, pre-verbal, stages of infant development. In turn these changes reflect the increase in the proportion of patients coming for psychoanalytic help, not with simpler neurotic problems stemming from later Oedipal stages, but with personality and character problems rooted in these earliest stages of development. They may be very unstable 'borderline personalities', easily tipped over the boundary into fragmentation and psychosis (Jackson & Tarnopolsky, 1990), or 'narcissistic personalities' precariously and rigidly guarding a very vulnerable self-esteem (Kernberg, 1975). Such people have suffered problems in the earliest stages of the parent–infant relationship. Balint has used a geological metaphor to describe such a failure of fit between mother and infant as leading to a *basic fault* – the consequence of a 'considerable discrepancy in the early formative phases of the individual between his bio-psychological needs and the material and psychological care, attention, and affection available during the relevant times' (Balint, 1968, p. 22). In consequence, analyses now usually last much longer than when Freud started.

Recent developments have also led to a further move away from early psychoanalytic views of seeing the task of therapy as 'removing the amnesias' (Freud, 1896) or aiding the return of repressed memories. Psychoanalysis is more concerned with splits in the mind, with deepened awareness of the present rather than an excavation and reconstruction of the past, and with capacity to reflect on the self instead of intellectually based insight. Parts of the self are considered to be isolated from each other or projected into the external world, leaving the sufferer impoverished, grandiose, or even manic. Therapy becomes a process through which lost parts of the self are returned (Steiner, 1993). Interestingly this aspect has been taken up in cognitive therapy for psychosis in which hallucinations are seen as parts of the self that can be controlled and tamed (Kuipers, Garety, Fowler, *et al.*, 1997). In psychoanalytic therapy whole states of mind come under scrutiny. The patient is helped to identify different states of mind through an understanding of the process of transference and countertransference and so is less controlled by them.

Reconstruction of the past no longer forms a central core of clinical work. Emphasis is on thoughts, feelings, fantasies, assumptions, and impulses in the here-and-now and how they dominate an individual's responses. The relationship between patient and therapist is an actualization of an unconscious wishful fantasy in which the therapist is pushed to play a specific role and to give particular responses. A 'role-responsiveness' (Sandler, 1976) on the part of the analyst therefore becomes a necessary aspect of therapy. Childhood memories become a *metaphor* through which present responses are observed in detail and are not assumed to be direct representations of the past. Reflection on the present and its continuity with the past become central in a struggle to make coherent sense of oneself throughout development. Fonagy *et al.* (1995) coined the term 'reflective self-function' (RSF) to encapsulate the ability to think about one's biography. Securely attached individuals talk coherently about themselves and their past relationships. In contrast insecure individuals may be preoccupied and their narratives are incoherent. They appear entangled in their past experiences. Alternatively they are dismissive of their past, have few memories, and show restricted emotional responses in talking about their intimate lives. Therapy becomes a process through which self-awareness is fostered, feelings are identified, and reflection is encouraged – an attempt to help the patient move from an insecure attachment to a more secure position.

These developments in psychoanalysis threaten to widen the gap between longer term psychoanalytic therapy in which the goals are extensive, and brief therapies in which they are more limited. Yet there remains considerable overlap. Role-responsiveness, for example, has been operationalized in Ryle's (1995) cognitive-analytic therapy (CAT) (see p. 230). Reciprocal role procedures identified in CAT are core self-concepts (e.g. I am worthless) which invoke complementary responses in others, which in turn reinforce the original self-concept. This perpetuates splits within the individual that are particularly likely to occur in intimate relationships and may be repeated within the therapeutic relationship. One task of therapy is to identify the main reciprocal role procedures and even to present them in diagrams. In this way CAT tries actively to grasp the unconscious functions of the individual rather than seeing them as being represented through derivatives as in psychoanalysis.

CAT continues efforts begun by Freud's disciple Ferenczi (1926) to speed up the process of analysis and to make it more widely available. Ferenczi's experiments with active techniques and relaxation, with the analyst adopting definite roles and attitudes, were forerunners of many present-day therapies but are not accepted as part of psychoanalysis, which continues to see the unconscious as resisting direct intervention. But Freud anticipated that 'the large scale application of our therapy will compel us to alloy the pure gold of analysis freely with the copper of direct suggestion'; he went on 'whatever form this psychotherapy for the people may take, whatever the elements out of which it is compounded, its most effective and most important ingredients will assuredly remain those borrowed from strict and untendentious psychoanalysis' (Freud, 1919, p. 168). This is true of analytic psychotherapy, which, as we have already emphasized, shares common ground with psychoanalysis. Psychoanalytic concepts and techniques can be applied to psychotherapy conducted in other than the classical psychoanalytic way. This does not mean reverting to pre-analytic common sense, to suggestion, or the mere dispensing of encouragement and advice. For example, it is possible to use knowledge of unconscious motives and transference without necessarily entering into detailed elucidation of the whole of a patient's present and past, or to bring psychodynamic understanding to bear on the management of cases where psychotherapy is not appropriate. Moreover methods have been developed (e.g. Malan, 1963, 1979; Sifneos, 1972, 1987; Mann, 1973; Davanloo, 1978) to limit the extent of exploration by focusing on key problems or conflicts in brief dynamic therapy.

Brief dynamic psychotherapy

Patients often receive brief dynamic psychotherapy (Table 8) as a crisis intervention, particularly when there is severe personal distress of recent onset arising from an obvious precipitant such as a death and when the individual has adequate social and family networks. This is particularly so in the NHS where psychotherapy departments are overwhelmed with referrals and only limited resources are available.

General indications for brief therapy include *a clearly defined focus, adequate motivation, limited goals,* and *mild levels of symptoms.* A more negative indication is the likelihood of reacting to

Table 8 Indications for brief dynamic psychotherapy

General	Specific
Ability to define symptom focus at assessment	Focal conflict related to interpersonal problems
Good motivation from outset	Stable personal history
Specified, achievable goals possible	Absence of behavioural responses to emotional problems (e.g. self-harm)
Neurotic problem diagnostically	Establishment of positive therapeutic alliance during assessment
Internal or interpersonal problems predominate	Responsiveness to tentative psychoanalytic interventions

long-term treatment by developing severe regression or a trans-ference psychosis, or having significant dependency needs. General contra-indications include psychotic illness, extreme self-destructive behaviour, severe personality disorder, and drug misuse. Specific indications for brief dynamic therapy are summarized in Table 8. They include:

1 A problem understandable as related to a focal intrapsychic conflict to do with separation, Oedipal issues, narcissistic injury, or uncomplicated post-traumatic disorder such as grief.
2 A clear goal of treatment usually related to circumscribed character change and symptom relief.
3 A capacity to develop a therapeutic alliance is important and this may be indicated by:
   • at least one significant early relationship;
   • the patient quickly and flexibly relates to the assessor and can freely express feelings;
   • the two can agree on a focal conflict, which becomes clearer as they explore it, the patient responding to inter-pretations about it;
   • the patient is motivated to understand and change, and to make sacrifices for it;
   • the patient can experience, tolerate, and discuss painful feelings;
   • the patient has relatively high ego-strength and verbal intelligence;
   • the patient shows capacity for self-scrutiny (Clarkin & Frances, 1982).

The boundaries of brief dynamic therapy are no different from long-term therapy. A contract is made between patient and therapist, the number of treatment sessions identified, and a time and setting are agreed. Some flexibility may be built into the contract to take into account any unavoidably missed sessions. In the initial sessions the focus adumbrated during the assessment is explored and revised if necessary. Of particular importance is the development of a positive therapeutic alliance, which is dependent on both patient and therapist. This is discussed in more detail on p. 68. The therapist needs to be more active in brief dynamic therapy than in longer term therapy, always keeping in mind the focal conflict and returning to it throughout treatment. The aim of interventions is to elucidate the focal conflict in relation to the present and the past. A wide range of material is linked to the dynamic focus through selective attention and selective neglect. Elicited affect is seen within an interpersonal context and related to therapy in transference interpretation. Some proponents of brief dynamic therapy advocate confrontation of defences. Davanloo (1978) is relentless in his challenge of defences and Sifneos (1987) suggests that successful challenge releases affects and memories, allowing further exploration. Whatever the merits of such challenges, there is no doubt that they must be made sensitively and empathically if they are to lessen overall defensiveness rather than to stimulate a paranoid reaction. Defence should be interpreted with respect for the underlying anxiety and impulse. The time available has to be kept in mind throughout, and final sessions focus on ending treatment and the experience of loss. This is essential in all short-term treatment and especially important if the patient presents with unresolved grief. The aim is to help the patient review the positive and negative aspects of treatment, to identify areas of continuing vulnerability and find new ways of coping with them, to lessen dependency, and to promote autonomy and responsibility.

As in all therapies, good outcome of treatment may not be for reasons supposed either by the therapist or by the theory. There is conflicting evidence for outcome of brief dynamic therapy being related to transference interpretation itself, in the same way as outcome in cognitive treatments does not correlate in a simple way to cognitive interventions themselves. Marziali (1984) found a positive association between a favourable outcome and the frequency with which therapist interpretations referred to emotions experienced in the transference relationship. However Piper *et al.* (1991) found an inverse relationship between the proportion of transference interpretations and favourable outcome in patients with relatively good psychological function. This may be because of a negative effect of inaccurate transference interpretation or because transference interpretation increases as therapy fails. In general it is important that interpretation is accurate and in context, since progress may depend on affective responsiveness of the patient to the therapist's interventions (McCullough, 1991). Affective responsiveness is heightened in transference interpretation but not if it is given at the wrong time or if it is inaccurate.

Following brief psychotherapy some patients later enter longer term treatment if their problems are more extensive than they at first thought or if they wish to explore them in more depth. It is to this process that we now turn.

The setting

The generalization that the setting for dynamic psychotherapy is the relationship with the therapist (p. 68) is especially true in psychoanalysis and analytic psychotherapy. Conditions are provided which foster a deepening concentration by both patient and therapist on their developing relationship.

For a patient to move safely to the deeper levels of therapy, the therapist has to pay careful attention to the reliability of the conditions he provides. While this is true at all levels of psychotherapy, here it is especially important. Great effort is made to ensure that the room is reasonably free from interruptions and intrusive noise. It is preferably furnished with a couch and comfortable chairs of comparable height, emphasizing the equality of the conversational exchange which, although asymmetrical with respect to what is talked about (Hobson, 1974), is mutual as regards genuineness of feeling. While the same room should be used for each session, even more important is the reliability of time, duration, and frequency of sessions. The time and place become part of the containing environment offered by the therapist which, together with his sensitivity to their importance, helps to foster trust in the patient, who comes to see them as his own and begins to use them as he needs.

Although therapists have to find their own way of working comfortably, a doctor, when beginning to work in a more psychotherapeutic way, may have to give up his more traditional models of sitting behind a desk and writing notes, or at least consider why he needs to retain them and the effect of doing so on the patient and his communications.

It will be remembered that Freud's psychological discoveries arose from his work as a neurologist (p. 10). He first used hypnosis to dispel symptoms by suggestion, but later used this method to assist exploration of the origin and meaning of such symptoms and to facilitate catharsis of the associated emotional disturbance. He soon gave this up because of the difficulty of hypnotizing some patients, and his fear that the findings could be attributed to suggestion. Instead, for a while, he urged his patients to recall disturbing memories, often with his hand on their forehead, but this in turn he relinquished as he developed the technique of free association (Jones, 1953, p. 265). Patients were encouraged to report whatever came into their mind, however trivial, irrational, or disturbing it might seem; this became known as the 'basic rule' of psychoanalysis. The emergence of this method of exploring the patient's experiences marked the beginning of the psychoanalytic technique.

The couch, used by Freud for neurological examination and then for the induction of hypnosis, was retained to help patients with free association. Many psychoanalysts give patients the freedom to choose whether or not they use the couch. Lying down comfortably, free from intrusion of external sights and sounds, including those of the analyst who sits behind him, the patient is enabled to attend increasingly to internal experiences; thoughts, feelings, and fantasies become available to be reported directly, or evaded. Sometimes, particularly in the early stages of analysis, a patient may be reluctant to use the couch. He may fear loss of control, or see it as seductive or humiliating, in which case, until the fear is understood and worked through, patient and analyst may use chairs, preferably set at an angle so that they can choose whether or not to look at each other. In less intensive or in briefer forms of analytic psychotherapy it is common to use chairs throughout.

Classically, psychoanalysis involves sessions of 50 minutes' duration four or five times a week, often for several years. This commonly accepted duration and frequency of sessions in analysis compared with psychoanalytic therapy, for example, has its basis in tradition. There is almost no empirical evidence to show that sessions of this length compared to sessions of, say, 30 minutes are better for the analytic process or for patient outcomes or even that the frequency of sessions, say between three or five times per week, makes a difference. Nevertheless the frequency and regularity of sessions contribute to the intensity of therapy, and therefore increase both the patient's ability to enter more fully into his inner experiences and his sense of security in facing those which involve a lot of anxiety and pain. This provides time for the unfolding and exploration of the whole person and his psychopathology. The unhurried pace of psychoanalysis fosters regression, transference of feelings towards the analyst, and the evocation of childhood memories. These become manifest within the patient–analyst relationship and thus available for mutual experience and exploration. The frequency of sessions, interrupted by the inevitable weekends and holiday breaks, allows for re-experiencing of the vicissitudes of attachment and separation, and recognition of their contribution to the genesis of patients' problems (Bowlby, 1977).

Patient's role

There are a number of factors to be considered if a patient is to get the most out of psychoanalysis or analytic psychotherapy: he needs to have some recognition that the source of his problems is at least partially within himself; he must consider that a fuller understanding of himself and his relationships can facilitate their solution; and he needs to be able to question what he has taken for granted and, where appropriate, change his attitudes and behaviour.

With motivation to understand and change, if only in embryo, the patient joins in a therapeutic or working alliance (p. 69) with the therapist, in which he undertakes to follow the basic rule (p. 145), or at least gradually to try to overcome the resistance to communicate more openly and spontaneously. The patient gives the joint search for understanding priority, even over the relief of symptoms and the avoidance of emotional discomfort. He attempts to talk about his feelings and fantasies as they emerge, and not to dismiss them or act them out, whether inside or outside therapy; for example, if angry with the therapist, the patient is encouraged to say so rather than express it by coming late for a session or driving recklessly.

Through increasing awareness of the different levels of his experience of himself and others, and aided by the therapist's interpretations and comments, the patient comes to appreciate the continuing influence of the past in the present, of unconscious wishes and fears, and of maladaptive defences against them. He develops his capacity to differentiate between the objective and subjective aspects of the therapeutic relationship – between how it is and how it seems to be. Beyond this, he needs to integrate what he discovers and test out new ways of viewing himself and others, and fresh methods of dealing with threats and opportunities, both within the therapeutic relationship and outside it.

Analytic psychotherapy, especially when of short duration, requires all these capacities of the patient, but also an ability to work hard in therapy, to think about it between sessions, and to tolerate the anxiety and frustration that can arise from waiting for up to a week between sessions. He needs the capacity for self-responsibility, self-appraisal, and persistence (Rayner & Hahn, 1964).

Therapist's role

The first responsibility of the therapist is to create and maintain the therapeutic setting. Whilst this is true in all forms of psycho-therapy, it is particularly so in those which allow for psychological regression. If the patient is to be enabled to relinquish his more adult and defensive ways of experiencing himself and the therapist, the latter must be very sensitive to the effect of the environment he provides. He must consider the impact of weekends, breaks for holidays or sickness, unexpected change of room or time, or the consequences of the patient seeing him or another of his patients outside the consulting room.

The therapist's attitude Freud (1912) described as one of 'evenly suspended attention', tuning in equally to the manifest and latent meanings of what the patient is saying, or has said in the past. He follows the flow of free associations, noting resistance and evasion as well as the ideas and feelings conveyed by what the patient says, and the way he talks, moves, and holds himself on the couch, in the chair, or at the door. He is open to his own associations, fantasies, and feelings as well as to the patient's, monitoring them to ascer-tain whether they are likely to be springing from his own preoccu-pations or those of the patient. His preparedness to respond to the roles that the latter draws him into has been called 'free-floating responsiveness' (Sandler, 1976), a parallel to free-floating attention.

In contrast with the patient, who is free to say whatever comes into his mind, the therapist's interventions are aimed at furthering recognition and understanding of what has previously been avoided; these interventions may include confrontation, clarification, and interpretation already defined on p. 103. He should intervene mainly if the patient is blocked and not just to assert his own presence or to satisfy his wish to help or be clever. Choice, timing, and form of intervention can be crucial. An interpretation often puts into words something the patient has been aware of himself, however dimly or fleetingly. Sometimes it is best to delay an interpretation to enable the patient to arrive at it himself. As Winnicott (1971, p. 117) said: 'Psychotherapy is not making clever and apt interpretations; by and large it is a long-term giving the patient back what the patient brings.' Just as the therapist should offer his interpretations with discrimination, so must he tolerate and use the countertransference feelings evoked rather than discharge them automatically (Heimann, 1950). While it is the patient's privilege to discharge feelings, the therapist's responsibility is to contain and make use of his countertransference feelings.

Thus, the passivity of the therapist is more apparent than real. It provides the opportunity for the patient to experience the therapist in transference terms, as though he were a figure in his internal world seen in a 'mirror' (Freud, 1912); and it gives the analyst the freedom to maintain free-floating attention, to listen with his 'third ear'. It enables him to retain a capacity for contemplation and detachment while at the same time remaining intuitively receptive. By letting himself be drawn into the patient's experience and then reflecting on it, he helps the patient to understand and modify his 'assumptive world' (Frank, 1961).

Therapeutic processes

Both psychoanalysis and analytic psychotherapy aim at the attainment by the individual of a fuller and more conflict-free experience of himself and his relationships by deepening and extending his contact with alienated parts of himself, and so furthering his individual development (see Understanding and Integration, pp. 101–109). Both forms of therapy involve a mutual exploration of the patient's problems within the developing relationship with the therapist. Ideally, in psychoanalysis there is time to explore all problems at all levels of personality development; in analytic psychotherapy aims are more modest, and are usually restricted to the resolution of certain key problems and conflicts, freedom from which would then permit normal development to proceed.

Transference phenomena are encouraged and explored as the patient's conflicts become built into his relationship with the therapist. This *transference neurosis* is a re-creation in the present of the neurotic distortions springing from the patient's past disturbed family relationships. Repetition in the transference enables its vividness to be mutually experienced and examined by patient and therapist. This is the arena of what Alexander (1957) called the 'corrective emotional experience'. Intense transference feelings are experienced in which the past is alive, but the fact that the therapist does not respond as parents originally did in reality or in fantasy, for example, with rejection, punishment, or intrusion, provides a corrective emotional experience. Another way of looking at this aspect of therapy is to liken it to 're-parenting'. The recognition and correction of transference distortions, as their nature and origin are discerned, deepen understanding and the patient's mastery of himself.

A man in his thirties was referred because of family difficulties, which had resulted in his wife feeling neglected and his young son being scared of him. His careful politeness seemed to conceal a powerful and rebellious competitiveness. It emerged that he had been an assertive and aggressive child until, at the age of 8, he was sent to a convent boarding school across the road from where his parents and younger sister still lived. Fearing that he had been punished for his aggression, he became scared of physical violence, fearful of monsters in the dark, and started to wet his bed. His intense ambivalence towards his authoritarian and repressive father – wanting his acceptance but fearing his criticism and rejection – continued from childhood into his adult relationship with employers and, in due course, was expressed in reverse with his own son.

During psychotherapy these conflicts came into focus in the transference. In the session before a holiday break he started covertly to attack the therapist by quoting his sister's view that psychiatrists do nothing to prevent cruelty in the world, such as the large-scale massacres in a far-off country being at that time reported in the newspapers. Then, in scarcely concealed revenge at the therapist for leaving him, he announced defiantly that today he himself was going on a trip with a girl-friend. He stopped talking and waited. After a few minutes he began to laugh with relief; later he said he had felt intoxicated, with heart pounding, so fearful had he been that, like his father, the therapist would attack him for his defiance.

His previously distorted perception of people in the outer world, including the therapist, came home dramatically to him in this session. It played a part in gradually changing his relationship with his employers, enabling him to give to his wife and son the interest he had previously withheld in revenge. His relationships were no longer so dominated by unconscious rage and guilt, as he began to modify his internal super-ego and his projected images of a harsh and punishing father.

Strachey (1934) is often thought to have held the view that ultimately the only helpful or *mutative interpretations* are those aimed at transference distortions in order to modify a patient's overstrict super-ego. This view of the analyst would now be regarded as unnecessarily restrictive and perhaps more often, especially in regressive states, he functions as an auxiliary ego. But most psychotherapists would agree with Strachey's assertion that the greatest therapeutic effect takes place when the transference comes alive in the 'here and now' of therapy, as in the case described above. Psychoanalysis and analytic psychotherapy do not dwell on the past for its own sake; they are concerned to reveal its continuing effects, so that patients can free themselves from those that distort or restrict life in the present and future. All forms of analytic therapy aim at the resolution of conflicts by coming to face them and understand their roots in unreasonable fears, often arising in earlier life. The gradual overcoming of resistance to fuller acknowledgement and deeper understanding is what Freud meant by the analytic aim of making the unconscious conscious. 'Where id was, there ego shall be' (Freud, 1933).

These forms of therapy allow, and even encourage, *regression*: the re-living and discovery in therapy of earlier experiences, and of more child-like and irrational modes of thinking and feeling. Recognizing the child in the adult allows a greater awareness of impulses and fantasies, dreams, and day-dreams. The purpose of regression is to regain contact with parts of oneself which have manifested themselves only indirectly, as a symptom, inhibition, or sense of being incomplete or false, and to re-experience some critical period of development in the more favourable setting of the therapeutic relationship. As this happens a tentative *reconstruction* is made possible of early events and relationships in the individual's life. 'Therapy in analysis results . . . from a . . . re-evaluation and reconstruction of the meanings of one's past, present and future in the crucible of transference' (Gill, 1977, p. 589).

The patient can begin to master conflicts and traumas as he comes to place them in historical perspective, and to understand his own part in unnecessarily perpetuating them. This usually requires *working through* – the repeated experiencing and resolving of them in different ways and at different times during therapy – until understanding and mastery are complete enough. The future can then be seen as a time of challenge and change, instead of only an extension of an imprisoning past. We return to the past in order to gather strength for a 'new beginning' (Balint, 1965). There is a new chance for the patient to re-evaluate himself, his relationships, and his family of origin – understanding often allows forgiveness to mitigate blame – and to approach relationships outside in a more flexible and understanding way.

Return to the past is not an end in itself. Of particular importance to dynamic therapists is not whether memories are recovered during therapy but whether the recovery of memory during therapy has a therapeutic effect. Most therapists are aware that memories, traumatic or not, may be recovered in treatment but there remains uncertainty that the 'return of the repressed' is itself therapeutic. Freud originally argued that undoing of repression and recovering memory into consciousness was a major goal of therapy. This view has been elaborated and modified over the years but many therapists believe that it is part of the therapeutic action of treatment. Fonagy has controversially suggested that there is no evidence for it (Fonagy, 1999). He believes that remembering past events is an epiphenomenon, which occurs as a result of exploring the patient's mental models of relationships within the transference. It is the latter that is therapeutic. Memory is the channel through which the nature of internal object relationships is explored, and whether it is an accurate or inaccurate account of earlier events is not of absolute importance. Of course both patient's and therapist's experience of therapy may be that the recovery of memories has been therapeutic, but this is not the same as it being the therapeutic ingredient itself. In essence there is an argument about whether therapeutic action takes place within the autobiographical memory of patients or whether the work within the implicit memory system is of equal or greater significance. This may seem to be primarily of academic importance, but if it is the case that therapeutic action takes place within implicit memory, through transference exploration of object relationships, then the debate about repression and recovery of traumatic memories is defused as far as psychodynamic therapy is concerned because they no longer form a crucial aspect of treatment.

Research and individual psychoanalytic therapy

We discuss many aspects of research on individual psychotherapy in the last section of the book (Outcome and Research) and some relevant outcome studies are outlined there. Clinical descriptions of brief dynamic therapy are plentiful and recent reports of outcome of treatment are encouraging (Abbas, Sheldon, Gyra, et al., 2008). One aspect that is relevant to this discussion about the process of psychoanalytic therapy are the differences between short-term and long-term psychoanalytic therapy. Crits-Christoph (1992), in a meta-analysis of brief dynamic psychotherapy, suggested that it demonstrated large effects relative to waiting-list conditions but only slight superiority to non-psychiatric treatments such as self-help groups and placebo and clinical management. Its effects were about equal to those of other psychotherapies and medication. Anderson and Lambert (1995), in a further meta-analysis, found no evidence that brief dynamic therapy is superior or inferior to other forms of treatment at post-treatment, but there was slight superiority at follow-up. Winston et al. (1994) found that brief dynamic therapy was effective for patients with certain types of personality disorder, with similar efficacy to brief adaptational therapy based on cognitive techniques (see Outcome and Research). A more recent meta-analysis has suggested that brief dynamic therapy for depression, when added to medication, significantly lowers recurrence rates (Maina, Rosso, & Bogetto, 2009).

In one of the most interesting field studies, the Stockholm Outcome of Psychotherapy and Psychoanalysis study (Blomberg, Lazar, & Sandell, 2001; Sandell, Blomberg, & Lazar, 2002), 405 patients in psychoanalysis or psychoanalytic psychotherapy were compared. The groups were matched on many clinical variables and followed for up to three years after treatment. Outcome was similar at the end of treatment irrespective of whether the patient received sessions four or five times (psychoanalysis) or once or twice a week (psychotherapy). But at the 3-year follow-up of 156 patients, psychotherapy patients did not change further; yet those who received psychoanalysis continued to improve almost to the point at which their scores were indistinguishable from a non-clinical sample. This suggests that so-called rehabilitative changes (i.e. permanent changes in personality function) were stimulated in patients who received high-duration/high-frequency treatment. Few other therapies can boast either such long-term follow-up or evidence for increasingly positive effects over time and there is increasing evidence that dynamic therapies are associated with longer term change, known as rehabilitative change.

GROUP PSYCHOTHERAPY

People have always lived in social and family groups. Individuals influence groups and, even more so, groups influence the individuals who constitute them. The understanding of this mutual influence calls for 'outsight' as well as 'insight', a recognition of our existence ininteracting systems.

Individual psychoanalysis concentrates on the individual and his 'inner world'. Group analysis and group psychotherapy (along with family, couple, and social therapy) view this inner world as composed of and profoundly affected by relationships with others, families, societies, and cultural patterns. The dynamic interplay is usually complex and in a state of flux (Burkitt, 1991; Elliott & Frosh, 1995). The validity of the apparent dichotomy between inner and outer worlds, an artefact of the Enlightenment, has long been questioned (Elias, 1991; Diamond, 1996).

In 1819 Goethe urged:

> In exploring nature always look at each thing and the whole;
> Nothing is inside and nothing outside, for what is within is without.
> Hurry then to grasp this holy open secret,
> Rejoice in the true illusion, in the earnest game,
> No living being is a single thing, it is always a many.
>
> (Smart, 1993, p. 64)

The development of object-relations theory in psychoanalysis has helped us to understand the distorting effects that internalized early family relationships can have on current adult relationships. We now recognize the often unconscious effects on families of trans-generational and transpersonal influences, including social pre-judice, upheaval, and trauma, in previous generations as well as the present (Wardi, 1992; Dalal, 1998). Also transcultural issues, the consequences of migration, and social change are arousing increasing interest (Kareem & Littlewood, 1992; Le Roy, 1994; Adams, 1996).

Groups are able to provide powerful support and encourage-ment, as well as a vivid setting in which problems based on such distorting effects can be explored and treated. That is, groups can be used at both the outer supportive levels and the deeper exploratory levels of psychotherapy.

The therapeutic use of groups in modern clinical practice can be traced to the early years of this century, when the American chest physician Pratt (1907), working in Boston, described forming 'classes' of 15–20 patients with tuberculosis who had been rejected for sanatorium treatment. Weekly social meetings provided instruc-tion and mutual support, which led to striking improvements in morale and physical health. Subsequently, in the 1920s and 1930s, a number of psychiatrists applied such didactic and supportive measures to groups of mental hospital patients (Rosenbaum, 1978; Ettin, 1988). The term 'group therapy', however, was first used around 1920 by Moreno, whose main contribution was the devel-opment of psychodrama (p. 212) in which groups were used as both cast and audience for the exploration of individual problems by re-enactment under the direction of the leader (Moreno, 1948).

By the 1920s Freud was applying psychoanalytic insights to anthropology and to social groups. In *Totem and Taboo* (Freud, 1913b) he had explored the universality of the incest barrier, and in *Group Psychology and the Analysis of the Ego* (Freud, 1921) he speculated on crowd behaviour, and the relationships of groups (such as Church and Army) to their leaders. The concept of the super-ego (Freud, 1923) recognized the internalization of social standards (p. 60) as well as the resolution of the Oedipal phase in childhood (p. 46). Freud did not undertake anthropological fieldwork or therapeutic work with groups himself; he left these to anthropologists such as Roheim (1950) and the psychoanalysts whose work is described in this section.

Adler parted from Freud in 1911, not only because he disagreed with Freud's view of instinct, but also because he attributed greater importance to social factors. He played a part in founding social and preventive psychiatry and had a direct influence on the development of day hospitals and therapeutic clubs (Bierer & Evans, 1969). However, Adler did not himself explore the therapeutic use of groups beyond such innovations as conversation classes in kindergartens and among mothers of children attending child guidance clinics.

Exchange of information, education, encouragement, and mutual support are fundamental functions of therapeutic groups in their widest sense. Informal, non-professional self-help groups such as Alcoholics Anonymous have been developed and are proving of value to many people who share problems such as alcohol and drug dependency, agoraphobia, bereavement, or the stress of caring for a disabled child (Shaffer & Galinsky, 1989, ch. 13). Groups for cancer sufferers and others with chronic and terminal conditions have been shown to be helpful; they may even prolong life (Spiegel, Bloom, Kraemer, *et al.*, 1989; Leszcz & Goodwin, 1998). It will be apparent that these groups are primarily supportive and ventilatory rather than exploratory in method, but can be profoundly helpful.

In considering group psychotherapy it is useful to distinguish between such *homogeneous* groups and more *heterogeneous* groups (Frances, Clarkin, & Marachi, 1980). The former are indicated when (a) patients share the same problem, (b) see their symptoms as the problem, and/or (c) do not have a sustaining social network. Heterogeneous groups, typical of analytic groups, are indicated when (a) patients have important problems in current interpersonal relationships, (b) are open to others and willing to share, or (c) are excessively intellectual or emotionally restricted, cannot tolerate dyadic intimacy, get locked into regressive transference, or elicit harmful countertransference responses in an individual therapist.

The more analytic and exploratory use of groups in both hospital and out-patient settings was pioneered by a few European psychoanalysts who emigrated to the USA, such as Paul Schilder who treated severely neurotic and mildly psychotic out-patients in small groups at Bellevue Hospital, New York. However, each of his patients was also seen individually throughout the course of treatment, which was largely focused on individual psychopathology. Nevertheless, Schilder considered that some of the patients 'could not have been treated individually with classical analysis.

They reacted only in the group. This is especially true of social neuroses' (Schilder, 1939, p. 97). In a group he found that patients 'realise with astonishment that the thoughts which have seemed to isolate them are common to all of them' (ibid, p. 91).

The power of groups was most influentially demonstrated in Britain during World War II, when several psychoanalysts and psychiatrists proved the value of group methods for officer selection in the War Office Selection Boards. A chance to run an Army psychiatric unit on group lines was then given to several of these pioneers, notably Bion and Rickman, followed by Foulkes, Main, and Bridger. The Northfield Military Hospital in Birmingham gave its name to what came to be called the two 'Northfield Experiments', which provided the impetus for the development since the war of social therapy (p. 191) – the therapeutic community movement (Main, 1946) – and of the use of small groups for the treatment of neurotic and personality disorders (Foulkes, 1948, 1964). Main (1977) and Bridger (1985) have given vivid accounts of these pioneering days.

Another important influence in group work was that of the psychologist Kurt Lewin, a refugee from Nazi Germany working at the Massachusetts Institute of Technology, who coined the expression 'group dynamics'. He inspired the evolution in the USA of Sensitivity Training Groups and Human Relations Laboratories, and developed his own field theory of social interaction, which involves the idea of psychological space and emphasizes the 'here and now' more than remote causes in the past. The effect of different styles of leadership on the functioning and social climate of groups was illuminated by his classic experiment comparing the effects of autocratic, democratic, and laissez-faire leadership (Lewin, Lippitt, & White, 1939). Children in autocratically led clubs are dependent on the leader and self-centred in relation to their peers. When led democratically, the same children not only showed more initiative, friendliness, and responsibility, but they worked better and continued to work in the leader's absence. In laissez-faire groups, as well as those led autocratically, aggression was more common. Lewin's main influence has been through T-groups (training groups) organized to help people working in industry and other organizations to become aware of the effects of interpersonal behaviour, including styles of leadership (Frank, 1964; Rice, 1965). However, many processes emphasized in that field occur in therapy groups of both analytic and Encounter (p.

205) type, such as 'self-disclosure', 'feedback', and 'unfreezing' – the process of disconfirming the belief system previously held by an individual (Kaplan, 1967).

Formal groups have been used for therapeutic and training purposes in many ways beyond analytic group therapy and T-groups: for example, Encounter, Gestalt, and psychodrama groups, which will be described in a later section, and groups used in transactional analysis and behaviour therapy. Shaffer and Galinsky (1989) have written a valuable exposition of these many different models of group therapy and training. We shall confine ourselves in what follows now to analytic group psychotherapy, which in the course of its development has been approached in three main ways: as analysis *in* the group, analysis *of* the group, and analysis *through* the group.

Analysis in the group makes the least use of group dynamics. The therapist conducts psychotherapy of individuals in a group setting, as Schilder did – a method developed particularly in the USA, most notably by Wolf and Schwartz (1962). Their patients had often had a good deal of individual therapy or preparation, and so already had important individual relationships with the therapist. Sessions were held four times a week, two of them ('alternate' sessions) without the therapist. In this approach, there is an emphasis on individual transference relationships, and the therapist is active in directing therapeutic work on transference and resistance. The emergence of more spontaneous group processes is probably inhibited by focusing so much attention on the individual members and on the therapist.

Analysis of the group is associated with the particular interest in group dynamics developed in Britain by Bion and Ezriel at the Tavistock Clinic in London; group processes are seen to reflect the common motives, anxieties, and defences of the individuals in the group. Bion (1961) has contributed the idea of *basic assumptions*, or primitive states of mind which are generated automatically when people combine in a group. The fantasies and emotional drives associated with these basic assumptions unconsciously dominate the group's behaviour in a way that is apt to interfere with its explicit work task and so prevent creative change and development. In the case of a therapy group, the 'basic assumption groups' interfere with exploration by the 'work group' of the feelings and problems of individuals in it. Bion names the basic assumptions as *dependence* (expecting solutions to be bestowed by the therapist leader), *fight–flight* (fleeing from or engaging in battle with adversaries, particularly outside the group), and *pairing* (encouraging or hoping for a coupling of individuals which could lead to the birth of a person or idea that would provide salvation). These three attitudes, Bion suggests, are institutionalized respectively in the Church, Army, and Aristocracy. The relationship between basic assumption groups and work groups could be seen as analogous to that between primary and secondary process thinking (p. 64). It is also possible to imagine the three basic assumptions of dependence, fight–flight, and pairing as linked by fantasy systems associated with the oral–dependent, separation–individuation, and Oedipal stages of individual development.

Bion worked with therapeutic groups for only a few years; his ideas have perhaps had more influence on our understanding of the dynamics of institutions, including therapeutic communities (p. 203), committees with their hidden agendas, and training groups such as the T-groups organized by the Tavistock Institute of Human Relations in its Leicester Conferences (Rice, 1965). Bion's ideas have helped us to understand the primitive factors disrupting group work rather than the positive processes promoting it. Whereas 'basic assumption' phenomena do occur, they may do so particularly in situations where 'democratic' dialogue is impossible, inappropriate, or not sought – as in some committees, institutions, and societies, and in 'autocratically' conducted therapy groups (Brown, 1985).

Ezriel (1950, 1952) coined the expression *common group tension* to describe the group conflict resulting from a shared, wished-for, but *avoided relationship* with the therapist, which arouses fear of the consequences if it were to be acknowledged (the *calamitous relationship*) and is resolved by the adoption of a compromise relationship with him (the *required relationship*). For example, hostility to the therapist for frustrating each patient's wish to be the only patient/child (avoided relationship) may lead to fear of retaliation by abandonment (calamitous relationship), and be resolved by concealing resentment under an attitude of helpful compliance (required relationship). Ezriel regarded the group therapist's task as first to discern the common group tension, and then to point out to each member of the group his own personal contribution and former solution to the conflict, based on his individual psychopathology. In this sense Ezriel combined analysis of the group and analysis in the group.

These ideas can be useful in most groups, but their relevance is greatest in groups conducted along the lines of Bion and Ezriel, in which the therapist emphasizes his importance by being frustratingly impassive, or by being active in encouraging transference to himself.

Analysis through the group is particularly associated with the other main approach in British group psychotherapy, developed by S. H. Foulkes (1898–1976). Like Bion and Ezriel, Foulkes was a psychoanalyst. Born Siegmund Heinrich Fuchs in Germany, he qualified in medicine, and before training as a psychiatrist and psychoanalyst in Vienna, he studied with the neurologist Kurt Goldstein in Frankfurt. Working with injuries to the central nervous system, Goldstein used the ideas of Gestalt psychologists – for example, the relation of parts to wholes and of figure and ground. From this time can be traced Foulkes's metaphor of the individual as a nodal point in a *network* of neurones.

Returning to Frankfurt as Director of the Psychoanalytic Clinic, he came into close contact with leading members of the Institute for Social Research, and in particular the sociologist Norbert Elias. Elias had shown how culture changes over time in ways that influence what is called 'human nature' (Mennell, 1989). Foulkes became deeply impressed by how context affects what happens within it. Thus, although a psychoanalyst, Foulkes was increasingly aware not only of intrapersonal processes but also interpersonal and *transpersonal* processes (Brown, 1998b).

Nazism in Germany led him to emigrate to England, where he became a prominent training psychoanalyst. Having made the experiment of seeing his individual analytic patients together in his waiting room, Foulkes (1948, 1964) discovered at Northfield Military Hospital, during World War II, that a freer, more democratic system could promote confidence and responsibility in previously demoralized and passively resentful patients. He regarded the group as the therapeutic medium, and the therapist's task as that of nurturing its therapeutic potential by allowing the individuals in it to function increasingly as active and responsible agents themselves. In group analytic psychotherapy 'the individual is being treated *in the context* of the group with the active participation of the group'. It is 'psychotherapy *by* the group, *of* the group, including its conductor' (Foulkes, 1975, p. 3).

Foulkes came to see the individual as a nodal point in a network of relationships, and illness as a disturbance in the network that comes to light through the vulnerable individual. This awareness of *transpersonal* phenomena anticipated the more recent developments in our understanding of family processes and therapy. Furthermore, Foulkes discerned the many levels at which groups function, often simultaneously:

1   The level of current adult relationships.
2   The level of individual transference relationships.
3   The level of projected and shared feelings and fantasies, often from early pre-verbal stages of development.
4   The level of archetypal universal images, reminiscent of Jung's archetypes of the unconscious.

It will be seen that these levels range from more conscious objective 'everyday' relationships to increasingly subjective and unconscious fantasy relationships – from more to less clearly differentiated and individual relationships (Foulkes & Anthony, 1957; Foulkes, 1964). Figure 9 illustrates the way these levels can be linked with the idea of parent, adult, and child parts of the personality (p. 161). Level 1 would be A↔A, level 2 C→P, level 3 C↔C, and level 4 would join an infinite number of individuals.

The group analytic approach of Foulkes is probably the most influential one in Britain today (Pines, 1983; Brown & Zinkin, 1994) and forms the basis of most of what follows in describing small-group psychotherapy. In 1967 Foulkes started the journal *Group Analysis*, and in 1971 played a key part in founding the Institute of Group Analysis, the major training organization in analytic group psychotherapy with courses now established throughout Britain and Europe. Trainees are expected to have long-term intensive analytic group psychotherapy.

A complementary, eclectic, but research-orientated view from North America is provided by Bernard and MacKenzie (1994) and by the *International Journal of Group Psychotherapy*. Where research has been conducted, group therapy has been shown to be as successful as individual therapy, and it is therefore both effective and economic.

Today, with increasing job insecurity and pressure, greater social mobility and migration, broken families, etc., changes in society often disrupt supportive networks or impede their development. Group therapy can help to restore or provide for the first time a sense of connectedness and confidently being oneself with others.

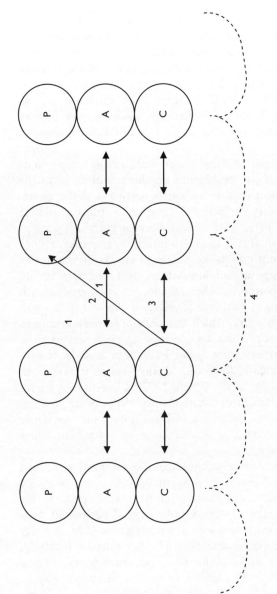

Foulkes's levels

1 Current adult relationships
   (working alliance)
2 Individual transference
3 Shared feelings and fantasies
4 Archetypal images

Figure 9

The setting

Six to eight patients, usually strangers to each other at the start, meet regularly for one and a half hours once or twice a week, for one to several years (most commonly two to three). The therapist (or pair of co-therapists) sits with them in a circle, in comfortable and equal chairs, perhaps with a small table in the centre as a focal point. Relative quietness and freedom from intrusion are as important as in individual psychotherapy, since the free flow of group discussion is the equivalent in a group of free association in individual therapy.

Patients are expected to view group membership as a major commitment, to treat as confidential anything spoken of in the group, and not to meet outside without reporting it to the group. They are asked to notify the group of unexpected absences, to take holidays during the periods of several weeks a year set aside for this, and preferably to give at least a month's notice if they wish to leave. Most out-patient groups are *slow-open* groups, in that membership slowly changes as individuals leave at a time appropriate for them, and are replaced by others. Some are *closed* groups, with all patients starting and finishing together at the end of a given time, say one or two years, which has been previously arranged. Closed groups are more common for training purposes, to fit in with academic terms or courses, but have been used in centres where pressure of demand for group therapy makes it expedient, with good results (Dick, 1975; Sigrell, 1992). Closed groups have the advantage that all members share the experience of termination together; on the other hand, in a slow-open group, the experience of moving from a position of newcomer to one of senior, 'older sibling', is also valuable.

Most groups are deliberately composed of equal numbers of men and women, with sufficient similarity of background or ways of expressing themselves for communication to be facilitated and for no one to feel too much an outsider. A range of personality type and experience is aimed for, as well as variety of problem, in order to provide an atmosphere where people can interact fruitfully, learn from each other, and together represent the human condition in miniature. The idea of a group can often be threatening to patients who have social problems, or fear that their problems could not possibly be understood or tolerated by other people unless it were their job to do so. It is therefore important to prepare patients for a group by explaining what to expect, and to discuss their anxieties and possible inclination to leave the group soon after joining (Whitaker, 1985, p. 183). Sometimes an initial period of individual therapy will help a patient to make better use of a group (Malan, 1976).

In certain circumstances specialized groups are helpful. Groups for adolescents and young adults and for older people can promote a greater degree of support and identification with each other's problems. Single-sex groups can free members from anxiety connected with the opposite sex (e.g. victims of abuse or rape) sometimes as an initial stage, say of a year, before moving into a mixed group. And, as mentioned earlier, problem-based groups can provide more focused support and advice than is appropriate in more open analytic groups.

The social nature of the setting provides opportunities to examine patients' difficulties in a situation reflecting the family and social networks in which their problems developed. In the National Health Service in Britain, group psychotherapy is the most generally available form of psychotherapy. This is not just an expedient; group psychotherapy is the treatment of choice for many people whose prime difficulty is relating to others.

Patient's role

The need for each patient to take responsibility for his problems and for seeking their solution through fuller understanding of himself and his relationships exists in all exploratory insight-orientated analytic therapy, including that conducted in groups. Agreement to participate in group therapy already involves a tacit recognition that solutions cannot be expected from passive dependence on the therapist functioning as a parent/magician, but patients with uncertain motivation can find it strengthened by the example, support, and challenge of others. The therapeutic alliance needs to be forged not only with the therapist but also with fellow patients, some of whom may be initially feared or even disliked, although the sharing of the endeavour on a more obviously equal footing can speed up the process, fostered by the discovery of how much each patient has in common with the others.

The greater his participation in the group, the more a patient will get from it. This involves being increasingly open about himself and his problems, but also increasingly responsive to and involved with others. Mere talking about himself, regardless of the needs or responses of others – 'hogging the limelight' – is usually counter-productive, leading to isolation and confirmation of stereotyped views of himself and others.

Some patients, silent for a while or for long periods, can still gain a lot from being in a group if they can allow themselves to think and feel in response to what is happening. In contrast with individual therapy, socially withdrawn and emotionally cut-off (schizoid) people can test themselves out gradually through involvement which is at first vicarious. What ultimately helps is joining in creating, responding to, and reflecting upon the experiences unfolding in the group, eventually putting into words what was previously unknown or inexpressible to themselves and others. Increasingly, each patient is enabled to take a therapeutic role in the group.

Therapist's role

The therapist is often called the *group conductor*. Like the conductor of an orchestra, he starts and finishes the proceedings, and helps to create an atmosphere in which honest communication can occur, with everyone giving of their best. By remaining relatively unobtrusive, he encourages the group to think, feel, and interact among themselves. This also allows him the opportunity to reflect on what is happening, using his own feelings and associations, including memories of previous sessions. He can attend not only to what individuals are saying, but how topics and associations link, and what the process reveals of common group preoccupations and conflicts. He may recognize that one individual is talking for others as well as for himself. For example, a more outspoken member might be able to criticize the conductor while others, more hostile but fearful, silently collude. Or he may discern that talk about events in the outside world really concerns something being avoided in the group; for example, general discussion may develop about refugees, while an impending holiday break is not mentioned.

In the early stages, when individuals have not yet got to know and trust each other, the group usually adopts a regressive or dependent relationship with the conductor, looking to him for leadership and gratification of infantile wishes (Scheidlinger, 1968). The group-analytic therapist, unlike those who follow the Tavistock model of Bion and Ezriel, will accept this as at first inevitable, because patients have to learn how to trust the new situation and to discover their own roles in it. The therapist may therefore facilitate, explain, and interpret more actively in the early stage, but relinquish this role of leadership when the group culture has become established.

However, the conductor's position as part of the group, yet different from the others, leaves him freer than the patients to maintain an analytic position of 'free-floating' attention. He can observe and may comment on how each person brings his problems into the group, creating a fresh blend in the 'here and now' of contributions from their current life outside and from their past, including early family relationships. He is also able to tune into the atmosphere of the group and might discern, in the separate contributions of individuals, a common preoccupation or conflict. Some conductors find the concept of *group focal conflict* (Whitaker & Lieberman, 1964) useful in orientating themselves. The conflict involves a *disturbing motive* in the group (such as the wish of each patient to have the therapist to himself), giving rise to a *reactive motive* (fear of disapproval by the therapist and fellow group members) and resulting in a *group solution*. Whitaker and Lieberman's group solution is not conceived as a fixed defence; it can change in the course of a session. A solution may be either *restrictive*, directed only at alleviating the fear, or *enabling*, in which case some expression of the disturbing motive will be allowed so that understanding and analysis is promoted. One common restrictive solution to the group conflict just described is that of 'spotlighting', where one patient at a time is given the whole group's attention. A more enabling solution is achieved when the hidden wish of all to be the only patient is acknowledged, so allowing a freer sharing of experiences. The concepts of group motives and solutions are really variants of those of wish, fear, and defence in classical psychoanalysis, and of Ezriel's avoided, calamitous, and required relationships mentioned earlier (p. 158), but these are broader and less therapist-orientated, as the examples demonstrate.

The conductor's task is to help in creating a therapeutic atmosphere and in the discovery by the group of such enabling solutions to the inevitable tensions it experiences. His interventions, including interpretations, may be especially needed when blockage occurs in the process of communication and exploration. It might be that issues are being avoided, or an individual is allowing himself to be ignored. Patients may still lack the confidence and skill to challenge someone (often the conductor), or to say something that they imagine would provoke a hostile or shaming response. At such times the conductor could intervene with a clarifying question, a confronting observation, or an interpretation. He might offer an encouraging comment or even divert attention if someone is too uncomfortably 'on the hook'. He does not confine himself to group interpretations, but talks to the group through the individual, and to the individual through the group. The conductor's interventions, like his attitude, have a modelling function from which patients increasingly find their own way of functioning as therapists, including interpreting wishes, feelings, and links with early family relationships.

As well as conveying a psychoanalytic attitude, the group con-ductor functions as a facilitator and model, in a rather more active role than the conventional picture of the psychoanalyst as a mirror, although even the latter is now an outdated view. His position, sitting in the group circle, would make it difficult and unnatural for him to hide himself and his feelings, even if he wanted to. However, therapists vary in their attitude to this issue of therapist trans-parency (Yalom, 1985), some choosing to reveal more, some less. Most group therapists judiciously vary the approach, even within the same session. Both ends of the continuum have their advan-tages. A constantly impassive stance encourages the emergence of transference responses to the conductor, but provides a poor model of active concern and emotional or imaginative freedom. On the other hand, although patients do not want to be burdened with the conductor's personal life and problems, they usually appreciate and benefit from his example of openness and confidence in expressing himself. When the conductor takes the option to express and report his countertransference feelings and fantasies in response to what is happening in the group, patients may be helped to use their own feelings and fantasies more freely.

The balance of the therapist's roles – activity versus passivity, transparency as opposed to opaqueness, and gratification con-trasted with frustration of patient demand – determines the atmo-sphere of the group. Yalom (1995) has outlined general principles of technique for group therapists which are more likely to create a group as an agent of therapeutic change. These are listed in Table 9.

Initially there has to be the creation of an atmosphere of hope and optimism about the group – as the place in which problems can be discussed and resolved. Patients are initially doubtful about this, often being more concerned with how they are seen in the group and

Table 9 Principles of group technique

Establish atmosphere of hope and optimism
Generate cohesiveness
Maintain and respect boundaries
Establish group norms – respect, honesty, industry, responsibility
Balance level of activity
Use the group as the basic resource
Accept subgrouping on issues and not on individuals
Focus on process rather than content
Generally keep comments closer to psychological surface
Attend to termination

what other people are like. The group therapist gradually builds up cohesiveness, maintaining respect for personal boundaries and, to some extent, social norms – it is not alright, for example, to insult someone in the group. The group therapist then focuses more on process than on the content of the group discussion, directing comments to enhancing group interaction rather than worrying about deeper meanings of the group process. The focus on process rather than content continues to divide group therapists and to some extent represents a North Atlantic rift, with American group therapists being more influenced by Yalom's proposals and European group therapists continuing to be influenced by Bion and his concern for the group as a whole. But most therapists nowadays use both aspects in their work in groups and it is likely that different interventions are useful for different groups of patients. For example, groups have been developed for patients with personality disorder using modified techniques while remaining true to the importance of the group as an agent of change. Mentalization-based treatment (MBT, see p. 236) has been operationalized in a group form for patients with borderline personality disorder. MBT is an example of a group psychotherapy combined with individual therapy running concurrently. When group and individual psychotherapy are run concurrently the same therapist may conduct both the group and the individual sessions. This is known as *combined* treatment. When different therapists offer the treatments it is known as *conjoint* treatment so potentially all patients in a group might have different individual therapists. Concurrent treatments tend to be used only for those patients who have severe difficulties in both social and interpersonal function.

To our knowledge there is only one study that has compared a conjoined versus a single modality approach for the same kind of therapy. The Italian group of Ivaldi and co-workers (Ivaldi,

Fassone, Rocchi, *et al.*, 2007) compared combined (same therapist) individual and group cognitive-evolutionary therapy for out-patients with personality disorders. The results seemed to favour the combined treatment on a range of outcome measures including overall social function. The study is in no way conclusive, but it is the first empirical indication of a superiority for combined psycho-therapy for patients with personality disorders.

Strictly speaking, then, we *suppose* that the two formats have a synergistic effect upon each other when implemented properly. However, it is important to underline that the two formats when operating together are not equal to the two formats when oper-ating alone. Individual psychotherapy when being conducted in concert with group psychotherapy has certain qualities which are different from individual psychotherapy as a single modality. The same is true for group psychotherapy. The therapist will of course explore the patient's experiences in the other modality but, more importantly, he/she will inhabit representations of the patient in the other modality in his/her mind as an ongoing and changing pro-cess. These representations are different from representations of the patient in relation to other attachment figures, since they are informed not only by stories told by the patient *but also by information and reflections provided by the other therapist(s)*. This point is highlighted in a study by Kegerreis (2007), who describes a conjoint individual–group psychotherapy programme with border-line patients from a British National Health Service out-patient psychotherapy department. Kegerreis emphasizes the *therapist couple* and how the mutual information-sharing is crucial for identifying and containing parts of the self that are being kept apart by being located in one of the modalities. The splitting makes it difficult to work towards an integration in the here-and-now in either of the modalities alone. However, the close cooperation between the therapist couple may make them more aware of these dynamics and facilitate containment, reflection, and change in the processes. It is now to the therapeutic process that we turn.

Therapeutic processes

Analytic psychotherapy in groups, like that conducted on an individual basis, aims to help the individual to resolve conflicts and gain greater understanding of himself and others, in the interest of fuller growth and development; the aim is insight, plus adjustment to relationships with others. The group setting in which these processes occur provides a context which has important consequences.

Because several people are taking part, interaction can be more varied and complex, at both conscious and unconscious levels, than in individual therapy. More experiences are drawn on from everyone's life situation, past and present, and a wider range of responses and attitudes is available. Because we are dealing with a multipersonal field, *multiple transferences* can develop: that is, each person may transfer feelings not only to the therapist, but also to fellow patients and to the group as a whole, which can represent a mother, womb, or breast. Other patients may be experienced as siblings in rivalrous competition for the therapist/parent's attention, as in the example on p. 76. At times, patients may experience others as though they represented unwelcome aspects of themselves, through projection and projective identification (p. 32). This is especially true of new members, who are experienced as strangers. The separateness of the conductor is particularly reinforced when new members join, echoing the power that parents have to produce another child, or the strength of their relationship despite the child's wish for merger with one or other of them (Bacha, 1997).

Patients learn a lot about themselves by feedback from fellow group members. They can discover how their behaviour and attitudes are often self-defeating, and how they lend themselves to be misunderstood and to misunderstand others, for example, coercing them to fit in with a transference distortion or expressing hostility to someone because they represent a feared aspect of themselves.

> *In one group, the mounting hostility between two members exploded in a session which allowed a homosexual man to see that he could not stand a recently married fellow member because he reminded him, in his gruff, withdrawn behaviour, of his rejecting and critical father. At the same time the other man recognized that he himself was identifying with his own withdrawn father, who could not respond to the patient's longing for him, and that he feared his own affectionate feelings as feminine and therefore homosexual.*

This is an example of what Foulkes called a *mirror reaction*. Through it the two patients saw more of themselves and their reactions, and thereby made contact with an important part of themselves. Following this they were able to communicate with and value each other better; and other patients had the opportunity to learn something too by sharing in the experience and applying it to their own developing understanding of themselves and others.

Neurotic conflicts can be seen as originating in relationships between the individual and his original family group. In the example given above, the two men were unable in childhood fully to express hostility or affection to their parents. Not only did they fear their fathers' responses, but also, the first man's mother had been temperamentally cold and critical, and the second man's had been unapproachable because of her chronic tuberculosis, which meant he was not allowed to give or receive demonstrations of love. The group provided a situation in which their previously private and incommunicable wishes and feelings could be expressed. As symptoms and inhibitions were translated into shared communication, they became understandable, and the outdated fears could be tested against the new reality of the therapy group and gradually relinquished.

Communication within and between people reverberates. Individual therapy allows for more detailed working within the single transference relationship with the therapist and more detailed reconstruction of each individual's developmental history, especially in its earliest infantile phase. But the setting of group therapy permits an analysis of the 'here and now' of the developing network of relationships, which for some can be both more varied and more vivid. Not only is there more input and response at both transference and non-transference levels, which enables very intense emotional experiences to occur, but contrasts between the experience and behaviour of different individuals, and between those of an individual now compared with an earlier occasion, can stand out very clearly. Therapeutic change is open to observation and comment.

In a group, people can *resonate* to what occurs at different levels of consciousness and regression, according to their needs and preoccupations. From the common pool of themes and feelings they pick out what is most meaningful to them at the time. They respond to different levels of meaning from conscious to deeply unconscious, from mature to primitively infantile, according to what is stirred up in them.

In a group with two new members, an old member had just married and another's wife had just had a child. These events prompted envy and hostility in some of the others, as well as more readily expressed pleasure. Then, the therapist had to announce an unpopular change of arrangements, and for several sessions bad mothering became a shared theme which evoked memories and group dreams that were both intensely moving and illuminating. The shared painful longing and ambivalence, which led the more emotionally detached members to withdraw and the more depressive ones to burden themselves with guilt and excessive reparative behaviour, became clearer to all. The intensity evoked the impact of early traumatic experiences, which were now more tolerable because they were shared.

One depressed professional woman, excessively devoted to her work in helping others, had been emotionally deprived as a child because her very beautiful mother was incapacitated by chronic asthma. She dreamt during this period in the group that she met another group member, a more obviously attractive woman (representing mother), wearing a dress which was the same as her own but brighter in colour. They went to a cafeteria where the other woman poured out two cups of coffee, which spurted over the dreamer's dress. Still wet, she went into the next room which was full of desks piled with papers. She set to work on them until a man (representing the therapist) came in and told her she did not need to work so hard. In talking about the dream, the group recognized its clear symbolism of envy of her attractive mother, her mixed feelings about being fed by her, and her need to work hard to compensate for them. The patient realized that the man in the dream stood for the therapist, from whom she had learned that she did not need to go on making reparation for feelings she had had for her mother, now evoked in the group in relation to the other woman.

This is an example of the *group dreams* which are especially useful in group therapy, since they can be understood and worked on by everyone sharing the same 'here and now' experience. The detailed analysis of dreams otherwise plays a less important part in group therapy than in individual therapy.

Group therapy is rooted in the experiences fed into and emerging from the group. These build up into a unique developing culture with its own history and memory, as members relate ever more deeply and intimately. Foulkes called this the *group matrix*. In it each individual can immerse himself in experiences which are personal, interpersonal, and transpersonal, that is, they spring from each individual's unique past and present outside the group, from

Table 10 Therapeutic factors of groups

Universality
Altruism
Instillation of hope
Imitative behaviour
Cohesiveness
Feeling of belonging to the group
Interpersonal learning and critical feedback
Recapitulation of family dynamics
Existential factors
Insight
Catharsis and self-disclosure

fresh engagements between members 'here and now' in the group, and from deep shared motives and responses which transcend their separate individualities. Garland (1982) has described the value of patients entering a new system – the group – quite different from that in which their problems arose. The new task, relating more fully and honestly with strangers, takes priority over the restricted 'world view' of the presenting problem, which when it emerges can be seen more clearly as foreground against a healthier background. As patients immerse themselves in the group matrix, each individual can question their own preconceptions, boundaries, and identity; they can regain aspects of themselves that they have disowned and projected, and re-emerge with fresh insights and ways of relating.

Yalom (1985) has described several therapeutic factors specific to groups and these are summarized in Table 10. *Universality* refers to the discovery of shared basic preoccupations, fears, and conflicts, so that what had previously isolated individuals is now found to unite them. *Altruism*, caring for and helping others in need, follows as individuals emerge from isolation and painful preoccupation with themselves alone; the group situation provides opportunities for people to develop their strengths at the same time as revealing their weaknesses, to function increasingly as therapists as well as patients. *Corrective recapitulation of the family group* implies that what went wrong in the early family group can be repeated and recognized in the group, where now, in a more open and experimental atmosphere, less maladaptive ways of coping can be worked out. Sometimes a group provides something lacking in the original family, such as acceptance and encouragement, or the right to differ and express hostility. *Imitative behaviour* refers to the opportunity other group members, including the conductor, provide of different models of behaving and relating that can be followed in choosing alternatives to old restrictive and neurotic ways. *Interpersonal learning* indicates the experience the social setting provides for increasing interpersonal skills by discovering new ways of being oneself with others, in an environment which is much nearer to everyday life than is individual psychotherapy. This is what Foulkes meant when he described group psychotherapy as involving 'ego training in action'. Problems can be observed and worked with *in vivo*. *Cohesiveness* is the sense of solidarity that binds a group together, and makes it attractive to its members. The sense of belonging enables members to work through difficulties together, and is thus part of the therapeutic or working alliance. *Existential factors* include recognition of responsibility in the face of our basic aloneness and mortality.

Skynner (1986) has emphasized the way in which group membership provides opportunities to make up for developmental deficits and overcome blocks based on neurotic conflict, as the group itself moves towards greater understanding and maturation. He believes the conductor's role needs to be appropriate to the stage the group is recapitulating: supportive and nurturant in the initial dependent stage; firmer, more frustrating, and confronting when group cohesion and confidence is better established; and more open, personal, and playful when it has moved towards fuller intimacy and individuation. Like Foulkes, he holds that the therapist who grows and learns through the group provides the most effective model.

Various stages of group development have been described in experimental group dynamic situations, well reviewed by Whiteley and Gordon (1979): Schutz (1958) related these to basic human needs for inclusion, control, and affection; Tuckman (1965) proposed four stages of forming, storming, norming, and performing that represent establishing a sense of belonging, emergence of conflict and resistance, arrival at intimacy, and new standards and roles, eventually sufficient for pursuit of group tasks. In an open-ended group, any such stages occur in a circular or spiral fashion, triggered by changing membership, crises, and destructive periods, but always hopefully in the direction of greater maturity.

Destructive forces in groups are based on primitive processes such as splitting, projection, and envy (Zinkin, 1983; Kreeger, 1992). Nitsun (1996) described destructive group forces as the anti-group which he considered as being rooted in failures of the earliest environment to contain and modify severe anxiety, pain, and rage.

This can also be linked to a hatred of sharing, within the Oedipal triangle or within a sibship. It has been observed that disturbed borderline parents split the children and promote sibling rivalry (Aggar, 1988). But to relate all group processes and problems to individual development, or even family pathology, is to ignore the huge effect of social problems, divisions, and struggles for power and resources, as occurs between social classes and economic groups (Dalal, 1998).

Group therapy constitutes a major part of long-term psychotherapy in the National Health Service in Britain today. Following assessment, when it becomes clear that a patient needs longer term help to understand and modify his neurotic and interpersonal difficulties, a period of group therapy may be indicated if he has sufficient motivation for insight, sufficient ego strength (see sections on Selection and Outcome and Research), and is prepared to commit himself to regular attendance for, say, at least a year. Where there is a range of psychiatric and psychotherapeutic facilities (still too rare in the NHS), group therapy can be part of an overall plan. It might be the first treatment offered; it may follow management of a crisis by supportive psychotherapy, medication, or hospital admission; or it might follow a shorter period of individual analytic therapy or cognitive-behavioural therapy (p. 228). Some patients who have responded to psychoanalytic therapy with only partial success can often begin to move, or apply what they have already learned, in the new atmosphere of a group.

It has been stated, aphoristically, that:

> after a successful psycho-analytic treatment a patient is definitely less neurotic (or psychotic) but perhaps not necessarily really mature; on the other hand, after a successful treatment by group methods the patient is not necessarily less neurotic but inevitably more mature.
>
> (Balint & Balint, 1961, p. 5)

This difference probably results from the greater availability of non-transference curative factors in group therapy, the greater similarity of the setting to the natural groups in which people live, in the family and in society, and the activation of mutual responsibility and concern (Brown, 1987). But aphorisms are of limited value nowadays in persuading patients and others that groups are an effective treatment, so an increasing amount of research is being undertaken.

Research and group psychotherapy

It has been difficult to examine group therapy from a research perspective primarily because of the variability and complexity of the intervention. Many group therapists practise in a pluralistic fashion using theories and techniques drawn from a range of perspectives about group function. Group psychotherapy is offered to a wide range of patients and in many different contexts, adding to the difficulties. Tschuschke (1999) extracted as many papers as possible studying the outcome of group therapy. The majority of empirical outcome studies were of cognitive-behavioural group psychotherapy in specific conditions. Nevertheless he analysed 62 studies examining psychodynamic and analytic group psychotherapy, finding that results were promising but that there was limited evidence. Most of the psychodynamic group therapies aimed to stimulate personality change in participants and yet there was no measure of this in most studies. Some naturalistic studies suggest that such changes do occur. Tschuschke and Anbet (2000), using a pre-post-test design, assessed changes of over 600 patients in either long-term out-patient group-analytic therapy or psychodrama. All patients did well and group-analytic psychotherapy showed a moderate to large effect size on the global assessment of functioning. This instrument assesses the overall function of an individual in society. Improvement over time suggests that the individual is increasingly likely to be able to cope with everyday stressors and so return to work, for example, or form constructive social and intimate relationships, all of which suggest permanent changes in personality function.

Group analysis is being increasingly used in the treatment of more specific populations of patients (see section on Personality Disorder). Valbak (2003) treated patients with bulimia nervosa and over the long term described positive results, but modification of the technique was needed. Consistent monitoring of eating habits and of the connection between self-esteem and the symptoms was necessary, along with considerable additional activity outside therapy sessions, to maintain the patient in treatment. Sandahl and colleagues (1998), in a randomized controlled design, compared patients with alcohol dependence treated either with psychodynamically orientated time-limited group treatment or with cognitive-behavioural group treatment. At 15 months' follow-up the patients in both groups had improved. Those in the psychodynamic group therapy had been able to maintain a more positive drinking pattern during the whole of the follow-up period.

Studies of what happens in groups have found that the development of a group milieu and the patient's ability to participate within the group may be crucial factors for good outcomes. In a study in Stuttgart, Tschuschke and Dies (1994) found that cohesion within the group, a feeling of belonging to the group, early self-disclosure, and criticial feedback from group members were predictors of a successful outcome. Seidler (2000) noted a correlation between reduction in psychosomatic symptoms and an increase in self-relatedness in patients receiving analytically orientated group psychotherapy in an in-patient setting.

FAMILY AND COUPLE THERAPY

The drama of family relationships has been the stuff of legend and literature since ancient times, but not until recently have psychiatrists recognized current family relationships as common sources of serious emotional disturbance, in addition to constitutional factors or intrapsychic conflicts and traumas rooted in early life. We can now think about disturbed *systems of relationship*, and attempt to influence them, rather than focusing only on an individual.

The treatment of family and couple systems has only emerged in the last half-century. Mittelman (1948), working in the USA, reported on his simultaneous but separate psychoanalytic treatment of husband and wife, which allowed him to understand their conscious and unconscious interaction and to treat successfully eleven out of twelve couples. At about the same time, the effect that some families have of predisposing children to schizophrenia was being studied. Fromm-Reichmann (1948) contributed the now discredited idea of the 'schizophrenogenic mother', and Lidz and Lidz (1949) that of parental 'marital schism and skew', with consequent blurring of generation lines and promotion of irrational ideas. This type of study was continued by workers in the USA and Britain, some of whom believed that the immediate family of schizophrenics may be at least as ill as the patient. They were thought to communicate in deviant ways, such as 'double binding' the patient (Bateson, Jackson, Haley, *et al.*, 1956) by presenting to him contradictory overt and covert injunctions to which there is no correct response and from which there is no escape: for example, the mother who repeatedly asks her son to kiss her, but walks away when he moves towards her, and then accuses him of not being a good son. Such families may have disturbed styles of thinking, including 'pseudo-mutuality' and illogicality, which conceal underlying hostility (Wynne, Ryckoff, Day, et al., 1958). Some believe that the family negate and virtually deny the patient's experience by 'mystification', so that a schizophrenic reaction is a natural self-protective response (Laing & Esterson, 1964). In consequence, schizophrenia is seen by some as a family problem, and family therapy therefore as appropriate in certain cases. Doubts were expressed about the validity of the observations on which this theory is based (Hirsch & Leff, 1975) and the theory is now known to have no basis in reality. What has become clear over time is that family conflicts do not have a primary role in the aetiology of schizophrenia. But equally it is well-established (Brown, Birley, & Wing, 1972; Leff & Vaughn, 1985) that patients who have had a schizophrenic breakdown are more liable to relapse in an emotionally charged family atmosphere (Pekkala & Merinder, 2002; Pilling, Bebbington, Kuipers, et al., 2002; Chien, Chan, & Thompson, 2006). In any event, these studies have aroused interest in the role of the family in psychiatric disorders in general. Family relationships are now widely accepted as relevant to the understanding of many emotional and developmental problems.

Although it had long been customary in child guidance clinics for a mother to be interviewed as well as her child, she was usually seen by a social worker while the child was interviewed and treated separately by a psychiatrist. However, in the 1950s, Ackerman (1966) began using family interviews in work with children and adolescents in the USA, and this has now become standard practice in many centres in Britain, where some child psychiatry clinics have been re-named departments of child and family psychiatry. Family therapy can be seen as a natural development of child psychiatry. Some departments of child psychiatry now offer a diagnostic interview to the whole family of any child newly referred (Bentovim & Kinston, 1978), rather than the traditional method of mother and child being first seen separately and involving families in assessment, and treatment is supported by research evidence (Heru, 2006).

The usefulness of systems theory in analysing the problems of individuals and the natural groups and communities in which they live has already been discussed (p. 66). Skynner (1976, 1986), a pioneer of family and marital therapy in Britain, developed his work through his interest in group psychotherapy and his practice as a psychiatrist in a child guidance clinic. He considered that what characterizes these newer forms of psychotherapy is their focus on the pathology and treatment of the natural systems formed by individuals in intimate relationships, rather than on individual psychopathology. The transgenerational history of the family may be an important part of the history of the individual, yet cut-off and repressed, as with secrets such as child abuse or the effects of forced migration and genocide. For this reason family therapists, and some individual psychotherapists and counsellors, will engage patients in drawing up genograms (Lieberman, 1979; McGoldrick, Gerson, & Petry, 2008).

Therapy ideally helps the natural system of the family to move towards the patterns of interaction that characterize healthy families. Skynner (1986) has summarized studies of these in the USA, particularly those of the Timberlawn Psychiatric Research Foundation (Lewis, 1979) which compared families at the extremes of health and dysfunction. At a level of statistical significance 'healthy' families (a) were affiliative rather than oppositional; (b) showed respect for separateness and individuality; (c) made open, clear communications; (d) had a firm, equal parental coalition; (e) used flexible, negotiable control; and (f) interacted spontaneously, with wit and humour.

The many techniques used in family therapy have been well described by Glick and Kessler (1974), Skynner (1976), Walrond-Skinner (1976), Hoffman (1981), Burnham (1986), Bentovim *et al.* (1987), Reimers and Treacher (1995), and Walsh (2003). As Bruggen and Davies (1977) pointed out in a review of the field, methods range in a spectrum from the more analytic to the more active techniques. At the analytic end of the spectrum, methods aim at insight through interpretation; at the other end, change in the disturbed system is sought through active intervention by the therapist using behavioural methods such as direct challenge and instruction, and active techniques such as role-playing, videotape feedback, and 'family sculpting'. (In family sculpting 'the members of a family create a physical representation of their relationships at one point in time by arranging their bodies in space', in a tableau vivant (Simon, 1972).) Overviews of the different methods of family therapy can be found in the family therapy textbooks of Nichols and Schwartz (2005) and Goldenberg and Goldenberg (2004).

The Milan school of family therapists (Selvini-Palazzoli, Boscolo, Cecchin, *et al.*, 1978) use their background as psychoanalysts to expose and undermine the unconscious 'rules of the game' which maintain family pathology. In their approach, psychoanalytic understanding is used for 'behavioural ends'. In contrast a more recent approach, *narrative therapy* (Epston & White, 1992), owes more to post-modern literary analysis (Legg, 1997). It is deliberately non-directive, avoiding interpretations based on scientific concepts. Instead, by telling stories about their lives, clients develop alternative views of their experiences which free them from the constraint of their previous explanatory stories (Byng-Hall, 1995). The family is no longer seen as a social system but more as a linguistic system. The narrative the family give about their lives is a linguistic construction that organizes past experiences and relationships, giving them significance or diminishing their importance. This idea is used in a number of differently named approaches which are essentially similar – for example the social constructionist approaches and the solution-focused approaches.

Family therapy is thus a fruitful meeting ground for dynamic and behavioural psychotherapists in many parts of the world. In 1977 they joined together to found the Institute of Family Therapy (London), now one of several organizations in the Family, Couple, Sexual, and Systemic Therapy Sections of UKCP (see Appendix).

Family or marital/couple evaluation (Clarkin, Frances, & Moodie, 1979) is almost always essential when the presenting complaint is a child or adolescent, the presenting problem is a sexual difficulty or dissatisfaction, the problem is clearly a family one, and when psychiatric hospitalization is being considered; it is commonly indicated when more than one family member is in psychiatric treatment at the same time, or when improvement in one leads to deterioration in another.

The setting

The common element in family and couple therapy is the focus on the family or couple as the disturbed unit. Usually one member has presented him or herself or (especially in the case of children) has been referred as the patient to be treated. The family or couple therapist will want to make a diagnosis at the level of the whole family system and to interview as many of the family members as possible; if there is a couple problem, he will want to see both partners. He will take pains to invite the cooperation of the other members of the family (or the partner), and if possible interview them together. This conjoint interview is often conducted by a pair of therapists, male and female, which is particularly useful in couple therapy, as it avoids some of the dangers of appearing to take sides. How cooperative partners or leading members of the family are – how willing they are to help and share in taking responsibility for the problems and their resolution – is itself of diagnostic importance; for example, their insistence on making one person the repository of all disturbance or blame suggests that they need to see and keep it that way. An extreme example is where a member of the family is falsely admitted to a mental hospital by relatives who want rid of him or her. This has been called the 'gaslight phenomenon' (Barton & Whitehead, 1969) after the play *Gaslight* written in 1931 by Patrick Hamilton, which portrayed a husband trying to convince his wife that she was mad. Family scapegoating is not new. In 1763, a Select Committee of the House of Commons reported that some people had been committed to asylums as a way of solving family and social problems (Leigh, 1961).

Sometimes family therapists will conduct their interviews in the family home, particularly when they work on the crisis intervention model. Psychiatric referral or requests for admission are then viewed as the result of a crisis in the network of relationships in which the adult or adolescent patient lives, usually at home, but perhaps also at school or work (Brandon, 1970; Bruggen & Davies, 1977). Such a crisis has usually already existed for a period of a few days to six weeks before either natural resolution or illness supervene. Timely therapeutic intervention can sometimes enable the crisis to be resolved in a way that promotes learning and change. Some psychiatrists recommend that all requests for urgent admission should be first investigated at home, in order to prevent unnecessary institutionalization. When patients are seen in the context of their families, their problems can often be encountered in vivo. This approach is probably more appropriate where there is a settled population and families are living together than in bedsitter-land in city centres.

With less acute problems, interviews can take place in a clinic or out-patient department, where it may be easier to provide a suitable setting: sufficient equal chairs set in a circle in a quiet room, with space in the centre for people to move around in if they so wish. A one-way viewing screen or video camera is often used to allow supervision of the process, which in some techniques is interrupted to allow consultation with observing members of the team. Diagnostic interviews merge into therapy sessions; two or three consultations at intervals of two or three weeks may suffice, or weekly or fortnightly sessions may continue for a year or two. Some family therapists, following the diagnostic interview with the whole family, may concentrate therapeutic work on the most responsive family member (often not the referred patient) or the parents only (Bowen, 1966); at the opposite extreme, others (Speck & Attneave, 1973) involve as many members as possible of the family and associated networks (work, school, neighbourhood, etc.) in meetings of up to 50 people! Yet others, especially in hospital settings for adolescents, may have multiple family groups discussing family relationships and intergenerational problems (Behr, 1996). Most limit themselves to the nuclear family, perhaps with key grandparents or with others sharing the home.

Couple therapy can also be conducted in various ways (Dicks, 1967): in conjoint sessions, in which both partners meet together with one or a pair of therapists; in groups in which three or four couples meet with one or two therapists; or by individual therapy conducted simultaneously with each partner by different therapists, who meet periodically to coordinate their work, a method developed particularly by the Institute of Marital Studies at the Tavistock Clinic (Pincus, 1960). Indications and contra-indications for conjoint and individually based approaches have been described by Skynner (1976). It is widely accepted that the conjoint approach is particularly valuable where the couple do not function as fully separate individuals; for example, each may represent a disavowed aspect of the other and make extensive use of projective identification (Main, 1966), as in the clinical example described below (p. 184). Skynner holds that the conjoint approach is less suitable for people who have not yet mastered the 'depressive position' (p. 133), that is, they have not learned to tolerate, without too much guilt, the co-existence of powerful feelings of love and hate.

Patient's role

Ideally members of a family or a couple accept that the problem they seek help with is a shared one, the solving of which is, at least to some degree, a joint responsibility. Often, however, some members exclude themselves, at least initially, but need to be kept in mind by the therapist. To establish a therapeutic alliance, which has to include other family members as well as therapists, there needs to be some residual mutual goodwill and some hope that things might improve.

Cooperation of relatives can often be gained by asking them to provide information about the presenting patient or to help in deciding the best way of coping with the difficulties caused by his or her 'illness'. Not uncommonly some key member refuses, most often a husband or father; but having at first granted this involvement reluctantly, they may often be willing to join in examining the problem and their own part in it, if they are guided in an understanding, clear, and firm way.

Given the opportunity and any necessary guidance, members can begin to talk and interact, revealing much of what their difficulties are. If they respond to the safety of this unusual situation and to the example of the therapist(s) in trying to face the truth impartially, family members may discover they can communicate more openly and confront each other with their views and feelings. Often it is the more 'ill' spouse or, in a family, one of the children who understands more or can provide the information or challenge which moves interaction on to a more creative plane, beyond the stereotyped complaint of symptoms or mutual blame.

If the initial interviews engage the family or couple, they may continue to communicate more openly between sessions, particularly as they come to recognize their mutual responsibility for change. This is one of the clear advantages of conjoint therapy: participants go on living together between sessions, and so have an opportunity to put into practice new ways of interacting begun in the sessions and to make the mutual adjustments which are necessary if the system is going to change for the better. When they slip back into the old maladaptive ways, they may point this out to each other; in other words they can continue as their own therapists. For this reason, family and marital therapy sessions are often held at less frequent intervals than in individual therapy, or group therapy with strangers.

Therapist's role

This depends in part on the level at which they choose to work and on their methods: whether they are working within a more psychoanalytic insight-seeking framework, or in a more action-based and behavioural one. Family and couple therapy is developing on the borders of several psychotherapeutic fields, but whatever their approach the therapists tend to adopt a more active and directive role than most other dynamic psychotherapists; they structure the interviews and use their power to challenge the existing family hierarchy and rules. As well as the more usual responsive and supporting role, they need to be authoritative and challenging because the disturbance of the family system is kept going by the interlocking of many relationships. Indeed the art of all psychotherapy is to find the right blend of support and challenge, or feminine and masculine elements. Too much of the former and the therapist might be overprotective, like a clucking mother-hen; too much challenge and invasion, and the patient may be driven away.

Family therapists discourage, and rarely draw attention to, transference feelings of family members towards themselves, unless they are interfering with the work in hand. Instead, to encourage interaction and exploration, they emphasize how members of the family or marriage are relating to each other consciously and unconsciously, and how members need to see others in certain ways, for example by repeating and avoiding patterns of relationship from their family of origin. Quite often therapists describe their own countertransference feelings evoked by the couple or family, either as a whole or by particular members. Also, more than most other therapists, they may talk about their own personal experiences. They function as models of openness and honesty, which can be particularly helpful when talking about sexual functions in a relaxed and direct way, so counteracting the influence of inhibited or restrictive parents.

Beels and Ferber (1969), in reviewing the work of many family therapists, gave a still useful description of three main types: *conductors*, *reactors*, and *systems-purists*. *Conductors* attempt as 'super-parents' to effect change in the family system towards more healthy functioning, educating by 'maternal' persuasion or 'paternal' criticism, whichever is more appropriate. *Structural family therapy* (Minuchin, 1974) uses this approach. Therapy consists of redesigning the family system so that it will approximate to the normative model of clear but open boundaries between the subsystems of parents and children, and the sibling sub-system will be organized so that children have tasks and privileges appropriate to their age and sex in the cultural supra-system to which they belong.

This approach originated in work with families in underprivileged inner-city areas of the USA.

Reactors, usually more psychoanalytically orientated, seek the family's own potential for change and growth and, by lowering their own defences, allow themselves to be drawn into its atmosphere and projections. This enables the therapists to experience the family members' disturbance within themselves, as they come to feel confused, unskilled, or angry. Skynner (1976, 1986), who was influenced by Foulkes's group analytic approach (p. 159), points out that such therapists are prepared to be drawn into the vulnerable role of child or patient rather than that of super-parent. Skynner himself, and Whitaker (1975), were prominent psychodynamic family therapists who make special use of their own subjective reactions.

> *The teenage son of a divorced couple was taken to his general practitioner by his father (with whom he lived) because of his gambling, which his father seemed to perpetuate by his over-solicitousness and by rescuing him from the scrapes he got into, so that the son never learned to be responsible for himself. Interviewed together with both parents, he was almost mute, while the estranged parents, sitting on either side of him, used the boy to complain about each other's failings. Mother claimed that father spoiled him. Father asserted he did this because she was as poor a mother as she had been a wife; he (father) was a much better mother. As they battled, each separately saying a lot that was true, one of the therapists felt himself increasingly oppressed and confused, and finally said so. He asked the son whether he felt the same. With relief the boy agreed, and turning to his father said: 'It looks as though we should be divorced.' The truth of this dawned on everyone, and father was enabled to give up some of his motherliness and to let his son separate and learn from his own mistakes.*

Reactor therapists often operate in pairs, one letting himself be drawn into the family pathology in this way, the other standing by in a more detached way as if at the end of a lifeline. In psychoanalytic therapy both these roles are carried out by the therapist, alternately identifying with the patient and withdrawing into objectivity. In family therapy dividing the roles allows one therapist to enter into a maelstrom that may be potentially strong enough to drive a vulnerable family member into confusion.

The third type of family therapist is the *systems-purist*, who attempts to discern the ground-rules the family uses for interaction, and how the family members attempt to engage the therapist. He counters them, does not play their game, and attempts to induce them to change their immature or pathological way of behaving. This approach characterizes 'strategic' family therapy (Haley & Hoffman, 1967; Watzlawick, Beavin, & Jackson, 1968) and the 'systemic' family therapy of the Milan School (Selvini Palazzoli, Boscolo, Cecchin, *et al.*, 1978).

Strategic family therapy originated in the USA. It uses active interventions designed to fit the specific problem presented and the details of how and when it occurs. Practitioners consider that symptoms are maintained by the family's habitual solution and seek ways to interrupt the vicious circle. These include issuing 'paradoxical injunctions', which challenge the family's declared wish to change, and use the oppositional qualities of most entrenched families by urging them to stay as they are or do the opposite of what would help them to change.

Systemic family therapy developed in Milan. Originally two therapists, a man and a woman, worked with a family while another two sat behind a one-way screen. More recently one therapist conducts the interview and one to three watch from behind the screen. The team discusses the referral or previous session beforehand, and carefully notes non-verbal communication during the hour-long session, which is videotaped. The team again consults, and the therapist rejoins the family to put the team's recommendations to them. These involve proposing counter-paradoxes to oppose the paradoxes in which severely abnormal families are trapped through a process of circular causality. Having established 'the family game' – that the whole problem is in a sick member – the therapist accepts it and even encourages it, but 'reframes it' in terms of the family needing a sick person. He then prescribes tasks or rituals to the family or part of it, which are designed to disrupt the systems of non-verbal signs that control collusive family denial, including 'double binds' (see p. 176).

Which of these three types (conductor, reactor, or systems-purist) a therapist fits into no doubt depends on his own personality and background, as well as on his theoretical training. Moreover recent developments, such as narrative therapy (p. 179), have moved away from so much directiveness, with its arrogation of power by the therapist, particularly for families and family members who have suffered real abuses of power. This perhaps represents a move towards a rapprochement with psychoanalysis (McFadyen, 1997).

Therapeutic processes

The theory and practice of family and couple therapy encompass counselling, behavioural, and action methods, as well as those based on analytic psychotherapy and group therapy. Therapeutic processes can therefore occur at all the levels of psychotherapy described earlier (pp. 115–125).

The outer level might suffice for less deeply entrenched problems and is common in a first interview or throughout a period of couple counselling. The opening up of communication, as members of the family or partnership allow themselves and each other to speak their minds and express their feelings to an unaccustomed degree, can lead to clarification of problems and recognition of mutual needs and responsibility, so that shared decisions can be reached and carried out by joint action. The so-called 'contract therapy' described by Crowe (1973) is a behavioural modification of this approach, involving agreement by spouses to reward one another for behaviour which each seeks from the other; for example a husband might help with the housework if his wife allows more sexual contact, which she might have previously withheld because she was so resentful about the unequal sharing of unwelcome domestic chores. Sexual problems such as impotence and frigidity can often be helped by the behavioural techniques pioneered by Masters and Johnson (1970), as long as they are not too deeply rooted in neurotic conflict or marital discord (Scharff, 1982; Skrine, 1989).

At a deeper level, when disturbance is more entrenched and resistances to change are greater, it may be necessary to work with less conscious processes, using concepts from psychoanalysis and group analysis. Avoided truths need to be faced and accommodated within the family so that collusive and coercive patterns of relating, such as mutual projection, are revealed and responsibility for them is acknowledged. For example, the exposure of unspoken family myths (Ferreira, 1963; Byng-Hall, 1973), such as 'safety is inside the family, danger outside' or 'a happy family is one where there are no disagreements', allows family members to discover their own ambivalence to each other, or permits an adolescent to begin to explore his own developing independence and sexuality. Family members may come to recognize their projection onto others of images of internalized parents or aspects of themselves, so allowing greater individuation and autonomy.

> *A middle-aged couple sought help after the wife's breakdown into a depressed state. The sale by her husband of his highly successful business, in order to start a second career as an artist, stirred up her anxieties stemming from a financially and emotionally insecure childhood. Their marriage had been based on her embodying the weak, helpless, and dependent parts of both of them, while he represented the tough and reliable parts; in consequence neither had achieved full separation and individuation. His change of career reflected an increasing dissatisfaction with being cut off from the previously feared intuitive and 'feminine' parts of himself, which he had associated with his mother. His wife was unprepared for this and reacted with anxiety and unexpressed resentment. In treatment they came to see the way they had both lost touch, through projective identification (p. 32), with important parts of themselves which they were able to re-own: he by becoming more comfortably intuitive and receptive, she by allowing herself to be more assertive and independent.*

Clarification of boundaries and re-distribution of power within a family system may have far-reaching effects. For example, recognition by parents that they have colluded with a child's wish to divide and rule the family may require them to acknowledge and work on their own marital problem. This could free them to cooperate in helping all to find more appropriate roles, which are likely to decrease the child's anxieties and his consequent need to behave omnipotently. Another example would be when the principal bond of affection in the family is between one parent and one child, so that problems over power, resentment by the excluded parent and siblings, and anxieties about incestuous attachments may have very distorting effects. The correction of these will require a clarification of the boundary between the parents' and children's sub-systems. Families often come to function better when a father, previously reduced to passivity and withdrawal, is enabled by the therapist to develop his authority and involvement (Skynner, 1976).

Such changes may necessitate overcoming powerful resistance to change in entrenched family pathology, but if successful this can lead to dramatic improvement in conditions as serious as schizophrenia and anorexia nervosa (Selvini-Palazzoli, Boscolo, Ceccin, *et al.*, 1978).

Changes in a family system may lead to distress in members other than the presenting patient, as they come to face their own responsibility for the problems and their own personal difficulties. The reality that they have sought to avoid, say, the poverty of their marriage or the loss of their children's dependence on them, may be hard to face and require a good deal of adjustment. Furthermore, some families cannot be helped by family therapy. They are locked in fixed or destructive patterns of interrelating, such as *child abuse* or *sado-masochistic relations*. They may have insufficient concern for each other or are too threatened by change. Then it may be necessary to help individual patients, often an adolescent or young adult, to separate from the family by involving them in therapy for themselves, either individually or in a group. Indeed a family is not necessarily the best place to be. One of the possible outcomes of a family or couple approach that has to be faced may be a decision to split up. Therapy in such cases can often help to ensure that this is done in a constructive way.

Separate therapy might be needed to help members to differentiate and develop more fully as individuals. This can be the case with couples where one or both partners need help to overcome their own problems originating in early family relationships, which may have determined the choice of partner and which the partnership perpetuates. It can also be appropriate for children. Children and adolescents often present with medical or educational problems, or with delinquency, rather than with overt emotional or psychiatric disturbance. Such children may respond to family therapy directed at correcting unhealthy family interaction. In order to overcome the effects of ongoing (as well as past) trauma and conflict, and to release their developmental potential, some children require a different sort of relationship from that which they have with their parents and siblings.

Child psychotherapy has grown in the last 70 years out of the pioneering work of psychoanalysts such as Hug-Hellmuth (1921), Klein (1932), Anna Freud (1966), and Winnicott (1975), who developed play techniques to analyse pre-school children not yet able to express themselves fully in words. With older children and adolescents it is possible to move towards more verbal communication in individual psychotherapy (Daws & Boston, 1981) and in group psychotherapy (Riester & Kraft, 1986; Evans, 1998), and there have been several therapeutic communities providing the benefits of social therapy (p. 191) for disturbed children and adolescents, who often present with learning difficulties (Rose, 1990). Most child psychotherapy in the UK takes place in community child guidance clinics and in hospital departments of family and child psychiatry, where a family approach is usual. In some, family therapy is emphasized; in others, parents are supported and guided while the main therapeutic effort is directed towards the child. A team approach is used, with the work of educational psychologists, teachers, educational therapists, and social workers integrated with that of psychiatrists and child psychotherapists.

Child psychotherapy is now a growing discipline, with its own professional organization. The Association of Child Psychotherapists is represented in the BPC and UKCP (p. 276) and has its own training programmes and its own journal, *Journal of Child Psychotherapy*. The interested reader is referred to such texts as Daws and Boston (1981) on the work of child psychotherapists in various settings, Laufer and Laufer (1988) on adolescent breakdown, and Sandler *et al.* (1990) on the work of Anna Freud and the Hampstead Child Therapy Centre.

Research and family therapy

In common with individual and group therapy it has been difficult to define the important components of family therapy and to ensure that therapists deliver the family intervention in a systematic manner. Equally there is uncertainty about what should be measured to assess the effect of a family intervention. Should it be a measure related to the overall functioning of the family or a more specific measure looking at symptoms expressed by a member of the family? In an early study of 18 London families treated in family therapy, Asen and colleagues (1991) applied a multidimensional set of measures to assess change at an individual, dyadic, and family level. They found no change at the family level of function, which included family communication, alliances, and boundaries, although there was change at the individual and dyadic level. It is difficult to conclude therefore exactly what has been achieved in relation to the family.

Most researchers have taken an easier route and only concentrated on, for example, a specific member of the family who is the defined patient, looking to see if family therapy affects an aspect of his difficulties. Many studies, for example, explore the effect of family interventions on the subsequent course of a patient with schizophrenia who lives with family members, most commonly the frequency of relapse as defined by admission to hospital. Basic psychoeducational packages about schizophrenia have been offered in the context of a single family or multiple-family groups. McFarlane and colleagues (1995b) have argued that they may be more effective than single family treatments on the basis that the social networking could enhance treatment effects. In a large multi-site trial McFarlane (1995a) compared multiple family with single family interventions, finding that there were indeed advantages to the former in terms of relapse rates, especially in patients with higher levels of positive symptoms such as delusions and hallucinations. For the clinician this suggests that seeing a number of families together might confer an advantage to the patient, as well as being less costly.

In another condition, eating disorders, a randomized clinical trial has also been of important benefit to clinicians. Patients were randomized to routine individual supportive psychotherapy or to family therapy following their discharge from an in-patient treatment programme to restore weight (Russell, Szmukler, Dare, *et al.*, 1987). Patients whose disorder had an earlier onset, before the age of 18 years, responded better to family therapy. Follow-up (Eisler, Dare, Russell, *et al.*, 1997) showed that patients presenting with a late onset or with an early onset but a long history tended to have poorer outcomes than patients with early onset and short history. Patients in this latter group who received family therapy did better than those who were given individual therapy.

These methodologically traditional studies of family interventions are being supplemented by less conventional research looking at narratives and the experiences of family members. Stern and colleagues (1999) studied the accounts of family members looking after a relative who was acutely psychotic. Narratives could be classified into two main themes. One involved a theme of reparation and integration of the illness into family life, whilst the other suggested the illness was a series of chaotic and unpredictable events. How these two different ways of processing a distressing situation within a family will impact on outcomes is not yet known.

SOCIAL THERAPY

The preceding three sections on individual, group, and family therapy have traced a widening perspective, from the individual and his inner world to his interpersonal and family relationships. This gives us different frames in which to view man, like using a microscope with lenses of varying powers of magnification. Parallel developments in psychoanalytic theory from 'one-body psychology' to two-, three-, and multi-body psychology were foreshadowed by Rickman (1951). How a person functions is dependent not only on his internalized family of origin, but also on the current family and social groups to which he belongs. His behaviour at any one time is affected by the social situation he finds himself in, including that in which he is treated when ill. When large groups such as institutions are studied, the insights of a psychoanalytic view can be usefully joined with the 'outsights' of a sociological one (Kreeger, 1975; Pines, 1975). Sociology was born out of the upheaval of the French Revolution and was christened by August Comte, who envisaged that it would contribute to a new social order; it studies the relation between man and society, the ways in which man both creates society and is moulded by it (Hopper & Weyman, 1975; Burkitt, 1991).

The less power individuals have, the more they are at the mercy of social forces and ideas imposed on them. For example, Karl Marx derived his concept of *alienation* from what he considered to be the helpless position of workers treated as 'hands', with no value or meaning in the social system other than in the work they produce. According to Marx, the more the worker produces materially, the poorer he will be in his inner life; similarly in the area of religious belief, the more he attributes to God, the less he has in himself (Marx, 1844). A sociological idea, readily linked with modern psychodynamic thinking, was Emile Durkheim's (1897) concept of *anomie*. This refers to the pathogenic vacuum of standards which results from the breakdown of stable social norms, familiar in the 'inner-city disease' of today; it reminds us of the individual's need for structured relationships, identifications, and roles for a sense of fitting into a meaningful scheme, in order to feel securely himself. Durkheim considered *anomie* an important cause of suicide. The more recent sociological work of George Brown also points to the social factors contributing to the high incidence of depressive states in working-class women, in particular the lack of social contact through having a lot of children, no work outside the home, little support from husbands, and early death of mother (Brown & Harris, 1978).

Social psychology and psychological sociology have flourished in the great social melting-pot of the USA. The pioneer psychologist William James (1890) recognized that the sense of self is bound up with the processes of social interaction, a view expounded and deepened by Erikson's (1965) more recent work on identity and psychosocial development (p. 47). An early sociologist, Cooley (1902), had proposed the idea of 'the looking glass self', according to which a person's self-image is built up from how he imagines others view and judge him, and his own subsequent feelings such as pride or mortification; this is not unlike Winnicott's (1971, p. 111) idea that the infant's self-image is built up through seeing himself reflected in his mother's face. Another influential American social psychologist was G. H. Mead (1934) through his contributions to self/other role theory. He saw language as the means by which a self comes into being through social processes of communication and symbolic interaction, and through mutual role-taking. As he put it, 'mind presupposes, and is a product of, the social process' (ibid, p. 243). Later sociologists (Parsons, 1964) have interested themselves in the two-way process between man and his social world. Social institutions reflect man's psychic structure, and vice versa; for example, the judiciary could be seen as representing man's collective external super-ego, while some social and cultural standards are internalized in everyone's individual super-ego. Both super-ego and judiciary are 'decider sub-systems' (p. 67) which maintain a powerful controlling function in the larger systems of personality and of society, respectively.

There can be a destructive as well as a creative interaction between man and the society he lives in, amply demonstrated by studies of closed institutions such as prisons and mental hospitals (Goffman, 1961; Foudraine, 1974), where humiliation and dispossession of familiar roles can destroy individuality and hope. Barton (1959) applied the term 'institutional neurosis' to these consequences of institutionalization, which can magnify or replace whatever disability brought a patient into hospital. The active rehabilitation and 'open doors' policies of the 1950s, reviving the 'moral treatment' of enlightened mental hospitals in the early nineteenth century, followed recognition of these adverse effects of prolonged hospital admission.

Main (1946) was one of the pioneers of the Northfield Experiments (p. 156) and on the strength of his experience there he gave the name *therapeutic community* to institutions where the setting itself is deliberately organized to restore morale and promote the psychological treatment of mental and emotional disturbance; he went on to create an influential example in the Cassel Hospital in Surrey, which has been one of the few units in Britain where inpatients undergo individual analytic psychotherapy for neurotic and personality disorders without recourse to drugs, in a setting where at the same time they engage in social learning.

In the 1950s Maxwell Jones (1952, 1968) founded the unit at Belmont, later to be called the Henderson Hospital, currently closed due to changes in health service provision and funding. He emphasized the opportunity for *living–learning* processes when people live and work together in a setting where social analysis, rather than psychoanalysis, is practised. At the Cassel Hospital, the community is an adjunct to individual therapy; at the Henderson, the community was the main focus (Norton, 1992). The Henderson Hospital accepted people who tended to show their problems more in disturbed social behaviour and relationships, for whom individual treatment is less appropriate than for those whose problems are neurotic and internalized. A social context was provided where these 'sociopathic' disturbances could be expressed, confronted, and explored. The Henderson Hospital regime was characterized by 'permissiveness, reality-confrontation, democracy and communalism' (Rapoport, 1960). Its permissiveness encouraged the expression and enactment of disturbed feelings and relationships, so that they could be examined by fellow patients and staff. The differences between patients and staff were minimized by staff discarding uniforms and titles (as has been done in many units since), and by each freely contributing their feelings and opinions of events. Decision-making was shared by the community as a whole, including issues of admission and discharge. Rules were kept to the minimum necessary for the safety and well-being of everyone. This type of residential community is the prototypical therapeutic community and has been subjected to research. There are other examples in many parts of the world, particularly in Britain, the USA, and Europe, although over the past few years many have had to close because of problems with funding for intensive treatment in in-patient settings. A few notable examples have survived, such as Austen Riggs in the USA, which continues to offer patients 'open-ended' residential therapy. Other units have adapted by offering therapeutic community treatment within a day hospital or community setting.

Clark (1977), in a valuable review of the history and status of the therapeutic community, distinguished between the therapeutic community, therapeutic milieu, and social therapy. The term therapeutic community or 'therapeutic community proper' (Clark, 1964) should be reserved for the specific type of therapeutic milieu developed by Jones and his followers: 'a small face-to-face residential community using social analysis as its main tool' (Clark, 1977). A therapeutic milieu is a social setting designed to produce a beneficial effect on those being helped in it: for example, a hospital ward, sheltered workshop, or hostel, each with a social structure different from the others. Social therapy (known as milieu therapy in USA) employed the idea that the social environment or milieu can be used as a mode of treatment. Of the three categories described by Clark, the therapeutic community was the most specific application of these principles; social therapy was the most general.

Clark pointed out that the enthusiastic idealism about the therapeutic community, widespread in the 1950s and 1960s, culminated in the founding of the Association of Therapeutic Communities in 1971. Such idealism has been tempered since then by recognition of the limitations of this means of treatment and by a move in society away from permissiveness. At the same time a clearer understanding of the principles of social therapy has led to their application in wider fields – such as the Richmond Fellowship hostels for psychiatric patients, and communities for adolescents with behavioural and learning difficulties – and to their adaptation to other special needs. Some self-governing hostels for ex-drug addicts, for example, while retaining 'democracy, communalism and reality-confrontation' (Rapoport, 1960), replace permissiveness by an authoritarian structure with harsher punishments and degradations than would be tolerated in most organizations run by doctors and nurses. They are communities and they are therapeutic, but because of their authoritarian structure they are not 'therapeutic communities proper'. In hospital psychiatric units the principles will also have to be adapted, but here to the broad range of psychiatric conditions, many of them acute. In such units, staff need to be free to make authoritative decisions in order to cope with emergencies and maintain the safe structure that is especially important for acutely ill patients who are not yet able to take much responsibility. Awareness of the principles of social therapy helps staff to remain flexible in their roles, and share responsibility as patients become ready to assume it. A vivid up-to-date review is provided by Kennard (1998).

The essence of social therapy is *openness of communication* and *shared examination of problems*. Patients are encouraged to use their initiative in running their own lives. Hierarchy is played down and responsibility shared as much as possible between patients and staff. Group meetings play an important part in facilitating these processes, both small groups of a dozen or so and large groups of the total unit (patients and staff), in the community meeting.

The relationship between social therapy and psychotherapy in the *community meeting* is still being debated. Edelson (1970) distinguishes between them, claiming that the function of the community meeting is not group psychotherapy but facilitation of the day-to-day functioning of the unit. Others such as Springmann (1970) argue that there can be distinct potential for individual insight and change in community meetings, although they are not a substitute for more intimate, small therapy groups. Springmann fosters a less structured and consequently more spontaneous meeting. However, large unstructured groups can produce a lot of anxiety even in 'normal' people; primitive anxieties of persecution and annihilation, and defences against them, such as withdrawal or omnipotent exhibitionistic behaviour, are not uncommon. In general psychiatric units, which cater for people with all degrees of disturbances and vulnerability, Pines (1975) favours a clear structure to the community meeting, particularly at its outset. This reduces anxiety and confusion induced by threats of anonymity, fear of loss of control, and of catching other people's madness. An elected chairman and an initial agenda of feedback reports from groups of patients and staff can provide a useful structure from which more spontaneous information, preoccupations, and conflicts emerge later in the meeting. This procedure was followed at the Henderson Hospital and has been adopted by many community meetings in psychiatric units.

Social systems can provide defences against primitive persecutory and depressive anxieties based on the paranoid-schizoid and depressive positions (p. 133), or they can increase them (Jaques, 1955). In creating a social system devoted to therapy, it is necessary to determine what level of anxiety and defence is appropriate for the patients and staff working together in it. The organization and methods used in a hospital or unit may be determined, understandably, by the need to provide staff with defences against anxiety, as much as by what is best for patients: for example, nursing hierarchies and rituals can protect nurses, many of them young and inexperienced, from the anxieties provoked by feeling too involved with the suffering they encounter (Menzies, 1961); or, to counteract staff anxieties, psychiatric patients may be given drugs to quieten them rather than an opportunity to express and talk about their problems (Stanton & Schwartz, 1954). Nevertheless, while social or institutional defences may be right and proper, they should not be so great as to hamper the therapeutic task of the institution. Getting the balance right can be a struggle (Hinshelwood, 1987).

The idea of social therapy has been applied in a number of different settings, for example, psychiatric hospitals, hostels for drug addicts, schools for emotionally disturbed and learning impaired adolescents, and even prisons. Indeed there has recently been renewed interest in its application to the management and treatment of offenders (Welldon, 1997) – small prison wings such as Grendon Underwood run on therapeutic community lines (Genders & Player, 1995), those with severe personality disorders (Whiteley, 1994; Dolan, Warren, & Norton, 1997), and the use of in-patient groups in helping patients with schizophrenia have been described as enabling patients with inadequate capacity for symbolizing to internalize helping figures (Rey, 1994). The methods used are even more numerous, and therefore description of them will be limited to a few general principles.

Following the Thatcher years of 'there is no such thing as society – only individuals and families', the benefits of communities are being promoted (Etzioni, 1993; Mulgan, 1997). The therapeutic value of communities in 'reconnecting' people, discovered by the pioneers of group psychotherapy (see pp. 156–161) and established at the Military Neurosis Centre at Northfield, is due for renaissance after a period of relative decline (Kennard, 1994; Knowles, 1995; Cox, 1998; Campling & Haigh, 1999).

The setting

The boundaries of the social system in which social therapy is practised need to be clear, whether it is a 'therapeutic community proper' or a 'therapeutic milieu' in an in-patient or day unit, hostel, residential home, or prison wing. This allows it to develop its own clear culture and rules. Clarity of the boundaries of the system also permits examination and understanding of happenings within it to be differentiated from events originating outside, such as intrusions from administrators, police, local inhabitants, or relatives.

The degree to which a unit can control its boundaries inevitably affects what happens inside it. This explains many of the differences between a 'therapeutic community proper' and a psychiatric unit operating as a 'therapeutic milieu'. A therapeutic community can control its admissions. It selects patients who, on the whole, want to play an active and responsible part in their own treatment, and are thought likely to fit into and benefit from the culture of the unit. In many therapeutic communities, more established patients play a part in deciding who will be admitted. Such control and selection is impossible in a general hospital unit, because it serves a local catchment area and has to admit patients of all types and ages, and all degrees of intellectual capacity and emotional disturbance. In such a unit, the structure has to allow for patients who need traditional nursing and doctoring, at least for a while. The most acutely disturbed patient might need the provision of a good deal of structured care, as does a newborn child, but as the patient improves he should be encouraged, like the growing child, to move towards the greatest autonomy possible.

The organization of any psychiatric unit should provide opportunities for sharing and learning from the reality of living together (Haigh, 2002b). Community meetings are held at least weekly, in some settings daily, attended by as many of the patients and staff as possible. It is important to have a room of sufficient size and shape for everyone to be accommodated, sitting comfortably in something approaching concentric circles, so that people can communicate with each other face to face. Decisions to exclude some patients (because, say, they are still too disturbed) or to agree that some staff do not attend (e.g. those not available all the time) need to be examined and faced openly, along with all other significant events.

In addition, small groups may exist for discussion of day-to-day problems in subdivisions of the unit (say wards) or for discussion of specific problems shared by a number of patients (arrival in the unit, impending discharge, women's rights, and so on). In a general psychiatric unit, more formal psychotherapy, which requires longer term commitment, is best conducted in small out-patient groups which people usually join after discharge. For in-patients, opportunities are created, in addition to discussion groups, for non-verbal expression and communication through occupational therapy and art or music therapy. These can be extremely valuable in contacting patients who are withdrawn, inhibited, or unused to talking about themselves and their feelings. Some people can use these methods to get in touch with previously unexpressed aspects of themselves. We have already quoted Winnicott (1971, p. 38) saying that 'Psychotherapy has to do with two people playing together'; he went on, 'The corollary of this is that where playing is not possible then the work done by the therapist is directed towards bringing the patient from a state of not being able to play into a state of being able to play.' Art, music, and dance therapy may help people to find they *can* play, and in so doing make fuller contact with themselves and others (Jennings, 1983, 1987).

Staff ideally meet together following (and sometimes before) community and small group meetings, to share and clarify their understanding of what has happened and to make any necessary decisions or contingency plans. In addition, staff often have their own meetings to discuss practical issues and general planning. The more of a therapeutic community the unit is, the more likely it is that staff will air and face up to interpersonal tensions and conflicts in these meetings; otherwise, it would be hypocritical to expect patients to do so, quite apart from the knowledge that unresolved conflicts between staff affect patients adversely (Stanton & Schwartz, 1954).

A common feature in 'therapeutic communities proper' is the crisis meeting of either the whole community or one of the sub-groups of patients and staff. This aims to examine a critical event – such as someone behaving in a disturbed or destructive way – in an honest and supportive manner. The extent to which this can happen might almost be a yardstick of how much a unit functions as a 'therapeutic community proper', that is, by sharing responsibility and treatment between all members of the community without slipping too much into the traditionally distinct roles of helpless sick patients and competent healthy staff.

Patient's roles

Patients learn that they have an active role to play in helping themselves and each other, by participating in communal life as they become able to do so. They have an opportunity to discover the personal and interpersonal nature of problems and conflicts which underlie symptoms. By facing up to the problems of living together and sharing in finding solutions, they can move away from isolation and a sense of abnormality. They have many chances to express feelings and talk honestly about themselves and others, and to learn new ways and attitudes. By playing an active role they have opportunities to rediscover, or discover for the first time, strengths and skills in handling problems. Being elected to the chair of the community meeting and filling the role adequately are often experienced as a graduation, particularly by previously unassertive patients and those with damaged self-esteem. Their success may encourage others.

Staff roles

In keeping with the ethos of social therapy, staff transcend the specific roles prescribed by their training in the disciplines of medicine, nursing, social work, occupational therapy, and so on. They work more as individuals in a multidisciplinary team. Although still practising their separate professional skills as necessary, they share socio-therapeutic attitudes and try to face up to any interdisciplinary tensions and rivalries which interfere with their work. As it is between disciplines, so it needs to be between different hierarchical levels within each staff subgroup; problems between seniors and juniors need to be resolved by honest confrontation and discussion. This is what is known as 'flattening of the authority pyramid' (Clark, 1964, p. 45). It does not mean that power and responsibility are dissipated; indeed, one of the paradoxes of the therapeutic community movement is that the aims of democratization and sharing of responsibility have often been best achieved under the 'benevolent dictatorship' of charismatic leaders. However, a therapeutic milieu encourages the sharing of decisions and power among staff of different disciplines; it also tends to reduce 'social distance' between them. The same trends can be seen in the organization of industry and higher education, where greater consultation and shared decision-making are increasingly being sought. Desirable ideals in any organization are that power and responsibility are open and clear, and that their diffusion is in the interest of helping its members, in our case staff and patients, towards autonomy and growth without losing direction and sight of the overall function of the unit.

Working in a therapeutic community demands openness and honesty. This means being able to say to fellow staff members, as well as to patients, things which are difficult to say and to accept, such as: 'I don't like the way you do that . . . Why on earth did you say that? . . . I feel it's your problem not the patient's.' An atmosphere and culture in which such confrontations can be made and received without feelings being too hurt is one which has to be built up and constantly maintained. Without it, destructive forces can prevail: for example, through splitting and projection between subgroups of staff and patients (Main, 1957).

Therapeutic processes

Social therapy involves open communication and confrontation of problems as they arise. Instead of using staff roles and hierarchies for unnecessary defence and evasion, it demands self-questioning and change. These characteristics produce an atmosphere which is lively and creative, but often stressful.

Not everyone, staff or patients, is comfortable in this atmosphere, although many adjust and learn to value it. The question of whether some may find it anti-therapeutic is still open to research. One of the disadvantages of social therapy is that it is difficult for patients to opt out if it does not suit them in the form provided in a particular unit, except by leaving or not cooperating. For this reason it is important for a general psychiatric unit aiming to function as a therapeutic milieu to have a range of programmes adaptable to a variety of different people and problems. Working well, a therapeutic milieu promotes the tackling of the inevitable problems of living with other disturbed people, in a way that facilitates their solution and promotes learning about personal relationships.

A community meeting in the psychiatric unit of a general hospital had revealed an undercurrent of explosive irritability among patients, whose feedback reports had glossed over several distressing events during the previous week, and hinted at shared anxieties and resentment about forthcoming staff changes. Some patients in particular, through the chairman of the community meeting, who was one of their number, complained that they were not seeing enough of their doctors. This implied that the nurses were not good enough, and incapable of discerning deterioration in the condition of their patients. It emerged, in the staff group following the meeting, that some nursing staff were themselves demoralized by intense feelings of unexpressed resentment at their senior nurse who had not communicated with them openly and directly about his temporary absence, nor made arrangements for his replacement. When these feelings were shared with colleagues, and the problem acknowledged as one which needed to be tackled, the nurses felt freer to take action, and their morale began to improve. Opening up these issues also led, in the following community meeting, to a useful exploration of patient attitudes to staff, including their reluctance to recognize that staff too could have problems. The need for doctors to be idealized as strong and omniscient was seen to reflect the wish for a good reliable father on the part of many patients (including the chairman), like the nurses' wish for a more reliable and concerned senior nurse.

The task of social therapy is to create a therapeutic milieu, and its paradigm is the therapeutic community, the core of which is the community meeting. Through it, Pines (1975, p. 303) has traced the link between the social system and individual psychotherapy:

The community meeting represents the creation of a new social system that accepts as its fundamental problem control, containment and treatment of mental illness. The attempt is made to foster the development of a society whose 'shared understanding and common intellectual and emotional discourse' are based on the insights of psychotherapy which state that mental illness results in, and may arise from, faulty communication, that mental illness has meaning that can be understood and that all persons, sick or well, have more in common than they can easily recognise. The psychotherapeutic viewpoint emphasises that emotional disturbances have roots in failed developmental tasks which centre on the resolution of issues of dependency, autonomy, authority and sexuality. The resolution of these issues is renegotiable in the transactions of psychotherapy, and it is expected that they will appear in the social transactions of the group, and thereby offer opportunities for psychotherapeutic work. The psychotherapeutic effort is to raise these issues to the level of conscious understanding where they can be acted upon in more mature and adaptive ways than have been open to the individuals heretofore.

The therapeutic processes of social therapy are thus the treatment of conflicts and blocks in communication within the unit, so creating a 'therapeutic milieu' in which practical problems can be solved, interpersonal skills developed, and the psychotherapeutic functions of the unit can flourish. Whether the latter are largely supportive or exploratory, both functions are needed in a comprehensive caring service, and should be available with the National Health Service. Needs vary from patient to patient, and often at different stages in the same patient's care.

Psychiatric units have come under increasing pressure over the last few years. The closure of large mental hospitals and inadequate re-provision of services has meant that patients are discharged as soon as possible, if indeed they are admitted at all. Patients are maintained in their homes throughout treatment unless considered as being at high risk to themselves or to others. The need for psychiatric units to keep the average length of stay down to a few weeks only discourages the development of a therapeutic milieu in acute psychiatric wards, which are no longer a place for a more gradual recovery.

Alternative ways of working through emotional crises exist. Those who work on the crisis intervention model aim to keep people out of hospital by sorting out emotional crises in the home (p. 176). In the group homes of the Arbours Housing Association (Berke, Masoliver, & Ryan, 1995) and the Philadelphia Association (Cooper, Friedman, Gans, *et al.*, 1989), followers of Laing claim that patients can be supported and helped to work through their psychological disturbance in a way felt to be more creative, facing the suppressed imaginative parts of themselves rather than sealing them off with a rapid 'cure'. This view has been increasingly questioned, especially for psychotic patients. But one does not need to accept Laing's view of mental illness *in toto* to recognize that people vary in the time and conditions they need to work through their problems in a way that is right for them.

At the exploratory end of the psychotherapeutic spectrum, the existence of 'therapeutic communities proper' depends on their being free from the pressures which constrain acute psychiatric units, so that they can make their facilities more widely available to patients likely to benefit from intensive psychotherapy and social therapy during a stay of 6–12 months. Ideally, perhaps, every region should have units of this type available for both in-patients and out-patients. At the opposite, supportive end of the spectrum, despite advances in psychiatric treatment, long-term care in conditions of true 'asylum' are likely to be needed for some chronically and severely disabled patients, if necessary for the rest of their lives. More long-term units or group homes are needed, and it is important that they have space, grounds, and adequate facilities for occupation and recreation.

There are disadvantages in trying to do everything together; neither support nor exploration can be easily provided, in full measure, in a compromise situation. Consequently there are dangers in a policy of concentrating psychiatric care in a uniform service based solely on acute psychiatric units, unless there is concurrent development of a wide range of psychotherapy services for out-patients and alternative therapeutic milieux. The needs of many types of patient will have to be catered for in a comprehensive psychiatric service: some with acute emotional disturbance, and others with chronic disability; some who need mainly support and medication, and others who can use an opportunity to work through problems and learn new solutions through psychotherapy, whether cognitive-behavioural or dynamic.

In many areas, however, psychotherapists are playing a growing part in the support and supervision of community psychiatric nurses, so helping in the psychodynamic management in the community of often very difficult patients. They are also cooperating with social workers, and others are already developing a more flexible service by adopting some of the principles of social therapy in facilities such as hostels and clubs. Units formerly offering in-patient therapeutic community treatment are now providing a therapeutic milieu in a day hospital or within a community setting. Patients come together for community groups on a regular basis but no longer sleep within a hospital. The idea of social therapy – that the social context affects what happens in it – can guide us in fitting the provisions to the needs of the patients for various types and levels of psychotherapy.

Research and therapeutic communities

Therapeutic communities argued strongly for many years that the process of treatment prevented the use of traditional research methods, which were seen as disruptive to the focus on equality, democracy, and communalism. Randomization of patients to an appropriate control group was also difficult, partly because therapeutic community treatment tends to be a long-term treatment and there is no obvious comparison. Nevertheless there has been some research on the use of therapeutic community treatment, primarily for antisocial personality disorder and drug addiction (Lees, Manning, & Rawlings, 1999), which concluded that therapeutic communities, particularly the so-called 'concept' communities in the USA, were effective but the positive effects were found mostly in substance misusers in secure settings in which there is a considerable degree of coercion.

In Europe no randomized trials have been carried out. However, Dolan and colleagues (1997) at the Henderson Hospital, in a creative attempt to find an appropriate control group, used a non-admitted comparison sample to assess the effectiveness of treatment on core symptoms of personality disorder: 137 patients were studied, of whom 70 were admitted and 67 not admitted, either for clinical or for financial reasons. However, this is not a strict comparison group as fewer than one in seven of those considered for the Henderson Hospital completed treatment (Rutter & Tyrer, 2003). There was significantly greater reduction in core features of personality disorder in the treated group than in the non-admitted group. A similar control group was used to see if treatment in a therapeutic community unit within Grendon Underwood Prison was useful for offenders. Taylor (2000) followed up 700 individuals over seven years, contrasting their outcomes with patients allocated to the waiting list for the unit and 1400 inmates from the general prison population. There were some indications of reduced rates of reoffending and there was a link between length of stay on the unit and better outcome. The stay had to be longer than a year to have an effect, suggesting that the therapeutic community belief in long-term treatment has some merit.

Further work suggested that therapeutic community treatment may show cost savings over treatment in general psychiatric services primarily because of reducing the need for hospital admission (Davies, Campling, & Ryan, 1999). As there are now many more treatments available for the treatment of personality disorder, therapeutic communities need to come into the frame of comparison studies and further research should be undertaken (Haigh, 2002a), but proponents will need to adopt acceptable experimental designs if they are to compete with other treatments.

Allied to therapeutic communities and their methods is a wide range of therapy movements which became known as the human potential movement, and it is to these historical developments that we now turn.

ENCOUNTER AND BEYOND

Psychoanalysis began as a radical movement, challenging the established view of orthodox medicine and psychiatry. This may be one reason why it was more readily accepted in North America, with its democratic spirit of equality and opportunity for all, than in the Old World. However, in time, it encountered the problem of all revolutionary movements as they are taken over by, and become part of, the established order. The 'human potential movement', or 'humanistic psychology' as it is sometimes called, may be seen as the next revolution, reacting to what was felt to be conservatism in psychoanalysis. It was in many ways typically American (Kovel, 1976), and with roots in inspirational religious revivalism (Marteau, 1976) takes a basically optimistic view of human nature and its perfectibility. This contrasts with the rather pessimistic view of Freud (1930), towards the end of his life, as expressed in *Civilization and its Discontents*, that man is inevitably in conflict between the demands of instinct and those of culture. These movements attract people who seek 'self actualisation' (Maslow, 1954); they do not regard themselves as ill, merely 'blocked' or 'alienated from their true selves'.

Perhaps another, indirect, influence on these newer therapies has been the Existential movement in philosophy (Heidegger, 1967), which has concentrated on *understanding* existence in contrast to the earlier Cartesian preoccupation with *thinking*; on *being* rather than *knowing*. In a sense it asserts *sum ergo cogito* as opposed to *cogito ergo sum*. The existential emphasis on the phenomena of the individual's experience and his need to face his mortality and aloneness has led some philosophers, like Sartre, to a position of stoicism in the face of anxiety and despair. It can also lead to a search for a meaningful 'I and Thou' relationship with God (Buber, 1971) or with other human beings. Existentialist thinking has influenced several psychiatrists and psychotherapists (May & Ellenberger, 1958; Laing, 1960), who put conscious *awareness* of the self and others before consideration of unconscious processes or biological aspects of human behaviour. The title of Rogers's (1961) early book, *On Becoming a Person*, proclaims this attitude. In psychoanalysis, this humanistic trend has always existed, but has manifested itself in a growing interest in the experience of the self, its development, and vicissitudes (Jacobson, 1964; Kohut, 1977), and in narcissistic problems of self-esteem (Kernberg, 1975). Wolf (1994) has reviewed the variety of disorders of the self and their origins from the perspective of self-psychology (see p. 62).

The 'human potential movement' was most typically represented by the Esalen Institute, founded in 1962, at Big Sur, California, where Rogerian psychotherapy, Encounter groups, Gestalt therapy, bioenergetics, meditation, Yoga, and Zen flourished side by side. Similar 'growth centres' were established elsewhere in the USA and in Europe with the help of American 'missionaries'. Through so-called transpersonal psychotherapy (Gordon-Brown & Somers, 1988) the movement even integrated esoteric elements and Eastern mysticism.

Whilst all this might sound 'whacky', there have been more recent attempts to integrate Eastern philosophy into psychotherapy. Marsh Linehan, a radical behaviourist, developed dialectical behaviour therapy (Linehan, 1993b) for the treatment of borderline personality disorder. This treatment has a judicious mix of behavioural techniques combined with ideas taken from Zen Buddhism. More specifically, she developed the technique of mindfulness to help patients manage highly arousing emotional states and this has now become a treatment in its own right, particularly for depression (Segal, Williams, & Teasdale, 2002).

Mindfulness

Mindfulness, explicated most thoroughly in the Buddhist literature (Hahn, 1975), has been defined recently for research purposes as 'an enhanced attention to and awareness of current experience or present reality' characterized by 'especially *open* or *receptive* awareness and attention' (Brown & Ryan, 2003, p. 822, emphasis in original). As a concept and technique it links with mentalizing (see p. 82). Attention is pivotal to mindfulness, as it is to mentalizing. Yet mindfulness, like thinking, is not restricted to any particular object; one can be mindful of a flower or of one's breathing. To bring the concepts closer together, we might construe mentalizing as *mindfulness of mind* (Allen & Fonagy, 2006). Although mindfulness is broader than mentalizing (i.e. pertaining to more than mental states), it is also narrower in being present-centred; by contrast, mentalizing also can be directed to past and future mental states. In addition, mentalizing explicitly is relatively deliberative, whereas mindfulness is construed as 'pre-reflective' as well as 'perceptual and non-evaluative' (Brown & Ryan, 2003, p. 843). Finally, befitting its Buddhist origins, mindfulness sometimes connotes relatively emotionally detached awareness, whereas a premium is placed on mentalizing in the midst of intense emotional states. Notwithstanding these conceptual distinctions, the term 'mindfulness' is not only extremely useful in its own right but also aptly captures the principles in dynamic therapy of *attending to and being mindful of* mental states. The careful definition of concepts also brings the use of 'alternative' techniques back into the scientific arena, which has not been central to the human potential movement.

Apart from such frank side-stepping of conventional scientific scepticism, the most important departures of the human potential movement from established psychotherapeutic practice have been in the nature of the therapist–patient relationship, the move from talk to action, and the emphasis on expression rather than on understanding. The basic elements of dynamic psychotherapy, as we have emphasized, are a relationship of trust, communication in words, understanding, and integration. A relationship of trust remains the cornerstone of all psychotherapy, including these newer manifestations which, however, involve the therapist in a more active and self-revealing role. Rather than listening receptively, he engages the client in a series of technical exercises. Instead of patiently interpreting and working through resistances to self-awareness and change, the therapist aims at expression of the client's feelings by the facilitation of intense experiences. Treatment is shorter term and often concentrated in weekend workshops or 24-hour 'marathons'. Feelings are considered to be more important than thoughts, and getting them out (catharsis) more important than reflecting upon their origins. These therapists emphasize (a) 'body language' and the unity of body and mind, (b) treatment in the 'here and now', and (c) the therapeutic impact of the real I–thou engagement between therapist and client. However, the following concepts are basic to psychoanalysis and its more conventional derivatives:

1   Psychoanalysis has always concerned itself with the interplay of psychological and physical processes.

2   The concept of transference implies that the past is alive in the present, and psychoanalysis has long recognized that it is the 'here and now' quality of the experience of transference phenomena which gives them therapeutic impact. It is a common misunderstanding that psychoanalysts are only interested in discussing their patients' childhood at a distance, rather than as it is manifest in the 'here and now'.

3   Analysts also are well aware of the importance of their own personality and the 'real' as opposed to the transference elements in the therapist–patient relationship (Klauber, 1981); it forms the basis of the therapeutic alliance (p. 68).

Certainly a more active and directive therapist may do things that another might not do while in a psychoanalytic stance, but conversely there are things he may not be able to do. He can challenge defences more forcibly, and engineer changes when a patient or family is stuck in repetitive behaviour; but the quicker pace may not allow him to reflect on transference and counter-transference phenomena, or attend to the slowly emerging communications of the patient. Further, there are dangers that the active, directive role will attract therapists who seek to gratify their own needs for power. It is to counter such dangers that personal analytic experience and supervision are considered such a vital part of most recognized forms of training in psychotherapy (Pedder, 1989a).

While analytic therapy may lend itself to defensive thinking rather than feeling, especially in schizoid or obsessional patients cut off from their feelings, feeling alone can also be defensive. The intense experience of more active treatments can lead to great relief or euphoria, but without working through the effect may be transient. Disregarding a person's need for defences can lead to psychiatric casualties – estimated at about 9 per cent – when such techniques as Encounter are used with people who are psychologically disturbed or vulnerable (Lieberman, Yalom, & Miles, 1973).

There have been many new developments (Rowan, 1988). Most of them, as can be seen from the following brief descriptions, reflect an aspect of Freud's thinking that was developed by one of his early followers. Whether such developments will die out, replace established methods, or be integrated into the mainstream of psychotherapeutic practice remains to be seen. Their methods, however, have stirred up a lot of interest and have enabled some people, especially those not formally designated as patients, to feel more fully alive and authentic; and they may help others, stuck in conventional therapy, to get moving again through the expressive methods of the creative therapies, using art, music, movement, and drama (Jennings, 1983). Action techniques may be useful in the early stages of group therapy with people unused to talking about feelings and relationships; later, as these people develop verbal skills, they may give up the action methods and concentrate on the more spontaneous and free-flowing discussion of analytic group psychotherapy. Tillett (1991) provides a more recent view of the value of active and non-verbal psychotherapeutic approaches in psychiatry.

Many of these approaches are included in forms of humanistic and integrative psychotherapy and their training programmes combine psychodynamic approaches with aspects of Gestalt, transactional analysis, body work, spiritual-awareness, and so on. They expect some personal therapeutic experience of their trainees.

Encounter

Carl Rogers, the American evangelist turned academic psychologist, who developed non-directive counselling (p. 119), later became a leading figure in the Encounter movement. As he pointed out (Rogers, 1970), this grew out of the confluence of two streams. One started from the establishment of summer T-groups in Bethel, Maine, in 1947, under the posthumous influence of Kurt Lewin (p. 156). This led to the foundation of the National Training Laboratories, whose training groups in human relations skills have concentrated on helping managers and executives in industry to become aware of their interaction with others and the group dynamics inevitable in any organization. In the UK this work has been specially developed by the Tavistock Institute of Human Relations (Rice, 1965; Neumann, 2007). The other stream was started at about the same time when Rogers and his colleagues at the Counselling Centre of the University of Chicago set up brief but intensive training courses for would-be counsellors in the Veterans Administration Hospitals, which were then wrestling with the problems of servicemen returning from the Second World War. The trainees met for several hours a day to help their self-understanding and awareness of personal attitudes, which, as counsellors, might be self-defeating. The training combined cognitive and experiential learning which often led, beyond improvement in inter-personal communication and relationships, to personal growth and development. Sensitivity or T-groups of this type are now being used in helping students and staff in psychiatric and many other institutions and businesses to learn about themselves and develop their skills. Coming to terms with oneself and learning through experience are part of the psychotherapeutic process, for therapists as well as for patients.

Encounter and sensitivity groups usually have 8–18 members and are relatively unstructured. They choose their own goals, which in Encounter groups proper would be an experience of personal authenticity and honesty in relation to others; in a staff sensitivity group it would be exploration of feelings and problems encountered in working together. Usually there is a leader, whose task is to help in the creation of a climate of safety which facilitates expression of members' feelings and thoughts in their immediate interactions. In this climate, trust can develop out of the freedom to express real feelings, hostile as well as appreciative, so that each member becomes more accepting of himself and others in the 'here and now', intellectually, emotionally, and bodily, without considering the past. With reduction of defensiveness, communication opens up, and new ideas and innovations can be welcomed rather than feared. Individuals learn to discard their masks and discover their hidden selves.

This is really another way of describing the communicative processes of all psychotherapy (see Figure 7, p. 96). However, a certain sequence of events is characteristic of Encounter groups conducted in Rogers's non-directive way. After a period of 'milling around', in which people engage in defensive 'cocktail talk', a spontaneous structure emerges, usually after a member says something like 'shouldn't we introduce ourselves?'. People then do so, but avoid real personal expression and exploration. When personal feelings finally do emerge, they are often feelings of hostility towards another member or the leader. The ice having been broken in this way, members begin to express and explore personal concerns; they may expose feelings of anxiety and pain which they have never shown to another person. The discovery that fellow group members respond in a spontaneously therapeutic way facilitates the extension and deepening of these revelations. As people feel more fully accepted as they really are, rather than for their social front, they can risk removing their masks more completely. The feedback that individuals get, sometimes with vigour and unwelcome honesty, enables them to take fuller stock of themselves and their behaviour. The counterbalancing sympathy and acceptance, sometimes with help extended outside the group situation, allows the increasing expression of closeness, affection, and gratitude. The real emotional and intellectual contact in the 'here and now' is what is meant *by basic encounter*.

To facilitate this basic encounter, certain techniques are sometimes used, such as guided day-dreams or group fantasies, role-playing, and psychodrama (see below). Some Encounter leaders, such as Schutz (1967), emphasize physical and non-verbal experiences. For example, the need to make contact is explored by exercises in which everyone is blindfolded and has to find and explore each other only by touch. Competition is expressed by two people clasping hands and pushing each other. Trust and affection are learned and expressed by 'rocking and rolling', whereby one person at a time allows himself to fall into the arms of the others gathered around, who cradle and pass him around and rock him rhythmically. Rogers himself is distrustful of the over-ready use of such methods, preferring to use them only when they emerge spontaneously, and not as deliberate 'gimmicks'.

There is no doubt that people attain intense experiences in Encounter groups, and that some feel more acceptable and authentic as a result of the opportunity to be utterly frank about themselves, and learn a lot through the feedback from others. Some esoteric 'cultish' movements developed, most of which have now ceased, like Erhard Seminar Training (EST) which offered a two-weekend (60-hour) course known officially as 'The *est* Standard Training'. The purpose of EST was to allow participants to achieve, in a very brief time, a sense of personal transformation and enhanced power. The first course happened at the Jack Tar Hotel in San Francisco, California, in October 1971. Within a year, trainings were being held in New York City, and other major cities in the USA followed soon after. EST and I Am, and other similar movements, used a mixture of Encounter techniques, group support, and pressure, along with suggestion and directive leadership, to enhance people's self-esteem and sense of mastery of their lives. But frankness and a superficial change of attitude do not in themselves ensure the elucidation and working through of deeply unconscious conflicts. Moreover, there are some casualties among the psychologically disturbed and vulnerable, as already mentioned. Adverse effects may be commoner in groups run by more directive, provocative, and charismatic leaders, who may use them for their own gratification. There is some indication that the initial naive enthusiasm of the 1970s led to disillusionment and a more modest and realistic practice in growth potential centres such as Spectrum in London (Wibberley, 1988).

Psychodrama

Psychodrama was the creation of Jacob Moreno (1892–1974). He was born in Romania and brought up in Vienna, where he not only studied philosophy and medicine, but became deeply involved in the arts and edited a literary journal. During the early 1920s he led impromptu play groups with children in the parks of Vienna, and went on to develop an improvised 'Theatre of Spontaneity' (Moreno, 1948). Davies (1976) describes how Moreno discovered that an actress in this theatre, who usually played gentle, naive roles, behaved as a vicious person at home after marrying an actor friend of his. Moreno gave her more violent unsympathetic roles to play in the theatre, with the result that her behaviour at home became transformed for the better!

After emigrating to the USA in 1925, Moreno applied his ideas to the treatment of emotional disturbance. He used groups (he is said to have coined the term 'group psychotherapy') in which members could explore and enact the role conflicts which he saw as the essence of their neuroses; for example, a young woman may need to play the part of a gentle submissive female to please her father, and at the same time act as a confident assertive person to satisfy her mother's need for a successful achiever, a substitute for the son she never had. A common example nowadays is the role-conflict experienced by women who seek to be traditional wives and mothers while striving to achieve in competitive occupations. This is reminiscent of some of the techniques used in interpersonal therapy (see p. 222).

The therapist functions as a director, literally as in the theatre, and in some institutions a raised circular platform serves as a stage on which members of the group, usually 6–12 in number, meet for one and a half to two hours and take turns to enact their problems. The patient chosen as 'protagonist' will help the 'auxiliaries' to take up a role by describing the scene of his psychodrama in great detail. At times the director will instruct a member of the audience to step into the protagonist's role ('role reversal'), in order to foster identification and improvisation. Several people, from direct experience, can then join in the subsequent discussion about the protagonist's role-conflicts and how they might be overcome. The enactment and discussion, in a supportive and cohesive group atmosphere, aim to redefine the key conflict and allow the person to approach it from a number of different angles, until he achieves a sense of mastery. The theory and practice of psychodrama continues to develop (Kellermann, 1992), and psychodramatists play an active part in the International Association of Group Psychotherapy.

The techniques of psychodrama (Karp, Holmes, & Bradshaw-Tauvon, 1998) may sometimes be useful in the course of more analytic individual or group therapy, to help patients work through a block in expression or communication (Kellermann, 1987). They can be particularly helpful in a hospital setting for those who are inhibited or find verbal expression difficult (Jennings, 1987). They capitalize on the potential extroverted qualities in a patient, and probably appeal particularly to more extroverted therapists. In some psychiatric units, occupational therapists have developed special skills in these techniques, which become part of the range of creative therapies, like art and music therapy, used in helping patients to become more spontaneous and outgoing (Jennings, 1983). Related role-playing exercises have been used in family therapy (p. 176) and in training staff to appreciate what it feels like to be a patient or a member of a disturbed family. They have also been integrated into Gestalt therapy.

Gestalt

Gestalt therapy was developed by Frederick (Fritz) Perls (1893–1970). He was a man of great energy and restlessness, both a rebel and a synthesizer, who moved from Germany to South Africa, to New York, to the Esalen Institute in California, and finally to Vancouver, where he established a Gestalt community. Trained in psychoanalysis in Germany, he felt it had become inflexible, particularly in its emphasis on mental and verbal processes. Like Foulkes, the pioneer of group psychotherapy, Perls had worked with the neurologist Kurt Goldstein. The latter had extended the concepts of Gestalt psychology to motivation, and saw human personality not as an aggregate of discrete habits but as striving for unity.

Perls considered neurosis to be caused by splitting in the Gestalten, that is the 'wholes', which unify mind and body, or an individual and his environment. Anxiety would be the manifestation of the organism's struggle for unification, not, as in classical psychoanalysis, a reaction to an inner danger. However, like Freud, and unlike Rogers, he considered that neurosis was caused by warding off forbidden trends or blocked-off needs of the total organism: mind plus body (Perls, Hefferline, & Goodman, 1951). In making particular use of bodily signs of tension and defence, Gestalt therapists followed the lead of Wilhelm Reich, an early adherent of Freud's who later left the psychoanalytic fold (p. 215).

Gestalt therapy is practised individually or, more usually, in groups; but rather than making use of group processes, some individuals watch and participate vicariously on the sidelines while one of them is helped to be more whole through expanding his awareness of himself. Nor is transference encouraged; instead, dramatization is used to explore and express fuller awareness of the self in the 'here and now', utilizing certain rules and 'games'.

Levitsky and Perls (1972) identify several basic rules. *The principle of now*, whereby awareness is concentrated on current feelings – on the 'what' and the 'how', rather than the 'why' of remote causes – implies that if the past needs attention, it has to be brought into the present, not 'talked about'. (This is also true of analytic therapy, although in the latter the 'here and now' and 'there and then' are seen as in dynamic interaction; too much talk about either may be considered defensive.) *I and thou is* another principle followed in the struggle for immediacy; patients are urged to talk *to* rather than *at* others. *It* language is eschewed; that is, when people talk about parts of their body they have to translate 'it' into 'I' language: for example, 'my legs are tense' becomes 'I am tense'. Passive expressions like 'I am choked' are translated into the active 'I am choking myself'. *No gossiping* means that people should be addressed directly, not talked about as though they were absent. Statements are demanded when questions distance the questioner and evade direct confrontation.

Gestalt 'games' are techniques devised to foster immediacy of awareness. In *Dialogue*, the patient is asked to create a conversation between two split parts of himself (e.g. over-conscientious and resentfully compliant, or masculine and feminine parts) or between himself and some other significant person who can be imagined sitting on an empty chair in the room. The patient will play both roles in turn. *Making the rounds* involves the patient in replacing a general remark about the group by a process of addressing the remark individually to each in turn, or translating it into more emotional body language (e.g. caressing, or giving vent to hostility). *Unfinished business* refers to bringing into the treatment situation, and facing directly there, unresolved feelings from the patient's earlier life, for example about parents or siblings. In *Exaggeration* a patient is asked to act out the feeling he complains of in accentuated form, and in *Reversal* to enact its opposite.

Gestalt therapy thus aims at an intense immediacy of awareness. Words tend to be distrusted as defensive 'bullshitting' (a characteristic phrase), and feelings and bodily expression tend to be regarded as more reliable. While psychoanalysts, too, watch out for wordy defensiveness in their own practice, they would nevertheless regard total reliance on immediacy and feeling as equally defensive and misleading. Perhaps in response to this danger, some Gestalt therapists have attempted to integrate such techniques with aspects of intersubjective self-psychology and 'dialogic therapy'. They aim to promote greater depth and authenticity in what they call 'person-to-person' relatedness (Hycner & Jacobs, 1995).

Bioenergetics

This has been called a 'biofunctional therapy', based on the assumption that neurosis involves interference with man's fundamentally biological nature, and that therapy should aim to remove the results of such interference. This had been Freud's original view of one type of neurosis that he called actual neurosis, based on his first anxiety theory (p. 24). Incomplete discharge of libido was thought to be converted into anxiety through unnatural sexual practices such as coitus interruptus. Wilhelm Reich (1897–1957), one of the original followers of Freud, became especially interested in the way that bodily tension and posture – 'character armour' – could reflect and maintain psychological character defences (Reich, 1933). Often these have to be confronted and interpreted before any repressed feelings and fantasies can emerge. Such ideas became part of psychoanalysis and influenced Anna Freud's (1936) view of defence mechanisms (p. 30). However, Reich eventually left the psychoanalytic fold as his own notions developed a more and more revolutionary flavour, equating the overthrow of Fascism with the overcoming of repressions which prevent the attainment of full 'orgastic potency' and sexual release. Perhaps because of his revolutionary zeal, Reich had the unique distinction of being expelled from both the Communist Party and the International Psychoanalytical Association (Rycroft, 1971). Reich even came to believe that he could record and store (in the famous Orgone box) the 'sexual energy' flowing freely within and between people.

Essentially, Reich seemed to be reverting to one-body psychology and to Freud's first anxiety theory. He ignored the importance of intrapsychic life and object relations. He adopted an active confrontational style to challenge a person's character defences. Interpreting a fixed smile or military bearing would sometimes release a flood of dammed-up emotion (e.g. rage or passive yearning for affection). He introduced physical techniques, such as massage and attention to breathing, to help the thawing of frozen postures and attitudes. This is a return to Freud's early cathartic methods for the release of 'strangulated affects' (Breuer & Freud, 1895) or even Freud's own early use of massage to promote free association. Catharsis still plays an important part in more orthodox therapies, perhaps most commonly when helping someone to ventilate previously unexpressed grief.

Reich's work has been continued as 'bioenergetic therapy' by his former pupil Lowen (1967), who has corrected some of the excessive physical bias of Reich's methods by using more varied physical exercises and verbal forms of psychotherapy, including group work. A good account of recent developments is given by Whitfield (1988) and by Boadella (1988). Many current 'body work' therapies, such as yoga and autogenic training, aim to correct the flow and balance of bodily forces and their integration with mental ones.

Primal therapy

The Primal Scream is the name of a book by Arthur Janov (1970) describing a theory and treatment of neurosis. He believed that all neurosis is an attempt to ward off mental pain which has been inflicted on the infant from outside and creates tension leading to secondary defences. Like Freud, he sees the neurotic as someone struggling with unresolved problems from the past. But he does not allow, as Freud later did, for the interaction between actual events and intrapsychic fantasies based on the child's instinctual wishes. Like Reich, who inflated Freud's early idea of 'actual neurosis' and the harm that can be caused by an unhealthy sexual life, Janov takes as the form of his treatment the discharge of intense emotion. In primal therapy, this is the 'scream' generated in infancy by intense pain, but not expressed sufficiently in an adequately supporting relationship, and consequently sealed off.

The pain experienced by the child as a sense of being intensely hurt or wronged has recently been traced by Janov and others, including Laing, to what they regard as the first trauma, that of birth. Freud (1926a) himself had proposed that the 'trauma' of birth was the prototype of traumatic neuroses, as opposed to those caused by internal conflict. This idea was exaggerated by another of Freud's early followers, Otto Rank (1929), who thought that the sudden expulsion from the protecting environment of the womb constituted a trauma which was the precursor of *all* later experiences of anxiety, and believed that many patients were seeking to re-experience their birth. The obstetrician Leboyer (1977) drew attention to the insensitivity with which children are often received into the world in hospital, with bright lights, clashing noises, and rapid removal from their mothers. He reintroduced quieter and less traumatic methods, which include putting mother and child into immediate skin contact. While still controversial, these ideas have a natural appeal to many obstetricians and paediatricians, and are nearer to the normal practice of most midwives doing home deliveries. There have been reports that minimization of the traumatic separation of mother and infant, and their early reintroduction, foster subsequent 'bonding' between them. Perhaps this seemingly romantic movement is no more than a timely reassertion of human values in the face of excessive hospital technology. It is also part of women's demand to have more say and control of how they give birth, a practical fruit of the Women's Movement.

Giving so much importance to birth trauma seems too reductionist; after all, everyone has to be born, but only some develop neuroses. Yet there are patients with a history of early trauma who experience a need to scream in therapy, and, in a regressed state, some do appear to experience birth-like bodily sensations. Although there have been reports of dramatic cures from severe neurosis and psychosomatic states following guided re-experience of birth (Lake, 1978), we cannot take them as proof of a causal connection; suggestion in a state of intense arousal and emotional vulnerability can have powerful effects.

In Janov's hands, primal therapy involved a full-time intensive initial phase lasting three weeks. This was followed by return to normal life, whilst continuing treatment for six months in a 'Primal Group', which provided a supportive background in which each individual sought repetition of his own primal experiences.

The more recent developments in theory and practice are well described by Rowan (1988), who makes the link between the catharsis and integration of deep affect in primal therapy with shamanistic practices and ancient Greek theatre.

Other therapies

In addition to the forms of therapy already described, all deriving historically from some elements of psychoanalysis (see Figure 10), several others have recently gained some prominence. We cannot fully do them justice, or include them in Figure 10, but will say something brief about them to extend our overview of current forms of therapy that have at least peripheral connections with the main forms of dynamic psychotherapy described in this book.

Hypnotherapy. It will be recalled (p. 10) that Freud first used hypnosis in an attempt to remove neurotic symptoms and later to release repressed memories and ideas by putting his patients into a light trance. He soon relinquished deliberate suggestion and replaced hypnosis by the technique of free association. Others, however, continued to investigate hypnotic phenomena (Heap, 1988) and to use it for therapeutic ends with neurotic, behavioural, and addictive problems, to help in the management of psychosomatic disorders and of pain in obstetrics and dentistry (Kroger, 1963; Erickson & Rossi, 1979), and as an aid to analytic psychotherapy (Karle & Boys, 1996). Good hypnotic subjects not only attain a heightened susceptibility to suggestion, but under its influence appear to 'regress' to earlier periods of their lives, and recall traumatic events, often with considerable emotional catharsis and vividness. They can then be reassured, 'forgiven', and offered explanations of a link between these experiences and their current difficulties. This can bring relief which, even if only short term, can break a cycle of symptoms and distress. The relationship of patient to therapist needs to be submissive and trusting. The power of transference is used in hypnosis rather than revealed by exploration and interpretation as in analytic psychotherapy. The practice of hypnosis as part of psychotherapy has been confined to the periphery of orthodox medicine, dentistry, obstetrics, and psychiatry. In this country, however, the British Society of Medical and Dental Hypnosis has continued as a focus for professional development, and there are now a few training bodies which are attempting to organize and control work in this field, represented in a separate Hypno-psychotherapy section within the UKCP.

Neuro-linguistic programming (NLP). An influential figure in hypnotherapy has been the powerful personality of Milton Erickson (Rossi, O'Ryan, & Sharp, 1998), whose language patterns, like those of other charismatic therapists (Perls, Satir), were studied by Bandler and Grinder (1981) to form the therapeutic system known as NLP (O'Connor & Seymour, 1990). This explores the models of the world that people create based on the pre-verbal raw material of their dominant perceptual mode – visual, auditory, or kinaesthetic-emotional. Hypnosis is used to varying extents by different NLP practitioners to help clients change their restricted models to more flexible and adaptive ones. Practitioners use close observation of sensory cues – eye movements, breathing, skin colour changes, head nods, and so on – to determine the deeper, unconscious responses of clients to questions and suggestions in establishing rapport, and in guiding themselves towards what is 'right' for the client.

Personal construct therapy (PCT) engages with patients to discover their maladapative ways of construing themselves and the world, using more cognitive and traditional verbal methods than does NLP. However, practitioners of these two types of therapy have recently joined together to form a separate section, Experiential Constructivist Therapies, within the UKCP. Both approaches have what they describe as an equality of interest between therapist and client, and emphasize the 'here and now' and 'continuing processes of reconstruction' in helping patients to free themselves from the 'prisons' of their past. However, while NLP requires a knowledge of well-developed techniques and interventions, in PCT techniques for helping the process of reconstruction are used more empirically. PCT uses the personal construct psychology of George Kelly (Fransella & Thomas, 1988), who devised the *repertory grid*. This studies the cognitive constructs underlying our evaluation of significant figures in our lives, past and present. Repertory grids have also been used by research-orientated psychotherapists to study transference problems, identification, and sense of identity (Ryle, 1982).

Mention will be made of three other approaches – psychosynthesis, co-counselling, and transactional analysis – which contrast with the detailed cognitive analysis and directiveness of the methods described so far in this section. All are represented in the Humanistic and Integrative section of the UKCP.

Psychosynthesis aims to be more creative and spiritual. Founded by Roberto Assagioli (1888–1974), an Italian psychiatrist known to both Freud and Jung, it is close to Jungian analytic psychology but influenced by existential and humanistic philosophies. Assagioli saw both the problems *and* the potential of the personality and of the human race as contained in the various areas of the unconscious. These include what he called 'the lower unconscious', the dynamic unconscious of psychoanalysis; 'the middle unconscious', approximating to the pre-conscious of psychoanalysis; and 'the higher unconscious' of transpersonal and spiritual awareness, including Jung's archetypes (p. 130).

The methods used are discursive and exploratory, looking at *subselves* or parts of the personality. Free drawing and writing are employed to symbolize deeper aspects of the self. These are rarely used in adult psychoanalysis, with notable exceptions (e.g. Milner, 1969). The emphasis that psychosynthesis puts on the third level of therapeutic work – the 'evolutionary unfoldment' of the problem – is also used by psychoanalysts, but less explicitly. (It is implicit in therapeutic regression in the transference (p. 70), *reculer pour mieux sauter*, and the interpretation of neurotic symptoms as compromise expressions of underlying strivings.) To psychosynthesists, therapeutic change involves working to actualize potentials in a higher integration and identity (Hardy & Whitmore, 1988), which is another way of talking about sublimation. In emphasizing creative potential they could be seen to counter a tendency to pathologize and stigmatize the patient, and downplay human destructive potential, including that in the therapeutic relationship.

Co-counselling carries mistrust of the asymmetry of power in the therapist–patient relationship to the extreme. The roles of counsellor and client are alternated. Founded in the 1950s by Harvey Jackins, it has spread from the USA to Europe, and was developed in Britain by John Heron at the Human Potential Research Unit at the University of Surrey. Like Gestalt, bioenergetics, and primal therapy described earlier, it aims to change repetitive developments and neurotic patterns of behaviour by cathartic methods, but claims evolutionary and learning theory perspectives. Existential tensions cause *primary* distress, accumulation of which leads to interpersonal tensions and hurt, or *secondary* distress.

In alternating pairs, those in the client role are encouraged to express their distress, and every cue is taken as an opportunity to facilitate more discharge. Those in the counsellor role facilitate this by showing approval, respect, confidence, even love; they should also be emotionally expressive and aware of and working on their own chronic patterns (Evison & Horobin, 1988). This could be seen as a highlighting or condensation of things that happen over time in psychoanalytic psychotherapy – both individual and group – which allows much more time for release and exploration. Although the psychoanalytic dyad do not change places, analysands are testing out their analysts who put themselves in the analysand's shoes. They do this by empathic identification and self-analysis, notably by attending to their countertransference (p. 79). In an analytic group, all members function as therapists to an increasing extent, as their insight increases and they are able to attend to the distress of others as much as their own. Interestingly, the term *group analysis* was first used by the American psychoanalyst Trigant Burrow, who in the teens of the twentieth century exchanged places on couch and chair with his student Clarence Shields.

Transactional analysis, referred to in Part I with regard to Models of the Mind and Therapeutic Relationships (pp. 59 and 68), is directly interactional and concentrates on restoring self-esteem, as indicated by two seminal books of the 1960s: Eric Berne's (1966) *Games People Play* and Thomas Harris's (1967) *I'm OK – You're OK*. Initiated by Berne (1910–1970), who had trained as a psychoanalyst, it has spread worldwide to influence humanistic psychotherapy.

Transactional analysis concentrates on the ego and social context, and is more indebted to Adler than to Freud. Typically it is practised in short-term groups of, say, 10 sessions. A focal contract is decided on at the first session, and apart from discerning each other's ego states of parent, adult, and child, and how they react with others, it emphasizes positive environmental responses ('strokes') to counter feelings of inferiority, rather than working on infantile conflicts or the repressed unconscious. Regression is discouraged, and transactions become playful 'games' which aim to unhook people from maladaptive patterns. Education involves a series of 'injunctions' and 'strokes'.

In recent years attempts have been made to integrate trans-actional analysis with intrapsychic dynamics and interpersonal behaviour patterns within a humanistic and existential framework (Clarkson, 1992). This mixing of therapies has become common and has blurred the boundaries between a number of therapies. It will be apparent to the reader that each therapy, at least in its early development, picks up and inflates one of the elements of Freud and of mainstream analytic psychotherapy, while excluding others. In Figure 10 we have attempted to show the derivation from Freud's ideas of most of the forms of therapy described in this book. They would not necessarily be acknowledged by those mentioned, nor do they always imply an apostolic succession of analyst and analysand. The 'family tree' illustrates our contention, expressed in the Intro-duction, that all forms of dynamic therapy derive from the work of Freud and psychoanalysis.

FURTHER THERAPIES

In this section we consider a variety of therapeutic movements which have emphasized, in a particular way, one aspect of therapy that has been present to some degree in classical psychoanalytic therapy, or was especially emphasized at some time in its devel-opment. These movements have attempted to correct what the proponents of each saw as a one-sided bias and limitation in psychoanalysis.

Interpersonal psychotherapy (IPT)

IPT developed out of the interpersonal tradition of psychoanalysis as espoused by Sullivan and Fromm-Reichmann (see p. 176). Originally conceived as a treatment for depression, it has now been adapted for use with other problems such as post-traumatic stress disorder and recently for personality disorder. We will give only a short description of the therapy here and the interested reader is referred to the extensive outline by Klerman et al. (1996) and to the more recent clinician's guide by Stuart and Robertson (2003).

IPT for depression is a brief (16 sessions), focused, structured, time-limited therapy that emphasizes the current interpersonal

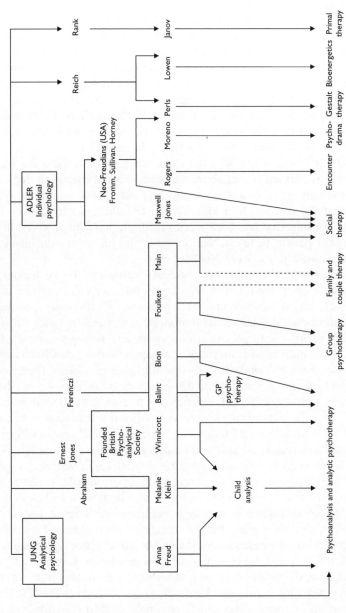

Figure 10

relations of the patient. Symptoms of depression are seen as being generated within an interpersonal context and, as such, to be amenable to change through transformation of relationships. To this extent it recognizes the importance of relationships in a person's well-being but does not place them at the centre of the treatment process in the way that dynamic therapy does. IPT does not harness the relationship of the patient and therapist through transference in order to bring about change. Focus is on the current life relationships of an individual and how they may be developed to improve mood. We tend to feel better either when we do things with others or when we help others to do things with us.

In IPT, like other brief therapies (see p. 141), a focus for treatment is formed in collaboration with the patient. Four foci are described: *grief*, *disputes*, *deficit*, and *role transition*. *Grief* is an inevitable reaction to a loss and the IPT therapist focuses on the relationship that has been lost to facilitate mourning, whilst helping the patient to re-establish interests and other relationships that can substitute for what has been lost.

Disputes are a common cause of depression. To be locked in persistent argument with a significant other, such as a partner, both lowers mood and perpetuates depression. IPT therapists consider interpersonal disputes to be at different stages and try to identify the stage in order to target therapy appropriately. Renegotiation implies that the individual is aware of the dispute and is actively trying to bring about a resolution. If no resolution appears likely, frustration develops and eventually the dispute leads to an impasse in which there is a smouldering resentment. A cold relationship results. Finally, the dispute may lead to an irretrievable breakdown. In each of these situations IPT focuses on the interpersonal relationship and how 'non-reciprocal role' expectations interfere with change. The term 'non-reciprocal role' describes a situation in which an expectation of someone else is not met by that person conforming to the assigned role. For example, a mother may both want and expect her adolescent daughter to confide in her about her worries, just as she did in her own mother, but her daughter feels that in order to grow up and become independent she has to work things out for herself. Such non-reciprocal roles may become evident in therapy itself: for example, the patient expecting something from the therapist that the therapist cannot provide. Under these circumstances the IPT therapist may point out the transference repetition to illustrate how the individual tries to insist on specific roles for others.

A focus on *deficit* implies that the individual has few, if any, relationships and this makes it problematic for a therapy which focuses on relationships outside therapy to help someone change. Under these circumstances the only relationship a patient may have is with the therapist and so transference may be used to help him develop an understanding of how to develop a social network outside.

Finally, a focus on *role transitions* is common in IPT. We have already emphasized aspects of the human life cycle (see p. 46) and the most frequently encountered role transitions occur as we move from one aspect of life to another – adolescence to adulthood, leaving home, becoming a mother or father, changing careers, becoming unemployed, retiring, growing old, and so on. These are normal events but sometimes an individual can feel he is failing in his new role or not adapting in a constructive way, and so becomes depressed. In IPT careful evaluation of the old role and its meaning to the individual is undertaken whilst exploring the advantages and disadvantages of the new role.

In summary, IPT takes a detailed look at the ways in which an individual both sees himself in relation to others and how he uses his 'personal network' constructively. It does this within a framework of a focus that is formed in collaboration with the patient. A number of research studies have looked at its efficacy, particularly in depression, showing it to be an effective therapy (see p. 264). This has led to questions about which patients do better with which therapy. There is an indication that patients who are single and not co-habiting with a partner do better with IPT than with other therapies (Barber & Muenz, 1996). This is discussed further in the sections on Selection and Outcome and Research (see p. 264). IPT has been adapted for use in groups and there is increasing evidence of its effectiveness in conditions other than depression – for example, post-traumatic stress disorder (Bleiberg & Markowitz, 2005; Krupnick, Green, Stockton, *et al.*, 2008) – and for different patient populations – for example, adolescents (Mufson, Weissman, Moreau, *et al.*, 1999; Mufson & Sills, 2006).

Conversational model or psychodynamic-interpersonal therapy

The conversational model of therapy was developed by Hobson (1985), an analytical psychologist. He sought to design a therapy that had a greater interpersonal and collaborative focus than traditional psychoanalytic therapy, which he saw as a one-sided and asymmetrical relationship. He drew on psychodynamic principles but added some humanistic and interpersonal elements. Originally a conversational model, because the aim was to develop a 'mutual feeling language' and a relationship of 'aloneness–togetherness', it has become known as *psychodynamic-interpersonal therapy* (PI) following its use in research trials (see p. 265) and perhaps because that name states more clearly its fundamental assumptions.

The model has been conceptualized as consisting of seven different, but integrated, components. These are summarized by Guthrie (1999). Although many of these form part of the non-specific aspects of therapy, together they form a discrete and definable therapy that is relatively easy to learn and is understandable to patients. Further, the therapy can be tailored to specific conditions such as depression and somatization (Guthrie, Creed, Dawson, *et al.*, 1991).

The seven components are: exploratory rationale, shared understanding, staying with feelings, focus on difficult feelings, gaining insight, sequencing interventions, and making changes. Developing an *exploratory rationale* requires the therapist to identify the patient's main interpersonal difficulties. Emotional symptoms are linked to the interpersonal difficulties and the therapist explores a rationale in conjunction with the patient that expressly links the emotional state with the problems. Together they seek to identify how the problems may have precipitated the symptoms, continue to contribute to them, or perpetuate them. This interpersonal focus forms the core of the therapy and shows a clear relationship to interpersonal therapy (IPT) developed separately in the USA (see above).

Shared understanding refers to a process by which the therapist and patient clarify what the patient is really experiencing and feeling. In order to do this a language of mutuality is developed by using the relationship between patient and therapist. The therapist expresses a more active involvement than is often recommended in psychoanalytic therapy but many of the interventions are similar, with the use of metaphor and interpretation. Interpretations are construed as tentative hypotheses and offered with less conviction than interpretations in classical psychoanalytic therapy. However, there may be little difference nowadays since interpretations in psychoanalytic therapy are often seen as hypotheses rather than veridical statements.

Staying with feelings requires sensitivity on the part of the therapist, who needs to help the patient recreate difficult feelings within the session. It is important that feelings are not discussed in the abstract or as something that only occurred in the past, but as really experienced in the 'here and now'. A *focus on difficult feelings* may occur at this point, but more often refers to situations in which the affect is hidden and the therapist needs to focus actively on the feeling. A patient may express a particular emotion but not be aware of it, or alternatively not feel something when it would be expected. This can be pointed out to the patient by contrasting the verbal and non-verbal cues, for example, or by highlighting the discrepancy between the content of the story and the expressed affect.

Gaining insight refers to an increased understanding of the present problems in terms of the patient's past and current relationships. Just as in psychoanalytic therapy, links are made between the patient's childhood and adult relationships. The patient–therapist transference relationship is drawn upon to focus this process and links are made between feelings that emerge within the session and those that occur outside the therapy. It is important that these links or explanatory hypotheses are only made after the emotional base of the symptoms and their interpersonal context has been established. This is known as *sequencing of interventions*. The use of transference in such an explicit way differentiates PI from IPT. However, *both* recommend that the therapist acknowledges *change* in an explicit way throughout therapy.

PI may be structured either as a short-term or a long-term therapy, although more often it is limited to 8–16 sessions. It is important that therapy is sequenced carefully but that the therapist works flexibly. Initial sessions establish the interpersonal links of the patient's symptoms and identify the main problem areas by exploring carefully the relationships of the patient, agreeing a focus, and establishing a symptom history. Intermediate sessions may explicitly use transference to explore hidden feelings, stay with feelings, and link change in symptoms with interpersonal events. This is followed by final sessions in which ending may be linked to earlier losses, negative feelings are scrutinized, gains are explicated, and ways in which the patient can continue working on himself afterwards are discussed.

It is obvious that PI lies between traditional psychoanalytic therapy and IPT, and that both PI and IPT have more in common with psychodynamic principles than with cognitive psychology. Both take an interpersonal or relationship focus and see emotions as central to human function. This is in stark contrast to the origins of cognitive-behavioural therapy, which initially placed cognition at the centre.

Cognitive-behavioural therapy (CBT)

Cognitive-behavioural therapy (CBT) is a therapy that has been developed by practitioners dissatisfied with both psychoanalytic therapy and behaviour therapy. A. T. Beck (1976), himself a psychoanalyst, became disappointed with the results of treating depressed patients with psychoanalytic therapy. He recognized that many depressed patients seemed to concentrate on thoughts that showed recurrent themes: for example, of being a failure. These cognitive themes were taken up as being part of the primary disorder. This was in contrast to hitherto when such thought processes were regarded as secondary to emotional change.

Similar disenchantment occurred within the world of behaviour therapy, the limitations of which were becoming increasingly apparent. In behaviour therapy symptoms are seen as maladaptive patterns of behaviour which have been learned – something akin to bad habits – and not part of a complex psychological system whose final pathway of expression is a symptom. Behaviour therapy aims at correction of 'habits' and may be particularly effective in monosymptomatic phobias. But too great an emphasis on behavioural components of psychiatric illness fails to encapsulate the complexity of most mental illness, particularly by avoiding less conscious aspects of motivation (see the case illustration on p. 107). So behavioural techniques have been combined with newly developed cognitive interventions in CBT, and their practitioners are jointly represented in the Behavioural Cognitive Therapy section of the UKCP.

Originally CBT failed to take into account unconscious processes but over the past decade there has been increasing recognition that many aspects of psychological function take place outside consciousness and these have to be taken account of in treatment. Of course there is not an acceptance of the unconscious as it is viewed within psychoanalytic therapy (see p. 14), but there is a realization that a simple focus on manifest behaviour and conscious thought is inadequate.

The general approach in CBT is strikingly similar to psychoanalytic therapy. Sessions are carefully structured, a relationship is developed with the patient, and regard is given to empathic understanding, careful listening, and formation of a therapeutic alliance (see p. 68). In contrast to psychoanalytic therapy the approach is active, with the therapist taking an expert role and having specific aims. These include a detailed analysis of the patient's difficulty by focusing on ways of thinking and their relationship to symptoms, a formulation of the problem for the patient to test in everyday life, and an identification of the antecedents, behaviour, and consequences of the actions. These aims are achieved through daily monitoring of thoughts to establish automatic thoughts, and through homework assignments, for example identifying triggers for particular thought patterns. Sometimes patients are asked to identify a whole series of thoughts and to map them into a ladder or hierarchy so that it will be obvious to a patient very early on that an anxiety attack may develop. This may enable an attack to be anticipated and prevented. In some ways this is a practical example of psychic determinism, in which all psychological states are seen as being preceded by and containing within them traces of earlier psychological processes.

These basic techniques have been developed for different disorders but the principles remain the same. An automatic thought in depression may be 'I am a failure'. Once it is established that this relies on a basic assumption that 'anything I do is useless', the therapist helps the patient look at the evidence for the thought and may focus on the advantages and disadvantages of holding such a view. Thus the approach is vigorous rather than contemplative and often is considered as collaborative. However it may become overly prescriptive in inexperienced hands. CBT probably has the most extensive evidence base of all the therapies and has become the therapy of choice in NHS services within the IAPT schemes (see p. 114). It is not within the scope of this book to review the research literature but the interested reader is referred to Roth and Fonagy's (2005) excellent summary of the research about the use of psychological therapies in the different psychiatric disorders.

It is interesting that in its early stages CBT differentiated itself from psychoanalytic therapy in a firm and rigid manner. It was as if independence could only be achieved by disavowal of the past, and separation had to be complete, threatening a schism between emotion and cognition. More recently there has been a rapprochement, as if adolescent conflicts have now been worked through and dialogue can occur with a recognition that the dynamically orientated parent therapy not only may have something to say but also may have something to learn from the new 'kid on the block'. As in all good families, it is to be hoped that constructive co-existence and cross-fertilization of ideas will result. Already there is an understanding in CBT of a rational system of processing information and an experiential system that is emotionally driven (Epstein, 1994). In psychoanalytic theory there is recognition that thought processes are not solely emotionally dependent and some dynamically determined change is itself cognitively processed. CBT has become more interpersonally based, with recognition of emotionally based 'hot cognition' as central to treatment. Thus emotion has returned to CBT and cognition to psychodynamic therapy. We are of the view that the distinction between a cognitive treatment and psychodynamic therapy is often difficult to establish even though the practitioner may be working within a different framework.

It was inevitable that two major therapies such as psychodynamic therapy and CBT would themselves generate further therapies attempting to integrate elements of both. In this way cognitive-analytic therapy was born.

Cognitive-analytic therapy (CAT)

Ryle (1982, 1990) first developed cognitive-analytic therapy (CAT) in an attempt to integrate both cognitive and psychoanalytic ideas. Since then, CAT has evolved into an emerging integrated theory restating aspects of psychoanalytic theory in cognitive terms, whilst developing a clear outline of clinical practice. It is cognitive in that some of the work in therapy takes place at an intellectual level, recognizing that self-awareness and conscious choice are central to change. In practice, self-monitoring and homework may be used. It is analytic in that it is concerned with internal objects which, as in psychoanalytic theory, are seen as being derived from early experience, modified in fantasy, and as influencing our present relationships. In practice, transference and countertransference inform the therapy and there is a focus on relationships rather than cognitions. Some attention is given to working conflicts through by repeatedly addressing those mechanisms that preclude healthy adaptation.

The emphasis in CAT on the relationships of the patient was present right from the beginning. Ryle suggested a *procedural sequence model* (PSM) in which intentional acts or the enactment of roles in relationships were governed by repetitive sequences of mental, behavioural, and environmental processes. So an individual may perceive someone as being friendly and appraise the situation in terms of knowledge, values, personal wishes, and predicted outcome. The relationship or interaction is then put into practice and the consequences evaluated, leading to a confirmation or disconfirmation of the original perception and expectation. It is at the appraisal stage that internal object relationships and conflict may govern the actions of the individual and how the perception is acted upon. In effect the model takes into account the interplay between *internal* and *external* processes, both of which govern our relationships.

This rather mechanistic approach was developed further in the idea of *reciprocal role procedures* (RRP). These are seen as being based on early relationships. The infant learns to respond to or to elicit a caretaker's actions and reactions, and to translate these into other relationships. A repertoire of reciprocal roles is built up and elaborated, and these structure all future relationships. They influence the types of people to whom we are attracted, since we want partners who have complementary roles. Each of us has the capacity to enact both roles (Freud, 1914) and we may enact them within ourselves: for example, by treating one's body as not part of oneself. It will be obvious to the reader that this idea is akin to contemporary psychoanalytic theory and self-psychology (see p. 44) but the difference in CAT is that the reciprocal roles are carefully mapped out in therapy and not only explored within the transference relationship. RRPs form the core of a reformulation and they are drawn out with the patient using loops and arrows, to show the recurring shifts between positions. Neurotic procedures may support or maintain RRPs by preventing modification of ineffective or harmful roles. These are often called traps, dilemmas, and snags. *Traps* refer to the way in which individuals reinforce negative beliefs and assumptions by acting in ways that elicit the negative belief. For example, a low self-esteem trap may be a feeling that if I go to a party no one will speak to me. I attend the party feeling hostile and defensive and respond to approaches in a surly manner, which in turn means that people do not speak to me for long. The negative belief of myself is confirmed. *Dilemmas* are conflictual. Choices are seen as polarized between two alternatives (false dichotomization) – if I get involved I will be hurt; if I stay alone I will be lonely. *Snags* lead to an inappropriate abandonment of personal aims as a result of a true or false prediction or perception of negative outcome – if I go out with my boyfriend my mother will think that I am abandoning her and will get ill or make me feel guilty.

These complex reformulations have superseded the PSM and form the *procedural sequence object-relations model* (PSORM). This is worked on throughout therapy, which is usually brief, lasting 12–16 sessions. Towards the end of therapy the therapist asks the patient to write a letter to bring to the following session describing his experience of therapy, what he has got out of it, what he has or has not got out of it, and where it leaves him. The therapist does the same and in the final session these letters are exchanged, read, and discussed. The letters provide an opportunity to express gratitude, disappointment, and anger at termination as well as forming a concrete summary of the work achieved and possible problems ahead. They also act as a 'transitional object' (see p. 137).

CAT continues to develop and has now been put into practice for the treatment of specific relationship disorders such as borderline personality. The interested reader is referred to Ryle (1995) for a more detailed outline about present developments, and to Ryle (1997) for a discussion of the treatment in borderline personality disorder.

PERSONALITY DISORDER

So far, in Part II of this book, we have covered different forms of psychodynamic treatments along with more recent developments of other therapies. In this section we will discuss the treatment of personality disorder simply because practitioners of dynamic therapy have laid claim to the idea that the process of therapy not only helps to reduce symptoms but also helps someone change their personality. This begs the question of what personality and its dysfunction actually is. Central to the concept of personality is how an individual functions within himself and how he relates to others. These two features are clearly the focus of dynamic therapy, with its technical emphasis on the relationship between the therapist and the patient, so it may indeed be a suitable treatment for a person who has problems relating to others and difficulties in how he feels about himself.

It is obvious that we all have a personality. We have a sense of who we are and others think of us as a particular type of person. The view we have of ourselves is not necessarily the same as the perspective that others have of us – we might think we are kindly whilst others see us as a little harsh, we might view our primary characteristic as modest whilst others see it as ambitious, and so on. What is being described here are our personality traits, which are often apparent in how we react to others and how we behave in social situations. There are some traits or factors that seem to be common between us all and these are known as the 'big five'. The five-factor model of personality consists of neuroticism, openness, extraversion, agreeableness, and conscientiousness (Costa & Widiger, 1994).

Neuroticism can be defined as an enduring tendency to experience negative emotional states. These individuals worry, experiencing such feelings as anxiety, anger, guilt, and depression. *Openness* involves active imagination, aesthetic sensitivity, attentiveness to inner feelings, preference for variety, and intellectual curiosity. *Extroverts* tend to be gregarious, assertive, and interested in seeking out excitement, whereas introverts tend to be more reserved, less outgoing, but are also marked by a richer inner world. They are not necessarily loners but they tend to have smaller circles of friends and are less likely to thrive on making new social contacts. Introverts are less likely to seek stimulation from others, enjoying their own thoughts and imagination. *Agreeableness* is a tendency to be pleasant and accommodating in social situations. Individuals are empathetic, considerate, friendly, generous, and helpful. People scoring low on agreeableness place self-interest above getting along with others. They are generally less concerned with others' well-being, report less empathy, and are therefore less likely to go out of their way to help others. Their scepticism about other people's motives may cause them to be suspicious and unfriendly. People very low on agreeableness have a tendency to be manipulative in their social relationships and are more likely to compete than to cooperate. *Conscientiousness* is the trait of being painstaking and careful. It includes such elements as self-discipline, carefulness, thoroughness, organization, deliberation (the tendency to think carefully before acting), and need for achievement. Inevitably these individuals are generally hard working and reliable. When taken to an extreme, they may also be workaholics, perfectionists, and compulsive in their behaviour. People who are low on conscientiousness are not necessarily lazy, but they tend to be more laid back, less goal oriented, and less driven by success.

We all tend to have a balance of these traits and it is only when one becomes dominant that personality function becomes distorted and we are considered to have a personality disorder. In a *personality disorder* the constellation of personality traits has become inflexible and maladaptive, leading to difficulties in work or interpersonal relations, and often causing subjective distress. This results in people with personality disorder presenting to services either because they become unhappy within themselves or because other people become unhappy with them. In general those people who internalize their feelings (e.g. people who self-harm) complain to the doctor about their relationships and difficulties, whilst those who externalize their problems (e.g. by being aggressive to others) are more likely to be referred for treatment than to request it.

A number of personality types have been described and now form part of diagnostic systems, of which the best known is the DSM – the *Diagnostic and Statistical Manual of Mental Disorders* by the American Psychiatric Association. An attempt was made to identify personality prototypes based primarily on clinical and academic experience and opinion. A significant number of such disorders were described and operational criteria for the diagnosis defined. The best known personality disorders are borderline personality disorder (BPD) and antisocial personality disorder (ASPD). People with BPD tend to internalize their problems and experience considerable subjective distress, which leads them to seek help. Descriptively they have difficulties in relationships, which are often volatile because they fear being abandoned; they experience problems with how they feel about themselves, leading them to self-harm or to try to kill themselves; they suffer rapidly fluctuating emotions which easily get out of control so they become inconsolable or inappropriately angry; and they are prone to oversensitivity to others, resulting in paranoid responses. In contrast, people with ASPD tend to externalize their problems and experience less internal distress. They do not conform to social expectation, are deceitful and lack remorse, fail to plan ahead, and are often irritable and aggressive. This leads them to get into fights, often with disregard for their own or others' safety. Not surprisingly, people with ASPD are found in large numbers in prison populations as they get into trouble with the law.

Psychodynamic therapy for personality disorder

Surprisingly, until relatively recently the natural history of personality disorder had not been systematically studied. Several major cohort follow-along studies have yielded surprising data concerning the rate of symptomatic remissions in a disorder that was supposed to have a life-long course (Cohen, Crawford, Johnson, et al., 2005). Taking just one dramatic example over a 10-year follow-along period, 88 per cent of those initially diagnosed with BPD appeared to remit in the sense of no longer meeting diagnostic criteria for BPD for two years (Zanarini, Frankenburg, Hennen, et al., 2006). The symptoms that remit most readily irrespective of treatment appear to be the acute ones such as parasuicide and self-injury, which are the most likely to trigger psychotherapeutic intervention. Temperamental symptoms, such as angry feelings and acts, distrust and suspicion, abandonment concerns, and emotional instability, appear to resolve far more slowly. They are associated with ongoing psychosocial impairment and are not specific to the diagnosis of BPD. People with ASPD may not show the same level of improvement with time and show persistent conflict with society for many years. In general, personality disorders are important statistical predictors of quality of life and are more important than socio-demographic variables, physical health, and other psychiatric disorder (Cramer, Torgersen, & Kringlen, 2006). People with BPD have highly significant, widespread reductions in their quality of life. This means that finding effective treatment is of considerable importance.

Initial studies of psychodynamic treatments were almost universally of in-patient treatment, which as we have mentioned is now rarely available to patients due to the costs and uncertainty of outcomes. A naturalistic five-year follow-up of individuals receiving in-patient treatment at the Cassel Hospital in London indicates the need for caution in ascribing benefits to in-patient treatment (Rosser, Birch, Bond, et al., 1987). Patients with BPD had a less favourable outcome than those with neurotic pathology, depression, high intelligence, and lack of chronic out-patient history. More recently Chiesa and colleagues found that shorter in-patient treatment with community follow-up yields better overall outcomes for patients with personality disorder and that differences in improvement are still discernable five years later (Chiesa & Fonagy, 2003; Chiesa, Fonagy, & Holmes, 2006).

There are a number of non-randomized trials of dynamic psychotherapy in the literature. The best of these are the studies of Stevenson, Meares, and colleagues (Stevenson & Meares, 1992, 1999; Stevenson, Meares, & D'Angelo, 2005). They report on patients receiving twice-weekly interpersonal-psychodynamic out-patient therapy (conversational therapy, see p. 225) over 12 months. Outcomes in 30 patients who completed one year of treatment were contrasted with patients placed on a 12-month waiting list: 30 per cent of the treatment group no longer met the DSM-III-R criteria for BPD at the end of treatment, with little indication of change in the waiting-list group.

Support for a psychodynamically based approach has come from a randomized study comparing the effectiveness of a psycho-analytically oriented day-hospital programme using mentalization-based treatment (MBT) with standard psychiatric care for patients with BPD (Bateman & Fonagy, 1999; Bateman & Fonagy, 2001; Bateman & Fonagy, 2008). Thirty-eight patients with BPD, diagnosed according to standardized criteria, were allocated either to MBT or to general psychiatric care (control group) in a randomized control design. Intensive treatment was for 18 months. Patients in the day-hospital programme showed a statistically significant decrease on all measures, in contrast to the control group which showed limited change or deterioration over the same period. Improvement in depressive symptoms, decrease in suicidal and self-mutilatory acts, reduced in-patient days, and better social and interpersonal function began after 6 months and continued to the end of intensive treatment at 18 months. Further follow-up for 18 months demonstrated further improvement, suggesting that rehabilitative effects were stimulated during the intensive treatment phase. Long-term follow-up five years after all experimental treatment ceased suggested that gains were maintained and differences between the groups continue, but general social function remains impaired for both groups.

An out-patient version of MBT (MBT-OP) has also shown that people with BPD can benefit from treatment (Bateman & Fonagy, 2009). A total of 134 patients evaluated for borderline and antisocial PD were randomized to MBT-OP or structured clinical management organized as best clinical practice within mental health services. Eleven mental health professionals, equal in years of experience and training, served as therapists. Six-monthly assessment was by independent evaluators blind to treatment allocation.

The primary outcome was the occurrence of crisis events, a composite of suicidal and severe self-injurious behaviours, and hospitalization. Secondary outcomes included social and interpersonal function and self-reported symptoms.

Substantial improvements were observed in both conditions across all outcome variables. Patients randomized to MBT-OP showed a steeper decline of both self-reported and clinically significant problems, including suicide attempts and hospitalization.

Another manualized dynamic therapy known as transference focused psychotherapy (TFP) has shown promising results. In a randomized trial comparing TFP, dialectical behaviour therapy (DBT), and supportive therapy (Clarkin, Levy, Lenzenweger, *et al.*, 2007) 90 patients, 92 per cent of whom were female, were randomized. At completion of treatment at one year there were no differences between groups on global assessment of functioning, depression scores, social adjustment, anxiety, and measures of self-harm. However, whereas TFP showed significant improvement in irritability and verbal and direct assault, this was not observed in either DBT or supportive psychotherapy. Further, patients who received TFP showed greatest improvement on reflective function, which is an operationalization of the mentalization construct (Levy, Meehan, Kelly, *et al.*, 2006). An important outstanding question is whether individuals whose reflective function improved will turn out to be more likely to have retained treatment gains upon follow-up. This study suggests that other treatments not focusing on the relationship between patient and therapist may be equally effective in helping people with personality disorder. It is possible that there may be many different roots to achieving similar outcomes in people with personality disorder. DBT is a behavioural treatment (Linehan, 1993a) and helps people who self-harm or try to commit suicide by focusing on their behaviours rather than their relationships. One aspect of the treatment is described on p. 206. Research on DBT as a treatment for BPD is the most extensive of all the treatments (Linehan, Armstrong, Suarez, *et al.*, 1991; Linehan, Heard, & Armstrong, 1993; Linehan, Comtois, Murray, *et al.*, 2006).

In our discussion about groups (see p. 153) we mentioned the importance of the group process in helping people to improve social interaction and their interpersonal skills through understanding how they relate to others in the group. So group psychotherapy has been offered to patients with personality disorder. Non-controlled studies with day-hospital stabilization for chaotic behaviour followed by out-patient dynamic group therapy indicate the utility of group psychotherapy in BPD (Karterud, Pedersen, Bjordal, *et al.*, 2003; Wilberg, Karterud, Pedersen, *et al.*, 2003). Marziali and Monroe-Blum have concentrated on group therapy without the additional milieu and social components of therapy. In a randomized controlled trial they found equivalent results between group and individual therapy, and concluded that on cost-effectiveness grounds group therapy is the treatment of choice (Marziali & Monroe-Blum, 1995).

Finally we should mention that therapeutic communities are commonly used to help people with personality disorder simply because they are designed to form a microcosm of society with groups of people living together and trying to manage their relationships with each other. Some evidence for the effectiveness of this treatment is discussed on p. 203.

SELECTION

For whom should psychotherapy be considered?

In order to answer this question we need to specify what type of psychotherapy for what sort of problem. Furthermore, since psychotherapy is not an impersonal medical technique, we cannot avoid taking into account the individual characteristics of patient and therapist (see p. 269), who must be able to work together. Ultimately a decision about embarking on psychotherapy with a particular therapist can only be arrived at when both patient and therapist show what they could bring to the therapeutic relationship.

In assessment of suitability for different types of psychotherapy, the doctor or therapist needs to go beyond diagnosis. Diagnosis itself is a poor indicator of which type of therapy is likely to be best for an individual. The doctor or therapist will listen attentively and try to enter imaginatively into the patient's experience. Comments by the doctor/therapist which show awareness of the patient's anxieties about the interview are often particularly helpful in establishing rapport. In attempting to understand and look below the surface of the presenting complaints, he may offer interventions (or trial interpretations) at varying levels. For example, he may say to a depressed and agitated middle-aged woman, devoted to caring for her aged parents, 'It seems that you are trying not to think about your feelings of resentment at the restrictions this imposes on your life'; or, to a promising student who always fails his examinations, 'I wonder if you are afraid of succeeding because that would be like triumphing over your unsuccessful father?'. The responses they make could help in assessing their preparedness to think about difficulties in a new way. Unthinking rejection or passive acceptance of an interpretation are usually bad auguries for dynamic psychotherapy; a thoughtful response, with expression of emotion or meaningful associations, or even 'I don't think so', are preferable. Sometimes it is possible to make transference interpretations linking a patient's attitude to the interviewer (e.g. fearful of criticism or anxious to please) to his attitude to a parent.

If the patient can make use of interpretations this suggests that he will continue to do so if he enters therapy. The therapist's personality and the extent to which he is interested and involved are key factors. Research work has shown that 'empathy, warmth, and genuineness' are therapist characteristics which predispose to favourable outcome in non-directive therapy. These factors are probably relevant to some degree in all types of psychotherapy, but even this cannot be seen in isolation. What matters is how patient and therapist get on together. This can often be assessed at a first interview by the degree of emotional contact, or rapport, that is made between them, by the feelings that the patient expresses (sometimes to his surprise), and by the therapist's own counter-transference responses.

We have already indicated that psychotherapy can occur at several levels, from supportive to exploratory, and that it can take place within both informal and professional relationships. Any person in difficulty benefits from support and help to maintain or restore morale; this is psychotherapy in the general sense (level 1). However, certain questions arise when considering exploratory psychotherapy in the special dynamic sense (level 3), which aims to promote change. These are as important as the formal psychiatric diagnosis, or presenting problem, in deciding who would make use of dynamic psychotherapy.

Are the person's difficulties understandable in psychological terms?

Beyond making a psychiatric diagnosis, based on the symptoms and signs elicited at the interview, it should be possible to make a tentative *psychodynamic formulation* of the patient's problems, taking into account both current life situation and earlier development. A dynamic formulation is a way of thinking about a patient's problems in psychological terms. Symptoms and behaviour are understood to have personal meaning and not to be alien to the individual. Why has this person got this problem at this time? Together the therapist and patient try to understand the internal mental model of the patient, its development, and its conscious and unconscious determinants.

What important factors in the past are relevant, what patterns are there to relationships that may provide hints of underlying conflict, and are there any obvious assumptions and beliefs that may help explain the form of symptoms? What are the major internal identifications of the patient and are they relevant to the symptoms? Finally, excessive or inappropriate use of defence mechanisms to deal with anxiety and conflict may lead to the development of symptoms, and it may be important to help the patient understand how he is using them to his disadvantage. The simplest way to organize a formulation is to think about predisposing, precipitating, and perpetuating factors whilst all the time trying to understand what they mean to the individual.

For example, the depressive state of Mrs A., described in the Prologue, became understandable when her response to the prospect of her daughter leaving home was viewed in the context of her own early history of separation. The patient's preparedness to think about problems in psychological terms is a parallel requirement. Response to test interpretations, as described above, can help in assessing this. Perhaps of greater significance is the way in which both interviewer and patient can enter into sharing the essence of a provisional psychodynamic formulation, before moving on to discuss treatment options at the end of the interview (Brown, 1991).

Is there sufficient motivation for insight and change?

A patient expresses his wish for insight by the way he asks for help and engages in discussion about himself and his problems. If he is rigidly defensive and remains very guarded, or restricts himself to complaining about symptoms, or to blaming someone else for his troubles, he is unlikely to want to understand his own contribution to his problems and how he can change. If he pours out his difficulties, as though using the interviewer as a wastebin, or he seems to be looking for 'magical solutions' from an omnipotent parent/therapist, he is probably not yet ready to join in an effective *working alliance* (p. 68), although he might do so in time. Mrs A.'s reappraisal of her separation experiences, past and present, in a joint exploration with the interviewer indicated her readiness for insight and augured well for her ability to use dynamic psychotherapy. A degree of introspectiveness, average intelligence, and verbal fluency is desirable if unmodified dynamic therapy is to be used. However, patients' capacities for introspection and verbal communication can develop during therapy and are not prerequisites for dynamic psychotherapy. Modified therapy is necessary for patients who find it difficult to reflect and to think about their feelings, as they may act them out impulsively, and their capacity to communicate through talking may be restricted. Sometimes these capacities are fostered by the use of action techniques in modified dynamic therapy, such as those mentioned in the previous section, particularly in the case of borderline patients.

A patient's *earliest* memories can be used in dynamic interviewing and formulation. A marked degree of childhood amnesia may indicate prominent repression and restriction of personality. The capacity to remember dreams is another useful indicator of the ability of patients to contact unconscious parts of themselves without feeling unduly disturbed. Resistance to insight and change can be based on anxieties about the danger of deep exploration or unwillingness to upset a balance which brings advantage to the patient or their family.

Has the patient adequate ego strength?

He must be able to evaluate his experience and integrate the competing demands of motivational drives (id), conscience (superego), and external reality, while coping with the tensions they create. He needs to take stock of perceptions arising from the external world and from within himself, and to distinguish between them. He has to be able to sustain feelings and fantasies without impulsively acting on them, without being overwhelmed by anxiety, and without losing, for long, the capacity to think and talk rationally. Further, he must keep in touch with his adult self and maintain the working alliance with the therapist, at the same time as he contacts the disturbed and often helpless child in himself. Then, before leaving a session, he must return to functioning as a reasonable coping adult until the next session, which during holiday breaks he may need to do for several weeks. If these capacities are not present at the beginning of therapy they must be fostered by the therapist through understanding and appropriate management: for example, in deciding if hospital admission or medication is necessary. Repeated hospital admissions or frequent suicidal attempts may suggest insufficient ego strength for out-patient psychotherapy or that the therapy has to be modified. Repeated risk-taking – an established and destructive pattern of addictive behaviour – or serious somatization into major psychosomatic disorder can also indicate overrunning of the person's capacity for integration. All are cues to question whether to modify technique and to ensure therapy is provided either within the right setting, such as a day hospital or in-patient unit, or with the use of medication. In addition, a history of repeated dropping-out of relationships and failure to complete ventures can be bad auguries for continuation in therapy.

In general, patients with acute psychotic disorders are not amenable to exploratory psychotherapy, because their ego functions are too impaired. During a schizophrenic breakdown, patients suffer impaired ego boundaries, and they are already flooded by unconscious primitive material. They may no longer be certain whether their thoughts and feelings are their own or someone else's (which gives rise to the phenomena of thought broadcasting and insertion). Severely depressed patients may be too slowed-up and unresponsive to engage in psychotherapy, while at the same time a hypercritical super-ego might produce severe guilt feelings or even delusions. Ego functions may be so impaired that the voice of conscience is no longer recognized as internal, but projected outwards and experienced as a hallucinatory voice making derogatory remarks. The transference relationships made by psychotic patients are often frighteningly intense, and cannot be seen by the patient in 'as if' terms; for them, the doctor or nurse *is* their mother or father. Primitive transference responses to the therapist are likely to overwhelm the working alliance. On the other hand, psychotic patients benefit from supportive psychotherapy aimed at strengthening the ego while they receive medication, often in hospital. At a later stage, when they have recovered from an acute episode, cautious exploration of underlying conflicts may sometimes be appropriate.

The importance of ego strength as an indicator that a patient will be able to hold onto his identity, despite experiencing psychic pain due to inner turmoil and conflict uncovered in psychotherapy, is supported by research. In the Menninger Psychotherapy Project, Kernberg (1972) found a significant relationship between ego strength and outcome in psychoanalytic psychotherapy. This study (Wallerstein, 1986), undoubtedly the outstanding example of the naturalistic studies of psychoanalysis, began in 1954 as a prospective study and spanned a 25-year period looking at assessment, treatment, and outcome in patients referred to the Menninger Clinic in the USA for psychoanalysis, 42 of whom were selected for intensive study. Patients, their families, and their therapists were subjected to a battery of tests, and process notes and supervisory records were kept, charting the progress of therapy.

A major thrust of Wallerstein's analysis of this enormous mass of data has been the attempt to compare classical psychoanalysis with psychoanalytic psychotherapy. He classified 22 of the cases as psychoanalysis and 20 as psychotherapy, but there was a clear spectrum from classical psychoanalysis, modified psychoanalysis, expressive-supportive psychotherapy (probably equivalent to the British category of psychoanalytic psychotherapy), supportive-expressive psychotherapy, to supportive psychotherapy. Some of Wallerstein's most important findings, many of which are consistent with results we have outlined from other studies, can be summarized as follows:

1   There was no evidence that psychoanalysis was more effective with this group of patients than supportive therapy: 12/22 (46 per cent) psychoanalytic cases and 12/20 (54 per cent) psychotherapy cases did well, with good or moderately good outcomes. The improvements brought about by supportive therapy were:

> . . . just as stable, as enduring, as proof against subsequent environmental vicissitudes, and as free (or not free) from the requirment for supplemental post-treatment contact, support, or further therapeutic help as the changes in those patients treated via . . . psychoanalysis.
>
> (Wallerstein, 1986)

2   Of the 22 cases initially started with psychoanalysis only six remained within the parameters of classical analysis; six had

'modified classical', which included some supportive elements such as sitting up, the analyst wrapping blankets round a rain-drenched anorexic, telephoning suicidal patients at home, and admissions to hospital in crisis; six were converted to supportive therapy, one of whom became a 'therapeutic lifer', receiving 25 years of continuous therapy from four different therapists.

3   A 'positive dependent transference' seemed to be the basis of *all* successful therapies, whether analytic or supportive.

4   Overall there was only a weak relationship between 'insight' and change, although psychoanalysis was particularly associated with the presence of insight – whether this was because analysis led to insight or that insightful patients were selected for analysis was unclear. In summary, 25 per cent showed neither insight nor change; in 45 per cent, change occurred with little insight (the majority of these were, unsurprisingly, in the psychotherapy group); in 25 per cent, insight and change went hand in hand (these were virtually all in the psychoanalysis group); and in 5 per cent there was insight but little change.

An important aim of Wallerstein's study was to elucidate the controversy about the 'widening scope' of psychoanalysis – the use of psychoanalytic techniques to treat much more severely disturbed patients than had previously been thought possible. Kernberg's (1975) contribution to the Menninger project suggested that a modified analytic approach, including the use of 'psychodynamically guided hospitalisation', early interpretation of negative transference, and a focus on the here-and-now interactions rather than reconstructions, enabled severe borderline and even some psychotic patients to be successfully treated. Wallerstein looked in detail at this group of 'heroic indication' patients. The overall results were not good. He identified 11 such patients with paranoid features, major alcohol or drug addiction, or borderline pathology. Six of these were in the psychoanalysis group: three died of mental-illness-related causes, two from alcoholism and one by suicide; three dropped out of analysis, of whom two did badly and one did well – the psychotherapeutic 'lifer' already mentioned. Five were in the psychotherapy group, of whom two had mental-illness-related deaths, four were total failures, and one did moderately well.

The conclusions about this group of patients, with whom psychodynamically minded psychiatrists will be all too familiar, were that: the best form of therapy is 'supportive-expressive' for however long it is necessary – a lifetime if needs be; periods of hospitalization will be required alongside long-term therapy; a network of informal support, often centred around the subculture associated with a psychiatric unit, is also an important ingredient if these patients are to survive at all, let alone thrive; and finally, 'even if they had little chance with psychoanalysis, they might have had no chance at all with other forms of treatment'.

Is there a capacity to form and sustain relationships?

It might seem paradoxical that this should be a criterion for dynamic psychotherapy. After all, most of the difficulties with which people come for help are ultimately relationship problems. However, as we have said, psychotherapy operates within or through the relationship of patient and therapist, without which there can be no working alliance, let alone analysis of transference. Even one sustained or reliable relationship in the patient's past or current life suggests a firmer basis from which to start therapy, which is particularly important in short-term analytic psychotherapy. In long-term analytic psychotherapy there is time to develop trust and become more fully engaged, whereas in brief therapy intense involvement is required from the start (p. 141).

Given that these criteria are satisfied, many people with neurotic and character problems, if they genuinely want to change, can be helped by analytic psychotherapy, either individually or in a group. Their problems may have been brought to light by life events or developmental crises, such as leaving home for the first time, parenthood, or bereavement. Others may be more chronically dissatisfied with themselves and their relationships, or may feel inhibited or unduly anxious. They may be unable to realize their potential or to cope with aggression or sexuality. If successful, benefit usually extends beyond any presenting symptoms.

> *For example, a man who initially complained only of impotence discovered that he was afraid of the consequences of his aggressive feelings towards women, a fear that originated through his relationship with his mother; as he resolved this conflict, he discovered that he could also be more appropriately assertive in other areas of his life.*

Some patients with psychosomatic disorders which are not too deeply ingrained in their physical or psychological constitution can be helped by dynamic psychotherapy if they are able to consider psychological causes and solutions. Likewise, some perversions and addictions can be modified if they are not symptoms of a seriously damaged personality or a defence against breakdown and disintegration.

Selection for psychotherapy may appear to some to involve an objectionable introduction of elitist values. Psychotherapists have been chided for tending to take on young, intelligent, and personable patients, but equally they are asked to take on difficult patients for whom psychiatrists have little to offer (Chiesa, Fonagy, & Bateman, 2007), such as those with severe personality disorders. While surgeons perform relatively brief operations on inert anaesthetized patients, psychotherapists spend a lot of time in a unique personal relationship with their patients. Personal feelings are therefore bound to influence who is accepted for treatment by therapists, just as referrals to them are influenced by the feelings of the family doctor or general psychiatrist. Indeed, referrals may be motivated either by a wish to do everything possible for someone, or conversely by a wish to get rid of a difficult or even untreatable patient. The therapist has to decide the level and type of psychotherapeutic help the patient is able to use, as well as who can best provide it. Part of the task is to engage the patient in this decision-making, and to respect his right to reject a therapist he does not feel he can work with. For this reason a network of therapists and a range of therapies are desirable in a full psychotherapy service.

Severity of problem

Many people think that the more severe the problem, the more difficult the individual will be to treat, and yet this does not seem to be true. Severity is a complicated term and for psychotherapy it is important to distinguish between the number of symptoms of a disorder, which might indicate severity, and the level of personal impairment that either results from or precedes the symptoms. Someone with a previous low level of function, for example few relationships and long-term unemployment, is likely to be less responsive to psychotherapy than someone with good pre-morbid function involving constructive and satisfying relationships and productive work and activity. In fact, low level of function is more predictive of poorer prognosis than severity of symptoms. The best predictor of response to IPT (see pp. 222 and 264) was emotional health prior to initiation of treatment (Rounsaville, Weissman, & Prusoff, 1981). Luborsky (1962) and Luborsky *et al.* (1980) found a significant link between psychological health and treatment outcome in a group of patients treated for 12 weeks with brief focal psychodynamic therapy. Clients who had shown the highest level of adaptive functioning before therapy showed the most improvement.

There is now general agreement that personality disorder, which is itself an indicator of a low level of social and interpersonal function, is a moderator of outcomes and so therapists should be aware that patients with personality disorder will be more difficult to help.

Personality variables

We might anticipate that someone who chose a particular therapy and had high expectations of treatment would do better than someone who was sent for treatment. Indeed this seems to be the case, but intriguingly patient expectation is more related to duration of treatment than it is to treatment outcome (Lorr & McNair, 1964). Frank (1971) considered the patient's confidence in his therapy and in the therapist as being the variable of most importance. It is likely that patient expectation is associated with therapeutic alliance (see p. 68) and that the alliance itself is the mediator of the outcome. In a study of brief psychotherapy patient expectation was only moderately related to treatment outcome but strongly related to treatment alliance (Joyce & Piper, 1998). The converse seems also to be true – the more difficult the patient and the more negative he is about therapy, the poorer the outcome, perhaps because he makes the therapist less competent (Foley, O'Malley, Rounsaville, *et al.*, 1987). Not surprisingly therapists tend to do less well when patients are unpleasant. This is a further example of how feelings in the therapist can be induced by the patient and lead to countertransference experiences (see p. 79) which interfere with the patient–therapist interaction.

Psychological mindedness

The question about whether a patient is 'psychologically minded' is often asked by practitioners of dynamic therapy, on the assumption that a patient who is already psychologically thoughtful is more likely to benefit from therapy. The term usually refers to a person's ability to understand his own and other people's problems in psychological terms. This is often exampled by showing more self-reflection and self-disclosure, and both of these have been related to treatment outcome (Baer, Dunbar, Hamilton, *et al.*, 1980). Piper and colleagues (Piper, Joyce, Rosie, *et al.*, 1994) also found that in short-term group psychotherapy psychological mindedness was directly correlated with patient outcome, but interestingly this was not the case in individual psychotherapy. In a later controlled trial, being psychologically minded was directly related to remaining and working in group therapy but not to extracting benefit from the process. The most likely explanation for all these conflicting results is that patients with high psychological mindedness do better with more interpretive psychotherapy offered at level 3. Conversely, patients with lower levels work better and gain more from supportive therapy offered at level 1.

An additional twist has been placed on these ideas about the psychological mindedness of a patient. Blatt compared patients who were predominantly what he called introjective (self-critical and perfectionistic) with patients who were anaclitic (mostly concerned with abandonment and loss) and found that pre-treatment perfectionism had a negative impact on therapeutic outcomes (Blatt, Quinlan, Pilkonis, *et al.*, 1995). In the Menninger project discussed on p. 243 anaclitic patients did better with psychotherapy than they did with psychoanalysis, whereas patients who were introjective did better with psychoanalysis (Blatt & Shahar, 2004).

Attachment patterns

Throughout this book we have discussed ideas developed from attachment theory (see p. 55). Since psychotherapy of any type involves the development of an attachment relationship between individuals, it is likely that the patient's and therapist's attachment histories and the quality of these attachments might influence outcomes. In a study on borderline personality disorder, patients with insecure-dismissive attachment histories responded better to intervention compared to patients with other attachment patterns (Fonagy, Leigh, Steele, *et al.*, 1996), but this might have been a result of the therapists offering modified treatment to manage patients with this style of relationship. Dozier (1990) found that patients with dismissing patterns are often problematic in treatment and have difficulty in asking for help; they avoid the involvement of being engaged in psychotherapy because they become disorganized when confronted with emotional interaction. Studies with patients with affective disorders and anxiety, and even those with drug addiction, have also suggested that patients with secure attachment styles report fewer symptoms prior to treatment and show greater improvement following treatment compared to those with insecure attachments (Meyer, Pilkonis, Proietti, *et al.*, 2001).

It is possible that these effects of the attachment patterns of the patient are mediated through the therapeutic alliance. Patients with confidence in their capacity to form relationships are likely to elicit positive responses from therapists (Hardy, Stiles, Barkham, *et al.*, 1998). But it seems that the therapist responses can also be influenced by their own attachment style. Therapists tend to adopt more emotional and relationship-orientated responses to patients with over-involved, preoccupied interpersonal styles but more cognitively focused interventions with patients who are under-involved and dismissing (Hardy, Stiles, Barkham, *et al.*, 1998). Therapist attachment styles might balance those of the patient. Patients in treatment for serious psychiatric disorder with therapists who were dissimilar to them in attachment style on the hyperactivation/deactivation dimension of attachment showed better therapeutic outcomes and stronger therapeutic alliances (Tyrell, Dozier, Teague, *et al.*, 1999). All this research on the patient–therapist relationship supports one central tenet of this book – that the doctor–patient relationship has a significant influence on the psychological state of the patient and their experience of their illness.

What type of psychotherapy?

We have already outlined different levels of psychotherapy. The *outer levels* (p. 115) involving unburdening, ventilation of feelings (catharsis), and discussion of problems – include counselling and supportive psychotherapy, and are indicated for those who do not want, or could not tolerate, deeper exploration and uncovering. Those who want help with particular problems relating to adolescence, unwanted pregnancy, or marital difficulties, for example, can get valuable help from special counselling agencies. Patients with long-term disability and impairment or a personality severely affected by early deprivation may need long-term supportive psychotherapy to help them cope with the inevitable stresses of life (see p. 116). Some patients with chronic psychosis may benefit from cognitively based therapy targeting some of their hallucinations and delusions (Kuipers *et al.*, 1997; Turkington & Kingdon, 2000). People who are reacting to an acute crisis in their lives, such as bereavement, divorce, or loss of a job, and whose personality is basically strong and capable of adjusting to difficulties might need only relatively short-term supportive psychotherapy or counselling to restore their defences and stability to the *status quo ante*. If after a while their emotional distress has not begun to resolve, it is possible that the crisis has thrown up underlying conflicts and problems which may be helped by more exploratory, dynamic psychotherapy. Therapists who work with a crisis model (p. 180) may attempt to intervene at an early stage in a family crisis, hoping thereby to increase the chances of constructive change and learning.

At *intermediate levels*, the question arises of whether the patient should be referred for general psychiatric treatment, cognitive-behavioural therapy, or dynamic psychotherapy. There are few indications to help us decide which patient should receive which therapy. Many people tend to think that diagnosis is the best guide but the evidence for such an approach to clinical decision-making is tenuous. How a patient views himself and his world may be a better guide. If a person has symptoms of anxiety and depression it is often appropriate to put it to him that there are different ways of viewing the problem. His symptoms could be seen as part of an illness of unknown cause, which will be relieved by medication; or he might want to try to discover why he has developed into the kind of person who reacted in this sort of way at this time, in which case dynamic psychotherapy may be more appropriate. The two views are not mutually exclusive – symptomatic relief from drugs might be helpful first and then further exploration via psychotherapy if desired. When given this choice people are very often able to decide what is best for themselves. As Balint and Balint (1961, p. 47) said:

> One of the chief aims of every diagnostic interview is, if at all possible, to enable the patient to decide for himself what his next step should be – a decision which, as a rule, he has been unable to take before the interview.

People differ according to age, education, and background. One patient may say: 'Give me the pills, doctor, there's no point in talking about it.' Another more reflective person may say: 'What's the good of suppressing symptoms with medication if they only recur? I want to get to the bottom of it and understand why I'm like this.' Psychotherapy is more akin to an educational process that engages the client as an active participant than to a conventional medical treatment where the patient remains a passive recipient.

Where there are marital difficulties, one couple might prefer to tackle a sexual problem, such as impotence or frigidity, by the sexual training techniques pioneered by Masters and Johnson (1970), while to another couple it may make more sense to view it as a reflection of something amiss in their relationship and of what each brings to it, and therefore to seek more dynamic couple therapy.

It is becoming increasingly apparent that attempts to link diagnosis to choice of therapy is too narrow an approach to deal with the complexity of problems that patients bring. As a result there is more interest in staging approaches according to the patient's difficulties. For example, a patient with an extensive history of impulsive and self-destructive behaviour may need the structure of a behavioural programme to begin to get the impulses under control. Following this, an exploration of the underlying causes may be appropriate to add depth to the gains and to integrate new ways of thinking about and experiencing himself and his relationships. Similarly, some socially inhibited and unassertive patients, who would at first be too overwhelmed by the idea of joining a group, are able to make use of analytic group psychotherapy following social skills training. Conversely, there are patients who improve in many ways through dynamic psychotherapy, without fully overcoming their symptoms, and subsequently obtain relief through techniques of behaviour modification, for example, desensitization for residual phobic symptoms.

At the *deeper levels* of exploratory psychotherapy we need to consider the developmental origin of the underlying conflicts and problems. Classically this has been seen in terms of the three developmental phases described in Part I (pp. 48–50). The more mature a patient's personality, and the later the developmental phase in which his principal conflicts and problems originated, the more likely he is to respond to shorter term analytic psychotherapy or group therapy. Conditions with roots in earlier phases or whose developmental traumas persist over time, such as those with personality disorder, are likely to need longer term treatment. Patients severely damaged by early environmental failure, if suitable for analytic therapy, might need over a long period to experience the analyst more concretely as mother and his words as feeds. At such a time the provision of a relationship may be more important than the intellectual content of interpretations. Such patients can be treated in groups, but often their need to regress, although in a new and more favourable environment, makes them extremely intolerant of other group members; or they may comply and make no deep therapeutic progress. Some therapists have used combined individual and group therapy for such very deprived patients, with good results.

Group psychotherapy is the treatment of choice for many patients with problems in relating to others, since the group setting provides particular opportunities for interpersonal learning. Even members who are initially reluctant to talk much about themselves learn from others. In the course of a few months, isolated or schizoid people may allow previously cut-off feelings to emerge. Those with character problems perpetuated by restricting their relationships may, in a group, discover for the first time how unsatisfactory their solutions have been to underlying problems; they can then begin to seek new solutions with the help of the group. However, patients who are extremely demanding, paranoid, or severely depressed have difficulty in tolerating or being tolerated by a group. Ultimately, whether they become part of the group depends on its composition, atmosphere, and stage of development.

In considering whether individual, group, or family therapy is appropriate, Skynner's (1976, p. 168) notion of *minimum sufficient network* can help in deciding whom to include in treatment when one member of a family presents or is presented as a problem. Skynner applies the idea that a well-functioning individual needs to have ego, super-ego, and id working in harmony. All three are needed in individual therapy to allow a reasonable degree of reality-testing, control of impulses, and emotional spontaneity, respectively. Working with families, often from deprived and chaotic backgrounds, he found that these families needed to integrate and harmonize their functions, which previously they had split off into different members of the family (e.g. sensible mother, critical father, and delinquent child) or had lodged in the family's relationship with the community (e.g. concerned school, punishing police, and demanding, violent family). What is needed is to reintegrate the parts so that they can begin to modify each other. As discussed in the section on Family and Couple Therapy, when a disturbance is located in the family or marriage, the presenting patient may not be the sickest member nor the one most open to change. Bringing the family together for treatment can often mobilize understanding and constructive change in the system, producing sufficient relief of stress for a more satisfactory adjustment to be achieved without deep exploration of individual members.

Skynner and Brown (1981) have pointed out that although it is individuals who are usually referred, and individual therapy that is most often thought of, a family approach (to diagnosis, if not therapy) has wide applicability in terms of types and level of pathology and capacity for insight. If it can be arranged, a family consultation provides information about the interaction of many key people in addition to the presenting patient, who may not be the sickest nor the most amenable to direct therapeutic influence. And even without motivation for insight, a few sessions can have a big effect by changing the whole system of interaction (Howells & Brown, 1986).

Group therapy of different types also has a wide spectrum of applicability, and in analytical group therapy even patients who initially have poor motivation for insight and little capacity for emotional expression can be helped; they can learn from others and change gradually over time. Individual therapy has the advantage of flexibility in that the needs of each person, including the frequency of sessions, can be catered for.

Why is help sought now?

This is often a pertinent question when a patient asks for help, from either family doctor or psychiatrist. The answer may throw light on factors which disturb the individual's adjustment, and give an idea of his ego strength and coping capacities. It could throw into relief the interaction between chronic and acute stresses: for example, between long-term frustration of needs or wishes and the final blow of disappointment or loss. It might reveal a sequence of successful attempts to cope with challenges, before tension and other non-specific signs of crisis arise prior to the final 'breakdown' into an organized psychological or physical disorder. The crisis may have been precipitated by some sudden or mounting stress in the family or at work, or even in the patient's relationship with his family doctor; in this case help may be most appropriately directed at a family or marital problem, or at supporting the doctor in coping with a burdensome long-term patient.

It may take more than one meeting but eventually, having defined and located the problem, patient and doctor/therapist are usually in a better position to decide whether ongoing psychotherapy is needed and, if so, which level and form of therapy makes most sense to both of them. The *level* will range from support and counselling, augmented if necessary by symptomatic relief with medication, to various levels of analytic exploration. In addition, the *form* of therapy may depend on the degree of directiveness likely to be required in order to influence the problem, and also on whether the patient is more likely to respond to behavioural and action methods rather than those based on insight and understanding.

Figure 11 places the psychotherapeutic methods described in Part II in a range from interpretation to action, between individual and group. Whatever the problem and however full the range of possible psychotherapeutic methods, assessment and selection for psychotherapy do not involve examination by an active doctor of a passive and inert patient, as in some areas of medicine. We need the patient's active cooperation. Moreover:

> The other cardinal difference is that in organic medicine it is sufficient if the therapy makes sense to the doctor; what is required from the patient is merely that he should reliably carry out the doctor's prescriptions. Contrariwise in psychological medicine it is essential that the therapy should make sense both to the patient and to the doctor.
>
> (Balint & Balint, 1961, p. 206)

OUTCOME AND RESEARCH

There has been a rapid increase in the amount of research in psychotherapy over the last decade. In this section we attempt to summarize some of the main findings and to answer some fundamental questions. The interested reader is recommended to refer to Lambert, Bergin, and Garfield (2004) and associated summaries in the fifth edition of Bergin and Garfield's *Handbook of Psychotherapy and Behaviour Change* (2004) for an extensive account of all research findings, and to Roth and Fonagy (2005) for a review of psychological treatments of the major mental disorders.

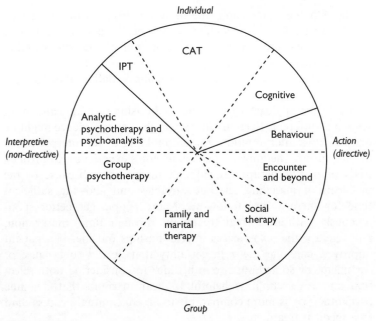

Figure 11

What evidence do we have that psychotherapy does any good?

This is as hard to answer simply as the question 'For whom should psychotherapy be considered?' – and for similar reasons. Few studies have taken into account all the relevant variables, such as the level and type of psychotherapy, the sort of patient and problem, the personality and skill of the therapist, and how patient and therapist get on together. It is difficult to measure the relevant changes in human adjustment and to standardize treatments which, by their nature, involve unique experiences at many levels. Controlled double-blind trials of drug treatments are simple in comparison, because every pill is the same, and control groups of patients can be given dummy pills without their realizing it, thus giving a measure of the 'placebo effect':

The more an illness resembles an accident, the better are the results of hospital medicine, and it is here in this field that the proper application and value of the double-blind experiment lie. On the other hand, the more an illness is due to a lack of integration the less effective will be the so-called scientific treatments and the less applicable will be the double-blind experiment.

(Balint & Balint, 1961, p. 126)

In psychotherapy each therapeutic relationship is unique and every session is different. Even in one session the key experience might be one *mutative* interpretation, the withholding of an interpretation, or, in a group, the impact of someone else's experience. Controlled trials of psychotherapy are difficult to construct because of the problems of matching relevant variables and allowing sufficient time for therapy and follow-up. Many people get better spontaneously without formal treatment, through time, maturation, and 'therapeutic' experiences in relationships outside. If a patient improves, can one say with certainty that he did so because of treatment, or something else in his life? In considering both selection and research, it is helpful to bear in mind that dynamic psychotherapy is more comparable to an educational process than to a medical treatment.

Psychoanalytic psychotherapy is a labour-intensive clinical intervention and, as such, requires considerable resources. Consequently, like all medical procedures, it has come under increasing scrutiny over the past decade and practitioners in the NHS have to justify provision of treatment and show cost-effectiveness relative to other interventions. Clinical judgement and professional recommendation are no longer sufficient justification for offering treatment. This is entirely proper, and a challenge to both detractors of psychotherapy (Aveline, 1984; Kolvin, Macmillan, Nicol, *et al.*, 1988). Ideology can blind, or at least lead to tunnel vision. This is particularly dangerous when narrow criteria are used to justify axing the still-too-rare psychotherapy provisions in the NHS, when their wider cost–benefits are not taken into account. In England, cost savings have been demonstrated at follow-up for patients with personality disorder (Bateman & Fonagy, 2003). In the USA, Gabbard *et al.* (1997) reviewed data on the impact of psychotherapy on costs of care for psychiatric disorders: 80 per cent of the 10 clinical trials with random assignment and 100 per cent of studies without random assignment suggested that psychotherapy reduces total costs. Cost–benefit was found in many psychiatric disorders, including schizophrenia, bipolar affective disorder, and borderline personality disorder. Much of this accrued from fewer hospital admissions and better work performance. In Germany this has been so well established that private in-patient and out-patient psychotherapy, including some psychoanalysis, is covered by government medical insurance. In Finland, psychotherapy is regarded as a form of rehabilitation by the National Social Insurance Institution, which subsidizes analytically orientated and supportive psychotherapy for two to three years to improve people's capacity to work and study. Careful assessment of the results indicates that more than 80 per cent benefited and about one-third were symptom-free; those suffering from neurotic disorders particularly benefited (Seppala & Jamsen, 1990).

The complex issues involved in assessing the efficiency of psychotherapy services have been analysed with great thoroughness by Fonagy and Higgitt (1989). They conclude that it is possible to find indicators that reflect the value of a psychotherapy service to the local community, and that we urgently need to agree on the appropriate parameters to evaluate this. Holmes and Lindley (1989) provide a powerful rebuttal of 'the case against psychotherapy' (ch. 2) in their own review of research findings. They make an eloquent plea for the more widespread availability of publicly funded psychotherapy services, comparing the current view that this is a luxury rather than a basic right with attitudes to education a century ago. However, psychotherapy will only remain a right within the present climate if there is an 'evidence base'.

Psychoanalytic therapy, with its reliance on the single case study, does not yet fully match up to requirements of an evidence base. Nevertheless there is a much larger evidence base for dynamic psychotherapy than many people recognize. But, as we shall see, there is a tension in psychotherapy research between quantification and meaning. Quantification is meaningful to a scientist but less meaningful to a therapist and patient. Conversely, clinical reality is meaningful to therapists but considered by researchers to be of limited value. To bridge the gap we need a third way that combines quantification and meaning.

Are there problems with the concept of an evidence base?

Fundamentally an evidence base implies that the value of an intervention can be judged by its consequences. Therapy is only good if a patient gets better. This has a number of problems for psychotherapy research.

First, there is difficulty in agreeing meaningful measures of outcome which accurately reflect improvement. Psychotherapy is an elaborate intervention targeting complex human problems. Faced with this, the tendency can be merely to measure symptoms, forgetting that they are part of a human experience affecting the internal world of the individual and his family and friends. For example, depression may be measured with the Beck Depression Inventory (BDI) or the Hamilton Rating Scale, but the measures are not the illness and cannot represent the complexity and hetero-geneity of depression and the individual's total situation.

Second, symptomatic improvement may be a poor measure of the benefit of treatment. A patient may not improve symptoma-tically but be helped not to commit suicide. If this is the case, it is an important effect of therapy that is essential but difficult to measure.

Third, it needs to be decided who is the arbiter of outcome. Is it the therapist, the patient, or an independent observer? Patient satisfaction has become increasingly important and yet most research relies on the clinician–researcher as the judge of outcome. On the other hand, reliance on client satisfaction alone is not acceptable even though it may be superficially attractive. Patients may select all sorts of inappropriate treatments simply because they are pleasurable.

Fourth, over-reliance on scientific empiricism using randomized controlled trials as the gold standard may perpetuate unethical or unacceptable treatments. Clearly, choice of treatment depends on many factors, of which only one is the result of a trial.

What are the general methodological problems found in psychotherapy research?

A major problem for evaluating evidence for the usefulness of psychotherapy is the gap between 'efficacy' and 'effectiveness'. *Efficacy* of treatment refers to the results that are achieved in carefully designed trials. Efficacy trials are designed to show inter-nal validity so that causal inferences can be made. As many factors as possible are controlled so that the major variable is the inter-vention itself. In this way any measured change is likely to be a consequence of the treatment rather than a result of another factor such as passage of time. But treatment found to be efficacious in carefully defined conditions does not necessarily generalize to other settings and might work poorly within a hard-pressed psychotherapy department with few fully trained staff. This is known as the *effectiveness* of a treatment or how it performs in everyday clinical practice. More research is needed into effectiveness to ensure research findings can be generalized to everyday clinical practice (external validity).

Psychotherapy research is not alone in trying to address the strain between internal and external validity. Pharmacological research has exactly the same problem but in many ways takes it less seriously. Supervised patients participating in carefully conducted trials may take medication with unpleasant but harmless side-effects because serum levels are monitored, whereas patients who are left to their own devices may often 'forget' to take their pills. No one is surprised that the effectiveness of antidepressants in clinical practice is lower than that found in trials. It is probably true to say that the schism between efficacy and effectiveness studies or internal and external validity, respectively, is overstated. All research is a compromise.

What are the specific problems?

Particular problems in psychotherapy research are dependent on the strategy used. Until recently psychodynamic psychotherapy has been reliant on single case studies which have been rich in clinical detail. Malan (1963, 1973) has demonstrated the value of designing outcome criteria appropriate to each patient. After careful psychodynamic assessment, but before therapy began, a decision was made by Malan's research team as to which changes would be accepted as evidence. In each case, focal conflicts underlying the patient's symptoms were identified. For therapy to be considered a success, resolution or modification of the conflicts needs to have taken place. For example, in the case of a socially anxious woman whose underlying conflict is related to fear of entering a relationship with a man, the evidence sought might be that, by the end of treatment or follow-up, she should have a long-term heterosexual relationship. Reduction in social anxiety alone would not be accepted as evidence of dynamic change.

Psychodynamic therapists have been severely criticized on the basis that knowledge gleaned from single case studies is less valid and less generalizable than that obtained from groups of individuals. Whilst there is some merit in this criticism, the situation is nothing like as straight-forward as some critics would like people to believe. Single case studies may be descriptive or quantitative and, whilst descriptive cases help in understanding complex unconscious processes, any interpretation and generalization of the findings are limited since interventions have a range of specific and non-specific effects and there is no contrasting intervention. Quantitative single case studies do not suffer from these problems. Appropriate baseline measures may be taken, interventions given or withdrawn in an organized manner, and the effects monitored. The patient acts as his own control. This has been used extensively in cognitive-behavioural therapy and to a lesser extent in psychoanalytic therapy (Fonagy & Moran, 1993). Single case designs are important and cannot be dismissed. When replicated across randomly sampled cases they have excellent generalizability, particularly about the effectiveness of interventions on specific symptoms. Despite the useful information that may be derived from such studies and their ease of implementation, greater emphasis has been given to the randomized controlled trial (RCT).

The application of the RCT to psychotherapy research may seem at first sight to be deceptively simple. A homogeneous group of patients are allocated randomly to different treatments targeting specific problems. Interventions are delivered by skilled therapists in a pure and measurable form in a specific 'dose' (e.g. 16 sessions) and outcome is reliably measured. But this is easier said than done and there are many limitations to the approach despite its present popularity.

Randomization of patients to different therapies does not represent normal patient entry into and continuation with treatment. Strict randomization may lead to patients being allocated to treatments they would otherwise not normally accept. There is some evidence that patient expectation of therapy is important for outcome (Horowitz, Rosenberg, & Bartholomew, 1993). Sample size is inevitably small, and attrition of patients may be significant, leading to a situation in which those patients remaining in a trial are far from random. Different patients respond differently to the same treatment, leading to variation in outcome within the same group which may distort the outcome (see SPP-1, p. 265). Further, the same 'named' treatment is often delivered by different therapists so, even if a manual is followed, patients may well be getting treatment that differs in significant respects. Fidelity of application is measured by recording the sessions. Although few studies record all sessions, they randomly transcribe them to ensure that therapists keep to the model of therapy. Therapists themselves are rarely matched to patients even though the patient–therapist fit is a potent influence on outcome. Finally, non-specific factors (see p. 69) and investigator allegiance powerfully influence outcome (Robinson, Berman, & Neimeyer, 1990; Gaffan, Tsaousis, & Kemp-Wheeler, 1995; Luborsky, Diguer, Seligman, *et al.*, 1999). Professionals heavily identified with a therapy are more likely to show a better outcome for that therapy than an alternative control. Again, blind evaluations are hard to achieve.

Perfect implementation of an RCT may not be necessary to determine adequately the outcome of treatment. It is possible to randomize patients recruited from within a 'clinical setting', thereby gaining the advantage of treatment being given within a context in which it will be applied in normal practice, but such studies are rare within any modality of therapy. RCTs favour short-term treatments since they are difficult to maintain over a prolonged period of time. Patients tend to drop out or begin to resent the intrusion on treatment and decline to take part. This is especially so in patients treated in longer term psychodynamic therapy who nowadays often have personality disorders. Nevertheless RCTs of longer term psycho-analytically orientated therapy for personality disorder have been done and a number are in progress. These are described on p. 236. These problems have meant that another method has been used more frequently in dynamic therapy to assess outcome: the 'open trial' or cohort study, which reflects a naturalistic approach to a group of patients undergoing treatment. Patients may have to fit strict criteria to enter the trial but there is no control group. As a result any change may be due to other factors such as passage of time. However, if the cohort of patients is large enough it is possible to draw conclusions about the relative value of a treatment. This method has been used particularly in the study of effectiveness of services such as the Cassel Hospital (Rosser, Birch, Bond, *et al.*, 1987) and Henderson Hospital (Dolan, Warren, & Norton, 1996) in the UK and the Austen Riggs Center in the USA (Blatt & Ford, 1994).

Some outcome studies

Having spelt out some of the problems of psychotherapy research, we will now mention some of the important studies that have been done over the years. Recently there has been a sea-change in the field of dynamic therapy. More and more research is being done in relation to both outcome of treatment and process of change.

Eysenck (1952), in his often-quoted reviews of evidence then available, asserted that two-thirds of neurotic patients improve whether they are treated or not, but his view has been sharply criticized. Indeed, it is amazing how much mileage these articles have had when one considers that they compared out-patients who improved in analysis with in-patients considered well enough to be discharged from state mental hospitals within a year; the groups were scarcely comparable in terms of type and severity of illness, social background, or criteria of change. The figures, if offered by anyone else, would hardly have escaped Eysenck's own criticism. Reanalysis of Eysenck's data (McNeilly & Howard, 1991) showed that the impact of a few months' psychotherapy was equal to the impact of two years of all other forms of help available to an individual, confirming the potency of psychotherapy. Nevertheless Eysenck's remarks challenged the complacency of psychotherapy and stimulated more detailed research.

Our contention that psychotherapy has more significant effects than simply removing symptoms is lent indirect support by findings that emerge from examination of an early study by Sloane and colleagues (1975) in Philadelphia. They studied patients suffering from a variety of moderately severe neuroses and personality disorders, who, after a lengthy initial assessment (which could itself be therapeutic), were randomly allocated to one of three groups for four months. One group was treated by behaviour therapists, one by analytically orientated psychotherapists, and the third remained on a waiting list with the promise of eventual treatment (and were kept in telephone contact). Within four months the severity of target symptoms had declined significantly in all three groups, but in both treated groups more than in the waiting-list group; and in both treatment groups the outcome was very much related to the quality of the relationship between patient and therapist. However, while only the behaviour therapy group had improved in four months on both work and social adjustment ratings, during the subsequent eight-month follow-up, *after treatment had stopped*, the analytical psychotherapy group continued to improve with regard to social adjustment. It seems that, despite the short duration of psychotherapy, they had internalized the learning process. These findings support those of an earlier study in Baltimore, comparing the outcome in patients who had six months of either individual, group, or supportive therapy, and were followed up for five years:

> The results add some confirmation to the supposition that psychoanalytic psychotherapy, which is of course insight-orientated, produces two distinguishable but related types of effect – relief of distress and improvement in personal functioning. Symptom relief results primarily from the patient's expectation of help, so that it occurs rapidly, is independent of the particular type of therapy, and can be duplicated in some patients by administration of a placebo. Improvement in personal functioning occurs more gradually and seems to be related to the kind of therapeutic experience, suggesting that it may be the result of a learning process.
>
> (Frank, 1961, p. 214)

Another more carefully crafted study looking at differential effectiveness of therapies was conducted by Snyder and Willis (1989). They compared behavioural marital therapy (BMT) to insight-orientated marital therapy (IOMT) and found both treatments to be more effective than no treatment but generally equivalent to each other at the end of the trial and at six-month follow-up. The couples were then followed up four years later (Snyder, Willis, & Grady-Fletcher, 1991). There was a marked difference in divorce rates between the two groups: 38 per cent in the BMT group but only 3 per cent in the IOMT group. It seems that there was something particular about the IOMT that had a continuing effect over time which was absent in the BMT. There are of course other possible explanations but therapist adherence to treatment was carefully monitored and it was established that both treatments, designed to have clear difference, had been given appropriately.

It would seem that successful psychotherapy initiates a process of learning which develops its own momentum. This starts in the relationship between patient and therapist, the crux of all dynamic psychotherapy, whether at the outer levels of support and counselling or the deeper levels of exploration and analysis. Effects occurring after the cessation of therapy are known as sleeper effects and they seem to be more apparent after longer term analytic therapy than after other therapies. This underscores the need to build in long-term follow-up when looking at the outcome of different therapies. Not only may some patients who improve at the end of therapy deteriorate, but also some may improve gradually over time.

There has been a recent surge in psychotherapy research incorporating long-term follow-up. A notable example in the USA is that conducted by the National Institute of Mental Health (NIMH) and called the Treatment of Depression Collaborative Research Programme (TDCRP) (Elkin, Shea, Watkins, *et al.*, 1989). We shall describe this in some detail. The study had two major aims. The first was to see if collaborative clinical trials of psychotherapy on a large scale were feasible. The second was to test the effectiveness of two brief psychotherapies for the treatment of out-patient depression.

Two hundred and fifty depressed patients were randomly assigned to four treatment conditions: cognitive-behavioural therapy (CBT, see p. 228), interpersonal psychotherapy (IPT, see p. 222), imipramine as a standard antidepressant plus clinical management (IMI-CM), and placebo plus clinical management (PLA-CM). Therapists were trained in their model, were supervised regularly, sessions were tape recorded to ensure that therapy was given according to the model, and adherence was carefully checked. Patients were assessed for levels of depression and social function before treatment and at 4, 8, 12, and 16 weeks, and followed up at 6, 12, and 18 months. Inevitably the results are complicated but in essence there was little difference in outcome between all the groups. Patients receiving IMI-CM were least symptomatic and those receiving PLA-CM the most symptomatic at the end of treatment. Patients receiving IMI-CM or IPT were most likely to recover. This was upsetting to those vociferously supporting CBT, who have argued that the CBT was inadequately given on one site, although there is little data to support this (Hollon & Beck, 1994), and so the results have been criticized and the data reanalysed. No doubt the criticism would have been more muted if CBT had been shown to be superior to other treatments, but reanalysis (Elkin, Gibbons, Shea, *et al.*, 1995) confirms the equivalence of treatment options for less depressed patients. However, there is greater differentiation among therapies for the more depressed sample. On measures of depression IMI-CM and IPT were equally effective, and IMI-CM was more effective than CBT or PLA-CM. Follow-up of patients suggested that relapse rates were similar across groups, although there was a trend towards fewer relapses in those patients receiving psychotherapy, suggesting some 'sleeper effects' for those given a psychological treatment.

Overall the results were disappointing to those adherents of brand-named therapies who had hoped to prove once and for all that their therapy was the best.

Similar results were found in three studies conducted in the UK which looked at the outcome of depression treated with either CBT or psychodynamic-interpersonal therapy (PI). The latter is a manualized therapy theoretically derived from psychodynamic principles with some humanistic and interpersonal elements. The studies are the Sheffield Psychotherapy Project (SPP-1; Shapiro & Firth-Cozens, 1987), the Second Sheffield Psychotherapy Project (SPP-2; Shapiro, Barkham, Rees, *et al.*, 1994; Shapiro, Rees, Barkham, *et al.*, 1995), and the Collaborative Psychotherapy Project (CPP; Barkham *et al.*, 1996). Again we shall describe them in some detail to illustrate some of the inevitable complexities in psycho-therapy research. All three studies were rigorously designed, conducted with independent assessors, used operationalized therapy which was monitored for adherence, and included careful follow-up. Subjects for all three studies had to have symptoms of depression, and in the SPP-2 and the CPP patients were stratified into mild, moderate, or severe, according to level of depression. In essence SPP-1 and SPP-2 were efficacy studies in that they involved the recruitment of white-collar workers who were then treated within a research clinic. The CPP was different and was designed to assess the effectiveness (generalisability) of the treatments, and so took place within a clinical setting.

The SPP-1 was a cross-over study. Patients were treated by the same therapists with CBT plus PI (eight sessions of each) or PI plus CBT (eight sessions of each) in order to mimic eclectic but professionally delivered therapy. There was no difference in outcome between the two groups and the order of therapy had no impact on outcome. Small differences on some measures were attributable to the effects of one therapist who was skilful in delivering CBT but less effective than other therapists in delivering PI. Perhaps this was because all the therapists had background training in CBT.

SPP-2 was a randomized controlled trial designed not only to assess overall outcome of CBT and PI in the treatment of depression, but also to explore the impact of investigator allegiance, the importance of symptom severity, and the speed of recovery or 'dose response'. Therapists were considered as being in 'equipoise' for CBT and PI, having no specific allegiance, and all delivered both treatments. Treatments were given for either 8 weeks or 16 weeks and patients were stratified according to level of depression. All the subjects who received CBT or PI showed substantial and broadly equivalent improvement. The effects of both psychotherapies were exerted with equal rapidity and were the same at all three levels of symptom severity. An interaction was found between initial symptom severity and duration of therapy, with the more severely depressed patients showing significantly better outcomes with 16 sessions compared to those receiving only 8 sessions. Although there were improvements following eight sessions of PI, it was not as effective as the other three treatments (8-session CBT, 16-session CBT, 16-session PI). Follow-up at one year found no differences in outcome or in maintenance of gains between CBT and PI, although those receiving only eight sessions of PI continued to do less well.

It has already been mentioned that it is all very well for treatments to work within a research setting when they are applied by well-trained workers, but this is not the same as their working within a clinical setting. The CPP was designed to test this. Subjects were recruited from NHS clinics and once again stratified according to severity of symptoms and given either 8 or 16 sessions of either CBT or PI. Not surprisingly the results were less good than those found in the SPP-2, although all subjects did show substantial gains. There were two main effects: patients did better with 16 sessions of treatment; and the immediate post-therapy gains were not maintained at three months nor at one year.

The consistent finding of equivalence of different therapies in a number of disorders is known as the 'dodo verdict' – 'everybody has won and all must have prizes'. This judgement has become so frequent that finding difference rather than similarity in outcome needs careful explanation. It may be that we just do not yet have the research capability to detect difference, but it remains possible that all therapies have many factors in common and that these factors in themselves are potent agents of change. They are often subsumed under the rubric of the therapeutic alliance or working alliance.

Outcome and the therapeutic alliance

We have already highlighted the importance of the relationship between therapist and patient as a contributor to the success of therapy (see p. 249). In a meta-analytic study (analysis of trends in large numbers of variously conducted trials), Horvath and Symonds (1991) concluded that there was a 26 per cent difference in level of therapeutic success dependent on the therapeutic alliance. Thus although most studies show little if any difference in outcome between therapies, when there is a difference this may simply be a reflection of the alliance between patient and therapist and not a differential effect of a therapy. In general the early alliance between patient and therapist is a better predictor of success than the strength of the alliance later in therapy, although this pattern is less evident in more recent studies. It may be thought that the alliance is likely to be of most importance in dynamic therapies since psychoanalytic therapy uses the relationship between patient and therapist as a mediator of change. In fact the alliance seems equally important in other therapies. Castonguay *et al.* (1996) reported significant associations between the alliance and outcome measures at mid- and post-treatment for patients receiving CBT and CBT plus an antidepressant. However a study by DeRubeis and Feeley (1990) implies that the alliance is less predictive in more highly structured interventions.

The impact of the alliance on outcome has been reported both for the NIMH and the Sheffield project discussed earlier (see p. 265). Krupnick *et al.* (1996) reported that the alliance level averaged over all the treatment sessions accounted for 21 per cent of the variance in the NIMH trial. Interestingly this factor showed equal impact across all the treatments, including pharmacotherapy. But this group was also given clinical management, which may itself be another name for therapeutic alliance. In the Sheffield study the results are more complex, but Stiles *et al.* (1998) also found a statistically significant association between a number of outcome measures and the alliance.

There seems little doubt that the alliance, when positive, makes a substantial contribution to the outcome of all forms of therapy. Of course this could be the result of patients reporting a positive alliance if their treatment is going well, but those studies that have looked at this possibility suggest this is not the case. There is no evidence that those patients with a good outcome view their therapy as more positive or as having more favourable interventions than those individuals whose treatment goes less well.

A positive alliance does not of itself ensure a good outcome. A lot of energy has been spent in trying to identify the potent factors of therapies in the hope that more of what is effective will improve outcome. This is rather simplistic and follows the 'drug metaphor' of therapy. If a little aspirin is good for a headache then increasing the dose may be more effective. Whilst this is true to an extent, there may of course be a therapeutic range in which the drug is effective. The same applies to psychotherapy. One can overdose or underdose! Further, it is no good simply increasing the number of transference interpretations or cognitive interventions during a session. Such activity may represent desperation on the part of the therapist and so be negatively correlated with improvement. Piper *et al.* (1991, 1993) explored the relationship between number (concentration) and accuracy of transference interpretation and outcome of therapy. The results are complex and tentative. Those patients with the most psychological-mindedness as measured on the Quality of Object Relations (QOR) scale had the best outcomes if interpretation was both *accurate* and of *low* concentration. Those patients with low quality of object relations did not do well, particularly if interpretations were inaccurate and of high concentration. Similar effects may occur in cognitive therapy since all interventions need to be given at the right time, in the right way, and within the right patient–therapist context if they are to be effective. For example, in a study by Horowitz and Marmac (1984) improvement for bereaved patients given short-term psychotherapy based on the principles of Malan (1976) was related to psychological maturity at the *beginning* of treatment. Those patients with good motivation and a stable, coherent sense of themselves did best with psychodynamic *exploration* of their difficulties. Those with a poor sense of self responded better to *supportive* therapy. In a later study Horowitz *et al.* (1993) suggested that patients who viewed their difficulties in interpersonal terms do best with psychodynamic therapy. These findings can be seen as supporting the impression of most clinicians.

Some recent research has considered the role of the therapist as a determinant of the outcome of treatment. Not surprisingly it turns out that there are good and bad therapists. One infrequently used method to investigate therapists involves profiling patient outcomes within therapy in order to find the empirically supported psychotherapist. Okiishi, Lambert, Nielsen, and Ogles (2003) examined data collected on 1841 clients seen by 91 therapists over a 2.5-year period in a University Counselling Centre. Clients were given the Outcome Questionnaire-45 (OQ-45) on a weekly basis. Okiishi *et al.*

first checked to see if theoretical orientation, type of training, professional role, and other factors could account for differences in clients' rate of improvement, but they did not, so they used statistical analysis to compare individual therapists to determine if there were significant differences in the overall outcome and speed of client improvement. There was a significant amount of variation among the clients' rates of improvement. The therapists whose clients showed the fastest rate of improvement had an average rate of change 10 times greater than the mean for the sample. The therapists whose clients showed the slowest rate of improvement actually showed an average increase in symptoms among their clients. Thus it looks like there are some super-therapists and some therapists who are a poor fit with a large group of patients who actually make their patients worse. Oddly, most therapists rate themselves as above average (Dew & Riemer, 2003).

Can therapists be helped to improve?

Cory-Harmon and colleagues (2007) gave psychotherapy patients a questionnaire about how they were feeling and functioning. They then randomly gave the patients' feedback to half of the therapists whilst the other half received strengthened feedback, which included patient self-assessment plus specific information about how the patients viewed their therapists and their social supports. These two groups were compared with a control group of patients whose therapists received no feedback. There were more than 1000 patients in the groups, giving the results additional importance. The researchers found that giving feedback to therapists clearly improved treatment outcome: with no feedback, 21 per cent of patients deteriorated; with regular feedback, 13 per cent of patients deteriorated; with strengthened feedback, 7 per cent of patients deteriorated. Thus feedback provided outside the clinical session, which is then used in the therapy itself, seems to reduce some of the harmful effects of therapy as well as increasing the beneficial effects. Often therapists think their patient is doing well when in fact the patient feels worse. The clear implication is that therapists are not always the best judge of how their patients are doing, perhaps because they are wedded to their theory – which can even suggest that deterioration during treatment is a sign of progress – blinded by their own optimism, or anxious about their own ineffectiveness.

Lambert (2005) and colleagues have described a system to measure, monitor, and feed back information about patient treatment. The clinician is provided with timely warnings when a patient's deviation from an expected treatment response foretells possible treatment failure. In summarizing four controlled studies, the collective results suggest that measuring, monitoring, and predicting treatment failure (feedback) enhance treatment outcomes for patients who have a negative response. They conclude that clinicians should be encouraged to employ feedback methods in routine practice despite their confidence in their own ability to predict patient outcome.

The quantification of meaning

These studies looking at the detail of the psychotherapeutic process represent an attempt to understand the complexity of the endeavour and to that extent move research away from quantification towards meaning. The most widely known attempt to put psychotherapeutic insights on a reliable, replicable, and scientifically reputable basis is the development of the Core Conflictual Relationship Theme (CCRT; Luborsky & Crits-Christoph, 1990). The method is laborious, but it yields psychodynamically meaningful data about the 'inner world'. It starts from the idea that every therapy session contains a number of unconscious personal themes which can be identified through studying transcripts of the sessions. Identifying CCRTs is a two-stage process. First, pairs of trained judges extract from the transcript a number of 'relationship episodes' (REs) which have been described or enacted by the patient in the session – a story about work, home, or his or her reactions to the therapist. Most patients generate about four such REs per session. The list of REs is then passed on to a second set of judges who analyse them into three components: (a) the patient's wishes, needs, or intentions; (b) the response elicited from others, either positive or negative; and (c) the reactions of the self to these others' reactions, again positive or negative. Common examples of wishes are for closeness, dominance, or autonomy; examples of responses are those of being rejected, controlled, or dominated; and examples of self-responses are anger, withdrawal, and disappointment. These categories are initially made freehand by the judges so as to produce 'tailor made' categories, which are then translated into a predetermined list of standard categories that allow for more reliable comparisons. From these emerges a CCRT or set of CCRTs which characterize the patient's core state – a typical example would be the wish for closeness, feeling rejected, and responding with withdrawal.

CCRT formulations are experience-near and do not use sophisticated psychoanalytic concepts or terminology, but are highly reliable (Crits-Cristoph, Luborsky, Dahl, *et al.*, 1988) and thus have considerable flexibility as a research tool. They can be modified into a set of statements which the patient can then use to think about himself. CCRTs correspond with the 'core beliefs' found to be important in cognitive therapy.

Luborsky has used CCRTs to research a number of important psychoanalytic issues. CCRT 'pervasiveness' decreases in the course of successful therapy, so that by the end of therapy patients are less dominated by their core themes. Wishes change less than responses, therapeutic change being associated particularly with the capacity to cope with negative responses and to elicit more positive ones from others, rather than some idealized 'resolution of underlying conflict'. Another study used CCRTs to look at the relationship between the 'accuracy' of interpretations, as measured by their closeness to CCRTs. In general the more skilful the therapist, the better the outcome, especially in so far as they were able accurately to identify wishes, responses elicited, and reactions. In this study, while accuracy of interpretation is related to good outcome, the type of interpretation was not, that is, non-transference interpretations were just as effective as transference ones (Fretter *et al.*, 1994).

Luborsky and Crits-Cristoph (1990) believe that the CCRT approach provides the first scientific confirmation and objective measure of the concept of transference (see p. 70). By comparing the features of CCRT with Freud's statements about transference they confirm that:

1   Individuals have only a few basic transference patterns.
2   These patterns are manifest both in their relationships generally and with the therapist.
3   They seem to derive from early parental relationship patterns.
4   Transference patterns are as evident outside therapy as in it.
5   These patterns are susceptible to gradual change in the course of treatment.

An important feature of any research method is its capacity to be used by all workers in the field, not just by those who devised it. This has not perhaps been the case with CCRT, but it is certainly true of a new instrument, the Adult Attachment Interview (AAI), devised by Mary Main and her colleagues (Main, 1991) based on the principles of attachment theory (Bowlby, 1988; Holmes, 1993), which is being widely used in psychodymamic psychotherapy research. The AAI also starts with interview transcripts, but, unlike most instruments, it is concerned not so much with the content as the *form* and *style* of the patient's narrative. Like therapy itself, the AAI tries to 'listen with the third ear' (Reik, 1922), but in a way that can be researched. A psychodynamic type of assessment interview is carried out, concentrating on the subject's past and present attachments and losses. It is assumed that a person's underlying relational dispositions (which may well be unconscious) will be evident in the structure of his narrative: its consistence, coherence, elaboration, or restrictedness.

Interviews are assigned to one of four major categories: *autonomous-free*, in which the subject can talk openly and coherently about his childhood and parents, including painful experiences from the past; *dismissive-detached*, in which narratives are not elaborated, and subjects have few childhood memories and tend to deny difficulty or devalue relationships in a grandiose way; *preoccupied-enmeshed*, in which the narrative style is muddled and confusing, and the individual appears to be dominated by affect from the past such as anger or overwhelming sadness; and *unresolved*, in which the subject shows lapses of reasoning and gives inconsistent information, particularly when discussing traumatic events such as physical or sexual abuse. The AAI also identifies significant 'breaks' or incoherence in any type of interview, which may reflect past trauma such as sexual abuse which has been repressed but momentarily surfaces during the interview. Many of these interviews may be classified as unresolved, although it has become apparent that it is impossible to classify some individuals.

The AAI has been used to track change in psychoanalytic therapy, showing how individuals can move from dismissive or enmeshed to secure narrative styles as therapy progresses (Fonagy *et al.*, 1995). It has also been used to trace the intergenerational transmission of attachment patterns, showing how the classification of prospective parents on the AAI before their babies are born correlates well with the subsequent child's attachment status at 1 year. An unexpected but important finding of this study was that infants appear to develop quite independent attachment patterns with each parent, so that they may be secure with father and insecure with mother, or vice versa, in line with the parent's AAI. This is consistent with the psychoanalytic view of an inner or representational world containing models or prototypes of relationships which may act independently of one another. Presumably similar internal models of attachment are built up in the course of therapy which then super-sede previous insecure relationship patterns.

Despite these attempts to move away from 'head-to-head' clashes of different psychotherapies, and to gain a better understanding of the subtlety and meaning of psychotherapy, we still have limited knowledge of patient, therapist, and therapy characteristics which are important for a favourable outcome to treatment. Certainly social class, age, ethnicity, and sex are not indicators either of outcome or of choice of therapy. Equally certain is that a friendly sympathetic attitude showing warmth and understanding is necessary on the part of the therapist, along with the development of a collaborative relationship, if therapy is to have any chance at all. A focus both on the patient's *negative feelings* towards the therapist (Reandeau & Wampold, 1991) and on attention to the patient–therapist relationship facilitates the therapeutic alliance. This factor, along with a well-motivated patient who views his problems both in interpersonal and intrapsychic terms, probably forms the most potent mix for effective therapy.

What sort of outcome can an individual patient look forward to at the end of psychotherapy?

We began with Mrs A. (see Prologue) as an example of someone helped by an initial psychotherapeutic approach. Where do we hope to have got to after more extensive psychotherapy? Freud defined mental health as the capacity to find satisfaction in work and love. Perhaps we should add a capacity for play or, in other words, define health as the ability to find satisfaction in work, play, and loving relationships. If this sounds rather ideal, it is less so than the definition adopted by the World Health Organization in its Charter that 'health is a state of complete physical, mental and social well-being' and more recent statements that there is no health without mental health. Such magical solutions psychotherapy cannot provide, but at best it can help to launch people in the direction of greater freedom and growth. We will give the last words to another patient.

> *Miss Z. was referred by her family doctor for psychotherapy in a depressive crisis, which followed a second termination. In the past she had lurched from one bad relationship or crisis to the next. Part of her was again inclined to 'pull herself together' as in the past, and forget about her difficulties till the next crisis arose. She had spent her life trying to be 'pleasant' to people and fulfil their expectations. Another part of her knew that this time she really needed help to break the cycle of failed relationships.*
>
> *During psychotherapy it became clear that the termination, which precipitated her depression, had revived her earlier childhood feelings of loss when her parents' marriage broke up, since when she had learnt to hide all her feelings behind a controlled and courteous front. Slowly she began getting in touch with the lost child part of herself and was able to develop a more appropriate and satisfying relationship with a man, whom she later married. After a comparatively brief period of psychotherapy, once or twice a week for 18 months, she felt, in her own words, 'the door had been pushed open a bit, the stiffness of the hinges overcome' and she both wanted and felt able to go on opening it herself.*
>
> *Some time after leaving she wrote: 'I would like to let you know that on leaving I felt none of the sadness of parting I had expected but, to my astonishment, quite the reverse: an immense cheerfulness at having found someone to talk with, past, present, and future. And so, for the first time I can remember a feeling of solid confidence in myself to face life itself, still confusing but not so frightening any longer. The feeling of being able to be and exist and give of myself without feeling the threat of an infinite void, of falling off a very high roof, but rather of having myself, and contact with the world all around, continues.'*

Appendix

Brief description of training and roles of some professionals in the field of the psyche

Psychiatrists are medically qualified doctors who have gained postgraduate experience and training in the treatment of emotional and mental disturbances. Like general physicians in the medical field, they have overall responsibility for the assessment and management of all types of psychiatric in-patients and out-patients, including those with organic and functional psychoses, neuroses, and personality problems. Their treatment may be more often physically based, especially for the psychoses, using drugs and ECT, but also offers the vital support of hospital admission or day-care that is essential in many conditions. Supportive psychotherapy is provided by the general psychiatrist and other members of his team, such as social worker, nurse, or occupational therapist. Some training in psychotherapy is recommended for every psychiatrist, who should now reach practitioner level in at least one specified psychotherapy and have a working knowledge of other therapies.

Psychologists are usually not medically qualified, but have a degree in psychology – the study of mental processes and behaviour, normal and abnormal. After graduation they may specialize in academic, educational, industrial, or clinical psychology. Clinical psychologists in the past were chiefly employed to administer intelligence, personality, and neurodiagnostic tests, but are now more autonomous offering important therapeutic roles. They have played a leading part in furthering behavioural psychotherapy and cognitive therapy (p. 228), many are active in dynamic psychotherapy, and some go on to train in the special fields of psychoanalysis, group analysis, and family and marital therapy.

Psychoanalysts may be medically qualified, and if so have usually trained as psychiatrists before seeking further training at a recognized institute of psychoanalysis, which includes having a personal psychoanalysis. Those who are not medically qualified come from backgrounds such as psychology and social work, but usually arrange for a doctor to take medical responsibility for the patients they treat. Psychoanalysis can be viewed as one type of psychotherapy, albeit the most radical and intense in its aims.

In the UK, *psychotherapist* as a designation implies no specific professional training as yet. This has disadvantages and advantages. The fact that anyone can call himself a psychotherapist means that untrained people can exploit those in emotional distress. Following concern about Scientology, the Foster (1971) Report recommended that in order to ensure professional and ethical standards a register of specialist psychotherapists should be set up, indicating those with recognized training such as qualified psychoanalysts, group analysts, and psychotherapists trained by certain established institutes.

To this end a Professions Joint Working Party was formed which led to the publication of the Sieghart (1978) Report, then a series of annual 'Rugby' psychotherapy conferences, evolving into the UK Standing Conference for Psychotherapy (UKSCP) in 1989 (Pedder, 1989a) and then the inauguration of the UK Council for Psychotherapy in 1993. However not all parties were entirely happy with these arrangements and some of the analytic wing broke away to found the British Confederation of Psychotherapists (BCP). Both the UKCP and the BCP, now renamed the British Psychoanalytic Council (BPC), are pursuing issues of standards of training, ethics, and registration. These developments were given impetus by the establishment of a single market within the European Community in 1992. Reciprocal arrangements will have to be arrived at whereby qualifications to practise psychotherapy are recognized between countries. In some, legislation exists to restrict practice and health insurance cover to registered psychotherapists and their clients.

At present there remains a pressing need to regulate the practice of psychotherapy in this country but, after many years of talking, nothing has yet been agreed, which is a sad reflection on the profession. Professional regulations and codes set out the values and standards expected of any professional psychotherapist and it is hoped that by the time this book is published they will be laid out so that all psychotherapists can accept a set of core values to which they adhere. They will then have an overarching professional duty to consider and respect them because they give structure to their professional identity. Openly expressed values also give an indication to clients and patients of what they can expect from their therapists and, more importantly, what they can expect *not* to happen.

Training and psychotherapy

In its *general* sense, the practice of psychotherapy should not be restricted to full-time psychotherapists. Everyone in the helping professions should have a psychotherapeutic attitude, be familiar with the simpler psychotherapeutic methods, and be aware of the scope and availability of more specialized forms of psychotherapy. Courses in communication skills and developing a therapeutic alliance are now routinely offered to health professionals to further this aim, but it is the more specialist courses which are beginning to think about training differently. In the past, training in psychotherapy followed an apprentice model during which trainees attended an academic course and applied their knowledge in clinical practice whilst undergoing supervision from a more senior practitioner. Nowadays, trainees are more likely to be assessed according to their competence in demonstrating the application of technical aspects of therapy within a clinical encounter. This begs the question of defining exactly what a therapist does and how we know that he does it with high quality. It is possible to engage in a therapeutic process that technically might follow recommendations but to do it in such a way that the quality is compromised. So practitioners have spent considerable time trying to outline the skills of psychotherapy, and these are currently being developed in a systematic manner by Skills for Health (2009).

Competencies are defined according to the ability of the therapist to maintain a therapeutic attitude, to be able to assess patients for different psychotherapies, to develop a therapeutic alliance, and to engage the patient in a therapeutic process. Whilst these statements might sound ill-defined, the detail of them forms the core of this book. It is necessary for all therapists to have a sound theoretical framework on which to base coherent therapeutic interventions, but above all it is a requirement that they treat people with respect and are able to join with their patients so that together they can try to relieve distress and solve problems.

References

Abbas, A., Sheldon, A., Gyra, J., & Kalpin, A. (2008). Intensive short-term dynamic psychotherapy for DSM-IV personality disorders: A randomized controlled trial. *Journal of Nervous and Mental Disease*, *196*, 211–216.

Acharya, S., Moorhouse, S., Kareem, J., & Littlewood, R. (1989). Nafsiyat: A psychotherapy centre for ethnic minorities. *Bulletin of Royal College of Psychiatrists*, *13*, 358–360.

Ackerman, N. W. (1966). *Treating the Troubled Family*. New York: Basic Books.

Adams, M. V. (1996). *The Multicultural Imagination: "Race", Colour and the Unconscious*. London: Routledge.

Aggar, E. M. (1988). Psychoanalytic perspectives on sibling relationships. *Psychoanalytic Inquiry*, *8*, 1–30.

Ainsworth, M. D. S., & Wittig, B. A. (1969). Attachment and exploratory behavior of one-year-olds in a strange situation. In B. M. Foss (Ed.), *Determinants of Infant Behavior* (pp. 113–136). London: Methuen.

Alexander, F. (1957). *Psychoanalysis and Psychotherapy*. London: George Allen & Unwin.

Allen, J. G., & Fonagy, P. (Eds.) (2006). *Handbook of Mentalization-Based Treatment*. Chichester: Wiley.

American Psychiatric Association (1994). *Diagnostic and Statistical Manual of Mental Disorders (DSM-IV)* (4th ed.). Washington, DC: American Psychiatric Association.

Anderson, E. M., & Lambert, M. J. (1995). Short-term dynamically oriented psychotherapy: A review and meta-analysis. *Clinical Psychology Review*, *15*, 503–514.

Ansbacher, H. L., & Ansbacher, R. R. (1957). *The Individual Psychology of Alfred Adler*. New York: Harper Torchbooks.

Apter, A., Plutchik, R., Sevy, S., Korn, M., Brown, S., & van Praag, H. (1989). Defense mechanisms in risk of suicide and risk of violence. *American Journal of Psychiatry*, *146*, 1027–1031.

Argyle, M. (1972). *The Psychology of Interpersonal Behaviour.* Harmondsworth: Penguin.

Asen, K. E., Berkowitz, R., Cooklin, A., Leff, J., Piper, R., & Rein, L. (1991). Family therapy outcome research: A trial for families, therapists and researchers. *Family Processs, 30,* 3–20.

Ashurst, P., & Hall, Z. (1989). *Understanding Women in Distress.* London: Tavistock Publications/Routledge.

Atwood, G. E., & Stolorow, R. S. (1984). *Structures of Subjectivity: Explorations in Psychoanalytic Phenomenology.* Hillsdale, NJ: Analytic Press.

Aveline, M. (1984). What price psychiatry without psychotherapy? *Lancet, 2,* 856–859.

Bacal, H. A., & Newman, A. (1990). *Theories of Object Relations: Bridges to Self Psychology.* New York: Columbia University Press.

Bacha, C. (1997). The stranger in the group. *Psychodynamic Counselling, 3,* 7–22.

Baer, P. E., Dunbar, P. W., Hamilton, J. E., & Beutler, L. E. (1980). Therapist perceptions of the therapeutic process: Development of a psychotherapy process inventory. *Psychological Reports, 46,* 563–570.

Balint, E., Courtenay, M., Elder, A., Hull, S., & Julian, P. (1993). *The Doctor, His Patient and the Group: Balint Re-visited.* London: Routledge.

Balint, M. (1957). *The Doctor, His Patient and the Illness.* London: Butterworth.

Balint, M. (1965). *Primary Love and Psychoanalytic Technique.* London: Tavistock Publications.

Balint, M. (1968). *The Basic Fault.* London: Tavistock Publications.

Balint, M., & Balint, E. (1961). *Psychotherapeutic Techniques in Medicine.* London: Tavistock Publications.

Balint, M., Ornstein, P. H., & Balint, E. (1972). *Focal Psychotherapy: An Example of Applied Psychoanalysis.* London: Tavistock Publications.

Bandler, R., & Grinder, J. (1981). *Neuro Linguistic Programming and the Structure of Hypnosis.* Moab, UT: Real People Press.

Baranger, M. (1993). The mind of the analyst: From listening to interpretation. *International Journal of Psycho-Analysis, 74,* 15–24.

Barber, J., & Muenz, L. (1996). The role of avoidance and obsessiveness in matching patients to cognitive and interpersonal psychotherapy: Empirical findings from the treatment of depression collaborative research programme. *Journal of Consulting and Clinical Psychology, 64,* 951–958.

Barkham, M., Rees, A., Shapiro, D. A., Stiles, W., Agnew, R. Halstead, J., *et al.* (1996). Outcome of time-limited psychotherapy in applied settings: Replication the Second Sheffield Psychotherapy Project. *Journal of Consulting and Clinical Psychology, 64,* 1079–1085.

Barton, R. (1959). *Institutional Neurosis*. Bristol: John Wright.

Barton, R., & Whitehead, J. A. (1969). The gas light phenomenon. *Lancet*, *1*, 1258–1260.

Bateman, A., & Fonagy, P. (1999). The effectiveness of partial hospitalization in the treatment of borderline personality disorder: A randomized controlled trial. *American Journal of Psychiatry*, *156*, 1563–1569.

Bateman, A., & Fonagy, P. (2001). Treatment of borderline personality disorder with psychoanalytically oriented partial hospitalization: An 18-month follow-up. *American Journal of Psychiatry*, *158*, 36–42.

Bateman, A., & Fonagy, P. (2003). Health service utilization costs for borderline personality disorder patients treated with psychoanalytically oriented partial hospitalization versus general psychiatric care. *American Journal of Psychiatry*, *160*, 169–171.

Bateman, A., & Fonagy, P. (2008). 8-Year follow-up of patients treated for borderline personality disorder: Mentalization-based treatment versus treatment as usual. *American Journal of Psychiatry*, *165*, 631–638.

Bateman, A., & Fonagy, P. (2009). Randomized controlled trial of outpatient mentalization based treatment versus structured clinical management for borderline personality disorder. *American Journal of Psychiatry*, *1666*, 1355–1364.

Bateman, A., & Holmes, J. (1995). *Introduction to Psychoanalysis: Contemporary Theory and Practice*. London: Routledge.

Bateson, G., Jackson, D., Haley, J., & Weakland, J. (1956). Toward a theory of schizophrenia. *Behavioural Science*, *1*, 251–264.

Beck, A. T. (1976). *Cognitive Therapy and the Emotional Disorders*. New York: International Universities Press.

Beels, C. C., & Ferber, A. (1969). Family therapy: A view. *Family Process*, *9*, 280–318.

Behr, H. (1996). Multiple family group: A group-analytic perspective. *Group Analysis*, *29*, 9–22.

Benjamin, J. (1990). *The Bonds of Love*. London: Virago.

Bentovim, A., & Kinston, W. (1978). Brief focal family therapy when the child is the referred patient. *Journal of Child Psychology and Psychiatry*, *19*, 1–12.

Bentovim, A., Gorell Barnes, G., & Cooklin, A. (1987). *Family Therapy*. London: Academic Press.

Berger, R. J. (1969). The sleep and dream cycle. In A. Kales (Ed.), *Sleep Physiology and Pathology*. Philadelphia: Lippincott.

Bergin, A. E., & Garfield, S. L. (Eds.) (1994). *Handbook of Psychotherapy and Behaviour Change* (4th ed.). Chichester: Wiley.

Bergin, A. E., & Garfield, S. L. (Eds.) (2004). *Handbook of Psychotherapy and Behaviour Change* (5th ed.). Chichester: Wiley.

Berke, J., Masoliver, C., & Ryan, T. (1995). *The Arbours Experience of Alternative Community Care*. London: Process Press.

Bernard, H. S., & MacKenzie, K. R. (1994). *Basics of Group Psychotherapy*. New York: Guilford Press.

Berne, E. (1961). *Transactional Analysis in Psychotherapy*. New York: Evergreen.

Berne, E. (1966). *Games People Play*. London: Andre Deutsch.

Bertalanffy, L. von (1968). *General System Theory*. New York: Brasiller.

Bettelheim, B. (1975). *The Uses of Enchantment*. Harmondsworth: Penguin (1978).

Bierer, J., & Evans, R. I. (1969). *Innovations in Social Psychiatry*. London: Avenue Publishing.

Bion, W. R. (1961). *Experiences in Groups*. London: Tavistock Publications.

Bion, W. R. (1962). *Learning from Experience*. London: Maresfield Reprints (1989).

Blatt, S., & Ford, T. Q. (1994). *Therapeutic Change: An Object Relations Approach*. New York: Plenum Press.

Blatt, S. J., & Shahar, G. (2004). Psychoanalysis: For what, with whom, and how: A comparison with psychotherapy. *Journal of the American Psychoanalytic Association, 52*, 393–447.

Blatt, S. J., Quinlan, D. M., Pilkonis, P. A., & Shea, M. T. (1995). Impact of perfectionism and need for approval on the brief treatment of depression: The National Institute of Mental Health Treatment of Depression Collaborative Research Program revisited. *Journal of Consulting and Clinical Psychology, 63*, 125–132.

Bleiberg, K. L., & Markowitz, J. C. (2005). A pilot study of interpersonal psychotherapy for posttraumatic stress disorder. *American Journal of Psychiatry, 162*, 181–183.

Bloch, S. (1979). *An Introduction to the Psychotherapies*. Oxford: Oxford University Press.

Bloch, S. (2006). Supportive psychotherapy. In S. Bloch (Ed.), *An Introduction to Psychotherapies* (pp. 215–235). Oxford: Oxford University Press.

Blomberg, J., Lazar, A., & Sandell, R. (2001). Long-term outcome of long-term psychoanalytically oriented therapies: First findings of the Stockholm Outcome of Psychotherapy and Psychoanalysis study. *Psychotherapy Research, 11*, 361–382.

Boadella, D. (1988). Biosynthesis. In W. Dryden & D. Rowan (Eds.), *Innovative Therapy in Britain*. Milton Keynes: Open University Press.

Boardman, J., Henshaw, C., & Willmott, S. (2004). Needs for mental health treatment among general practice attenders. *British Journal of Psychiatry, 185*, 318–327.

Bowen, M. (1966). The use of family therapy in clinical practice. *Comprehensive Psychiatry, 7*, 345–374.

Bowlby, J. (1952). *Maternal Care and Mental Health*. Geneva: World Health Organization.

Bowlby, J. (1960). Separation anxiety. *International Journal of Psycho-Analysis, 41*, 89–113.

Bowlby, J. (1969). *Attachment and Loss. I. Attachment*. London: Hogarth Press.

Bowlby, J. (1973). *Attachment and Loss. II. Separation: Anxiety and Anger*. London: Hogarth Press.

Bowlby, J. (1977). The making and breaking of affectional bonds. II. Some principles of psychotherapy. *British Journal of Psychiatry, 130*, 421–431.

Bowlby, J. (1980). *Attachment and Loss. III. Loss: Sadness and Depression*. London: Hogarth Press/Penguin.

Bowlby, J. (1988). *A Secure Base: Clinical Applications of Attachment Theory*. London: Routledge.

Bowlby, J. (1990). *Charles Darwin: A New Biography*. London: Hutchinson.

Brandon, S. (1970). Crisis theory and possibilities of therapeutic intervention. *British Journal of Psychiatry, 117*, 627–633.

Brazelton, T., & Cramer, B. (1991). *The Earliest Relationship*. London: Karnac Books.

Breuer, J., & Freud, S. (1895). *Studies on Hysteria. The Standard Edition of the Complete Psychological Works of Sigmund Freud, Vol. 2*. London: Hogarth Press/Institute of Psychoanalysis.

Bridger, H. (1985). Northfield revisited. In M. Pines (Ed.), *Bion and Group Psychotherapy*. London: Routledge.

Brown, D. G. (1977). Drowsiness in the countertransference. *International Review of Psycho-Analysis, 4*, 481–492.

Brown, D. G. (1985). Bion and Foulkes: Basic assumptions and beyond. In M. Pines (Ed.), *Bion and Group Psychotherapy*. London: Routledge.

Brown, D. G. (1987). Change in the group analytic setting. *Psychoanalytic Psychotherapy, 3*, 53–60.

Brown, D. G. (1991). Assessment and selection. In J. Roberts & M. Pines (Eds.), *The Practice of Group Analysis*. London: Routledge.

Brown, D. G. (1998a). Fairshares and mutual concern: The role of sibling relationships. *Group Analysis, 31*, 315–326.

Brown, D. G. (1998b). Foulkes's basic law of group dynamics 50 years on: Abnormality, injustice and the renewal of ethics, 21st S. H. Foulkes Lecture. *Group Analysis, 31*, 391–419.

Brown, D. G., & Zinkin, L. (1994). *The Psyche and the Social World: Advances in Group-Analytic Theory*. London: Routledge.

Brown, G. W., & Harris, T. O. (1978). *Social Origins of Depression: A*

Study of Psychiatric Disorder in Women. London: Tavistock Publications.

Brown, G. W., Birley, J. L. T., & Wing, J. K. (1972). Influence of family life on the course of schizophrenic disorders: A replication. *British Journal of Psychiatry, 121*, 241–258.

Brown, J. R., Donelan-McCall, N., & Dunn, J. (1996). Why talk about mental states? The significance of children's conversations with friends, siblings, and mothers. *Child Development, 67*, 836–849.

Brown, K. W., & Ryan, R. M. (2003). The benefits of being present: Mindfulness and its role in psychological well-being. *Journal of Personality and Social Psychology, 84*, 822–848.

Bruch, H. (1974). *Learning Psychotherapy.* Cambridge, MA: Harvard University Press.

Bruggen, P., & Davies, G. (1977). Family therapy in adolescent psychiatry. *British Journal of Psychiatry, 131*, 433–447.

Buber, M. (1971). *I and Thou* (trans. W. Kaufmann). Edinburgh: Clark.

Bureau, J., Easterbrooks, M. A., & Lyons-Ruth, K. (2009). Maternal depression in infancy: Criticial to children's depression in childhood and adolescence? *Development and Psychopathology, 21*, 519–537.

Burkitt, I. (1991). *Social Selves: Theories of the Social Formation of the Personality.* London: Sage Publications.

Burnham, J. (1986). *Family Therapy: First Step Towards a Systemic Approach.* London: Routledge.

Butler, S. (1872). *Erewhon.* London: Jonathan Cape.

Byng-Hall, J. (1973). Family myths used as defence in conjoint family therapy. *British Journal of Medical Psychology, 46*, 239–249.

Byng-Hall, J. (1995). *Rewriting Family Scripts: Improvisation and Systems Change.* London: Guilford Press.

Campling, P., & Haigh, R. (Eds.) (1999). *Therapeutic Communities: Past, Present and Future.* London: Jessica Kingsley.

Casement, P. (1985). *On Learning from the Patient.* London: Tavistock Publications.

Castonguay L. G., Goldfried, M. R., Wiser, S., Raue, P. J., & Hayes, A. M. (1996). Predicting the effect of cognitive therapy for depression: A study of unique and common factors. *Journal of Consulting and Clinical Psychology, 64*, 497–504.

Cawley, R. H. (1977, January). The teaching of psychotherapy. *Association of University Teachers of Psychiatry Newsletter*, pp. 19–36.

Chien, W. T., Chan, S. W., & Thompson, D. R. (2006). Effects of a mutual support group for families of Chinese people with schizophrenia: 18-Month follow-up. *British Journal of Psychiatry, 189*, 41–49.

Chiesa, M., & Fonagy, P. (2003). Psychosocial treatment for severe personality disorder: 36-Month follow-up. *British Journal of Psychiatry, 183*, 356–362.

Chiesa, M., Fonagy, P., & Holmes, J. (2006). Six-year follow-up of three treatment programs to personality disorder. *Journal of Personality Disorders*, *20*, 493–509.

Chiesa, M., Fonagy, P., & Bateman, A. (2007). Differences in clinical characteristics between patients assessed for NHS specialist psychotherapy and primary care counselling. *Psychology and Psychotherapy: Treatment, Research and Practice*, *80*, 591–603.

Chodorow, N. (1994). *Femininities, Masculinities, Sexualities: Freud and Beyond*. London: Free Association Books.

Clark, D. H. (1964). *Administrative Therapy*. London: Tavistock Publications.

Clark, D. H. (1977). The therapeutic community. *British Journal of Psychiatry*, *131*, 553–564.

Clarkin, J. F., & Frances, A. (1982). Selection criteria for the brief psychotherapies. *American Journal of Psychotherapy*, *36*, 166–180.

Clarkin, J. F., Frances, A. J., & Moodie, J. L. (1979). Selection criteria for family therapy. *Family Process*, *18*, 391–403.

Clarkin, J. F., Levy, K. N., Lenzenweger, M. F., & Kernberg, O. (2007). Evaluating three treatments for borderline personality disorder. *American Journal of Psychiatry*, *164*, 922–928.

Clarkson, P. (1992). *Transactional Analysis Psychotherapy: An Integral Approach*. London: Routledge.

Cloninger, C. R. (1994). Somatoform and dissociative disorders. In G. Winokur & P. Clayton (Eds.), *Medical Basis of Psychiatry* (pp. 169–192). Philadelphia: W. B. Saunders.

Cohen, P., Crawford, T. N., Johnson, J. G., & Kasen, S. (2005). The children in the community study of developmental course of personality disorder. *Journal of Personality Disorders*, *19*, 466–465.

Cooley, C. H. (1902). *Human Nature and the Social Order*. New York: Scribner.

Cooper, R., Friedman, J., Gans, S., Heaton, J. M., Oakley, C., Oakley, H., et al. (1989). *Thresholds: Between Philosophy and Psychoanalysis*. London: Free Association Books.

Cory-Harmon, S., Lambert, M., Smart, D., Hawkins, E., Nielsen, S., Slade, K., et al. (2007). Enhancing outcome for potential treatment failures: Therapist–client feedback and clinical support tools. *Psychotherapy Research*, *17*, 379–392.

Costa, P., & Widiger, T. (1994). *Personality Disorders and the Five-Factor model of Personality*. Washington, DC: American Psychological Association.

Cox, J. L. (1998). Reflections on contemporary community psychiatry: Where is the therapy? The 1st Maxwell Jones Lecture. *Therapeutic Communities*, *19*, 3–10.

Cramer, V., Torgersen, S., & Kringlen, E. (2006). Personality disorders and quality of life. A population study. *Comprehensive Psychiatry*, *47*, 178–184.

Crisp, A. H. (1967). The possible significance of some behavioural correlates of weight and carbohydrate intake. *Journal of Psychosomatic Research*, *11*, 117–131.

Crits-Christoph, P. (1992). The efficacy of brief dynamic psychotherapy: A meta-analysis. *American Journal of Psychiatry*, *159*, 325–333.

Crits-Cristoph, P., Luborsky, L., Dahl, L., & Popp, C. (1988). Clinicians can agree in assessing relationship patterns in psychotherapy. *Archives of General Psychiatry*, *45*, 1001–1004.

Crowe, M. J. (1973). Conjoint marital therapy: Advice or interpretation? *Journal of Psychosomatic Research*, *17*, 309–315.

CSIP (2007). Commissioning a brighter future: Improving access to psychological therapies. Retrieved from http://www.dh.gov.uk.

Dalal, F. (1998). *Taking the Group Seriously: Towards a Post-Foulkesian Group Analytic Theory*. London: Jessica Kingsley.

Darwin, C. (1871). *The Descent of Man*. London: Prometheus Books (1997).

Darwin, C. (1872). *The Expression of the Emotions in Man and Animals*. Chicago: University of Chicago Press (1965).

Das, A., Egleston, P., El-Sayeh, H., Middlemost, M., Pal, N., & Williamson, L. (2003). Trainees' experiences of a Balint group. *Psychiatric Bulletin*, *27*, 274–275.

Davanloo, H. (Ed.) (1978). *Basic Principles and Techniques in Short-Term Dynamic Psychotherapy*. New York: Spectrum Publications.

Davies, M. H. (1976). The origins and practice of psychodrama. *British Journal of Psychiatry*, *129*, 201–206.

Davies, S., Campling, P., & Ryan, K. (1999). Therapeutic community provision at regional and district levels. *Psychiatric Bulletin*, *23*, 79–83.

Daws, D., & Boston, M. (1981). *The Child Psychotherapist: Problems of Young People*. London: Karnac Books.

DeRubeis, R. J., & Feeley, M. (1990). Determinants of change in cognitive therapy for depression. *Cognitive Therapy Research*, *14*, 469–482.

Dew, S., & Riemer, M. (2003). Why inaccurate self-evaluation of performance justifies feedback interventions. In L. Bickman (Chair), *Improving Outcomes Through Feedback Intervention. A System of Care for Children's Mental Health: Expanding the Research Base*. Tampa: University of South Florida.

Diamond, N. (1996). Can we speak of internal and external reality? *Group Analysis*, *29*, 303–317.

Di Ceglie, D. (1998). *A Stranger in My Own Body: Atypical Gender Identity Development*. London: Karnac Books.

Dick, B. M. (1975). A ten year study of out patient analytic group therapy. *British Journal of Psychiatry*, *127*, 365–375.

Dicks, H. V. (1967). *Marital Tensions: Clinical Studies Towards a Psychological Theory of Interaction*. London: Routledge.

Dixon, N. F., & Henley, S. (1991). Unconscious perception: Possible implications of data from academic research for clinical practice. *Journal of Mental Disease*, *79*, 243–251.

Dolan, B., Warren, F., Menzies, D., & Norton, K. (1996). Cost-offset following specialist treatment of severe personality disorders. *Psychiatric Bulletin*, *20*, 413–417.

Dolan, B., Warren, F., & Norton, K. (1997). Change in borderline symptoms one year after therapeutic community treatment for severe personality disorder. *British Journal of Psychiatry*, *171*, 272–279.

Dozier, M. (1990). Attachment organisation and treatment use for adults with serious psychopathological disorders. *Development and Psychopathology*, *2*, 47–60.

Dunn, J. (1995). Intersubjectivity in psychoanalysis: A critical review. *International Journal of Psycho-Analysis*, *76*, 723–738.

Durkheim, E. (1897). *Suicide: A Study in Sociology* (trans. J. A. Spaulding & G. Simpson, 1952). London: Routledge & Kegan Paul (1952).

Edelman, G. M. (1989). *The Remembered Present: A Biological Theory of Consciousness*. New York: Basic Books.

Edelson, M. (1970). *Sociotherapy and Psychotherapy*. Chicago: University of Chicago Press.

Eisler, I., Dare, C., Russell, G. F. M., Szmukler, G., le-Grange, D., & Dodge, E. (1997). Family and individual therapy in anorexia nervosa: A 5-year follow-up. *Archives of General Psychiatry*, *54*, 1025–1030.

Elias, N. (1991). *The Society of Individuals* (trans. from German by E. Jephcott). Oxford: Blackwell.

Elkin, I., Shea, M. T., Watkins, J. T., Imber, S. D., Sotsky, S. M., Collins, J. F., et al. (1989). National Institute of Mental Health Treatment of Depression Collaborative Research Program: General effectiveness of treatment. *Archives of General Psychiatry*, *46*, 971–982.

Elkin, I., Gibbons, R. D., Shea, M. T., Sotsky, S. M., Watkins, J. T., Pilkonis, P. A., et al. (1995). Initial severity and differential treatment outcome in the National Institute of Mental Health Treatment of Depression Collaborative Research Program. *Journal of Consulting and Clinical Psychology*, *63*, 841–847.

Ellenberger, H. F. (1970). *The Discovery of the Unconscious*. London: Allen Lane.

Elliott, A., & Frosh, S. (1995). *Psychoanalysis in Contexts*. London: Routledge.

Emde, R. (1988). Development terminable and interminable I and II. *International Journal of Psycho-Analysis*, *69*, 23–42, 283–296.

Engel, G. L. (1967). A psychological setting of somatic disease: The giving up, given-up process. *Proceedings of the Royal Society of Medicine, 60,* 553–555.

Epstein, L., & Feiner, A. H. (1979). *Countertransference.* New York: Jason Aronson.

Epstein, S. (1994). Integration of the cognitive and the psychodynamic unconscious. *American Psychologist, 49,* 709–724.

Epston, D., & White, M. (1992). *Experience, Contradiction, Narrative and Imagination.* Adelaide, South Australia: Dulwich Centre Publications.

Erickson, M. H., & Rossi, E. L. (1979). *Hypnotherapy.* New York: Irvington Publishers.

Erickson, S. J., Feldman, S. S., & Steiner, H. (1996). Defense menchanisms and adjustment in normal adolescents. *American Journal of Psychiatry, 153,* 826–828.

Erikson, E. H. (1965). *Childhood and Society.* Harmondsworth: Penguin.

Ernst, S., & Maguire, M. (1987). *Living with the Sphynx: Papers from the Women's Therapy Centre.* London: The Women's Press.

Ettin, M. F. (1988). "By the crowd they have been broken, by the crowd they shall be healed": The advent of group psychotherapy. *International Journal of Group Psychotherapy, 38,* 139–167.

Etzioni, A. (1993). *The Spirit of Community.* New York: Crown.

Evans, J. (1998). *Active Analytic Group Therapy for Adolescents.* London: Jessica Kingsley.

Evison, R., & Horobin, R. (1988). Co-counselling. In W. Dryden & J. Rowan (Eds.), *Innovative Therapy in Britain.* Milton Keynes: Open University Press.

Eysenck, H. J. (1952). The effects of psychotherapy: An evaluation. *Journal of Consulting Psychology, 16,* 319–324.

Ezriel, H. (1950). A psycho analytic approach to group treatment. *British Journal of Medical Psychology, 23,* 59–74.

Ezriel, H. (1952). Notes on psychoanalytic group psychotherapy: II. Interpretations and research. *Psychiatry, 15,* 119–126.

Fairbairn, W. R. D. (1952). *An Object-Relations Theory of the Personality.* New York: Basic Books.

Fazio, R., Jackson, J. R., Dunton, B., & Williams, C. J. (1995). Variability in automatic activation as an unobtrusive measure of racial attitudes: A bona fide pipeline? *Journal of Personality and Social Psychology, 69,* 1013–1027.

Ferenczi, S. (1926). The further development of an active therapy in psychoanalysis. In *Further Contributions to the Theory of Psychoanalysis.* London: Hogarth Press.

Ferreira, A. (1963). Family myth and homeostasis. *Archives of General Psychiatry, 9,* 457–463.

Findlay, A. (1948). *A Hundred Years of Chemistry.* London: Duckworth.

Foley, S. H., O'Malley, S., Rounsaville, B. J., Prusoff, B. A., & Weissman,

M. M. (1987). The relationship of client difficulty to therapist performance in interpersonal psychotherapy of depression. *Journal of Affective Disorders*, *12*, 207–217.

Fonagy, P. (1999). Memory and therapeutic action. *International Journal of Psycho-Analysis*, *80*, 215–223.

Fonagy, P., & Higgitt, A. (1989). Evaluating the performance of departments of psychiatry. *Psychoanalytic Psychotherapy*, *4*, 121–153.

Fonagy, P., & Moran, G. (1993). Selecting single case research designs for clinicians. In N. E. Miller, L. Luborsky, J. P. Barber, & J. P. Docherty (Eds.), *Psychodynamic Treatment Research: Handbook for Clinical Practice*. New York: Basic Books.

Fonagy, P., Steele, M., Steele, H., Leigh, T., & Kennedy, R. (1995). Attachment, the reflective self, and borderline states; the predicitive specificity of the adult attachment interview and pathological development. In S. Goldberg (Ed.), *Attachment Theory: Social, Developmental, and Clinical Perspectives*. New York: Academic Press.

Fonagy, P., Leigh, T., Steele, M., Steele, H., Kennedy, R., Mattoon, G., *et al*. (1996). The relation of attachment status, psychiatric classification, and response to psychotherapy. *Journal of Consulting and Clinical Psychology*, *64*, 22–31.

Fordham, M. (1978). *Jungian Psychotherapy*. London: Wiley.

Foster, S. J. (1971). *Practice and Effects of Scientology*. London: HMSO.

Foudraine, J. (1974). *Not Made of Wood*. London: Quartet Books.

Foulkes, S. H. (1948). *Introduction to Group-Analytic Psychotherapy: Studies in the Social Integration of Individuals and Groups*. London: Maresfield Reprints.

Foulkes, S. H. (1964). *Therapeutic Group Analysis*. London: Allen & Unwin.

Foulkes, S. H. (1975). *Group Analytic Psychotherapy*. London: Gordon & Breach.

Foulkes, S. H., & Anthony, E. J. (1957). *Group Psychotherapy: The Psychoanalytic Approach*. Harmondsworth: Penguin.

Frances, A., Clarkin, J. F., & Marachi, J. (1980). Selection criteria for outpatient group psychotherapy. *Hospital and Community Psychiatry*, *31*, 245–250.

Franco, F. (2005). Infant pointing: Harlequin, servant of two masters. In N. Eilan, C. Hoerl, T. McCormack, & J. Roessler (Eds.), *Joint Attention: Communication and Other Minds*. New York: Oxford University Press.

Frank, J. D. (1961). *Persuasion and Healing*. Baltimore: Johns Hopkins University Press.

Frank, J. D. (1964). Training and therapy. In L. P. Bradford, J. R. Gibb, & K. D. Benne (Eds.), *T Group Theory and Laboratory Method: Innovation in Education*. New York: Wiley.

Frank, J. D. (1971). Therapeutic factors in psychotherapy. *American Journal of Psychotherapy*, *25*, 350–361.

Fransella, F., & Thomas, L. (1988). *Experimenting with Personal Construct Psychology*. London: Routledge & Kegan Paul.

Fraser, C. (1976). An analysis of face to face communication. In A. E. Bennett (Ed.), *Communication between Doctors and Patients*. London: Nuffield Provincial Hospitals Trust/Oxford University Press.

Fretter, P., Bucci, W., Broitman, J., Silberschatz, G., & Curtis, J. (1994). How the patient's plan relates to the concept of transference. *Psychotherapy Research*, *4*, 58–71.

Freud, A. (1936). *The Ego and the Mechanisms of Defence*. New York: International Universities Press.

Freud, A. (1958). Adolescence. *Psychoanalytic Study of the Child*, *13*, 255–278.

Freud, A. (1966). *Normality and Pathology in Childhood*. London: Hogarth Press.

Freud, A. (1976). *Changes in psychoanalytic practice and experience*. New York: International Universities Press.

Freud, S. (1894). *The Neuro Psychoses of Defence (I). Standard Edition of the Complete Psychological Works of Sigmund Freud*, Vol. 3. London: Hogarth Press.

Freud, S. (1896). *Aetiology of Hysteria. Standard Edition*, Vol. 3. London: Hogarth Press.

Freud, S. (1900). *The Interpretation of Dreams. Standard Edition*, Vols. 4 and 5. London: Hogarth Press.

Freud, S. (1901). *The Psychopathology of Everyday Life. Standard Edition*, Vol. 6 (pp. 1–190). London: Hogarth Press.

Freud, S. (1905). *Three Essays on the Theory of Sexuality. Standard Edition*, Vol. 7. London: Hogarth Press.

Freud, S. (1912). *Recommendations to Physicians Practising Psychoanalysis. Standard Edition*, Vol. 12. London: Hogarth Press.

Freud, S. (1913a). *On Beginning Treatment. Standard Edition*, Vol. 12 (pp. 121–144). London: Hogarth Press.

Freud, S. (1913b). *Totem and Taboo. Standard Edition*, Vol. 13. London: Hogarth Press.

Freud, S. (1914). *Remembering, Repeating and Working Through. Standard Edition*, Vol. 12. London: Hogarth Press.

Freud, S. (1917a). *Introductory Lectures on Psycho-Analysis: Part III, General Theory of the Neuroses. Standard Eedition*, Vol. 16 (pp. 243–463). London: Hogarth Press.

Freud, S. (1917b). *Mourning and Melancholia. Standard Edition*, Vol. 14. London: Hogarth Press.

Freud, S. (1919). *Lines of Advance in Psycho-Analytic Therapy. Standard Edition*, Vol. 17. London: Hogarth Press.

Freud, S. (1920). *Beyond the Pleasure Principle. Standard Edition*, Vol. 18 (pp. 1–64). London: Hogarth Press.

Freud, S. (1921). *Group Psychology and the Analysis of the Ego. Standard Edition*, Vol. 18. London: Hogarth Press.

Freud, S. (1923). *The Ego and the Id. Standard Edition*, Vol. 19. London: Hogarth Press.

Freud, S. (1925a). *An Autobiographical Study. Standard Edition*, Vol. 20 (pp. 7–74). London: Hogarth Press.

Freud, S. (1925b). *Some Psychical Consequences of the Anatomical Distinction Between the Sexes. Standard Edition*, Vol. 19 (pp. 248–258). London: Hogarth Press.

Freud, S. (1926a). *Inhibitions, Symptoms and Anxiety. Standard Edition*, Vol. 20. London: Hogarth Press.

Freud, S. (1926b). *The Question of Lay Analysis. Standard Edition*, Vol. 20 (pp. 77–172). London: Hogarth Press.

Freud, S. (1930). *Civilization and its Discontents. Standard Edition*, Vol. 21. London: Hogarth Press.

Freud, S. (1933). *New Introductory Lectures. Standard Edition*, Vol. 22. London: Hogarth Press.

Freud, S. (1940). *Splitting of the Ego in the Process of Defense. Standard Edition*, Vol. 23 (pp. 275–278). London: Hogarth Press.

Friedli, K., King, M., Lloyd, M., & Horder, J. (1997). Randomised controlled assessment of non-directive psychotherapy versus general practitioner care. *Lancet*, *350*, 1662–1556.

Fromm-Reichmann, F. (1948). Notes on the development of treatment of schizophrenics by psychoanalytic psychotherapy. *Psychiatry*, *11*, 263–273.

Frosh, P. (1987). *The Politics of Psychoanalysis: An Introduction to Freudian and Post Freudian Theory*. London: Macmillan Educational.

Gabbard, G. O., Lazar, S. G., Hornberger, J., & Spiegel, D. (1997). The economic impact of psychotherapy: A review. *American Journal of Psychiatry*, *154*, 147–155.

Gaffan, E. A., Tsaousis, I., & Kemp-Wheeler, S. M. (1995). Researcher allegiance and meta-analysis: The case of cognitive therapy for depression. *Journal of Consulting and Clinical Psychology*, *63*, 966–980.

Garland, C. (1982). Group analysis: Taking the non-problem seriously. *Group Analysis*, *15*, 4–14.

Garland, C. (1998). *Understanding Trauma: A Psychoanalytic Approach*. London: Duckworth.

Gaston, L. (1990). The concept of the alliance and its role in psychotherapy: Theoretical and empirical considerations. *Psychotherapy*, *27*, 143–153.

Gawronski, B. (2007). Attitudes can be measured! But what is an attitude? *Social Cognition*, *25*, 573–581.

Genders, E., & Player, E. (1995). *Grendon: A Study of a Therapeutic Prison*. Oxford: Clarendon Press.

Gergely, G., & Watson, J. (1996). The social biofeedback model of parental affect-mirroring. *International Journal of Psycho-Analysis, 77,* 1181–1212.

Giesbrecht, T., Smeets, T., & Merckelbach, H. (2007). Depersonalization experiences in undergraduates are related to heightened stress cortisol responses. *Journal of Nervous and Mental Disease, 195,* 282–287.

Gill, C. (1973). Types of interview in general practice: "The Flash". In E. Balint & J. S. Norell (Eds.), *Six Minutes for the Patient*. London: Tavistock Publications.

Gill, M. M. (1977). Psychic energy reconsidered: Discussion. *Journal of the American Psychoanalytic Association, 25,* 581–597.

Giovacchini, R. L. (1989). *Countertransference Triumphs and Catastrophes*. New York: Jason Aronson.

Gittings, R. (1975). *Young Thomas Hardy*. London: Heinemann.

Glick, I. D., & Kessler, D. R. (1974). *Marital and Family Therapy*. New York: Grune & Stratton.

Goffman, E. (1961). *Asylums: Essays on the Social Situation of Mental Patients and Other Inmates*. Harmondsworth: Penguin.

Goldenberg, I., & Goldenberg, H. (2004). *Family Therapy: An Overview* (6th ed.). Pacific Grove, CA: Thomson.

Gordon-Brown, I., & Somers, B. (1988). Transpersonal psychotherapy. In D. Dryden & J. Rowan (Eds.), *Innovative Therapy in Britain*. Milton Keynes: Open University Press.

Greenberg, J. R., & Mitchell, S. A. (1983a). *Object Relations in Psychoanalytic Theory*. Cambridge, MA: Harvard University Press.

Greenberg, J. R., & Mitchell, S. A. (1983b). *Psychoanalysis and Object Relations Theory*. New York: Basic Books.

Greenson, R. R. (1967). *The Technique and Practice of Psychoanalysis*. London: Hogarth Press.

Greer, S., Morris, T., & Pettingale, K. W. (1979). Psychological response to breast cancer: Effect on outcome. *Lancet, ii,* 785–787.

Grosskurth, P. (1985). *Melanie Klein: Her World and Her Work*. London: Hodder & Stoughton.

Guntrip, H. (1961). *Personality Structure and Human Interaction*. London: Hogarth Press.

Guntrip, H. (1971). *Psychoanalytic Theory, Therapy and the Self*. London: Hogarth Press.

Guthrie, E. (1999). Psychodynamic interpersonal therapy. *Advances in Psychiatric Treatment, 5,* 135–145.

Guthrie, E., Creed, F., Dawson, D., & Tomenson, B. (1991). A controlled trial of psychological treatment for the irritable bowel syndrome. *Gastroenterology, 100,* 450–457.

Hahn, T. N. (1975). *The Miracle of Mindfulness: A Manual on Meditation*. Boston: Beacon Press.

Haigh, R. (2002a). Therapeutic community research: Past, present and future. *Psychiatric Bulletin*, *26*, 68–70.

Haigh, R. (2002b). Modern milieux: Therapeutic community solutions to acute ward problems. *Psychiatric Bulletin*, *26*, 380–382.

Haley, J., & Hoffman, L. (1967). *Techniques of Family Therapy*. New York: Basic Books.

Hamilton, J. W. (1976). Early trauma, dreaming and creativity: The works of Eugene O'Neill. *International Review of Psycho-Analysis*, *3*, 341–364.

Hampson, J. L., & Hampson, J. G. (1961). The ontogenesis of sexual behaviour in man. In W. C. Young (Ed.), *Sex and Internal Secretions*. London: Baillière Tindall.

Hardy, G. E., Stiles, W. B., Barkham, M., & Startup, M. (1998). Therapist responsiveness to to client interpersonal styles during time limited treatments for depression. *Journal of Consulting and Clinical Psychology*, *66*, 304–312.

Hardy, J., & Whitmore, D. (1988). Psychosynthesis. In D. Dryden & J. Rowan (Eds.), *Innovative Therapy in Britain*. Milton Keynes: Open University Press.

Harlow, H. F. (1958). The nature of love. *American Journal of Psychology*, *13*, 67–85.

Harlow, H. F., & Harlow, M. (1962). Social deprivation in monkeys. *Scientific American*, *207*, 136–146.

Harris, T. (1967). *I'm OK – You're OK*. New York: Grove Press.

Hartmann, H. (1939). *Ego Psychology and the Problem of Adaptation*. London: Imago.

Hawthorne, N. (1850). The Scarlet Letter. In *The Scarlet Letter and Selected Tales*. Harmondsworth: Penguin (1970).

Heap, M. (1988). *Hypnosis: Current Clinical, Experimental and Forensic Practices*. London: Croom Helm.

Heidegger, M. (1967). *Being and Time*. Oxford: Blackwell.

Heimann, P. (1950). On counter-transference. *International Journal of Psycho-Analysis*, *31*, 81–84.

Heru, A. (2006). Family psychiatry: From research to practice. *American Journal of Psychiatry*, *163*, 962–968.

Hinshelwood, R. D. (1987). *What Happens in Groups: Psychoanalysis, the Individual and the Community*. London: Free Association Books.

Hirsch, S. R., & Leff, J. P. (1975). *Abnormalities in Parents of Schizophrenics*, Maudsley Monograph no. 22. London: Oxford University Press.

Hobson, J. A. (1999). The new neuropsychology of sleep: Implications for psychoanalysis with commentaries by M. Solms, A. Braun, M. Reiser and reply by J. A. Hobson, E. Pace-Schott. *Neuro-Psychoanalysis, 1,* 157–225.

Hobson, J. A., & McCarley, R. W. (1977). The brain as a dream state generator: An activation-synthesis hypothesis of the dream process. *American Journal of Psychiatry, 134,* 1335–1348.

Hobson, R. F. (1974). Loneliness. *Journal of Analytical Psychology, 19,* 71–89.

Hobson, R. F. (1985). *Forms of Feeling: The Heart of Psychotherapy.* New York: Basic Books.

Hoenig, J. (1985). The origin of gender identity. In B. Steiner (Ed.), *Gender Dysphoria: Development, Research, Management.* New York: Plenum Press.

Hoffman, L. (1981). *Foundations of Family Therapy.* New York: Basic Books.

Holland, R. (1977). *Self and Social Context.* London: Macmillan.

Hollon, S. D., & Beck, A. T. (1994). Cognitive and cognitive-behavioural therapies. In A. F. Bergin & S. L. Garfield (Eds.), *Handbook of Psychotherapy and Behaviour Change* (4th ed.). New York: Wiley.

Holmes, J. (1992). *Between Art and Science: Essays in Psychotherapy and Psychiatry.* London: Routledge.

Holmes, J. (1993). *John Bowlby and Attachment Theory.* London: Routledge.

Holmes, J. (1995). Supportive psychotherapy: The search for positive meanings. *British Journal of Psychiatry, 167,* 439–445.

Holmes, J., & Lindley, R. (1989). *The Values of Psychotherapy.* Oxford: Oxford University Press.

Home, J. H. (1966). The concept of mind. *International Journal of Psycho-Analysis, 47,* 42–49.

Hopkins, P. (1972). *Patient-Centred Medicine.* London: Balint Society/Regional Doctor Publications.

Hopper, E., & Weyman, A. (1975). A sociological view of groups. In L. Kreeger (Ed.), *The Large Group.* London: Constable.

Horowitz, L. M., Rosenberg, S. E., & Bartholomew, K. (1993). Interpersonal problems, attachment styles and outcome in brief dynamic therapy. *Journal of Consulting and Clinical Psychology, 61,* 549–560.

Horowitz, M. J., & Marmac, C. (1984). Brief psychotherapy of bereavement reactions: The relationship of process to outcome. *Archives of General Psychiatry, 41,* 438–448.

Horvath, A. O., & Symonds, B. D. (1991). Relation between working alliance and outcome in psychotherapy: A meta-analysis. *Journal of Consulting and Clinical Psychology, 38,* 139–149.

Howells, J. G., & Brown, W. (1986). *Family Diagnosis.* Madison, WI: International Universities Press.

Hug-Hellmuth, H. von (1921). On the technique of child analysis. *International Journal of Psycho-Analysis*, *2*, 287–305.

Hycner, R., & Jacobs, L. (1995). *The Healing Relationship in Gestalt Therapy: A Dialogic/Self Psychology Approach*. Highland, NY: Gestalt Journal Press.

Ivaldi, A., Fassone, G., Rocchi, M. T., & Mantione, G. (2007). The integrated model (individual and group treatment) of cognitive-evolutionary therapy for outpatients with borderline personality disorder and axis-I/II comorbid disorders: Outcome results and a single case report. *Group*, *31*, 63–88.

Jackson, M., & Tarnopolsky, A. (1990). Borderline personality. In R. S. Bluglass & P. M. A. Bowden (Eds.), *Forensic Psychiatry* (ch. 27). London: Churchill Livingstone.

Jacobs, J. (1999). Countertransference past and present: A review of the concept. *International Journal of Psycho-Analysis*, *80*, 575–594.

Jacobson, E. (1964). *The Self and the Object World*. New York: International Universities Press.

James, W. (1890). *The Principles of Psychology*. Cambridge: Harvard University Press (1983).

Janov, A. (1970). *The Primal Scream*. New York: Dell Publishing.

Jaques, E. (1955). Social systems as a defence against persecutory and depressive anxiety. In M. Klein (Ed.), *New Directions in Psychoanalysis*. London: Tavistock Publications.

Jaques, E. (1965). Death and the mid life crisis. *International Journal of Psycho-Analysis*, *46*, 502–514.

Jennings, S. (1983). *Creative Therapy*. Banbury: Kemble Press.

Jennings, S. (1987). *Dramatherapy*. London: Routledge.

Joffe, W. G., & Sandler, J. (1965). Notes on pain, depression and individuation. *The Psychoanalytic Study of the Child*, *20*, 394–424.

Jones, E. (1953). *Sigmund Freud: Life and Work*, Vol. I. London: Hogarth Press.

Jones, E. (1955). *Sigmund Freud: Life and Work*, Vol. II. London: Hogarth Press.

Jones, E. (1957). *Sigmund Freud: Life and Work*, Vol. III. London: Hogarth Press.

Jones, E. (1997). Modes of therapeutic action. *International Journal of Psycho-Analysis*, *78*, 1135–1150.

Jones, M. (1952). *Social Psychiatry: A Study of Therapeutic Communities*. London: Tavistock Publications.

Jones, M. (1968). *Social Psychiatry in Practice: The Idea of the Therapeutic Community*. Harmondsworth: Penguin.

Joyce, A. S., & Piper, W. E. (1998). Expectancy, the therapeutic alliance, and treatment outcome in short term individual psychotherapy. *Journal of Psychotherapy Practice and Research*, *7*, 236–248.

Jung, C. G. (1933). *Modern Man in Search of a Soul*. London: Routledge & Kegan Paul.

Jung, C. G. (1946). *Psychological Types*. London: Routledge & Kegan Paul.

Jung, C. G. (1964). *Man and His Symbols*. London: Aldus Books.

Kafka, F. (1920). *Diary: Kafka Shorter Works*, Vol. I (trans./ed. Malcolm Pasley). London: Secker & Warburg.

Kalucy, R. S., Brown, D. G., Hartman, M., & Crisp, A. H. (1976). Sleep research and psychosomatic hypotheses. *Postgraduate Medical Journal*, *52*, 53–56.

Kaplan, S. (1967). Therapy groups and training groups: Similarities and differences. *International Journal of Group Psychotherapy*, *17*, 473–504.

Kaplan-Solms, K., & Solms, M. (2007). *Clinical Studies in Neuropsychoanalysis: An introduction to a Depth Neuropsychology*. New York: Other Press.

Kareem, J., & Littlewood, R. (1992). *Intercultural Therapy*. Oxford: Blackwell Science.

Karle, H. W. A., & Boys, J. H. (1996). *Hypnotherapy: A Practical Handbook*. London: Free Association Books.

Karmiloff-Smith, A. (1992). *Beyond Modularity: A Developmental Perspective on Cognitive Science*. Cambridge, MA: MIT Press.

Karp, M., Holmes, P., & Bradshaw-Tauvon, K. (Eds.) (1998). *Handbook of Psychodrama*. London: Routledge.

Karterud, S., Pedersen, G., Bjordal, E., Brabrand, J., Friis, S., Haaseth, Ø., et al. (2003). Day treatment of patients with personality disorders: Experiences from a Norwegian treatment research network. *Journal of Personality Disorders*, *17*, 243–262.

Keats, J. (1817). Letters, 32, To G. and T. Keats. 21 Dec. 1817. In *Letters of John Keats* (selected by F. Page). London: Oxford University Press (1954).

Kegerreis, D. (2007). Attending to splitting: The therapist couple in a conjoint individual group psychotherapy program for patients with borderline personality disorder. *Group*, *31*, 89–106.

Kellermann, P. F. (1987). Outcome research in classical psychodrama. *Small Group Behaviour*, *18*, 459–469.

Kellermann, P. F. (1992). *Focus on Psychodrama: The Therapeutic Aspects of Psychodrama*. London: Jessica Kingsley.

Kennard, D. (1994). The future revisited: New frontiers for therapeutic communities. *Therapeutic Communities*, *15*, 107–113.

Kennard, D. (1998). *An Introduction to Therapeutic Communites* (2nd ed.). London: Jessica Kingsley/Routledge.

Kennedy, R. (1998). *The Elusive Human Subject*. London: Free Association Books.

Kernberg, O. F. (1972). Psychotherapy and psychoanalysis: Final report of the Menninger Foundation's Psychotherapy Research Project. *Bulletin of the Menninger Clinic*, *36*, 1–275.

Kernberg, O. F. (1975). *Borderline Conditions and Pathological Narcissism*. New York: Jason Aronson.

Kernberg, O. F. (1984). *Severe Personality Disorders: Psychotherapeutic Strategies*. New Haven, CT: Yale University Press.

Kernberg, O. F., Clarkin, J. F., & Yeomans, F. E. (2002). *A Primer of Transference-Focused Psychotherapy for the Borderline Patient*. New York: Jason Aronson.

Kestenberg, J. S. (1982). A metapsychological assessment based on an analysis of a survivor's child. In M. S. Bergmann & M. E. Jucovy (Eds.), *Generations of the Holocaust* (pp. 137–158). New York: Columbia University Press.

Klauber, J. (1981). *Difficulties in the Analytic Encounter*. New York: Jason Aronson.

Klein, G. S. (1976). *Psychoanalytic Theory: An Exploration of Essentials*. New York: International Universities Press.

Klein, M. (1928). Early stages of the Oedipus conflict. In *Love, Guilt and Reparation* (pp. 186–198). London: Hogarth (1975).

Klein, M. (1932). *The Psycho-Analysis of Children*. London: Hogarth Press.

Klerman, G. L., Weissman, M. W., Rounsaville, B. J., & Chevron, E. S. (1996). *Interpersonal Psychotherapy of Depression*. Northvale: Jason Aronson.

Knight, L. (1986). *Talking to a Stranger: A Customer's Guide to Therapy*. London: Fontana/Collins.

Knowles, J. (1995). Therapeutic communities in today's world. *Therapeutic Communities*, *16*, 97–102.

Koestler, A. (1964). *The Act of Creation*. London: Hutchinson.

Kohut, H. (1971). *The Analysis of the Self*. New York: International Universities Press.

Kohut, H. (1977). *The Restoration of the Self*. New York: International Universities Press.

Kohut, H. (1979). The two analyses of Mr Z. *International Journal of Psycho-Analysis*, *60*, 3–27.

Kohut, H., & Wolf, E. S. (1978). The disorders of the self and their treatment: An outline. *International Journal of Psycho-Analysis*, *59*, 413–426.

Kolvin, I., Macmillan, A., Nicol, A. R., & Wrate, R. M. (1988). Psychotherapy is effective. *Journal of the Royal Society of Medicine*, *81*, 261–266.

Kovel, J. (1976). *A Complete Guide to Therapy*. New York: Pantheon.

Kraemer, S., & Roberts, J. (1996). *The Politics of Attachment*. London: Free Association Press.

Kreeger, L. (1975). *The Large Group: Dynamics and Therapy*. London: Constable.

Kreeger, L. (1992). Envy pre-emption in small and large groups. 16th S. H. Foulkes Lecture. *Group Analysis, 25*, 391–408.

Kroger, W. S. (1963). *Clinical and Experimental Hypnosis in Medicine, Dentistry, and Psychology*. Philadelphia: Lippincott.

Krupnick, J. L., Sotsky, S. M., Simmons, S., Moyer, J, Elkin, I., Watkins, J., *et al.* (1996). The role of the therapeutic alliance in psychotherapy and pharmacotherapy outcome: Findings in the NIMH Collaborative Research Programme. *Journal of Consulting and Clinical Psychology, 64*, 532–539.

Krupnick, J. L., Green, B. L., Stockton, P., Miranda, J., Krause, E., & Mete, M. (2008). Group interpersonal psychotherapy for low-income women with posttraumatic stress disorder. *Psychotherapy Research, 18*, 497–507.

Kuipers, D., Garety, P., Fowler, D., Dunn, G., Bebbington, P., Freeman, D., *et al.* (1997). London–East Anglia randomised controlled trial of cognitive-behavioural therapy for psychosis. *British Journal of Psychiatry, 171*, 319–327.

Laing, R. D. (1960). *The Divided Self*. London: Tavistock Publications.

Laing, R. D., & Esterson, A. (1964). *Sanity, Madness and the Family*. London: Tavistock Publications.

Lake, F. (1978). Treating psychosomatic disorders related to birth trauma. *Journal of Psychosomatic Research, 22*, 228–238.

Lambert, M. (2005). Emerging methods for providing clinicians with timely feedback on treatment effectiveness: An introduction. *Journal of Clinical Psychology, 61*, 141–144.

Lambert, M. J., Bergin, A., & Garfield, S. (2004). Introduction and historical overview. In M. J. Lambert (Ed.), *Bergin and Garfield's Handbook of Psychotherapy and Behaviour Change*. New York: Wiley.

Langs, R. J. (1979a). The interactional dimension of countertransference. In L. Epstein & A. H. Feiner (Eds.), *Countertransference*. New York: Jason Aronson.

Langs, R. J. (1979b). *The Therapeutic Environment*. New York: Jason Aronson.

Laufer, M. (1975). *Adolescent Disturbance and Breakdown*. Harmondsworth: Penguin.

Laufer, M., & Laufer, M. E. (1988). *Developmental Breakdown and Psychoanalytic Treatment in Adolescence*. New Haven, CT: Yale University Press.

Leboyer, F. (1977). *Birth without Violence*. London: Fontana.

Lees, J., Manning, N., & Rawlings, B. (1999). *Therapeutic Community Effectiveness. A Systematic International Review of Therapeutic Community Treatment for People with Personality Disorders and Mentally*

Disordered Offenders (CRD Report 17). NHS Centre for Reviews and Dissemination: University of York.

Leff, J. P., & Vaughn, C. (1985). *Expressed Emotion in Families: Its Significance for Mental Illness*. New York: Guilford Press.

Legg, C. (1997). Science and family therapy. *Journal of Family Therapy, 19*, 401–415.

Leigh, A. D. (1961). *The Historical Development of British Psychiatry, Vol. 1. The Eighteenth and Nineteenth Century*. Oxford: Pergamon Press.

Le Roy, J. (1994). Group analysis and culture. In D. Brown & L. Zinkin (Eds.), *The Psyche and the Social World*. London: Routledge.

Leszcz, M., & Goodwin, P. L. (1998). The rationale and foundations of group psychotherapy for women with metastatic breast cancer. *International Journal of Group Psychotherapy, 48*, 245–273.

Levitsky, A., & Perls, F. (1972). The rules and games of Gestalt therapy. In J. Huber & L. Millman (Eds.), *Goals and Behaviour in Psychotherapy and Counselling*. Columbus, OH: Charles Merrill.

Levy, K. N., Meehan, K. B., Kelly, K. M., Reynoso, J. S., Weber, M., Clarkin, J. F., et al. (2006). Change in attachment patterns and reflective function in a randomized control trial of transference-focused psychotherapy for borderline personality disorder. *Journal of Consulting and Clinical Psychology, 74*, 1027–1040.

Lewin, K., Lippitt, R., & White, R. K. (1939). Patterns of aggressive behaviour in experimentally created social climates. *Journal of Social Psychology, 10*, 271–299.

Lewis, I. M. (1979). *How's Your Family?* New York: Brunner/Mazel.

Lidz, R., & Lidz, T. (1949). The family environment of schizophrenic patients. *American Journal of Psychiatry, 106*, 322–345.

Lieberman, M. A., Yalom, I. D., & Miles, M. B. (1973). *Encounter Groups: First Facts*. New York: Basic Books.

Lieberman, S. (1979). Transgenerational analysis: The geneogram as a technique in family therapy. *Journal of Family Therapy, 1*, 51–64.

Linehan, M. M. (1993a). *Cognitive-Behavioural Treatment of Borderline Personality Disorder*. New York: Guilford Press.

Linehan, M. M. (1993b). *The Skills Training Manual for Treating Borderline Personality Disorder*. New York: Guilford Press.

Linehan, M. M., Armstrong, H., Suarez, A., Allmon, D., & Heard, H. (1991). Cognitive-behavioural treatment of chronically parasuicidal borderline patients. *Archives of General Psychiatry, 48*, 1060–1064.

Linehan, M. M., Heard, H. L., & Armstrong, H. E. (1993). Naturalistic follow-up of a behavioral treatment for chronically parasuicidal borderline patients. *Archives of General Psychiatry, 50*, 971–974.

Linehan, M. M., Comtois, K. A., Murray, A. M., Brown, M. Z., Gallop, R. J., Heard, H. L., et al. (2006). Two-year randomized controlled trial and follow-up of dialectical behavior therapy vs therapy by experts for suicidal behaviors and borderline personality disorder. *Archives of General Psychiatry*, *63*, 757–766.

Little, M. (1951). Countertransference and the patient's response to it. *International Journal of Psycho-Analysis*, *32*, 32–40.

Little, M. (1957). "R": The analyst's response to his patient's needs. *International Journal of Psychotherapy*, *38*, 240–258.

Littlewood, R., & Lipsedge, M. (1989). *Aliens and Alienists: Ethnic Minorities and Psychiatry* (2nd ed.). London: Unwin/Heinemann.

Lorenz, K. (1966). *On Aggression*. London: Methuen.

Lorr, M., & McNair, D. M. (1964). Correlates of length of psychotherapy. *Journal of Clinical Psychology*, *20*, 497–504.

Lowen, A. (1967). *The Betrayal of the Body*. London: Collier Macmillan.

Luborsky, L. (1962). Clinicians judgments of mental health: A proposed scale. *Archives of General Psychiatry*, *7*, 407–417.

Luborsky, L., & Crits-Christoph, P. (1990). *Understanding Transference: The CCRT Method*. New York: Basic Books.

Luborsky, L., Mintz, J., Auerbach, A., Christoph, P., Bachrach, H., Todd, T., *et al.* (1980). Predicting the outcome of psychotherapy: Findings of the Penn Psychotherapy Project. *Archives of General Psychiatry*, *37*, 471–481.

Luborsky, L., Diguer, L., Seligman, D. A., Rosenthal, R., Krause, E. D., Johnson, S., *et al.* (1999). The researcher's own therapy allegiances: A 'wild card' in comparisons of treatment efficacy. *Clinical Psychology: Science and Practice*, *6*, 95–106.

Luft, J. (1966). *Group Processes: An Introduction to Group Dynamics*. Palo Alto, CA: National Press.

Lyons-Ruth, K., Dutra, L., Schuder, M., & Bianchi, I. (2006). From Infant attachment disorganisaton to adult dissociation: Relational adaptations or traumatic experiences? *Psychiatric Clinics of North America*, *29*, 63–86.

Maeterlinck, M. (1901). *The Life of the Bee* (trans. by A. Sutro). London: Allen & Unwin.

Mahler, M. S., Pine, F., & Bergman, A. (1975). *The Psychological Birth of the Human Infant*. London: Hutchinson.

Main, M. (1991). Metacognitive knowledge, metacognitive monitoring, and singular (coherent) vs. multiple (incoherent) model of attachment: Findings and directions for future research. In C. M. Parkes, J. Stevenson-Hinde, & P. Marris (Eds.), *Attachment Across the Life Cycle* (pp. 127–159). London: Tavistock Publications/Routledge.

Main, M., & Goldwyn, R. (1991). *Adult Attachment Classification System. Version 5*. Berkley: University of California.

Main, T. F. (1946). The hospital as a therapeutic institution. *Bulletin of the Menninger Clinic*, *10*, 66–70.

Main, T. F. (1957). The ailment. *British Journal of Medical Psychology*, *30*, 129–145.

Main, T. F. (1966). Mutual projection in a marriage. *Comprehensive Psychiatry*, *7*, 432–449.

Main, T. F. (1968). Psychoanalysis as a cross bearing. *British Journal of Psychiatry*, *114*, 501–507.

Main, T. F. (1977). The concept of a therapeutic community: Variations and vicissitudes. *Group Analysis*, *10* (suppl.), 1–16.

Main, T. F. (1989). *The Ailment and Other Psychoanalytic Essays*. London: Free Association Press.

Maina, G., Rosso, G., & Bogetto, F. (2009). Brief dynamic therapy combined with pharmacotherapy in the treatment of major depressive disorder: Long-term results. *Journal of Affective Disorders*, *114*, 200–207.

Malan, D. H. (1963). *A Study of Brief Psychotherapy*. London: Tavistock Publications.

Malan, D. H. (1973). The problem of relevant variables in psychotherapy research. *International Journal of Psychiatry*, *11*, 336–346.

Malan, D. H. (1976). *The Frontier of Brief Psychotherapy*. New York: Plenum Press.

Malan, D. H. (1979). *Individual Psychotherapy and the Science of Psychodynamics*. London: Butterworth.

Mann, J. (1973). *Time-Limited Psychotherapy*. Cambridge, MA: Harvard University Press.

Marteau, L. (1976). Encounter and the new therapies. *British Journal of Hospital Medicine*, *15*, 257–264.

Martin, D. J., Garske, J. P., & Davis, K. M. (2000). Relation of the therapeutic alliance with outcome and other variables: A meta-analytic review. *Journal of Consulting and Clinical Psychology*, *68*, 438–450.

Marx, K. (1844). Economic and philosophical manuscripts. In K. Thompson & J. Tunstall (Eds.), *Sociological Perspectives*. Harmondsworth: Penguin Educational (1971).

Marziali, E. A. (1984). Three viewpoints on the therapeutic alliance: Similiarites, differences and associations with psychotherapy outcome. *Journal of Nervous and Mental Disease*, *172*, 417–423.

Marziali, E. A., & Monroe-Blum, H. (1995). An interpersonal approach to group psychotherapy with borderline personality disorder. *Journal of Personality Disorders*, *9*, 179–189.

Maslow, A. (1954). *Motivation and Personality*. New York: Harper and Row.

Masson, J. M. (1985). *The Assault on Truth: Freud's Suppression of the Seduction Theory*. Harmondsworth: Penguin.

Masters, W. H., & Johnson, V. E. (1970). *Human Sexual Inadequacy*. London: Churchill.

May, R. A. E., & Ellenberger, H. (1958). *Existence: A New Dimension in Psychiatry and Psychology*. New York: Basic Books.

McCullough, J. P. (1991). Psychotherapy for dysthymia: A naturalistic study of ten patients. *Journal of Nervous and Mental Disease, 179*, 734–740.

McFadyen, A. (1997). Rapprochement in sight? Postmodern family therapy and psychoanalysis. *Journal of Family Therapy, 19*, 241–262.

McFarlane, W. R., Link, B., Dushay, R., Marchal, J., & Crilly, J. (1995a). Psychoeducational multiple family groups: Four year relapse outcome in schizophrenia. *Family Process, 34*, 127–144.

McFarlane, W. R., Lukensm, E., Link, B., Dushay, R., Deakins, S. A., & Newmark, M. (1995b). Multiple family groups and psychoeducation in the treatment of schizophrenia. *Archives of General Psychiatry, 52*, 679–687.

McGoldrick, M., Gerson, R., & Petry, S. (2008). *Genograms: Assessment and Intervention*. New York: Norton.

McNeilly, C. L., & Howard, K. I. (1991). The effects of psychotherapy: A re-evaluation based on dosage. *Psychotherapy Research, 1*, 74–78.

Mead, G. H. (1934). *Mind, Self and Society*. Chicago: University of Chicago Press.

Meares, R., & Hobson, R. F. (1977). The persecutory therapist. *British Journal of Medical Psychology, 50*, 349–359.

Mearnes, D., & Thorne, B. (2007). *Person-Centred Counselling in Action*. London: Sage.

Mennell, S. (1989). *Norbert Elias: An Introduction*. Oxford: Blackwell.

Menzies, I. E. P. (1961). *The Functioning of Social Systems as a Defence against Anxiety: A Report on a Study of the Nursing Service of a General Hospital* (Tavistock Pamphlet no. 3). London: Tavistock Publications.

Menzies Lyth, I. (1989). The aftermath of disaster: Survival and loss. In *The Dynamics of the Social*. London: Free Association Books.

Merskey, H., & Spear, F. G. (1967). The concept of pain. *Journal of Psychosomatic Research, 11*, 59–67.

Meyer, B., Pilkonis, P. A., Proietti, J. M., Heape, C. L., & Egan, M. (2001). Adult attachment styles, personality disorders, and response to treatment. *Journal of Personality Disorders, 15*, 371–389.

Michaels, R. M., & Sevitt, M. A. (1978). The patient and the first psychiatric interview. *British Journal of Psychiatry, 132*, 288–292.

Milner, M. (1969). *The Hands of the Living God*. London: Hogarth Press.

Milner, M. (1971). *On Not Being Able to Paint* (2nd ed.). London: Heinemann.

Minuchin, S. (1974). *Families and Family Therapy*. London: Tavistock Publications.

Mitchison, S. (1999). The value of eliciting dreams in general psychiatry. *Advances in Psychiatric Treatment, 5*, 296–302.

Mittelman, B. (1948). The concurrent analysis of married couples. *Psychoanalytic Quarterly*, *17*, 182–197.

Money, J., Hampson, J. G., & Hampson, J. L. (1957). Imprinting and the establishment of gender role. *Archives of Neurology and Psychiatry*, *77*, 333–336.

Moreno, J. L. (1948). *Psychodrama*. New York: Beacon House.

Mufson, L., & Sills, R. (2006). Interpersonal psychotherapy for depressed adolescents (IPT-A): An overview. *Nordic Journal of Psychiatry*, *60*, 431–437.

Mufson, L., Weissman, M. M., Moreau, D., & Garfinkel, R. (1999). Efficacy of interpersonal psychotherapy for depressed adolescents. *Archives of General Psychiatry*, *56*, 573–579.

Mulgan, G. (1997). *Connexity – How to Live in a Connected World*. London: Chatto & Windus.

Nemiah, J. (1978). Alexithymia and psychosomatic illness. *Journal of Clinical and Experimental Psychiatry*, *29*, 25–37.

Neumann, J. E. (2007). Becoming better consultants through varieties of experiential learning. In M. Reynolds & R. Vince (Eds.), *The Handbook of Experiential Learning in Management Education*. Oxford: Oxford University Press.

NHS Executive (1996). *NHS Psychotherapy Services in England: Review of Strategic Policy*. London: Department of Health.

NICE (2009). Borderline personality disorder: Treatment and management. Retrieved from http://www.nice.org.uk/Guidance/CG78/Nice Guidance/pdf/English.

Nichols, M., & Schwartz, R. (2005). *Family Therapy: Concepts and Methods* (7th ed.). Needham Heights: Allyn & Bacon.

Nitsun, M. (1996). *The Anti-Group: Destructive Forces in the Group and their Creative Potential*. London: Routledge.

Norton, K. (1992). A culture of enquiry – its preservation or loss. *Therapeutic Communities*, *13*, 3–25.

O'Connor, J., & Seymour, J. (1990). *Introducing Neuro-Linguistic Programming*. Bodmin, Cornwall: Crucible.

Ogden, T. H. (1994). *Subjects of Analysis*. London: Karnac Books.

Okiishi, J., Lambert, M., Nielsen, S., & Ogles, B. (2003). Waiting for supershrink: An empirical analysis of therapist effects. *Clinical Psychology and Psychotherapy*, *10*, 361–373.

Oldham, J., Phillips, K., Gabbard, G., & Soloff, P. (2001). Practice guideline for the treatment of patients with borderline personality disorder. American Psychiatric Association. *American Journal of Psychiatry*, *158*, 1–52.

Onishi, K. H., & Baillargeon, R. (2005). Do 15-month-old infants understand false beliefs? *Science*, *308*, 255–258.

Palmer, R., Coleman, L., Chaloner, D., & Smith, J. (1993). Childhood sexual experiences with adults. *British Journal of Psychiatry, 163,* 499–504.

Parker, I. (1997). *Psychoanalytic Culture: Psychoanalytic Discourse in Western Society.* London: Sage.

Parkes, C. M. (1972). *Bereavement: Studies of Grief in Adult Life.* London: Tavistock Publications.

Parsons, T. (1964). *Social Structure and Personality.* London: Collier Macmillan.

Pedder, J. R. (1977). The role of space and location in psychotherapy, play and theatre. *International Review of Psycho-Analysis, 4,* 215–223.

Pedder, J. R. (1982). Failure to mourn, and melancholia. *British Journal of Psychiatry, 141,* 329–337.

Pedder, J. R. (1987). Some biographical contributions to psychoanalytic theories. *Free Associations, 10,* 102–116.

Pedder, J. R. (1989a). Courses in psychotherapy: Evolution and current trends. *British Journal of Psychotherapy, 6,* 203–221.

Pedder, J. R. (1989b). The proper image of mankind. *British Journal of Psychotherapy, 6,* 70–80.

Pekkala, E., & Merinder, L. (2002). *Psychoeducation for Schizophrenia (Cochrane Review),* Vol. 4. Oxford: The Cochrane Library.

Perls, F., Hefferline, R. F., & Goodman, P. (1951). *Gestalt Therapy: Excitement and Growth in the Human Personality.* New York: Dell.

Piaget, J. (1953). *The Origins of Intelligence in the Child.* London: Routledge & Kegan Paul.

Piaget, J. (1962). *Plays, Dreams and Imitation in Childhood.* New York: Norton.

Pilling, S., Bebbington, P., Kuipers, E., Garety, P., Geddes, J., Martindale, B., *et al.* (2002). Psychological treatments in schizophrenia: II. Meta-analyses of randomized controlled trials of social skills training and cognitive remediation. *Psychological Medicine, 32,* 783–791.

Pincus, L. (1960). *Marriage: Studies in Emotional Conflict and Growth.* London: Methuen.

Pines, D. (1986). Working with women survivors of the Holocaust. *International Journal of Psycho-Analysis, 67,* 295–307.

Pines, M. (1975). Overview. In L. Kreeger (Ed.), *The Large Group.* London: Constable.

Pines, M. (1983). *The Evolution of Group Analysis.* London: Routledge & Kegan Paul.

Piper, W. E., Azim, H. F. A., Joyce, A. S., McCallum, M., Nixon, G., & Segal, P. (1991). Quality of object relations vs. interpersonal functioning as predictors of therapeutic alliance and psychotherapy outcome. *Journal of Nervous and Mental Disease, 179,* 432–438.

Piper, W. E., Joyce, A. S., McCallum, M., & Azim, H. (1993). Concentration and correspondence of transference interpretations in short term psychotherapy. *Journal of Consulting and Clinical Psychology*, *61*, 586–595.

Piper, W. E., Joyce, A. S., Rosie, J. S., & Azim, A. F. (1994). Psychological mindedness, work, and outcome in day treatment. *International Journal of Group Psychotherapy*, *44*, 291–311.

Pirandello, L. (1954). *Six Characters in Search of an Author* (trans. F. May). London: Heinemann.

Pontalis, J. B. (1974). Freud in Paris. *International Journal of Psycho-Analysis*, *55*, 455–458.

Pratt, J. H. (1907). The class method of treating consumption in the homes of the poor. *Journal of the American Medical Association*, *49*, 755–759.

Racker, H. (1968). *Transference and Countertransference*. New York: International Universities Press.

Raikes, H. A., & Thompson, R. A. (2006). Family emotional climate, attachment security, and young children's emotional knowledge in a high risk sample. *British Journal of Developmental Psychology*, *24*, 89–104.

Rangell, L. (1954). Similarities and differences between psychoanalysis and dynamic psychotherapy. *Journal of the American Psychoanalytic Association*, *2*, 734–744.

Rank, O. (1929). *The Trauma of Birth*. London: Routledge & Kegan Paul.

Rapoport, R. N. (1960). *Community as Doctor: New Perspectives on a Therapeutic Community*. London: Tavistock Publications.

Rayner, E. H., & Hahn, H. (1964). Assessment for psychotherapy. *British Journal of Medical Psychology*, *37*, 331–342.

Reandeau, S. G., & Wampold, B. E. (1991). Relationship of power and involvement to working alliance: A multiple case sequential analysis of brief therapy. *Journal of Consulting and Clinical Psychology*, *38*, 107–114.

Reich, W. (1933). *Character Analysis*. London: Vision Press (1950).

Reik, T. (1922). *The Inner Eye of a Psychoanalyst*. London: Allen Unwin (1949).

Reimers, S., & Treacher, A. (1995). *Introducing User-Friendly Family Therapy*. London: Routledge.

Reiser, M. (2001). The dream in contemporary psychiatry. *American Journal of Psychiatry*, *158*, 351–359.

Repacholi, B. M., & Gopnik, A. (1997). Early reasoning about desires: Evidence from 14- and 18-month-olds. *Developmental Psychology*, *33*, 12–21.

Rey, H. (1994). *Universals of Psychoanalysis in the Treatment of Psychotic and Borderline States*. London: Free Association Books.

Rice, A. K. (1965). *Learning for Leadership*. London: Tavistock Publications.

Rickman, J. (1951). Number and the human sciences. In W. C. M. Scott

(Ed.), *Selected Contributions to Psycho-Analysis*. London: Hogarth Press (1957).

Ridley, M. (1996). *The Origins of Virtue*. London: Viking.

Riester, A. E., & Kraft, I. A. (1986). *Child Group Psychotherapy*. Madison, WI: International Universities Press.

Robertson, J. (1952). *Film: A Two-Year-Old Goes to Hospital*. London: Tavistock Publications.

Robinson, L. A., Berman, J. S., & Neimeyer, R. A. (1990). Psychotherapy for the treatment of depression: A comprehensive review of controlled outcome research. *Psychological Bulletin*, *108*, 30–49.

Rogers, C. R. (1961). *On Becoming a Person*. London: Constable.

Rogers, C. R. (1970). *Encounter Groups*. Harmondsworth: Penguin.

Rogers, C. R., & Dymond, R. F. (1954). *Psychotherapy and Personality Change*. Chicago: University of Chicago Press.

Roheim, G. (1950). *Psychoanalysis and Anthropology*. New York: International Universities Press.

Roland, A. (1988). *In Search of Self in India and Japan: Towards a Cross-Cultural Psychology*. Princeton, NJ.: Princeton University Press.

Rose, M. (1990). *Healing Hurt Minds: The Peper Harrow Experience*. London: Tavistock Publications/Routledge.

Rosenbaum, M. (1978). Group psychotherapy: Heritage, history and the current scene. In H. Mullan & M. Rosenbaum (Eds.), *Group Psychotherapy: Theory and Practice*. New York: Free Press of Glencoe.

Rosenblatt, A. D., & Thickstun, J. T. (1977). Energy, information and motivation: A revision of psychoanalytic theory. *Journal of the American Psychoanalytic Association*, *25*, 537–558.

Rosser, R., Birch, S., Bond, H., Denford, J., & Schachter, J. (1987). Five year follow-up of patients treated with in-patient psychotherapy at the Cassel Hospital for Nervous Diseases. *Journal of the Royal Society of Medicine*, *80*, 549–555.

Rossi, E. L., O'Ryan, M., & Sharp, F. A. (1998). *The Seminars, Workshops and Lectures of Milton H. Erikson*, Vols. I–IV. London: Free Association Books.

Roth, A., & Fonagy, P. (2005). *What Works for Whom? A Critical Review of Psychotherapy Research* (2nd ed.). New York: Guilford Press.

Rounsaville, B. J., Weissman, M. M., & Prusoff, B. A. (1981). Psychotherapy with depressed outpatients. Client and process variables as predictors of outcome. *British Journal of Psychiatry*, *138*, 67–74.

Rowan, J. (1988). Primal integration therapy. In W. Dryden & J. Rowan (Eds.), *Innovative Therapy in Britain*. Milton Keynes: Open University Press.

Rowland, N. (1993). What is counselling? In D. R. Corney & R. Jenkins (Eds.), *Counselling in General Practice* (pp. 17–30). London: Routledge.

Rowley, J. (1951). Rumpelstiltskin in the analytic situation. *International Journal of Psycho-Analysis, 32,* 190–195.

Royal College of Psychiatrists (1997). Reported recovered memories of child sexual abuse: Recommendations for good practice and implications for training, continuing professional development and research. *Psychiatric Bulletin, 21,* 663–665.

Russell, G. F. M., Szmukler, G., Dare, C., & Eisler, I. (1987). An evaluation of family therapy in anorexia nervosa and bulimia nervosa. *Archives of General Psychiatry, 44,* 1047–1056.

Rustin, M. (1991). *The Good Society and the Internal World: Psychoanalysis, Politics and Culture.* London: Verso.

Rutter, D., & Tyrer, P. (2003). The value of therapeutic communities in the treatment of personality disorder: A suitable place for treatment? *Journal of Psychiatric Practice, 9,* 291–302.

Rycroft, C. (1966). Causes and meaning. In *Psychoanalysis Observed.* Harmondsworth: Penguin (1968).

Rycroft, C. (1971). *Reich.* London: Fontana.

Rycroft, C. (1972). *A Critical Dictionary of Psychoanalysis.* Harmondsworth: Penguin.

Rycroft, C. (1979). *The Innocence of Dreams.* Oxford: Oxford University Press.

Ryle, A. (1982). *Psychotherapy: A Cognitive Integration of Theory and Practice.* London: Academic Press.

Ryle, A. (1990). *Cognitive Analytic Therapy: Active Participation in Change.* Chichester: Wiley.

Ryle, A. (1995). *Cognitive Analytic Therapy: Developments in Theory and Practice.* Chichester: Wiley.

Ryle, A. (1997). The structure and development of borderline personality disorder: A proposed model. *British Journal of Psychiatry, 170,* 82–87.

Safran, J. D., & Muran, J. C. (2000). *Negotiating the Therapeutic Alliance: A Relational Treatment Guide.* New York: Guilford Press.

Samuels, A. (1985). *Jung and the Post Jungians.* London: Routledge & Kegan Paul.

Sandahl, C., Herlitz, K., Ahlin, G., & Ronnberg, S. (1998). Time-limited group psychotherapy for moderately alcohol dependent patients: A randomized controlled clinical trial. *Psychotherapy Research, 8,* 361–378.

Sandell, R., Blomberg, J., & Lazar, A. (2002). Time matters: On temporal interactions in long-term follow-up of long-term psychotherapies. *Psychotherapy Research, 12,* 39–58.

Sander, L. (1998). Boston Process of Change Study Group: Interventions that Effect Change in Psychotherapy: A Model based on Infant Research. *Infant Mental Health, 19,* 277–353.

Sanders, K. (1986). *A Matter of Interest: Clinical Notes of a Psychoanalyst in General Practice*. Strath Tay: Cluny Press.

Sandler, J. (1974). Psychological conflict and the structural model: Some clinical and theoretical implications. *International Journal of Psycho-Analysis, 55,* 53–72.

Sandler, J. (1976). Countertransference and role-responsiveness. *International Review of Psycho-Analysis, 3,* 43–47.

Sandler, J. (1983). Reflections on some relations between psychoanalytic concepts and psychoanalytic practice. *International Journal of Psycho-Analysis, 64,* 35–45.

Sandler, J. (1987). The concept of projective identification. In *Projection, Identification, and Projective Identification*. London: Karnac Books.

Sandler, J., & Joffe, W. G. (1969). Towards a basic psychoanalytic model. *International Journal of Psycho-Analysis, 50,* 79–90.

Sandler, J., & Sandler, A.-M. (1984). The past unconscious, the present unconscious, and interpretation of the transference. *Psychoanalytic Inquiry, 4,* 367–399.

Sandler, J., Holder, A., Dare, C., & Dreher, A. (1973). *The Patient and the Analyst: The Basis of the Psychoanalytic Process*. New York: International Universities Press.

Sandler, J., Kennedy, H., & Tyson, R. L. (1990). *The Technique of Child Psychoanalysis: Discussions with Anna Freud*. London: Karnac Books.

Sandler, J., Dare, C., Holder, A., & Dreher. (1997). *Freud's Models of the Mind: An Introduction*. London: Karnac Books.

Scharff, D. E. (1982). *The Sexual Relationship*. London: Routledge & Kegan Paul.

Scheidlinger, S. (1968). The concept of regression in group psychotherapy. *International Journal of Group Psychotherapy, 18,* 3–20.

Schilder, P. (1939). Results and problems of group psychotherapy in severe neurosis. *Mental Hygiene, 23,* 87–98.

Schoenberg, P. (2007). *Psychosomatics: The Uses of Psychotherapy*. Basingstoke: Palgrave Macmillan.

Schutz, W. C. (1958). *FIRO: A Three Dimensional Theory of Interpersonal Behaviour*. New York: Holt, Rinehart & Winston.

Schutz, W. C. (1967). *Joy: Expanding Human Awareness*. New York: Grove Press.

Scoville, W. B., & Milner, B. (1957). Loss of recent memory after bilateral hippocampal lesions. *Journal of Neurology, Neurosurgery, and Psychiatry 20,* 11–21.

Searles, H. F. (1979). *Countertransference and Related Subjects*. Madison, CT: International Universities Press.

Segal, H. (1964). *Introduction to the Work of Melanie Klein*. New York: Basic Books.

Segal, Z. V., Williams, J. M. G., & Teasdale, J. D. (2002). *Mindfulness-*

Based Cognitive Therapy for Depression: A New Approach to Preventing Relapse. New York: Guilford Press.

Seidler, G. H. (2000). The self-relatedness construct: Empirical verification via observation in the context of inpatient group therapy. *Group Analysis, 33,* 413–432.

Selvini-Palazzoli, M., Boscolo, L., Cecchin, G., & Prata, G. (1978). *Paradox and Counterparadox.* New York: Jason Aronson.

Seppala, K., & Jamsen, H. (1990). Psychotherapy as one form of rehabilitation provided by the Finnish Social Insurance Institution. *Psychoanalytic Psychotherapy, 4,* 219–232.

Shaffer, J. B. P., & Galinsky, M. D. (1989). *Models of Group Therapy and Sensitivity Training* (2nd ed.). Princeton, NJ: Prentice-Hall.

Shapiro, D., & Firth-Cozens, J. (1987). Prescriptive v. exploratory therapy: Outcomes of the Sheffield Psychotherapy Project. *British Journal of Psychiatry, 151,* 790–799.

Shapiro, D. A., Barkham, M., Rees, A., Hardy, G. E., Reynolds, S., & Startup, M. (1994). Special feature. Effects of treatment duration and severity of depression on the effectiveness of cognitive-behavioral and psychodynamic-interpersonal psychotherapy. *Journal of Consulting and Clinical Psychology, 62,* 522–534.

Shapiro, D., Rees, A., Barkham, M., Hardy, G., Reynolds, S., & Startup, M. (1995). Effects of treatment duration and severity of depression on the maintenance of gains after cognitive-behavioral and psychodynamic-interpersonal psychotherapy. *Journal of Consulting and Clinical Psychology, 63,* 378–387.

Sieghart, P. (1978). *Statutory Registration of Psychotherapists: Report of a Professions Joint Working Party.* Cambridge: Plumridge.

Sifneos, P. E. (1972). *Short-Term Psychotherapy and Emotional Crisis.* Cambridge, MA: Harvard University Press.

Sifneos, P. E. (1987). *Short-Term Dynamic Psychotherapy: Evaluation and Technique* (2nd ed.). New York: Plenum Press.

Sigrell, B. (1992). The long-term effects of group psychotherapy: A 13 year follow-up study. *Group Analysis, 25,* 333–352.

Simeon, D., Knutelska, M., & Yehuda, R. (2007). Hypothalamic-pituitary-adrenal axis function in dissociative disorders, post-traumatic stress disorder, and healthy volunteers. *Biological Psychiatry, 61,* 966–973.

Simon, R. (1972). Sculpting the family. *Family Process, 11,* 49–57.

Skills for Health (2009). Psychological therapies. Retrieved from http://www.skillsforhealth.org.uk/competences/competences-in-development/psychological-therapies.aspx.

Skrine, R. L. (1989). *Introduction to Psychosexual Medicine.* London: Montana Press.

Skynner, A. C. R. (1976). *One Flesh: Separate Persons.* London: Constable.

Skynner, A. C. R. (1986). *Explorations with Families*. London: Methuen.

Skynner, A. C. R., & Brown, D. G. (1981). Referral of patients for psychotherapy. *British Medical Journal, 282*, 1952–1955.

Skynner, A. C. R., & Cleese, J. (1983). *Families and How to Survive Them*. London: Methuen.

Sloane, R. B., Staples, F. R., Cristol, A. H., Yorkston, N. J., & Whipple, K. (1975). Short-term analytically oriented psychotherapy versus behaviour therapy. *American Journal of Psychiatry, 132*, 373–377.

Smart, N. (1993). *Buddhism and Christianity*. London: Macmillan.

Snyder, D., & Willis, R. (1989). Behavioural versus insight-oriented marital therapy: Effects on individual and interspousal functioning. *Journal of Consulting and Clinical Psychology, 57*, 39–46.

Snyder, D. K., Willis, R. M., & Grady-Fletcher, A. (1991). Long-term effectiveness of behavioral versus insight-oriented marital therapy: A 4-year follow-up study. *Journal of Consulting and Clinical Psychology, 59*, 138–141.

Solms, M. (2000). Dreaming and REM sleeping are controlled by different brain mechanisms. *Behaviour and Brain Sciences, 23*, 843–850, 904–1121.

Speck, R., & Attneave, C. (1973). *Family Networks*. New York: Pantheon.

Spiegel, D., Bloom, J. R., Kraemer, H. C., & Gottheil, E. (1989). Effect of psychosocial treatment on survival of patients with metastatic breast cancer. *Lancet, ii*, 888–891.

Springmann, R. R. (1970). The application of interpretations in a large group. *International Journal of Group Psychotherapy, 20*, 333–341.

Stanton, A. H., & Schwartz, M. S. (1954). *The Mental Hospital: A Study of Institutional Participation in Psychiatric Illness and Treatment*. New York: Basic Books.

Steiner, J. (1993). *Psychic Retreats. Pathological Organisations in Psychotic, Neurotic and Borderline Patients*. London: Routledge.

Stern, D. N. (1985). *The Interpersonal World of the Infant: A View from Psychoanalysis and Developmental Psychology*. New York: Basic Books.

Stern, D. N. (1998). The process of therapeutic change involving implicit knowledge: Some implications of developmental observations for adult psychotherapy. *Infant Mental Health, 19*, 300–338.

Stern, S., Doolan, M., Staples, E., Szmukler, G. L., & Eisler, I. (1999). Disruption and reconstruction: Narrative insights into the experience of family members caring for a relative diagnosed with serious mental illness. *Family Process, 38*, 353–369.

Stevenson, J., & Meares, R. (1992). An outcome study of psychotherapy for patients with borderline personality disorder. *American Journal of Psychiatry, 149*, 358–362.

Stevenson, J., & Meares, R. (1999). Psychotherapy with borderline patients: II. A preliminary cost benefit study. *Australian and New Zealand Journal of Psychiatry, 33,* 473–477.

Stevenson, J., Meares, R., & D'Angelo, R. (2005). Five-year outcome of outpatient psychotherapy with borderline patients. *Psychological Medicine, 35,* 79–87.

Stiles, W. B., Agnew-Davies, R., Hardy, G. E., Barkham, M., & Shapiro, D. A. (1998). Relations of the alliance with psychotherapy outcome: Findings in the second Sheffield Psychotherapy Project. *Journal of Consulting and Clinical Psychology, 66,* 791–802.

Storr, A. (1976). *The Dynamics of Creation.* Harmondsworth: Penguin.

Storr, A. (1979). *The Art of Psychotherapy.* London: Secker & Warburg.

Strachey, J. (1934). The nature of the therapeutic action of psychoanalysis. *International Journal of Psycho-Analysis, 50,* 275–292.

Stuart, S., & Robertson, M. (2003). *Interpersonal Psychotherapy: A Clinician's Guide.* London: Edward Arnold.

Sutherland, J. D. (1968). The consultant psychotherapist in the National Health Service: His role and training. *British Journal of Psychiatry, 114,* 509–515.

Symington, N. (1986). *The Analytic Experience: Lectures from the Tavistock.* London: Free Association Books.

Taylor, G. J. (1987). *Psychosomatic Medicine and Psychoanalysis.* Madison, CT: International Universities Press.

Taylor, R. (2000). A seven year reconviction study of HMP Grendon therapeutic community. In J. Shine (Ed.), *HMP Grendon, a Compilation of Grendon Research.* Thornhill: Leyhill Press.

Tillett, R. (1991). Active and non-verbal therapeutic approaches. In J. Holmes (Ed.), *Textbook of Psychotherapy in Psychiatric Practice.* Edinburgh: Churchill Livingstone.

Tschuschke, V. (1999). Empirische Studien mit verhaltenstherapeutischen und psychoanalytischen Gruppenpsychotherapie-Behandlungen. Ein literatur-Uberblick. *Praxis Klinisch Verhaltensmedizin und Rehabilitation, 48,* 11–17.

Tschuschke, V., & Dies, R. R. (1994). Intensive analysis of therapeutic factors and outcome in long-term inpatient groups. *International Journal of Group Psychotherapy, 44,* 183–214.

Tschuschke, V., & Anbet, T. (2000). Early treatment effects of long-term out-patient group therapies: Preliminary results. *Group Analysis, 33,* 397–412.

Tuckman, B. W. (1965). Developmental sequences in small groups. *Psychological Bulletin, 63,* 384–399.

Turkington, D., & Kingdon, D. (2000). Cognitive-behavioural techniques for general psychiatrists in the management of patients with psychoses. *British Journal of Psychiatry, 177,* 101–106.

Tylee, A. (1997). Counselling in primary care. *Lancet, 350,* 1643–1644.

Tyrell, C., Dozier, M., Teague, G., & Fallot, R. (1999). Effective treatment relationships for persons with serious psychiatric disorders: The importance of attachment states of mind. *Journal of Consulting and Clinical Psychology, 67,* 725–733.

Vaillant, G. E. (1992). *Ego Mechanisms of Defense: A Guide for Clinicians and Researchers.* Washington, DC: American Psychiatric Association.

Valbak, K. (2003). Specialised psychotherapeutic group analysis: How do we make group analysis suitable for 'non-suitable' patients? *Group Analysis, 36,* 73–86.

Van Marle, S., & Holmes, J. (2002). Supportive psychotherapy as an integrative psychotherapy. In J. Holmes & A. Bateman (Eds.), *Integration in Psychotherapy: Models and Methods.* Oxford: Oxford University Press.

Vernon, P. E. (1970). *Creativity.* Harmondsworth: Penguin.

Volkan, V. D. (1998). *The Need to Have Enemies and Allies.* Northvale, NJ: Jason Aronson.

Volkan, V. D., & Ast, G. (1997). *Siblings in the Unconscious and Psychopathology.* Madison, CT: International Universities Press.

Wallerstein, R. (1969). Introduction to panel on psychoanalysis and psychotherapy. *International Journal of Psycho-Analysis, 50,* 117–126.

Wallerstein, R. (1986). *Forty-Two Lives in Treatment: A Study of Psychoanalysis and Psychotherapy.* New York: Guilford Press.

Wallerstein, R. (1989). Psychoanalysis and psychotherapy: An historical perspective. *International Journal of Psycho-Analysis, 70,* 563–591.

Wallerstein, R. (1999). A half-century perspective on psychoanalysis and psychotherapy: The historical context of Joseph Sandler's contribution. In P. Fonagy, A. Cooper, & R. Wallerstein (Eds.), *Psychoanalysis on the Move: The Work of Joseph Sandler.* London: Routledge.

Walrond-Skinner, S. (1976). *Family Therapy: The Treatment of Natural Systems.* London: Routledge & Kegan Paul.

Walsh, F. (2003). Family resilience: A framework for clinical practice. *Family Process, 42,* 1–18.

Ward, E., King, M., & Lloyd, M. (2000). Randomised controlled trial of non-directive counselling, cognitive-behaviour therapy, and usual general practitioner care for patients with depression. *British Medical Journal, 321,* 1383–1388.

Wardi, D. (1992). *Memorial Candles: Children of the Holocaust.* London: Routledge.

Watzlawick, P., Beavin, J. H., & Jackson, D. D. (1968). *Pragmatics of Human Communication.* London: Faber.

Welldon, E. (1997). Let the treatment fit the crime: Forensic group psychotherapy. 20th S. H. Foulkes Lecture. *Group Analysis, 30,* 5–26.

Whitaker, C. (1975). Psychotherapy of the absurd. *Family Process, 14,* 1–16.

Whitaker, D. S. (1985). *Using Groups to Help People*. London: Routledge & Kegan Paul.

Whitaker, D. S., & Lieberman, M. (1964). *Psychotherapy through the Group Process*. New York: Atherton.

Whiteley, J. S. (1994). Attachment, loss and the space between: Personality disorder in the therapeutic community. 18th S. H. Foulkes Lecture. *Group Analysis*, *27*, 359–381.

Whiteley, J. S., & Gordon, J. (1979). *Group Approaches in Psychiatry*. London: Routledge & Kegan Paul.

Whitfield, G. (1988). Bioenergetics. In J. Rowan & W. Dryden (Eds.), *Innovative Therapy in Britain*. Milton Keynes: Open University Press.

Whyte, L. L. (1962). *The Unconscious before Freud*. London: Tavistock Publications.

Wibberley, M. (1988). Encounter. In D. Dryden & J. Rowan (Eds.), *Innovative Therapy in Britain*. Milton Keynes: Open University Press.

Wilberg, T., Karterud, S., Pedersen, G., Urnes, T., Irion, T., Brabrand, J., et al. (2003). Outpatient group psychotherapy following day treatment of patients with personality disorders. *Journal of Personality Disorders*, *17*, 510–521.

Winnicott, D. W. (1947). Hate in the countertransference. In D. W. Winnicott (Ed.), *Through Paediatrics to Psycho-Analysis*. London: Hogarth Press (1975).

Winnicott, D. W. (1960). Ego distortion in terms of true and false self. In D. W. Winnicott (Ed.), *The Maturational Processes and the Facilitating Environment*. London: Hogarth Press (1965).

Winnicott, D. W. (1965). *The Maturational Processes and the Facilitating Environment*. London: Hogarth Press.

Winnicott, D. W. (1971). *Playing and Reality*. London: Tavistock Publications.

Winnicott, D. W. (1975). *Through Paediatrics to Psycho-Analysis*. London: Hogarth Press.

Winston, A., Laitkin, M., Pollack, J., Samstag, L., McCullough, L., & Muran, J. (1994). Short-term psychotherapy of personality disorders. *American Journal of Psychiatry*, *151*, 190–194.

Wolf, A., & Schwartz, E. K. (1962). *Psychoanalysis in Groups*. New York: Grune & Stratton.

Wolf, E. S. (1994). Varieties of disorders of the self. *British Journal of Psychotherapy*, *11*, 198–208.

Wolff, H. H. (1971). The therapeutic and developmental functions of psychotherapy. *British Journal of Medical Psychology*, *44*, 117–130.

Wynne, L. C., Ryckoff, L., Day, J., & Hirsch, S. (1958). Pseudomutuality in the family relations of schizophrenics. *Psychiatry*, *21*, 205–223.

Yalom, I. D. (1985). *The Theory and Practice of Group Psychotherapy* (3rd ed.). New York: Basic Books.

Yalom, I. D. (1995). *Theory and Practice of Group Psychotherapy* (4th ed.). New York: Basic Books.

Yerkes, R. M., & Dodson, J. D. (1908). The relation of strength of stimulus to rapidity of habit formation. *Journal of Comparative Neurology and Psychology, 18,* 459–482.

Zanarini, M. C., Frankenburg, F. R., Hennen, J., Reich, D. B., & Silk, K. R. (2006). Prediction of the 10-year course of borderline personality disorder. *American Journal of Psychiatry, 163,* 827–832.

Zane, N., Nagayama Hall, G. C., Sue, S., Young, K., & Nunez, J. (2004). Research on Psychotherapy with culturally diverse populations. In M. Lambert (Ed.), *Bergin and Garfield's Handbook of Psychotherapy and Behavior Change* (pp. 767–804). New York: Wiley.

Zinkin, L. (1983). Malignant mirroring. *Group Analysis, 16,* 113–129.

Name index

Abbas, A. 152
Acharya, S. 97
Ackerman, N.W. 177
Adams, M.V. 154
Aggar, E.M. 174
Agnew, R. 265
Agnew-Davies, R. 267
Ahlin, G. 175
Ainsworth, M.D.S. 57
Alexander, F. 1, 149
Allen, J.G. 206
Allmon, D. 237
American Psychiatric Association 35
Anbet, T. 175
Anderson, E.M. 152
Ansbacher, H.L. 131
Ansbacher, R.R. 131
Anthony, E.J. 160
Apter, A. 29
Argyle, M. 99
Armstrong, H. 237
Armstrong, H.E. 237
Asen, K.E. 189
Ashurst, P. 97
Ast, G. 50
Attneave, C. 181
Atwood, G.E. 82
Auerbach, A. 247
Aveline, M. 256
Azim, A.F. 248
Azim, H. 268
Azim, H.F.A. 144, 268

Bacal, H.A. 63
Bacha, C. 169
Bachrach, H. 247
Baer, P.E. 248
Baillargeon, R. 85
Balint, E. 80, 122, 174, 250, 254, 256
Balint, M. 42, 61, 80, 122, 139, 151, 174, 250, 254, 256
Bandler, R. 219
Baranger, M. 80
Barber, J. 225
Barkham, M. 249, 265, 267
Bartholomew, K. 260
Barton, R. 180, 192
Bateman, A. 126, 236, 246, 256
Bateson, G. 176
Beavin, J.H. 66, 185
Bebbington, P. 139, 177, 250
Beck, A.T. 228, 264
Beels, C.C. 183
Behr, H. 181
Benjamin, J. 26
Bentovim, A. 177–8
Berger, R.J. 104
Bergin, A. 254
Bergin, A.E. 3, 254
Bergman, A. 49, 132
Berke, J. 202
Berkowitz, R. 189
Berman, J.S. 261
Bernard, H.S. 160
Berne, E. 6, 63, 131, 221
Bertalanffy, L. von 66

Subject index